2-23-77

YALE SERIES IN ECONOMIC HISTORY

SEA

N O R T H   S E A

GRONINGEN
• Leeuwarden
• Groningen

FRIESLAND
• Assen

DRENTHE

Den Helder •
• Koevoorden

• Hoorn

OVER-
Zwolle • Vechte
IJSSEL
• Almelo
• Hengelo

NORTH
HOLLAND
ZUIDERZEE

IJmuiden •
Haarlem •
• Zaandam
Amsterdam •

• Deventer
Enschede •

UTRECHT
GELDER-
• Zutphen
LAND

• Leyden
• The Hague
Utrecht •

Arnhem •

Delft •
SOUTH
Rotterdam •
HOLLAND
Dordrecht •

Lek
Waal
• Nijmegen
Rhine

Middelburg •
Flushing •

Bergen op Zoom •

NORTH
BRABANT

• Bois-Le-Duc

Meuse

Lippe

• Breda
• Tilburg
Helmond •

Rhine

• Venlo

Terneuzen •

• Eindhoven

DUTCH LIMBURG

Ruhr

• Düsseldorf

Ostend •
Bruges •
Antwerp •
St. Nicholas •
• Turnhout
• Roermond

Dunkirk •

WEST
FLANDERS

EAST
Ghent •
FLANDERS

ANTWERP
• Lier

Mechelen •

Demer

LIMBURG
Hasselt •

Cologne •

• Maastricht

• Aachen

• Ieper
Lys

Kortrijk •

Scheldt

• Brussels
SOUTH BRABANT
• Louvain

Meuse

Koblenz •

Lille •

• Waterloo
• Nivelles

Tournai •
HAINAULT
Mons •
• Charleroi

• Liège
Seraing •
LIÈGE

Vesdre
• Verviers

Sieg

Namur •
Sambre

NAMUR

Ourthe

Beaumont •

GERMAN CONFEDERACY

F R A N C E

LUXEMBOURG

GREAT
DUCHY
OF
LUXEMBOURG

Meuse

• Sedan

• Luxembourg
Moselle

The Low Countries after 1814

■ United Kingdom of the Netherlands

▨ The Netherlands since 1839

□ Belgium since 1839

Scale: 1:1,610,000

Ems

INDUSTRIALIZATION IN THE LOW COUNTRIES, 1795–1850

JOEL MOKYR

NEW HAVEN AND LONDON
YALE UNIVERSITY PRESS
1976

Library of Congress catalog card number: 75-43326
International standard book number: 0-300-01892-4

Designed by Sally Sullivan
and set in Monophoto Plantin type.
Printed in the United States of America by
The Murray Printing Co.,
Westford, Massachusetts.

Published in Great Britain, Europe, Africa, and Asia (except Japan)
by Yale University Press, Ltd., London.
Distributed in Latin America by Kaiman & Polon, Inc., New York City;
in Australia by Book & Film Services, Artarmon, N.S.W., Australia;
in Japan by John Weatherhill, Inc., Tokyo.

*Every economist goes through a phase where he is dissatisfied
with the deductive basis of economic theory, and feels sure
that a much better insight into economic processes could be
obtained by studying the facts of history. The instinct is
sound; yet the enthusiasms of this phase seldom survive any
serious attempt to get to grips with the facts of history in the
relevant sense. We mean by this . . . that the "facts" which
would interest the theorist are not what happened but why
it happened.*

W. Arthur Lewis

CONTENTS

LIST OF FIGURES AND TABLES

FIGURES

TABLES

PREFACE

The "New Economic History" is by now about to reach its adolescence. Yet its introduction to European economic history has been thus far rather tardy. Some recent work by cliometricians on English economic history is a hopeful sign that change is imminent, but meanwhile quantitative studies on the continental countries, especially on the period prior to 1850, are quite rare.

The present study cherishes the hope of being a contribution to the economic history of continental Europe before 1848. The Low Countries provide a convenient point to attack the intellectual *Westwall* of "good old economic history." The Netherlands and Belgium are small enough for the amount of material to remain manageable, while at the same time the advantages of a systematic comparison between two economies displaying widely different behavior patterns are retained. Throughout, I have attempted to emphasize the quantitative-comparative aspects of the industrialization process in the two countries. A large amount of quantitative information was assembled which to some may be useful in itself.

However, my main purpose was not to write the economic history of the industrial sectors in the Low Countries in the first half of the nineteenth century. Rather, my principal aim was to try to establish a causal relationship between economic conditions at the outset of the era of modern industrial technology and the actual rate of capital accumulation that transformed a traditional economy into a modern, industrialized one. The central issue is straightforward: Belgium and the Netherlands were two economies of similar size and location with comparable lingual and cultural traditions. Yet while Belgium became within four or five decades the leading industrial nation on the Continent, the Netherlands lagged behind and no industrialization of noticeable dimensions can be discerned before the last decades of the nineteenth century. Why did this process of "uneven development" occur? In order to come to grips with this issue, it is necessary to formulate a logical framework in which causal relationships can be deduced from fairly simple yet hopefully not unrealistic assumptions. At present, no satisfactory model for early industrialization in the West exists, and an attempt has been made to fill this lacuna. The model developed points clearly to a few factors as the likely causes for the emergence of a large gap between Belgium and the Netherlands, and it is shown that the available quantitative evidence is consistent with the hypotheses derived from the model.

Most of the sources used in the research for this study are printed. The vast amounts of raw, largely uninventoried manuscript material in various archives between Amsterdam and Liège have not been explored system-atically in view of the scope of the subject and the length of the reference period. On the other hand, there is a wealth of material in printed sources, both primary and secondary. As to the former, heavy use is made of statistical material collected by the various governments which ruled the two countries between 1795 and 1850. In addition, much valuable source material has been published in the last decades by various agencies. Another indispensable source of information are the opinions and accounts written by well-informed contemporaries. As to secondary sources, a large and diverse body of literature representing the fruits of a century of historical research exists. If the present study has made a positive contribution, it is only because it could stand on the shoulders of those who meticulously compiled this treasure of knowledge, to paraphrase Newton's aphorism. In this respect, I owe much to the resourcefulness of the Interlibrary Loan Department of Yale University's Sterling Memorial Library, which has miraculously produced scores of extremely rare books. The librarians and personnel of the following libraries have also been of great help: the Widener and Baker Libraries at Harvard University, the New York Public Library, the Library of Congress, Princeton University Library, the Koninklijke Bibliotheek in The Hague, the University of Leyden Library, the Library of the Economisch Historisch Archief in Amsterdam, the Royal Library in Brussels, the Library of the University of Ghent, the Library of the University of Leuven, and the Library of the National Archive in The Hague. The archivists of the Belgian and Dutch National Archives and the Ghent Municipal Archives have also been very helpful.

Throughout this study, all direct quotes from French and Dutch sources have been translated. The titles of Dutch works cited in footnotes are accompanied by English translations. As to place names, the following procedure was followed. As far as English names were available, they have been used (e.g., The Hague, Ghent, Brussels). For other place names, the present Belgian language border has been observed (e.g., St. Nikolaas, Kortrijk, Aalst, Limburg, but Liège, Tournay, Luxembourg).

It is a pleasant task to mention the many individuals who have helped me in many different ways to complete this work. First and foremost, I would like to mention Professor William N. Parker, whose insightful advice and constant encouragement were often the sole stable element in the research and writing processes. Professor John C. H. Fei helped to clarify the theoretical issues untangled in chapter 4 and was especially helpful in alerting me to the basic needs of any economic model in terms of consistency and determinacy. My friend and colleague, Professor Stephen DeCanio, has been a tireless source of inspiration; without the many conversations I have had with him, this study would have been much poorer. Many of my fellow students have been made to suffer through half-baked versions of it, and much is owed to their comments and criticisms. Especially valuable were the suggestions of Richard C. Levin, Mark Gersovits, and Daniel A. Seiver. Outside Yale, I have greatly benefited from discussions with Professor Jan de Vries of the University of California at Berkeley. Others who have read parts of the manuscript in various degrees of rawness include Professor Jon S. Cohen of the University of Toronto, Dr. Shlomo Maital of the University of Tel Aviv, and Professor Donald N. McCloskey of the University of Chicago. Their comments and suggestions are greatly appreciated. A special debt is acknowledged to Dr. Yoav Kislev of the Hebrew University. Without Dr. Nachum Gross of the same institution, my graduate studies would not have been possible. Members of the seminars in Economic History at Harvard, the University of Pennsylvania, Queens University, the University of Groningen, and the University of Leuven made valuable comments and criticisms of various parts, as did members of Yale's Economic Growth Center during several presentations of parts of the model. During my stay in the Netherlands, I enjoyed the hospitality of Professor M. R. Mok and his family in Wassenaar. I greatly benefited from discussions with Professor J. H. van Stuijvenberg of the University of Amsterdam and Professor Henri Baudet of the University of Groningen. In Belgium, I enjoyed the invaluable assistance of Mrs. Hilda Coppejans-Desmedt, who has also been so kind as to make her unpublished dissertation available to me. Professor Herman van der Wee and Mr. Karel Veraghert extended their hospitality to me during a conference on Belgian economic history in Leuven. Miss Liliane Viré of the Free University of Brussels provided me with good advice. I would like to thank the Yale Concilium on International and Area Studies for the financial support that made this study possible. Mrs. Cheryl Hunt has competently typed the final version of the manuscript. Last, but most decidedly not least, my wife Margalit's dedication and patience have set new standards even for the proverbial graduate student's wife.

LIST OF ABBREVIATIONS

A.A.G. Bijdragen: Afdeling Agrarische Geschiedenis (Wageningen), Bijdragen

AER: American Economic Review

AHN: Acta Historiae Neerlandica

Annales: Annales: Économies, Sociétés, Civilisations

ARCLM: Académie Royale de Belgique, Classe des Lettres, Mémoires

ARM: Académie Royale de Belgique, Mémoires

ARMC: Académie Royale de Belgique, Mémoires Couronnés

BCCS: Bulletin de la Commission Centrale de Statistique (Brussels)

BCRH: Bulletin de la Commission Royale d'Histoire (Brussels)

BIAL: Bulletin de l'Institut Archéologique Liégeois

BISEL: Bulletin de l'Institut des Sciènces Économiques, Louvain—currently named Bulletin de l'Institut des Recherches Économiques

DRSAC: Documents et Rapports de la Société Royale Paléontologique et Archéologique de Charleroy

EEH: Explorations in Economic History

EHJ: Economisch Historisch Jaarboek (Amsterdam)—currently named Economisch en Sociaal-Historisch Jaarboek

EHR: Economic History Review

EJ: Economic Journal

HMGOG: Handelingen der Maatschappij voor Geschiedenis en Oudheidkunde te Gent

JEEH: Journal of European Economic History

JEH: Journal of Economic History

JNS: Jahrbücher fur Nationalökonomie und Statistik

KVAV: Koninklijke Vlaamsche Academie, Klasse der Letteren, Verhandelingen

MPSH: Mémoires et Publications de la Société des Sciènces, des Arts et des Lettres de Hainaut

MSLEL: Mémoires de la Société Libre d'Émulation de Liège

MS: The Manchester School

OEP: Oxford Economic Papers

P and P: Past and Present

RBHC: Revue Belge d'Histoire Contemporaine
RBPH: Revue Belge de Philologie et d'Histoire
ReStud: Review of Economic Studies
RGP: Rijks Geschiedkundige Publicatiën (The Hague)
RH: Revue Historique
RHMC: Revue d'Histoire Moderne et Contemporaine
RN: Revue du Nord
RS: Revue de Sociologie (Brussels)
TBN: Tijdschrift ter Bevordering van Nijverheid
THB: Textiel Historische Bijdragen (Hengelo)
TSS: Tijdschrift voor Staathuishoudkunde en Statistiek
TVG: Tijdschrift voor Geschiedenis (Amsterdam)
VSWG: Vierteljahrschrift für Sozial- und Wirtschaftsgeschichte

1 THE STARTING POINT

The greatest beneficiary of seventeenth century concentration, the
Netherlands, was in many respects a "feudal business" economy,
a Florence, Antwerp, or Augsburg on a seminational scale....
Dutch profits did not depend greatly on capitalist manufacture....
In Belgium ... the opposite was true. Thus the Belgians compensated
for their loss of trade and finance to the Dutch in the late sixteenth
century, and therefore became a major industrial power before them.

Eric J. Hobsbawm

DUTCH ECONOMIC CONDITIONS AROUND 1795

By the end of the eighteenth century the "golden age" in Dutch history was a thing of the past. There seems to be agreement on this among economic historians concerned with the period. It is less clear, however, when the decline started, whether it was absolute or relative, and what its causes were. It may be argued that the process of decline, which eroded the Dutch domination of shipping and international trade, was a completely natural phenomenon, the restoration of an equilibrium rather than a "traverse" between two steady states. The emergence of Holland as the major trading and shipping nation in the Western world, as well as the development of a large industrial sector associated with the maritime sector, was unviable in the very long run in the sense that the position attained by this small country was disproportionate to its dimensions and resources. The decline experienced in the eighteenth century was therefore nothing more than the assumption of a more modest role—appropriate to the country's size and endowments.

Commerce and Industry

The present state of research indicates that there is not much evidence of an overall, absolute decline.[1] While other countries expanded their

---

1. Johan de Vries, *De Economische Achteruitgang der Republiek* [The economic decline of the Republic] (Amsterdam: J. van Campen, 1959), pp. 19–30.

trade and output, the Dutch stagnated. The result was that the Dutch position as leader in international trade was lost to England and France. As noted, this could be regarded as disastrous only if one views the Dutch supremacy in the seventeenth century as a viable, long-run equilibrium position. Most of this supremacy was based on the position of the Dutch as middlemen, which was the essence of the so-called "entrepôt" (carrying) trade. It was this function that made the divergence between the dimensions of Dutch commerce and the country's actual output possible. Yet, as Charles Wilson observed, middlemen have rarely been popular.[2] Political considerations combined with economic or pseudoeconomic arguments to result in restrictive trade policies in most European countries. Thus the momentum of Dutch commercial growth was arrested, although it is not certain that its volume actually diminished.

Nonetheless, the impact of the large maritime sector (trade, shipping, banking, insurance, finance) on the Dutch economy had remained largely intact in the period ending in 1795. The special structure of the economy, as it had emerged in the sixteenth and seventeenth centuries, changed only very slowly if at all during the eighteenth century. Most relevant to the present study is the special structure of Dutch industry.

The importance of trade made it profitable for the Dutch to concentrate their industry on activities based on raw materials that were imported and then largely reexported. A more or less unique sector emerged, often referred to as *trafieken* ("traffics") as opposed to *fabrieken* (manufactures). The "traffics" were inseparably connected to the maritime sector. For most practical purposes, one could view them as a form of trade, in the process of which some value was added by the refinements of the goods, in addition to the act of exchange. Some of the important "traffics" were paper mills, sugar refineries, breweries, distilling plants, soap boilers, calico printers, and the tobacco industry. Shipbuilding and related activities could also be viewed as "traffics," although a larger proportion of the value was added in the Netherlands. In these industries the commercial and industrial elements are intertwined and it becomes impossible to distinguish between the merchant's profit (the payment for the middleman's service and arbitrage) and the industrialist's profit.

The fortunes of the traffics were strongly correlated with those of commerce and shipping. Commerce and shipping did not decline in absolute terms before 1795 and neither did the traffic industries taken as a whole. Needless to say, some industries did distinctly better than

2. C. Wilson, "The Decline of the Netherlands," in *Economic History and the Historians* (London: Weidenfeld and Nicolson, 1969), p. 23.

others, but the evidence available suggests a picture less dismal than it seemed to some contemporaries.[3]

The manufactures, which were less dependent on the maritime sector, fared far worse. A conspicuous example is the famous woolen industry in Leyden. Between 1700 and 1795 total output of cloth fell from 70,000 pieces to 4,000, which was only partially compensated by an increase in production of rough woolen fabrics.[4] The same is true for other urban textile industries, notably the silk industry.[5] Other manufactures which underwent severe crises were the ceramic industries of Delft,[6] the saw mills in the Zaan area (a province of North Holland), and the sailcloth industry.[7] The cause for this decline was in part the increasingly prohibitive policies of Holland's trading partners. Virtually every country in Europe imposed at some stage or another heavy import tariffs on finished goods as well as export duties on raw materials. Smuggling could in part counteract these policies, but even when successful, smuggling constituted an additional cost to the manufacturer. Other arguments put forward by historians are the relatively higher production costs in Holland resulting from a higher wage level and the scarcity of raw materials.[8] How serious these claims are as explanations for the stagnation of the traffics and the decline of the manufactures still remains to be seen. After all, Dutch wages were probably not lower in the seventeenth century than in the eighteenth, nor did raw materials become scarcer over time. Yet in the seventeenth century industry had flourished in the Netherlands.[9] It seems that the problem was not so much high costs in the Netherlands as such, but rather that a shift in the international structure of comparative advantage had occurred, which made Holland lose its

3. Z. W. Sneller, "De Toestand der Nijverheid te Amsterdam en Rotterdam" [The situation of industry in Amsterdam and Rotterdam], in *Bijdragen tot de Economische Geschiedenis* (Utrecht-Antwerp: Het Spectrum, 1968), p. 164. J. G. van Dillen, *Van Rijkdom en Regenten* [On wealth and regents] (The Hague: Martinus Nijhoff, 1970), p. 545.

4. N. W. Posthumus, *De Geschiedenis van de Leidsche Lakenindustrie* [History of the cloth industry in Leyden] (The Hague: Martinus Nijhoff, 1939), 3: 1096.

5. L. van Nierop, "De Zijdenijverheid van Amsterdam, Historisch Geschetst" [Historical sketch of the silk industry of Amsterdam], *TVG* 46 (1931): 113–43.

6. Joh. de Vries, *Economische Achteruitgang*, pp. 86–87.

7. Van Dillen, *Van Rijkdom en Regenten*, pp. 543–44. The decline of the sailcloth industry (as well as other parts of the shipbuilding industry) was a direct result of the stagnation (not necessarily decline) of the volume of shipping. The mechanism behind this phenomenon is the well-known acceleration principle.

8. Wilson, "The Decline," pp. 31–33. Joh. de Vries, *Economische Achteruitgang*, p. 107.

9. For example, one author explains the decline of the Dutch cotton-printing industry by the high wages paid in that industry, while admitting at the same time that "Holland was known already in the seventeenth century for its high wages. The eighteenth century did not bring any change"; W. J. Smit, *De Katoendrukkerij in Nederland tot 1813* [The cotton-printing industry in the Netherlands before 1813] (Rotterdam: Ontwikkeling, 1928), p. 196. To the

position as exporter of some industrial goods. It may not be deemed in-
conceivable that this shift was due to events occurring largely outside
the Dutch borders.

An indication that technological and institutional changes abroad
were largely responsible for the decline of Dutch manufactures is the
increase in industrial imports to the Netherlands after 1770, though no
discernible transformation occurs within the Dutch economy in this
period. Attempts to raise a nationalistic reaction against imported goods
failed completely.[10] For some commodities both the external and internal
markets were lost while for others both were retained. It is debatable
whether this was really decay or perhaps nothing more than a healthy
process of elimination of inefficient activities.

All in all, the Netherlands entered the nineteenth century with a
formidable industrial sector. Yet it was an extremely vulnerable part
of the economy. The traffic industries were highly dependent on the
maritime sector, which was itself becoming more vulnerable due to the
loss of naval supremacy to England. Dutch industry was also obsolete;
its techniques had altered very little since the seventeenth century. True,
there had been attempts in the late eighteenth century to introduce various
machines from England into Dutch industry.[11] But the adoption of these
machines was extremely tedious and in all but a few cases resulted in
utter failure. In some industries, notably the paper industry for which
the Dutch had been famous in the early eighteenth century, inventions
made abroad were ignored by the Dutch.[12] The same is true for the
cotton printing industry.[13]

Another characteristic feature of the Dutch economy in the eighteenth
century was the growth of a capital market that made Amsterdam into
the "bank of Europe." It seems that the capital market was stimulated
by the decreasing attractiveness of industry and commerce. With the
volume of commerce more or less stationary, incremental investments in
the maritime sector were likely to yield a diminishing rate of profit. Slowly
but surely many entrepreneurs (or their descendents) were transformed
into *rentiers*. Johan de Vries pinpoints the start of this transformation

extent that the suppliers imposed export duties on them, raw materials can be said to have
become scarcer. Since the raw materials of the Dutch industry came from a variety of sources,
not all of which levied export duties, the restrictive policies of its suppliers cannot account for
the whole phenomenon.

10. J. Bierens de Haan, *Van Oeconomische Tak tot Nederlandsche Maatschappij voor
Nijverheid en Handel* [History of the Dutch society for industry and commerce] (Haarlem:
Tjeenk-Willink, 1952), pp. 24–50.

11. Joh. de Vries, *Economische Achteruitgang*, pp. 111, 128–36.

12. B. W. de Vries, *De Nederlandse Papiernijverheid in de Negentiende Eeuw* [The Dutch
paper industry in the nineteenth century] (The Hague: Martinus Nijhoff, 1957), pp. 83–89.

13. Smit, *Katoendrukkerij*, p. 198.

at the beginning of the eighteenth century.[14] During the subsequent decades, the total assets of Dutch financiers grew to dimensions that stunned contemporaries. Modern historians seem inclined to accept Luzac's estimate of 1.5 billion florins in foreign loans,[15] plus about one billion in domestic national debt, at the end of the eighteenth century.[16] In addition to these assets, a large insurance sector emerged, absorbing even more savings. A huge financial sector was thus created.

Agriculture and Rural Industry

The maritime sector and traffic industries were mostly located in the Western Provinces, Holland (North and South), Zeeland, and Utrecht. In the other parts of the country industry was of limited significance. The only exception was the rural-domestic industry (also known as cottage industry or "protoindustry") in the South and East. The discussion of these industries requires a short digression into agricultural conditions.

To start with, the Netherlands is quite sharply divided into alluvial clay soils in the West and North and the diluvial sandy soils of the South and East.[17] Between 1500 and 1650, agricultural production in the alluvial provinces underwent a profound transformation. A process of double specialization took place: the peasants specialized in the production of goods in which the Netherlands had a comparative advantage, while at the same time confining themselves to agriculture, which left most other activities such as textile production, transportation, and construction to specialists. The result was a marked rise in productivity that turned Dutch agriculture into one of the most prosperous agrarian sectors of Europe.[18] One student of Dutch agriculture states:

> Fully as remarkable as the commercial and industrial achievements of the Northern Netherlands, and closely connected to it, was a thoroughgoing transformation of the rural economy. In the course of the sixteenth and seventeenth centuries a rural economy emerged which differed qualitatively as well as quantitatively from that of the preceding era. . . . It is worth noting that the restructured rural

14. Joh. de Vries, *Economische Achteruitgang*, p. 63.

15. E. Luzac, *Holland's Rijkdom* [Holland's wealth] (Leyden: Luzac and van Damme, 1783), 4:310.

16. W. M. Keuchenius, *Inkomsten en Uitgaven der Bataafsche Republiek Voorgesteld in eene Nationaale Balans* [The income and expenditures of the Batavic republic presented in a national balance] (Amsterdam: Holtrop, 1803), p. 3.

17. Z. W. Sneller, "Landbouwtoestanden in Nederland in het laatst der achttiende Eeuw" [Agricultural conditions in the Netherlands at the end of the eighteenth century], in *Geschiedenis van den Nederlandschen Landbouw, 1795–1940* [A history of Dutch agriculture], ed. Z. W. Sneller (Groningen: J. B. Wolters, 1943), pp. 17–18.

18. This discussion is based on Jan de Vries, *The Dutch Rural Economy in the Golden Age* (New Haven and London: Yale University Press, 1974).

economy during the sixteenth and seventeenth centuries endured long after the urban economy fell into decay. The enhanced productivity of agriculture and related rural activities provided the material basis for the development of the Dutch economy in the nineteenth century, when the commercial and industrial glories of the "Golden Age" were but memories.[19]

Agriculture in the Low Countries became the model that others were to imitate—the English experience comes immediately to mind.[20] During the eighteenth century there was slow but continuous technological progress, with introduction of the potato and the inoculation against cattle plague (a discovery of the Dutchman Reinders) being the two single most important innovations. Other new inventions such as the seed driller were diffused rather slowly.[21] Nonetheless, in comparison with other countries and keeping in mind the state of agricultural science in the eighteenth century, the Dutch peasant was at the outer frontier of productivity. A recent article argues that the level of technology in agriculture attained by Dutch peasants could hardly be improved upon.[22] Agricultural production in the alluvial provinces was heavily export oriented. Dairy products were the most important high-productivity export, but madder, flax, rapeseed, and vegetables were of importance too.

Agriculture in the sandy soils in the East and South was far less prosperous. The peasants of both eastern Overijssel and North Brabant are generally described as far poorer than those in the West and North.[23] The quality of the soil was inferior in these areas, and techniques were primitive. The result was the emergence of a cottage industry, in which peasants were active whenever their earnings in agriculture fell short of their opportunity cost, the latter defined by their earnings in the domestic industry.[24]

The cottage industries in Twente and North Brabant (mostly fustian and linen in the former, wool in the latter) were relatively small compared

19. Ibid., pp. 119–20.

20. See, e.g., C. Wilson, *England's Apprenticeship 1603–1763* (London: Longmans, 1965), p. 28. G. E. Fussell, "Low Countries' Influence on English Farming," *English Historical Review* 74 (October 1959): 611–22.

21. Van Dillen, *Van Rijkdom en Regenten*, p. 537.

22. J. M. G. van der Poel, "De Landbouw in de Bataafse Tijd—Illusie en Werkelijkheid" [Agriculture in the Batavic period, illusion and reality], *EHJ* 35 (1972): 65–80.

23. Sneller, "Landbouwtoestanden," pp. 24–25.

24. B. H. Slicher van Bath, *Een Samenleving onder Spanning, Geschiedenis van het Platteland in Overijssel* [A society under tension, history of the countryside of Overijssel] (Assen: van Gorcum, 1957), pp. 200–10. Id., "Historische Ontwikkeling van de Textielnijverheid in Twente" [Historical development of the textile industry in Twente], *THB* 2 (1960): 23–24.

with the traffic industries, but they were less dependent on the fragile structure of international trade and therefore more resistant to exogenous disturbances. Most of the rural industries were of the putting-out type, in which the merchant-manufacturer bought the raw materials, had them spun or woven by the peasants at a piece rate, and then took care of the sale of the final product. The entrepreneurs active in North Brabant lived mostly in the provinces of Holland, while those in the Twente area were local. In general it seems that the forms the putting-out system took in the Netherlands were relatively mild. The tools were owned in many cases by the peasants, and there is not much evidence of the exploitation that was presumably occurring in other putting-out industries all over Europe.[25]

The Netherlands in 1795

An intriguing characteristic of the "periwig economy," to paraphrase Charles Boxer, was the extremely slow rate of population increase in the Netherlands, excepting the southern and eastern parts.[26] In Holland, the growth of population between 1650 and 1800 may well have been negative. The causes for this are not fully clear, but the heavily urbanized structure of the Dutch economy certainly was a factor. The Dutch cities, in which mortality rates were in general very high, partially absorbed increments in rural population.[27] The net result was a very low population growth rate for the country as a whole. The conspicuous exception is the province of Overijssel, in which urban centers were less significant than in the maritime provinces, and where population increased by some 90 percent between 1675 and 1795.[28] In the other provinces, especially in the West, urbanization had attained exceptional dimensions in the seventeenth and eighteenth centuries. In 1815, after two decades of severe depression during which thousands had fled the Dutch cities, the proportion of population living in cities in the Netherlands was still 28 percent,[29]

25. Z. W. Sneller, "De Twentsche Weefnijverheid Omstreeks het Jaar 1800" [The weaving industry in the Twente area around the year 1800], *TVG* 41 (1926): 415–16. W. A. J. M. Harkx, *De Helmondse Textielnijverheid in de Loop der Eeuwen* [The textile industries of Helmond during the centuries] (Tilburg: Stichting Zuidelijk Historisch Contact, 1967), p. 89.

26. J. A. Faber et alii, "Population Changes and Economic Developments in the Netherlands: A Historical Survey," *A.A.G. Bijdragen* 12 (1965): 47–113.

27. A. M. van der Woude and G. J. Mentink, "La Population de Rotterdam au XVIIᵉ et XVIIIᵉ Siècles," *Population* 21 (1966): 1186–87. J. H. F. Kohlbrugge, "Over de Invloed der Steden op hare Bewoners en op de Bewoners van het Platteland" [On the influence of the towns on urban and rural population], *De Economist* (1907), pp. 381–83. De Vries (*Dutch Rural Economy*, pp. 116–17) terms the demographic structure of the Dutch economy an "urban safety valve."

28. Slicher van Bath, *Een Samenleving onder Spanning*, p. 56.

29. E. Smits, *Statistique Nationale, Développement des 31 Tableaux* (Brussels: H. Tarlier, 1827), annex table I.

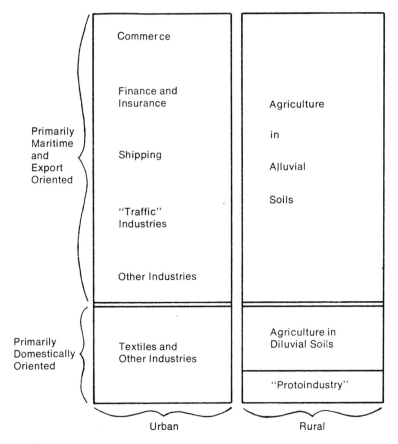

Figure 1.1   Schematic Diagram of the Structure of the Dutch Economy around 1795

and therefore was probably higher than in England and certainly was far higher than in any other country on the Continent.

To summarize, a simple sketch describing the structure of the Dutch economy by the end of the eighteenth century is presented in figure 1.1. The sketch is intended as a frame of reference only, and no inference should be made from it with respect to the relative economic significance of the various sectors.

BELGIAN ECONOMIC CONDITIONS AROUND 1795

The Southern Netherlands was, next perhaps to Poland, politically the most hapless area in Europe. Virtually every major war between 1500 and 1945 has been fought on its territory. In the sixteenth century, after the Northern Netherlands had revolted successfully, the Spanish managed to retain the area which today is Belgium. This had disastrous effects on the once wealthy economies of Brabant, Flanders, and the Walloon provinces. Spanish mercenaries devastated the land, a huge tax burden crippled the economy, and the relentless persecution of Protestants prompted thousands of highly skilled artisans to flee abroad, where they strengthened their homeland's competitors. Moreover, the Dutch, after their victory over Spain and their stunning ascent to economic prominence, used their newly acquired power to smother their former rivals. Antwerp, at one time the heart of Western commerce and finance, had its access to the North Sea blocked by the Dutch navy, which controlled the mouth of the river Scheldt (1585). The peace of Westphalia (1648) perpetualized the closure of the Scheldt, thereby dealing a mortal blow to Belgian commerce and industry. In the seventy years that followed, the country enjoyed little rest. Louis XIV's wars were once again largely fought on Belgian territory.

In 1713, the major part of the Southern Netherlands was transferred from Spain to Austria. The rest of what is today Belgium consisted mostly of the principality of Liège (ruled by a Prince-Bishop) and the sovereign abbatial territory of Stavelot-Malmédy. The eighteenth century was a period of slow economic recovery for most of these regions. The figures on population growth, though scarce, are suggestive in this context. The evidence suggests that rural population growth was very fast in this period. One source mentions that rural population in Brabant doubled between 1709 and 1784.[30] Other inquiries show that population in Flanders in the eighteenth century increased by 78 percent, the bulk of it in the countryside.[31] The urban sector in Belgium remained small and insignificant compared with the Northern Netherlands. Urban population seems to have diminished between 1700 and 1730, remained stationary between 1730 and 1755, and after that recovered slowly, reaching by 1790 the level of 1700.[32]

What were the mechanisms that made this population growth in the rural areas possible? The first was an increased agricultural productivity for which there is scattered but convincing evidence. Probably the increase in acreage under cultivation was as important as the creation and

30. H. Pirenne, *Histoire de Belgique* (Brussels: La Renaissance du Livre, 1948), 3: 143.
31. F. Mendels, "Industrialization and Population Pressure in Eighteenth Century Flanders" (Ph.D. diss., University of Wisconsin, 1969), p. 96.
32. H. van Werveke, "De Curve van het Gentse Bevolkingscijfer in de 17de en 18de Eeuw" [The population curve in Ghent in the seventeenth and eighteenth centuries], *KVAV* 10, no. 8 (1948): 52. H. Coppejans-Desmedt, "Economische Opbloei in de Zuidelijke Nederlanden" [Prosperity in the southern Netherlands], in *Algemene Geschiedenis der Nederlanden*, ed. J. A. van Houtte et alii (Utrecht: W. de Haan, 1955), 8:264.

diffusion of new techniques in agriculture. Enclosures (in Hainault, Namur, and Brabant) as well as drainage and poldering (in Flanders) made new lands available for cultivation.[33] A second factor was the introduction of the potato, which contributed to the increase in the amount of calories produced per acre.[34]

Most important, rural industry grew rapidly under the continuous stimulation of population increase. More precisely: the existence of a rural industry made the unchecked expansion of rural population possible by removing the Malthusian check of diminishing returns. Incremental population could thus be absorbed by the rural industry or "Z-good industry" as we will call it henceforth.[35] The peasants produced industrial commodities, sold them at the markets, to merchants, or in some cases received a wage from the "putters out." With the income from this industrial activity the peasants were able to purchase food which their own landholding or agricultural wage could not provide adequately. A formalization of this simple model will be presented at a later stage, but it will be intuitively obvious that the decisive feature of the Z-good industry was that it was basically a one-input activity and hence not subject to diminishing returns. The seasonal nature of agriculture and the choice between income and leisure, stressed by Mendels,[36] complicates this picture but does not alter it in any essential way.

33. Coppejans-Desmedt, "Economische Opbloei," p. 266. H. van der Wee, "De Industriële Revolutie in België" [The industrial revolution in Belgium], in *Historische Aspecten van de Economische Groei* (Antwerp-Utrecht: Nederlandsche Boekhandel, 1972), p. 176.

34. F. Mendels, "Agriculture and Peasant Industry in Eighteenth Century Flanders," in *European Peasants and Their Markets*, ed. William N. Parker and Eric L. Jones (Princeton: Princeton University Press, forthcoming). The nutritional value of the product of a unit of land planted with potatoes was about double the nutritional value of the alternative crops, wheat or rye. Therefore, Mendels argues, the increase in food production due to potatoes alone cannot have been larger than the proportion of land allocated to potatoes. This is an overly formalistic assertion. It ignores the fact that the potato was a popular food, grown largely by small peasants, while wheat was until the end of the eighteenth century an important export good. The substitution of potatoes for wheat may therefore have increased domestic food supply by a factor larger than two. Nor does Mendels provide evidence that the increased acreage did come in fact at the expense of cereals. Coppejans-Desmedt, "Economische Opbloei," p. 268, claims that the potato came largely at the expense of legumes (which were becoming less essential since protein production increased with the increase in livestock and cattle). In addition cereals were used for industry and fodder while potatoes were almost exclusively consumed by humans.

35. The term has been borrowed from S. Hymer and S. Resnick, "A Model of an Agrarian Economy with Nonagricultural Activities," *AER* 59, no. 4, part 1 (September 1969): 493–506. The term "protoindustry" will also be employed. It should be noted that Hymer and Resnick use the term Z-goods to denote goods which are consumed within the household, rather than exchanged for food at the market.

36. F. Mendels, "Protoindustrialization: The First Phase of the Industrialization Process," *JEH* 32, no. 1 (March 1972): 242. Idem, "Industrialization and Population Pressure," pp. 224–25.

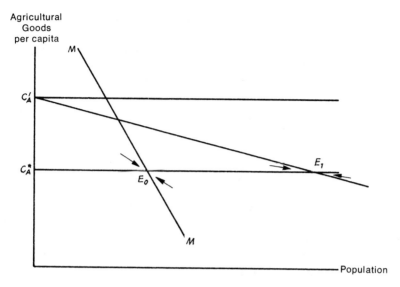

Figure 1.2   Protoindustry in a Simple Malthusian Model

The simple setup is demonstrated in figure 1.2. All we have to assume is that the rate of population growth is a continuous and rising function of the consumption of agricultural goods. Under these assumptions we can always define a level of consumption, $C_A^\star$, at which population is constant. Let the marginal product of labor in the production of agricultural goods be represented by MM.

An economy without a Z-good sector will end up at a point like E_0, the Malthusian trap (there is no need for the economy to remain at E_0—continuous overshooting could occur). Suppose now that the protoindustrial sector produces an industrial good, Z, which is exchanged at the world market for food (A). If the relative price of Z in terms of A is constant, the consumption of food per capita will be independent of the absolute size of population. This consumption level is depicted by C_A'. As long as $C_A' > C_A^\star$, population will increase continuously. Prices need not be constant even if the economy is a perfect price taker, but as long as price fluctuations are independent of the population size, we might as well ignore them. Such a procedure would not be satisfactory, however, if the economy was an imperfect price taker, that is, if the economy faces a downward sloping demand curve at the world market. Under that assumption, the consumption of agricultural goods declines with population, since the terms of trade deteriorate as more and more Z is supplied. Thus the economy will eventually reach a point like E_1 in figure 1.2. At that point population is stationary again, unless new ways are found to evade the threat of diminishing returns. In passing it should be noted that protoindustry can serve as a hedge against Malthusian mechanisms only in relatively small regions. The greater an economy, the less elastic the world demand curve it faces, and the more rapidly a point like E_1 is reached.

The question arises as to what were the special conditions that made it possible for Belgium to develop such a large Z-good sector. It is not easy to provide a satisfactory answer, but it seems that this area had three important advantages that played a role in this development. First, in some areas, especially in the Waas region in East Flanders, the soil was well suited to flax cultivation. Second, the traditional links that Belgium maintained with Spain helped it create easily accessible markets in Spain itself as well as in the Spanish colonies in South America. Third, the age-old tradition of domestic industry, a remnant of the woolen industry which had made Flanders famous in the Middle Ages, should not be underestimated as a factor in determining the economic and professional structure of Belgium.

The three major centers of the Z-good industry in Belgium were the linen industry in Flanders (including the lace industry, in part located in the urban areas of Brabant), the woolen industry in Verviers and other places along the river Vesdre in the eastern Walloon provinces, and the rural metallurgical industries in the Liège area, Namur, and Hainault.

The Linen Industry

The linen industry was particularly significant in the sandy soils of interior Flanders, although it could be found in most parts of western Belgium. In the maritime area, where the soils were of a different quality (mostly clay), it played a less crucial role.

The most salient feature of the Flemish linen industry was its sheer size. The number of people active in some way or other in the industry can be approximated by relying on well-informed contemporaries. An estimate from 1765 puts the total number of workers employed in the manufacturing of linen cloth at 200,000 plus 50,000 occupied in growing and preparing the raw material.[37] Only 5 percent of the total land was allocated to flax, but this was land of high quality since flax severely exhausts the soil. Labor requirements were high since flax needed much preparatory work (retting, hackling, etc.) before the raw flax could be sold to the spinners. The French administration estimated in the first years of the nineteenth century the number of spinners in the *département*

---

37. Cited by G. Willemsen, "Contribution à l'Histoire de l'Industrie Linière en Flandre au XVIIIe Siècle," *HMGOG* 7 (1906): 261.

Escaut (East Flanders) at 101,033, and the number of weavers at 21,821.[38]
For the province of West Flanders the number of weavers was estimated
at 23,133[39] and that of spinners at about 100,000.[40] An estimate of 250,000
workers, not counting the activity of children in winding yarn and other
auxiliary activities, would not be far off the mark. This amounts to a
quarter of the population.

The linen industry, like most Z-good production, was related to the
seasonal nature of agriculture. It still remains to be seen, however, if
seasonality was indeed the major force behind the emergence of the linen
industry in Flanders.[41] After all, seasonality in Flanders was not much
more pronounced than in most other agrarian regions of Europe. It may
be true that innovation in Flemish agriculture in the eighteenth century
had a seasonal bias,[42] but it seems that the adoption of such a work pattern
was in part the *result* of the availability of an alternative occupation during
the slack seasons. In any case, the phenomenon of seasonality should be
viewed analytically as a special case of the more general phenomenon of
diminishing returns. A theoretical analysis of the possible significance
of seasonality in enhancing the development of protoindustries is
presented in chapter 4.

If we accept the hypothesis that the formation of a Z-good sector was
enhanced by the existence of rapidly diminishing returns to labor in agriculture, the rapid growth of the linen industry in Flanders in the eighteenth
century is more easily understood. The rapid increase of rural population
mentioned above implied a continuous fragmentation of landholdings.
In the villages of Schorisse and St. Kornelis Horebeke in 1711, the proportion of farms smaller than one hectare was 48.6 percent and 44.1
percent respectively. In 1790 these figures had risen to 65.9 percent and
57.8 percent respectively. The proportion of farms smaller than five
hectares increased from 89.3 percent and 90.7 percent to 90.7 percent
and 92.1 percent respectively over the same period.[43] Clearly the process
of fragmentation was especially severe among small farmers, although

38. M. Faipoult, *Mémoire Statistique du Département de l'Escaut*, originally published in
the year XIII [1804], ed. Paul Deprez (Ghent: Oostvlaams Verbond van de Kringen voor de
Geschiedenis, 1960), p. 165.

39. C. Viry, *Mémoire Statistique du Département de la Lys* (Paris: Imprimerie Impériale,
year XII [1803]), p. 146.

40. E. Dubois, *L'Industrie du Tissage du Lin dans les Flanders* (Brussels: J. Lebègue, 1900),
p. 16.

41. This seems to be the opinion of Mendels. Cf. his "Agriculture and Peasant Industry,"
p. 5.

42. Mendels, "Industrialization and Population Pressure," p. 134.

43. C. De Rammelaere, "Bijdrage tot de Landbouwgeschiedenis in Zuidoost Vlaanderen"
[A contribution to the agrarian history of southeastern Flanders], *HMGOG*, n.s. 16 (1962):
33–40.

a similar process was taking place among large farmers as well. The results of a century of fragmentation are clear-cut. In the beginning of the nineteenth century the French prefect Faipoult observed that the Flemish farms were very small, not more than two to three hectares on the average.[44] It would be correct to say that population increase coupled with equal-share inheritance made the protoindustry the only hedge against starvation, but it is important to remember that the growth of population in Flanders was made possible in the first place by the existence of the protoindustry.

The Z-good sector can thus be seen as a passive factor which permitted population growth in Flanders. Similar relationships have been observed for other regions in Europe, including, as was shown above, Overijssel in the Eastern Netherlands. Mendels argues that the link between population growth and Z-good production is to be sought in a lowered marriage age. He explains that

> ... where industry was diffusing into the cottages, households could be sustained on smaller land parcels and the capital ... necessary before one could form a household was smaller. Marriages could take place at a younger age and respond more immediately to improved opportunities.[45]

In addition, changes in mortality were an explanatory factor of population movement in the longer run, though not of year-to-year variations with which Mendels's regression equations are concerned. Other writers tend to attribute the association of Z-good production with rapid population growth to changes in the social structure resulting from the spread of protoindustry.[46]

A particular feature of the Flemish linen industry was the fact that, in contrast to many other protoindustries, the entrepreneurial unit was small—in general, the household. Most spinners purchased the flax at the market and after spinning either sold the linen yarn or had other members of the household weave it into linen cloth. In general, spinning was performed by women, weaving by men. The relative absence of putting-out entrepreneurs implied that the risk was fully borne by peasants, but that on the other hand they were free from extortions and other monopsonistic practices used by the "putters-out."[47] The tools and implements used by spinners and weavers were either owned by them or

44. Faipoult, *Mémoire Statistique*, p. 108.
45. Mendels, "Industrialization and Population Pressure," p. 249.
46. R. Braun, "The Impact of Cottage Industry on an Agricultural Population," in *The Rise of Capitalism*, ed. David S. Landes (New York: Macmillan, 1966), pp. 53–64.
47. Willemsen, "Contribution," pp. 226–30.

rented cheaply.[48] The number of large-scale entrepreneurs not directly involved in production was very small.[49]

The total annual output of the linen industry is not easy to estimate since only part of the finished cloth ended up at the urban markets. A small but increasing part was bought up by traveling merchants known as *kutzers*. A large part of the exports went to Spain, which reexported the linen cloth to its colonies for slave clothing, coffee bags, and similar products. Italy, Holland, England, France, and the Ottoman Empire were important customers too, though the distribution of exports varied considerably over time. An estimate for the year 1765 puts total output at 159,000 pieces.[50] The size of an average piece of linen was 80 ells by $\frac{5}{4}$ ells (the Flemish ell was about 2′ 5″). The market value of this output was estimated at 5.4 million florins or 11.5 million francs. These figures probably refer to exports alone rather than to total output. The year 1765 was a bad year, and a year later exports rose to 200,000 pieces.[51] The average volume of exports of linen cloth between 1777 and 1791 was 163,000 pieces.[52] An estimate from 1804 referring to East Flanders only, puts total output at 175,000 pieces with a market value of 10.5 million francs. Since East Flanders produced something like half the total output of Flanders, it can be concluded that output had grown rapidly in the last third of the eighteenth century. Mendels estimates total output (including local consumption) at 350,000 pieces for the same period.[53] In addition, 130,000 pounds of yarn were exported annually. Ignoring the latter and estimating an average price of 70 francs per piece,[54] of which $\frac{1}{4}$ is to be deducted for raw materials,[55] it can be calculated that the average yearly earnings of a linen worker were slightly less than 74 francs, which does include the imputed value of the production consumed on the spot. Spread out over about 180 days, this amounts to a daily wage of 0.41 francs. Since there were about 4 spinners to a weaver and since the wage of spinners was about half the wage of weavers, the daily wage of weavers can be estimated at

48. Mendels, "Protoindustrialization," p. 243.
49. Willemsen, "Contribution," p. 230.
50. Ibid., p. 257.
51. Mendels, "Agriculture and Peasant Industry," p. 4.
52. Dubois, *L'Industrie du Tissage*, p. 13.
53. Mendels, "Industrialization and Population Pressure," p. 178.
54. The implicit price in Faipoult's figures is 64 francs per piece. The prices cited by Viry for West Flanders are higher, around 90 francs per piece sold in Kortrijk. Since the quality of linens sold in West Flanders was somewhat higher, the average price is closer to the lower figure. Cf. Viry, *Mémoire Statistique*, p. 155. Faipoult, *Mémoire Statistique*, p. 166.
55. N. Briavoinne, *De l'Industrie en Belgique, Causes de Décadence et de Prosperité, sa Situation Actuelle* (Brussels: Société Typographique Belge, 1839), 2: 343–44. Faipoult (*Mémoire Statistique*, p. 165) puts the proportion of raw materials in total value at 2/5, which would imply even lower wages.

0.68 francs daily, that of spinners at 0.34. Needless to say, these figures are crude estimates and fluctuated considerably with the prices of output and raw materials. Nonetheless, they reflect the extremely low standards of living which the protoindustry provided to those it saved from the jaws of the Malthusian monster. It seems therefore not implausible to suggest that around the year 1795 Flanders was probably not far from point E_1 in figure 1.2.

The extreme poverty of the Flemish linen producer in the last third of the eighteenth century is an undisputed fact. A memorandum written in the year 1765 by the *Keure* of Ghent (the institution in charge of inspecting the quality of the linen cloth) describes the condition of the Flemish rural industrial workers as follows:

> More than half of the producers and weavers of linen cloth live in cottages and huts in the countryside where they are occupied in weaving, especially in wintertime by lamplight. The women and children prepare and spin the flax. It is estimated that a weaver with his family can earn together seven to eight *sols* [0.63–0.72 francs] by working, as they always do, from four a.m. to nine p.m. They subsist on rye bread, potatoes, buttermilk, a little bacon on Sundays and water. That is all their food. There is no one more wretched than them in the whole world . . . they work absolutely for minimal subsistence. . . . One wonders whether at the end of the year the weavers will have as much as six écus [18 francs].[56]

These figures are probably too low, as 1765 was an exceptionally unfavorable year. In 1787 spinning is quoted as paying a daily wage of at most 5 *sols* (0.45 francs).[57] Another estimate put the income of a family of five, exclusively engaged in linen production, at 34 *groten* (1.56 francs) daily for the end of the eighteenth century. At around the same time (1801), the cost of bread for two adults was about 0.75 francs daily.[58]

Related to the Flemish linen industry was the lace industry, which used high quality linen yarn as its raw material. The centers of this industry were in the cities of Brabant and Flanders (Antwerp, Mechelen, Brussels, Kortrijk). Total employment was on the order of 25,000 persons, almost exclusively women.[59] Wages were even lower than in the rural industry.[60] The lace industry is an example of a successful urban industry employing

56. Cited by Willemsen, "Contribution," p. 229.
57. L. Varlez, *Les Salaires dans l'Industrie Gantoise* (Brussels: J. Lebègue, 1901–04), 2: xx.
58. Mendels, "Industrialization and Population Pressure," pp. 201, 206.
59. Coppejans-Desmedt, "Economische Opbloei," p. 282.
60. P. Bonenfant, "Le Problème du Paupérisme en Belgique à la Fin de l'Ancien Régime," *ARCLM* 35 (1934): 49.

traditional, manual techniques, and possibly should be viewed as a factor in the recovery of Belgian towns after 1760.

The Woolen Industry

The Belgian woolen industry originated and prospered in Flanders in the Middle Ages. The events of the sixteenth and seventeenth centuries virtually destroyed these industries. Eventually they resettled in the eastern part of Belgium in the region along the river Vesdre, with the town of Verviers as its main center. The growth of the woolen industry during the eighteenth century was probably slower than the growth of the linen industry in Flanders, but here even less is known with regard to quantitative evidence.[61]

The total number of workers in the woolen industry relative to total population was less significant than in Flanders. In 1800, the total number of rural workers in the woolen industry in this region was estimated at 37,000 or about 10 percent of the total population of the *Département de l'Ourthe* (today the province of Liège),[62] as compared with 25 percent employed in the Flemish Z-good sector. There were other differences as well between the two protoindustries. By its very nature, some phases in the production of woolen cloth needed to be done in a centralized mill. Fulling, for example, needed water mills which were built on the banks of the Vesdre. The entrepreneurs who owned the mills put out the weaving and spinning of wool, while performing the carding of the raw wool, as well as the finishing of the product (scouring, fulling, brushing, dyeing, etc.) in the plant. In most cases the entrepreneur retained the ownership over the raw materials throughout the process and owned the workers' implements as well.

In the second half of the eighteenth century a process of concentration started in the woolen industry of the Verviers area. In some firms workers were concentrated in *manufactures* (that is, workshops which brought the workers together, though the techniques remained basically unaltered) presumably to avoid embezzlement[63] and to enforce stricter quality control. Weaving especially became concentrated in a fashion similar to

---

61. P. Lebrun, *L'Industrie de la Laine à Verviers* (Liège: Bibliothèque de la Faculté de Philosophie et Lettres de l'Université de Liège, 1948), pp. 332, 518–19, and diagram IV. Lebrun finds that between 1747–50 and 1786–89 output increased by 30 percent. The oscillations of the series are, however, so large that choosing different starting and ending points reverses the conclusion. The trend over time is insignificant.

62. L. F. Thomassin, *Mémoire Statistique du Département de l'Ourthe*, written between 1806 and 1812 (Liège: Grandmont-Donders, 1879), p. 479. J. P. B. de Montalivet, *Exposé de la Situation de l'Empire* (Paris: Imprimerie Impériale, 1813), p. 5. Montalivet estimates the number of workers around 1784 at about 26,000.

63. Lebrun, *L'Industrie de la Laine*, p. 285. Mendels, "Protoindustrialization," p. 244.

what happened in England at the same time.[64] The concentration process was by no means general, however, and by the end of the eighteenth century the woolen industry was still primarily a domestic industry. Wool spinning was almost exclusively rural, while in weaving about 40 percent of the workers lived in the countryside, the rest in the townlets.[65]

The impact of the Z-good sector on the population and overall economic structure of the region that constitutes today the province of Liège is not as clear as in Flanders, mainly because of the absence of appropriate data. Therefore, the effects of the putting-out system in Liège (as contrasted with the self-employed Z-good sector in Flanders) cannot be unambiguously established. There are signs of imperfections in the putting-out labor markets indicating that monopsonistic entrepreneurs attempted to pay their rural employees less than their marginal product. In 1794 six *fabriquants* in Verviers controlled 50 percent of total cloth output. Another sign of an imperfect labor market was the (infrequent) occurrence of the notorious "truck system" under which the entrepreneur coerced the workers to accept payment in kind so that he made a double profit (many of the woolen cloth manufacturers were merchants as well). Moreover, there were many labor conflicts and strikes during the eighteenth century, indicating that workers as well as employers were well organized.[66]

Increasing exploitation, though not very plausible, is the only rescue for Lebrun's data, which are otherwise inconsistent. Lebrun's figures show that prices of woolen cloth rose 36 percent between 1770 and 1795. Yet nominal wages were constant until the closing years of the century while prices of agricultural goods showed an upward trend, especially in the late 1790s.[67] Part of the paradox can be resolved by the rise in the prices of raw wool, but since this rise was less than the rise in output prices, it cannot account for the whole phenomenon. Nor does it make sense to argue that the supply of labor for some reason shifted out, since then a clear-cut increase in employment and in output should be observed, which was not the case. The only possibilities are increasing imperfections in the labor market or possibly a very severe case of money illusion on the part of the workers. The alternative is to disbelieve Lebrun's data, which unfortunately seems the more logical choice.

The rural spinners, who comprised the majority of the protoindustrial workers, were, as in Flanders, mostly part-time workers occupied in some seasons in agriculture. Here, too, it was the low productivity of

---

64. Van der Wee, "Industriële Revolutie," p. 174. Lebrun, *L'Industrie de la Laine*, pp. 285–87.
65. Lebrun, *L'Industrie de la Laine*, pp. 217, 270, 272.
66. Ibid., p. 264.
67. Ibid., pp. 322–25, 516–18..

labor in agriculture that made protoindustry necessary: starvation and subsequent contraction of population being the only alternative. It is true that there are less clear indications of population pressure on the land than in Flanders, but there can be little doubt that a similar mechanism was in operation. The trans-Meuse region was mainly pastoral and its output primarily dairy products. But the prosperity that marked Dutch dairy farming was wholly absent. One contemporary writes:

> This type of agriculture requires little labor and little care, the country is very populated and labor is cheap; this leaves place for the introduction of various kinds of industries, especially the spinning of wool.[68]

The little historical research done in this area tends to confirm the conclusion that productivity in this region was very low. It seems relatively obvious that, taken as a whole, Walloon agriculture was far behind Flemish in its techniques and had as yet not adopted the three-crop rotation, the potato, intensive manuring, and other measures which made Flemish agriculture so productive.[69] It has also been demonstrated that population density was clearly associated with the geographical distribution of rural industry.[70]

The factors which made it possible for a large Z-good sector to emerge in the Walloon provinces are less easy to pinpoint than in Flanders. The raw wool was not locally produced but largely imported from Spain. The river Vesdre, which was utilized by means of canals that carried the water into the plants, provided water with a low calcium content, a considerable advantage. In addition, the constantly humid air and the proximity of cheap fuel (lumber) could be regarded as favorable factors for the Vesdre region. The crucial advantage seems, however, to have been the long tradition of woolen cloth manufacturing which the Vesdre region had inherited from medieval Flanders.

Most of the output of woolen cloth was exported. Thomassin reports that of a total output of 60 million francs, exports comprised no less than 55 million.[71] Most of the output went to France, Italy, and Germany. As in the linen industry, the cloth manufacturers operated in a competitive world market in which they were essentially price takers.

The wages in the Walloon industry cannot be said to have been simply

68. Thomassin, *Mémoire Statistique*, p. 475.

69. P. Lindemans, *Geschiedenis van de Landbouw in België* [History of Belgian agriculture] (Antwerp: de Sikkel, 1952), 1:42, 432.

70. J. Ruwet, *L'Agriculture et les Classes Rurales au Pays de Herve sous l'Ancien Régime* (Liège: Bibliothèque de la Faculté de Philosophie et Lettres de l'Université de Liège, 1943), pp. 240–42.

71. Thomassin, *Mémoire Statistique*, p. 475.

determined by the product of the workers' productivity and the price of the final output. The rural workers produced only a stage of the final product. The entrepreneurs earned profits on their circulating and fixed capital as well as a wage for the labor spent in organizing production and trading. In addition, as argued above, it is not clear whether, in fact, the rural worker received the value of his marginal product. In any case, the wages of the rural workers in the woolen industry do not seem radically higher than the wages earned in the Flemish protoindustry. They were without doubt far lower than wages in the Netherlands, either maritime or diluvial. A source from 1741, comparing wages in the woolen industries of Leyden (South Holland), Tilburg (North Brabant), and Verviers estimates them as relating to each other as 3 : 1.5 : 1.[72] Lebrun, too, mentions low wages in the Verviers area as a major factor in the development of the woolen industry.[73] In the first decade of the nineteenth century (a relatively prosperous period) skilled workers averaged 1.22 francs daily, while rural spinners earned a daily wage of only 0.70 francs.[74]

The Metallurgical Industry

The third major protoindustry in Belgium was the rural iron industry, which produced mainly nails, pins, and cutlery. Unfortunately, very little exact information is available about the industry. Its principal centers were the Northeast in what constitutes today the provinces of Liège and Limburg and in the South in the valley of the Sambre (Hainault and Namur). The total number of workers active in the nail industry is estimated by contemporaries at about thirty thousand.[75] This figure probably includes all members of the families of the workers, but since in fact the whole family participated in the production process, it probably represents the right order of magnitude.[76]

The similarity between the rural iron industry and other Z-good sectors has caused one writer to call the nail industry the "counterpart

72. N. W. Posthumus, "De Industrieele Concurrentie tussen Noord-en Zuid-Nederlandsche Nijverheidscentra in de XVIIe en XVIIIe Eeuw" [The industrial competition between northern and southern Netherlands in the seventeenth and eighteenth centuries], in *Mélanges d'Histoire offerts à H. Pirenne* (Brussels: Vromant, 1926), p. 376.

73. Lebrun, *L'Industrie de la Laine*, p. 192.

74. Thomassin, *Mémoire Statistique*, p. 474.

75. Of these about 15,000 were in the East and about the same in the South. Cf. A. Warzée, "Exposé Historique de l'Industrie du Fer dans la Province de Liège," *MSLEL*, n.s., vol. 1 (1860): 514. Id., "Exposé Historique et Statistique de l'Industrie Métallurgique dans le Hainaut," *MPSH*, 2d ser. 8 (1860–62): 127.

76. Thomassin, *Mémoire Statistique*, p. 439, mentions only 3,379 *cloutiers*. He notes, however (p. 440), that each manufacturer employed 4–8 workers (probably mostly family members) so that the acceptance of the latter figure by Hansotte is unwarranted. Cf. G. Hansotte, *La Clouterie Liégeoise au XVIIIe Siècle* (Brussels: 1972), p. 13.

of the Flemish linen industry."[77] Nail-making, too, was largely an export
industry. A large part of its output was sold to the Netherlands, probably
mostly for shipbuilding.[78] The rest was exported to Germany, Spain,
Portugal, and the Ottoman Empire.[79] A further parallel between the nail
industry and other protoindustries was the low wages paid in general in
the nail industry, though these wages varied substantially with the quality
of the nails produced.[80]

The nail industry was a putting-out industry. The merchants bought
the raw materials, sold the final product, and employed special middlemen
(*marchotais*), who acted on their behalf and supervised the production.
The merchants did not actually engage in the production process and
should not be regarded as industrial entrepreneurs, in contrast to the
entrepreneurs in the woolen industry. Moreover, in general the workers
owned the few implements and the little forge used in the production
process. Consequently, profits, mainly a return to risk-taking and to
circulating capital, were very low.[81] Many entrepreneurs attempted to
exploit their workers in various ways.[82] Monopolistic practices like
prohibiting workers from working for more than one employer and confining workers to fixed quality classes of nails were widespread. Especially
in the Liège area, exploitation of the workers was rampant and the truck
system widely employed. On the other hand, embezzlement of raw
materials was an important part of the worker's income. It is thus not
very meaningful to estimate daily wages. The available evidence does,
however, suggest that wages were extremely low.[83] These low wages,
as well as the monopolistic behavior of the merchants, were the source of
a prolonged wave of strikes that hit the Liège region in the second half
of the eighteenth century. Consequently, the center of gravity of the nail
industry drifted slowly to the Charleroi area in the Sambre Valley. While
it is not clear whether the decline of the nail industry in the Liège area
in this period was absolute or relative, it is clear that both the Liège and
the Charleroi areas entered the nineteenth century with a large "proto-
metallurgical" industry, employing tens of thousands of workers.

77. Coppejans-Desmedt, "Economische Opbloei," p. 281.
78. Thomassin, *Mémoire Statistique*, p. 439.
79. C. Génart, *L'Industrie Cloutière en Pays Wallon* (Brussels: J. Lebègue, 1900), p. 25.
80. Hansotte, *Clouterie*, pp. 15–16. Génart, *L'Industrie Cloutière*, p. 26.
81. Hansotte, *Clouterie*, p. 87.
82. Génart, *L'Industrie Cloutière*, pp. 24f.
83. A document from 1768 puts the maximum wage at 17–30 *sous Liègeois* (1.1–2.0 francs) a day. This lasted only for about 6–8 weeks each year, after which the wage dropped to 10–13 sous (0.66–0.86 francs). In the seasons in which the forges were idle, the wages dropped to even lower levels. Cf. Génart, *L'Industrie Cloutière*, p. 26.

Belgium in 1795

The Z-good sector has been described in considerable detail because of the unique role it played in subsequent industrial development in Belgium, as will be explained at a later stage. This is not to say that there were no other industries in Belgium before 1800. First and foremost, there was the large metallurgical industry. This industry had two main centers: one in the Liège region and the other in the area around Charleroi known as the Borinage. Total output of the sixty-three blast furnaces in Belgium around 1795 was 18.5 thousand tons of cast iron.[84] Most of the iron was sold to the nail and other domestic iron industries, including the armament industry in the city of Liège. The latter, however, did not fare very well in the relatively peaceful decades preceding the French Revolution.[85]

In the second half of the eighteenth century, some new industries were introduced in Belgium that did remarkably well. One of the most conspicuous of these was the calico printing industry that was centered in Ghent and that grew rapidly. Most of the calico printing firms were comparatively large and introduced some important technological innovations, most of them smuggled from England.[86] It has to be emphasized, however, that calico printing was still in its infancy in the eighteenth century and that most of the pathbreaking innovations were introduced only after 1795.[87] In other industries, too, important beginnings were made during the Austrian period. Some examples of these were paper, sugar, glass, and earthenware.[88] The locational patterns of industry had already started to crystallize. Most of the new industries were located in Flanders or in the industrial areas of Liège and Hainault.

Compared with the Netherlands, the urban industries in Belgium looked insignificant in 1795. The bulk of all industrial activity in this period was still performed by a large, semiagrarian rural proletariat. This activity was, as emphasized above, still using archaic technologies and was to some degree dependent on the seasonal nature of agriculture. Labor was virtually the only input in this industry, and its productivity was accordingly low. In spite of differences in organizational setup and market structure, the Belgian protoindustries had three important characteristics in common: they were all largely export-oriented, they interacted

84. N. Briavoinne, "Sur les Inventions et Perfectionnements dans l'Industrie," *ARMC* 13 (1838): 121–22.
85. P. Lebrun, "La Rivoluzione Industriale in Belgio," *Studi Storici* 2, nos. 3–4 (December 1961): 609.
86. Van der Wee, "Industriële Revolutie," p. 174.
87. Briavoinne, "Sur les Inventions," p. 81.
88. Coppejans-Desmedt, "Economische Opbloei," p. 284.

with demographic variables, and they determined essentially the labor supply to other sectors. The former two were discussed in some detail above, while the latter will be considered at length in chapters 4 and 5.

Concluding Remarks

Simplifying somewhat, it could be argued that Malthusian checks were the major force governing the dynamics of population and per capita consumption during the Middle Ages and much of the early modern period. Only in the modern period did various ways "to beat Malthus" emerge.[89] As was recently reemphasized, the Netherlands were the first region in Western Europe to succeed in this.[90]

The key to understanding the differences between the Northern Netherlands and Belgium at the end of the *ancien régime* is to be found in the different fashions by which they managed to escape the Malthusian trap. Initially, they started on more or less the same paths. A constant intensification of agriculture took place, together with a rapidly growing nonagricultural urban sector producing both industrial goods and services. The Low Countries specialized mainly in commerce, shipping, and finance. They were selling the means to reduce the world's transaction costs, to use a fashionable term. At some point, however, the paths of the two countries parted. A partial explanation of this may have been the lower fertility of the land in Belgium, but the main cause undoubtedly was the destructive series of wars that plagued the Belgian provinces between 1568 and 1714.

After the virtual destruction of its commercial and industrial urban centers, Belgium found itself at a crossroads. Either it was to enter a Malthusian stationary state, in which high mortality rates kept the size of population at a more or less constant level, or it had to find a way to avoid the Malthusian trap. The solution to the dilemma became more and more visible in the late seventeenth century and especially after the termination of the wars of Louis XIV, when protoindustry became an increasingly important part of the traditional sector.

In the Netherlands, and especially in the provinces of Holland, no Z-good sector was needed. They had succeeded in escaping the population checks by expanding the nonagricultural sector while at the same time revolutionizing the agrarian sector. Moreover, the large urban sector

89. For a powerful restatement of this generalization see Emmanuel Le Roy Ladurie, *The Peasants of Languedoc*, trans. John Day (Urbana: University of Illinois Press, 1974), pp. 309–11.

90. D. C. North and R. P. Thomas, *The Rise of the Western World* (Cambridge: At the University Press, 1973), p. 132.

which emerged as a result of the specialization of the Dutch in services and traffic industries, served by itself as a regulator of population. Only in those areas which were not amenable to the high standards of productivity of alluvial agriculture and which were relatively remote from the urban sectors in which the maritime economy was centered, did a small Z-good sector emerge. In these provinces, indeed, the rural population grew at a rapid rate. The unresolved question is why rural population in the rich alluvial soils of Holland did not grow faster than it did—the absorption by the towns of excess rural population can only partly account for the slow growth of population in these regions. It must have been the case that for some reason the level of consumption of agricultural goods at which population was constant ($C^\star_A$ in figure 1.2) was higher in the Netherlands than in Belgium. This implies that the whole population response mechanism in the Netherlands may have obeyed a different set of rules.

In any event, by 1795 the Netherlands enjoyed a comparatively high standard of living with a slowly growing population. According to contemporaries, the level of consumption in the Netherlands was the highest in Europe. This stands in sharp contrast with Belgium where in many areas severe poverty coexisted with a relatively rapid population growth.

Observing the Netherlands and Belgium in the closing years of the eighteenth century, it seems surprising that it was Belgium and not the Netherlands that followed in England's footsteps in the adoption of new and mechanized techniques in industrial production. At first glance, the Netherlands appear to have enjoyed many of the same advantages that are often used to explain England's initial leadership. A large and wealthy bourgeoisie, a singularly high rate of urbanization, a prosperous and relatively efficient agrarian sector, a commercial and financial superstructure that was without peer in Europe, and above all an abundance of capital that dwarfed any other country in Europe including England—all these would provide the Netherlands with a considerable headstart on its neighbors. Belgium had none of these. Governed by foreigners, the traditional battlefield of Europe, the country consisted largely of impoverished peasants. The benefits of Dutch maritime activities were almost wholly absent, nor did Belgium have the essential features of efficient transportation, finance and insurance, or even a deepwater harbor. Yet by 1850 Belgium was by far the most industrialized nation on the European continent, whereas the Netherlands experienced little industrialization before the last third of the nineteenth century.[91] The present study will try

91. This question baffles even W. W. Rostow. Cf. W. W. Rostow, "The Beginning of Modern Growth in Europe," *JEH* 33, no. 3 (September 1973): 573n.

to shed some light on the possible causes of this rather remarkable example of uneven development.

The two decades around the *fin de siècle* were the years in which many innovations introduced earlier in England were diffused in the Continent. How can we isolate the factors that determined which countries on the continent would follow the British example of mechanization *cum* accumulation and which would stay behind? What is necessary at this stage is a logical structure that makes it possible to sort the various facts that are relevant to the discussion and to establish tentative links of causality. The paucity and circumstantiality of the evidence does not permit in most cases a rigorous test of the hypotheses derived from the model. All that can be done at the present stage of research is to structure a model on relatively few plausible assumptions and then use what little quantitative information is available to examine whether the causal relationships derived from the model are consistent with the observed facts.

2 INDUSTRIALIZATION IN BELGIUM, 1795–1850

Belgium is a tragicomic genre-picture akin to a caricature in the great historical tableau. . . . the model state of the bourgeois monarchy. . . .

Karl Marx, 1849

In 1794 the French armies decisively defeated the Austrians at the battle of Fleurus and thereby terminated the Austrian rule over the Southern Low Countries. The episcopal principality of Liège was likewise overrun and the whole area which today constitutes Belgium was annexed to the French Republic. The first years were confused, even chaotic, especially in Flanders.[1] The French revolutionaries destroyed many of the ancient, venerable institutions: the guilds were abolished, clerical estates confiscated, monetary, legal, and measures-and-weights systems unified. The new fiscal order consisted mainly of the merciless squeezing of the bourgeoisie in Brabant and Flanders.[2] The new monetary system was soon discovered to be based on rapidly depreciating *assignats*. Arbitrary confiscations and conscriptions triggered peasant uprisings and political rest was not restored until 1799.

During the following years, however, the Belgian economy gathered momentum. Until 1810 or 1811, a process of rapid growth of modern industry can be discerned which has no precedent in the history of continental Europe. Although there can be little doubt that the development of industry in the first decade of the nineteenth century was related to the stormy political events of the era, it will be attempted in this study to lay bare the economic factors which provide the background of the sudden "takeoff" in Belgium in the first years of the nineteenth century.[3]

In 1814, the Belgian provinces were separated from the disintegrated

---

1. J. E. Nève, *Gand sous la Domination Française, 1792–1814* (Ghent: A. Buyens, 1927), pp. 158–66.

2. V. Fris, *Histoire de Gand* (Brussels: G. van Vest et Cie, 1913), p. 22.

3. No Rostovian quantification is implied by this term, except for some connotation of discontinuity.

Napoleonic Empire and given to William I of Orange, King of the Netherlands. Together the two countries constituted the "United Kingdom of
the Netherlands." The first years of the newly created monarchy were a
period of depression for Belgian industry, but by the end of the second
decade recovery set in. By the early 1820s, the process of technological
innovation, paired to the accumulation of fixed capital, resumed over a
wide range of industries. The political turmoil resulting from the Belgian
Revolution in 1830 (creating the independent kingdom of Belgium)
caused another temporary halt in economic growth. Again, however,
recovery was rapid, and although some shifts in the internal balance of
the industrial structure of the country can be observed, the overall trend
climbed upward until 1850, which is the end of our period of reference.
By that time, Belgium was the only country on the Continent which could
be said to compete with England in its degree of industrialization, an
observation agreed upon by historians and contemporaries alike.

In spite of its importance and interest, no satisfactory account exists of
Belgian industrialization. The present chapter is an attempt to fill this
lacuna. As will be realized, the economic transformation of Belgium was
not confined to industry. Commerce, transportation, financial markets,
and agriculture took part in the overall process of growth. A major event
was the reopening of the Scheldt in 1795, and the subsequent development
of the Antwerp harbor as one of the most important ports on the Continent.
It is, however, not possible to give adequate treatment to nonindustrial
aspects of the process of economic growth in Belgium, and the discussion
below will be confined to industry. Specifically, the three major industries
will be discussed in some detail: the textile industries in Flanders, the
textile industries in the Verviers area, and the heavy industries of the
Walloon provinces. Some attention will be paid to other industries as well.

THE COTTON INDUSTRY IN FLANDERS

If discontinuity is one of the conditions for spectacularity, the cotton
industry in Ghent can certainly claim to be spectacular. In 1795 the cotton
industry in this region was virtually nonexistent, except for calico printing
and some cotton weaving in the countryside which formed part of the
Z-good sector. It was in cotton that the spillovers of the industrial revolution in England at first attained significance.

The man who introduced the first mules in Flanders was a tanner from
Ghent, Lieven Bauwens.[4] Thanks to his close relations with English

---

4. The most recent biography is F. Leleux, *Liévin Bauwens, Industriel Gantois* (Paris:
S.E.V.P.E.N., 1969).

merchants, in 1798 Bauwens succeeded in smuggling out a prototype of a mule. Initially, he produced mules for the textile industry in Passy (near Paris), by reproducing the machines brought over. In 1801 the first spinning mill was established in Ghent in a confiscated monastery. From this moment on, cotton spinning in Ghent grew at a rapid rate. The first cotton mill in Ghent employed 227 workers in 1802.[5] By 1808 the number of spinners in Ghent exceeded 2,000, with probably another 1,000 in the other towns of East Flanders. The total number of spindles in 1808 was already 50,000.[6] A few years later, the number of spinners in Ghent reached 3,880, while the cotton industry as a whole employed more than 10,000 workers. The number of spindles in 1810 was estimated at 115,810, a figure sustained for approximately two years.[7]

Cotton spinning soon became a competitive industry, although Bauwens initially tried to dominate the sector by means of his control over the production of mules, most of which was in his hands, as well as through the fact that many new entrepreneurs were his relatives. After 1806, however, the influx of new entrepreneurs in the production of mules as well as the spinning of cotton became stronger and the number of firms in Ghent, as well as in Drongen, Termonde, St. Nikolaas, and Ronse, proliferated. The hectic activity of this period is reflected in the letter written in 1807 by the prefect Faipoult, who was keenly interested in the process of industrial expansion:

> When I arrived in Ghent [1801], only one spinning mill was in existence, that of Mr. Bauwens. Today there are seven or eight establishments in the *département* [Escaut, i.e., East Flanders] which are of equal importance if not more. In three years there will be thirty, judging by the growth of the last eighteen months ... if three new workshops [constructing mules and other capital goods] have been formed in the last fifteen months, there is no reason why in the next fifteen months three or six more will not be established. Each existing workshop could supply two or three workers who could be directors of new ones ... never has industry marched forward so rapidly.[8]

With the rapid expansion of cotton spinning, forward as well as backward linkages operated on other activities. The weaving of cotton grew almost *pari passu*, though its most rapid expansion came only after 1806. The major technological breakthrough in weaving was the introduction

5. Varlez, *Les Salaires*, 1:26.
6. J. Dhondt, "L'Industrie Cotonnière Gantoise à l'Époque Française," *RHMC* 2 (1955): 251.
7. Municipal Archives, Ghent, file K 1–2, bundles P and G.
8. Cited by Dhondt, "L'Industrie Cotonnière," p. 245.

of the flying shuttle. Bauwens had observed flying shuttles in England
and successfully reproduced them. Some cotton weaving had existed in
Ghent prior to the annexation to France. In 1795, according to a professional survey, 400 persons were employed in cotton weaving.[9] Output
consisted of crude cotton cloth, almost all for local consumption.[10] The
number of looms in the city was still only 500 in 1808 but grew to 3,600
in 1812.[11] These figures are, however, misleading since most of the weaving
was put out to the countryside where it formed part of the large Flemish
protoindustry. In 1816 a total of 15,000 weavers were reported for the
Ghent area, of which only 5,000 lived in the city itself. All weavers worked
at home.[12] The interaction between the Z-good sector and modern
industry can thus be seen to take various forms, the division of labor
between them being one possibility. Modern industry also helped the
Z-good industry. In cotton weaving (contrary to linen) the flying shuttle
was rapidly diffused.[13] The adoption of the flying shuttle doubled the
productivity of a domestic weaver.[14] The quality of the cotton fabric
changed as well: instead of rough cotton cloth, the main product became
calicoes.[15] The output of calicoes increased from virtually nil before 1800
to about 100,000 pieces annually in 1810. Total output of cotton goods
was about 150,000 pieces.[16]

   The third important activity in the cotton industry was calico printing.
As was noted above, this industry already had developed some momentum
before the Fench period. Output in 1769 was already 78,000 pieces
printed.[17] In 1803 this figure had risen to 180,000 pieces.[18] Employment
in printing increased from 881 workers in 1793 to 2,257 workers in 1816.[19]
In this industry, too, some important innovations occurred. The miraculous Lieven Bauwens introduced from England Patrick Bell's copper
cylinder system (patented in 1785), which was improved upon by means
of engraving on the cylinder's plates in relief. The Lefevre system, which
used a large copper roller, was adopted in 1807.[20]

   9. Municipal Archives, Ghent, file K 1–2, bundle A–B.
   10. Dhondt, "L'Industrie Cotonnière," p. 246.
   11. Municipal Archives, Ghent, file K 1–2, bundle i.
   12. Ibid., bundle C. C.
   13. Briavoinne, "Sur les Inventions," p. 78.
   14. Leleux, *Liévin Bauwens*, p. 142.
   15. Dhondt, "L'Industrie Cotonnière," p. 246.
   16. Municipal Archives, Ghent, file K 1–2, bundle G-bis.
   17. Coppejans-Desmedt, "Economische Opbloei," p. 285.
   18. H. Coppejans-Desmedt, "De Gentse Textielnijverheid van 1795 tot 1835" [The
textile industry in Ghent from 1795 to 1835] (Ph.D. diss., University of Ghent, about 1955),
p. 177.
   19. Dhondt, "L'Industrie Cotonnière," pp. 235, 266.
   20. Briavoinne, "Sur les Inventions," pp. 81–83.

To sum up, the cotton industry in Ghent increased by something on the order of a factor of ten in the first decade of the nineteenth century with respect to the number of workers employed, and probably by a much larger factor with respect to fixed capital goods. Total fixed assets in 1816 were evalued at 3.3 million francs, about half of it in buildings.[21] It should be emphasized, however, that the process of capital accumulation and output expansion was by no means a continuous, smooth process.[22] Severe crises occurred in 1806, 1808, 1810, and 1813. Not all of these crises had deep economic causes and some of them were of an obvious transitory character, and are therefore not pertinent to the discussion here.

The depression of 1813 was, however, far more severe than the preceding downswings. Some term it unjustly the "collapse" of the Ghent cotton industry,[23] probably because Bauwens and a few others went bankrupt. It should be noted, however, that most bankruptcies took place among producers of capital goods, which is to be blamed on the operation of the acceleration principle. Although the rapid growth was arrested with the collapse of the First Empire, the Flemish industry survived, in contrast with many other "hot-house" industries.[24] In fact, the cotton industry in Ghent seems in 1816 to be as large as in 1812 with respect to employment and the number of firms operating, although production was curtailed substantially.[25] The few bankruptcies in the cotton industry had no long run effects; often a bankruptcy did not imply at all a cessation of production. For instance, Bauwens's factory at the *Chartreux* monastery in Ghent was taken over by the brothers Bossaert after his bankruptcy and production continued without much difficulty.[26]

The expansion of the Ghent cotton industry during the French period can be documented with quantitative data. Unfortunately, there are no data available for the first years of the Dutch period. It is quite clear, however, that the five years following the fall of Napoleon and the severance of Belgium from the French Empire were a hard time for the Flemish

21. H. Coppejans-Desmedt, "De Statistieken van Emmanuel Carolus van der Meersch over de Katoenindustry in Oost Vlaanderen" [The statistics of E. C. van der Meersch on the cotton industry in East Flanders], *BCRH* 128, no. 3 (June 1962): 150.

22. This is stressed by J. Craeybeckx, "Les Débuts de la Revolution Industrielle en Belgique et les Statistiques de la Fin de l'Empire," in *Mélanges Offerts à G. Jacquemyns* (Brussels: Université Libre de Bruxelles, Éditions de l'Institut de Sociologie, 1968), pp. 115-27.

23. J. Dhondt and M. Bruwier, "The Industrial Revolution in Belgium and Holland, 1700-1914," in *The Fontana Economic History of Europe*, ed. Carlo M. Cipolla, vol. 4, sec. 1 (1970): 25.

24. F. Crouzet, "Wars, Blockade and Economic Change in Europe, 1792-1815," *JEH* 24, no. 4 (December 1966): 579.

25. Dhondt, "L'Industrie Cotonnière," p. 266.

26. Coppejans-Desmedt, "Gentse Textielnijverheid," p. 301.

cotton industry. The French market was abruptly closed to Belgian cotton goods, while at the same time the continental markets were overflooded with English cottons from stocks that had accumulated during the continental blockade and were dumped on European markets after 1814. It is remarkable, however, that those spinning mills that were able to survive the initial shock (1813–15) managed to stay in business for a long period thereafter.[27] The noted Dutch political economist, van Hogendorp, found in 1817 in Ghent many impressive machines and industrial implements, and although he states that industry was virtually at a standstill, he also describes a large mechanic spinning mill in operation.[28] The year 1817 was, in any event, an exceptionally bad year, the industrial crisis compounded by a severe harvest failure producing acute shortages everywhere in Flanders. The price of wheat, rye, and potatoes rose by an average of close to 100 percent between 1815 and 1817.[29] The food shortage was particularly serious for industry because by now the cotton industry was to a much larger extent dependent on the domestic market.

After 1817 the situation gradually improved. The recovery was to some extent due to the efforts of the Dutch government. King William I extended a personal loan of 150,000 florins to Rosseel, a leading cotton manufacturer (1 Dutch florin = 2.12 francs). In the same year the government lent 400,000 florins to the province of East Flanders. This loan was explicitly intended to relieve the severe unemployment in the cotton industry.[30] The government also helped in the marketing of the finished goods and took an active part in the sale of Flemish cotton goods to Germany.[31] Still, the process of recovery was painstakingly slow: employment in spinning rose between 1817 and 1819 from 4,000 to 6,000, while capacity was far larger.

The resumption of the process of expansion accelerated after the possibilities of the Dutch East Indies as a market for Flemish cotton goods were realized. The Dutch Indies had been taken over by England during the Napoleonic Wars, and although they were returned to the Netherlands in 1814, the demand for calicoes in Java and Madura was satisfied by

27. Varlez, *Les Salaires*, 1:38.
28. K. G. van Hogendorp, *Bijdragen tot de Huishouding van Staat in het Koninkrijk der Nederlanden* [Contributions to the political economy of the kingdom of the Netherlands] (Amsterdam: K. H. Schadd, 1825), 2:235.
29. C. Vandenbroeke and W. Vanderpijpen, "Gentse Merkuriale van Granen etc." [Price movements in Ghent], in *Documenten voor de Geschiedenis van Prijzen en Lonen in Vlaanderen en Brabant*, vol. 3, ed. C. Verlinden and E. Scholliers (Bruges: "De Tempel," 1972), pp. 101, 110, 141.
30. R. Demoulin, *Guillaume Ier et la Transformation Economique des Provinces Belges* (Liège: Bibliothèque de la Faculté de Philosophie et Lettres de l'Université de Liège, 1938), p. 158.
31. Coppejans-Desmedt, "Gentse Textielnijverheid," p. 296.

English manufacturers. A Belgian adventurer by the name of Wappers Melis, a former employee of the English East India Company, first suggested to the Dutch government in 1818 that the Dutch Indies could be used as a market for the Belgian calico industry.[32] After some hesitation, the Dutch authorities were convinced of the soundness of the plan. In 1824, the Governor-General of the Dutch East Indies imposed a tariff of 25 to 35 percent on all textile goods from Europe and the U.S., exempting the Dutch of course. A few months later, King William founded the Nederlandsche Handelsmaatschappij (Dutch Commercial Company, henceforth abbreviated as N.H.M.). The new organization was put in charge of the purchase of colonial goods from the East and the sale of Dutch goods in the colonies.

The N.H.M. can thus be seen to be complementing the tariffs in the attempts of the Dutch government to facilitate exports to the Dutch Indies. The result of these policies can be verified from table 2.1. There was a marked rise in the percentage of Dutch goods in total cotton imports to the Dutch East Indies. All Dutch calicoes until 1830 originated in Flanders. With an export market that displayed relative stability, the pace of investment and technological change in Flanders accelerated. Yet, it is important to realize that the slump in the Flemish cotton industry was in

Table 2.1   Cotton Imports to Java and Madura
(in millions of florins)

	Foreign	Dutch	Total	Dutch Percentage of Total
1823	3.4	0.1	3.5	3
1824	2.3	0.2	2.5	8
1825	1.48	0.21	1.69	12
1826	0.96	1.26	2.22	56
1827	1.97	0.86	2.83	30
1828	1.89	2.95	4.84	61
1829	1.63	3.49	5.12	68
1830	1.51	2.37	3.88	61
1831	1.55	1.39	2.94	47
1832	1.89	0.07	1.96	3

SOURCES: 1823–24—N. W. Posthumus, ed., *Documenten betreffende de Buitenlandsche Handelspolitiek van Nederland in de Negentiende Eeuw* [Documents concerning the Dutch commercial policy in the nineteenth century] (The Hague: Martinus Nijhoff, 1921), 2: 90–91. 1825–32— H. Muller, *De Nederlandsche Katoen-nijverheid en het Stelsel van Bescherming in Nederlandsch Indië* [The Dutch cotton industry and the system of protection in the Dutch Indies] (Rotterdam: H. A. Kramers, 1857), pp. 26–27.

32. H. R. C. Wright, *Free Trade and Protection in the Netherlands, 1816–1830* (Cambridge: At the University Press, 1955), pp. 196 ff.

fact already overcome in the early 1820s, *before* exports to Java started. A report from 1822 still sounds cautious: "Those of our factories which survived the strains of 1813–1815 are doing now quite well although some may eventually have to shut down." Less than a year later, the tone sounds more confident: "Profits are being made; although they are not as large as under the French government, they are steady and certain, and for that reason preferable to those that originated in the convulsions which plagued Europe [during the Empire]."[33] The resumption of the process of technical innovation can be pinpointed to 1819–20. In 1820, one Thomas Hurell came from England to Ghent to assist in the construction of the first power looms. Hurell became entangled in legal complications and ended up in jail, but his activities triggered a power loom rush which engulfed Ghent between 1822 and 1825 (before the boom in calico exports to the Indies). F. J. Voortman, one of Ghent's leading businessmen and a prominent cotton printer, became a leading power loom producer as well as a prominent weaver.[34] Voortman was surpassed, however, by J. J. Huytten-Kerremans as a producer of power looms. Huytten-Kerremans's workshop, later called De Phoenix, soon produced a variety of capital goods which were as good as the most advanced English equipment.[35]

The use of steam power became more and more widespread in the same period. In 1825 seventeen firms already made use of steam engines—some of them locally produced, others originating from Verviers, Liège, and Seraing in the Walloon provinces. Most of these machines were still quite small, between six and twenty-four horsepower.[36]

In addition to the introduction of steam power, there were many other improvements in the spinning process in the 1820s. Around 1825, an automatic beater and a beater-spreader (*batteur-étaleur*) came into use, as well as wetting and rolling machines. New and larger mules (up to 400 spindles) were diffused at the same time.[37] It should be emphasized that most of the new capital goods were manufactured in Ghent by the above-mentioned De Phoenix and others. Especially the former grew at a dazzling rate during the late 1820s.

The revolution of 1830 constituted a severe blow to the Flemish cotton industry. The Dutch government, in retaliation for the uprising, closed the Dutch East Indies to Belgian goods. The motive behind this action was political, not economic. At first, the Belgians managed to circumvent

33. Cited by Demoulin, *Guillaume Ier*, pp. 325n, 326n.
34. H. Coppejans-Desmedt, "Incidenten rond de Constructie van de Eerste Mechanische Weefgetouwen te Gent" [Some details concerning the construction of the first mechanical looms in Ghent], *HMGOG* 13 (1959): 163–77.
35. Coppejans-Desmedt, "Gentse Textielnijverheid," pp. 316–18.
36. Ibid., pp. 323–24.
37. Briavoinne, "Sur les Inventions," pp. 75–76.

the prohibition of imports of textiles from all "parts of the nation that are in revolt against the lawful government" by various smuggling practices. The Dutch government then reduced the 1824 tariff, in the hope that English cotton goods would supplant the Belgian. Remarkably enough, this policy failed completely. By this time, Belgian cotton production was fully competitive with English with respect to price and quality. Until 1834 Ghent and its surroundings continued to supply most of the cotton goods consumed in Java and Madura. In 1834, however, the Dutch, in an act dictated by vindictiveness rather than by economic reasoning, declared a tariff of 50–70 percent on all textiles imported to the East Indies from nations that did not have friendly relations with the Dutch. This decree terminated for a while the commercial ties between Ghent and its most important customer.[38]

As a consequence of the loss of the market in the Dutch East Indies, the Flemish cotton industry went through a deep depression in the mid-1830s. The number of spindles in the cotton industry actually declined from around 300,000 in 1830 to 280,000 in 1835, and a quarter of the latter figure were "inactive."[39] Output of finished cotton cloth fell from 350,000 pieces in 1829 to 112,000 pieces in 1835.[40]

In spite of the crisis (and, according to one author, *because* of the crisis),[41] technical change and accumulation of fixed capital continued at high speed. The number of power looms increased from 700 in 1830 to 2,900 in 1838.[42] The number of steam engines employed in the cotton industry increased from 55 to 110 between 1830 and 1838 alone, with probably a more than proportional increase in capacity. After 1838 the growth of steam power in the cotton industry slowed considerably—between 1838 and 1850 the growth in the number of machines was only 10 percent, while capacity increased by 28 percent.[43] Some notion of the overall trend in the cotton industry can be derived from foreign trade statistics, although this source should be treated with caution.

Table 2.2 shows the increasing dependence of the cotton industry on

38. H. Coppejans-Desmedt, "De Betekenis van Gent voor de Expansie van de Katoennijverheid in de Nederlanden, 1799–1834" [The significance of Ghent for the expansion of the cotton industry in the Netherlands], *THB* 11 (1969): 25–27.

39. X. Heuschling, *Essai sur la Statistique Générale de la Belgique*, 2d ed., (Brussels: Établissement Géographique Faubourg de Flandre, 1841), p. 95. Coppejans-Desmedt, "Gentse Textielnijverheid," p. 416.

40. Varlez, *Les Salaires*, 1: 42.

41. P. Schöller, "La Transformation Économique de la Belgique de 1832 à 1844," *BISEL* 14, no. 4 (1948): 585.

42. Briavoinne, *De l'Industrie*, 2: 383.

43. *Statistique Générale de la Belgique, Exposé de la Situation du Royaume 1841–1850* (Brussels: Ministère de l'Intérieur, 1852), p. 113. Henceforth referred to as *Exposé de la Situation*.

Table 2.2 Quinquennial Averages of Raw Cotton Imports and Finished
Cotton Goods Exports, 1831–50
(in thousands of kilograms)

	Imports of Raw Cotton	Exports of Finished Goods
1831–35	4.5	0.702
1836–40	7.2	0.512
1841–45	7.4	0.571
1846–50	9.0	0.922

SOURCE: *Statistique de la Belgique, Tableau Général du Commerce avec des Pays Etrangères* (Brussels: Ministère de l'Intérieur, 1838 and subsequent years), passim.

1948534

the domestic market, as indicated by the discrepancy between the growth in exports of the finished cotton cloth and the imports of raw cotton. Exports of yarn were of relatively minor importance. The increasing reliance of the cotton industry on domestic demand in the 1830s was no doubt related to the overall boom experienced in Belgium in the late 1830s, with the construction of the railroad network.

A summary of the quantitative history of the Ghent cotton industry is presented in table 2.3. Like most histories of this type, the case of Ghent resembles a jigsaw puzzle with most of the pieces missing. The overall trends reveal, however, a singularly rapid advance of mechanization. As might be expected, employment grew at a slower pace than output. The data are particularly bad on this issue, especially since the process of

Table 2.3 Development of the Cotton Industry in Ghent, 1801–38

	1801–02	1807–08	1810–12	1817	1826	1830	1838
Labor							
Spinners	227	1,838	3,790	n.a.	n.a.	n.a.	
Weavers	400	2,000	4,105	n.a.	n.a.	n.a.	18,700
Printers	1,700	1,135	1,350	n.a.	n.a.	n.a.	
Capital							
Spindles	—	78,022	115,000	n.a.	150,000	300,000	283,000
Looms[a]	n.a.	500	3,600	n.a.	n.a.	2,200	2,900
Output							
Yarn spun[b]	55	320	693	374	1,700	2,700	4,600
Cloth[c]	n.a.	n.a.	101	n.a.	410	n.a.	n.a.

[a]Including power looms
[b]In thousands of kilograms
[c]In thousands of pieces
SOURCES: Coppejans-Desmedt, *Gentse Textielnijverheid*, p. 508; van der Wee, "Industriële Revolutie," p. 192; Demoulin, *Guillaume Ier*, p. 329; Briavoinne, *De l'Industrie*, 2: 374 ff.

modernization consisted to a large extent of the shift of weaving from the countryside (which is not included in most data for Ghent) to the city. The earlier figures are thus probably downward biased.

At the end of the French period, the total number of workers employed in the Ghent cotton industry was about 10,000. A source from 1830 estimates total employment in the Flemish cotton industry at the end of the Dutch period at 26,588, of which Ghent itself accounted for 11,600.[44] Briavoinne estimates total employment in the cotton industry at 28,000, of which about two-thirds were located in Ghent.[45] Other estimates are at times dramatically different. Heuschling's estimate of 122,000 workers is fantastically high and even his corrected figure in the second edition of his book, 50,000 workers, is highly exaggerated.[46] On the other hand, the industrial survey of 1846 puts the number of employees in the cotton industry at 10,681 adults and 3,999 children. This figure is downward biased because of the omission of domestic workers from the survey.[47] All in all, an estimate of 25,000 workers in the mid-1840s is not far off the mark. This is certainly an impressive size by European standards of the period.

Where did the labor and the capital that built the Flemish cotton industry come from? These questions will have to be coped with if we are ever to understand the mechanisms that underlay the industrialization of Flanders. The labor was mobilized to some extent from the urban lumpenproletariat and to some extent from population growth, but mostly from the surroundings of Ghent, that is to say, the traditional (agricultural *cum* Z-good) rural sector. The capital came in part from short-term loans, government support in various forms, and personal resources, but the bulk of capital accumulated originated in the modern industrial sector itself, through an active policy of the plowing-back of profits. Since both processes, the mobilization of labor and the accumulation of capital, constitute the backbone of the emergence of modern industry in Flanders, it is worthwhile to examine them in some detail.

The late Professor Jan Dhondt has addressed himself to the issue of the sources of the labor force in the industrial revolution in Ghent.[48] Dhondt rejects the hypothesis that the labor for the cotton industry came

44. Municipal Archives, Ghent, file K 7/1.
45. Briavoinne, *De l'Industrie*, 2: 378.
46. Heuschling, *Essai*, 1st ed. (1838), p. 122. 2d ed. (1841), p. 96.
47. *Statistique de la Belgique, Recensement Général 1846* (Brussels: Ministère de l'Intérieur, 1851), "Industrie," p. xviii. B. Verhaegen, *Contribution à l'Histoire Économique des Flanders* (Louvain-Paris: Nauwelaerts, 1961), 1: 183.
48. J. Dhondt, "Notes sur les Ouvriers Industriels Gantois à l'Epoque Française," *RN* 36 (1954): 309-24.

from immigration from the countryside, as well as the hypothesis that the labor came from the class of urban artisans and shopkeepers. Instead, Dhondt argues that the labor employed in the cotton industry was drawn primarily from the urban lumpenproletariat, a class of the "most miserable, the starving, the vagabonds, the beggars."[49] There is, no doubt, a kernel of truth in Dhondt's argument. The number of persons subsisting on public relief during the last years of the *ancien régime* and the first years of French domination was about 11,000–12,000. However, in 1801, this number had fallen to 8,000.[50] Unfortunately, no data are available for the period between 1801 and 1818, so that it cannot be verified how many paupers were absorbed in the industrial labor force. In 1818, admittedly a period of depression, the number of *indigents* (i.e., paupers) had risen back to approximately 11,000. In 1826, when the cotton industry in Ghent was growing rapidly, the number of persons classified as paupers was 11,772, so that the same proportion of population was on relief as in 1801 before the "big spurt forward." Dhondt describes in great detail the various means by which the slum dwellers of Ghent were attracted to industrial employment and stresses the use of force to prevent them from switching employers. This by itself, however, does not establish Dhondt's point. In a rapidly growing industry, the supply of labor usually lags behind the demand for labor, so that for some period wages rise very rapidly, a phenomenon which the entrepreneurs tried to counteract by collusion and legal restrictions. In other words: the short-run elasticity of labor supply might have been much smaller than the long-run elasticity, and many of the facts observed by Dhondt should be interpreted as short-run equilibrium phenomena or disequilibrium situations.

Dhondt's main point, that the urban poor of Ghent constituted the main source of labor for the modern industry, is probably overstated. Though it is indisputable that some workers in the Ghent cotton industry were mobilized from the local paupers, this does not warrant the rejection of the immigration hypothesis, as Dhondt claims. It is difficult to see why the two hypotheses should be mutually exclusive. The importance of immigration in Ghent's economic development is demonstrated in table 2.4.

In the French period alone, total immigration to Ghent exceeded the maximum possible contribution of the paupers to the labor force. Needless to say, the proportion of those fit to work among the paupers and prisoners is likely to have been lower than among the new immigrants. Little is known about these immigrants. Coppejans-Desmedt, in her dissertation,

49. Ibid., p. 313.
50. P. C. van der Meersch, "De l'État de la Mendicité et de la Bienfaisance dans la Province de la Flandre Orientale," *BCCS* 5 (1853): 50, 73.

Table 2.4   Population Growth and Migration in Ghent, 1801-43

	Population at Starting Date	Population at Final Date	Births	Deaths	Immigration (residual)
1801-15	55,161	62,738	30,677	31,129	8,029
1815-30	62,738	83,843	39,480	30,105	11,730
1830-36	83,843	89,950	18,596	17,318	4,829
1836-43	89,950	108,451	24,863	22,749	16,387
1801-43	55,161	108,451	113,616	101,301	40,975

SOURCES: 1801-36—Coppejans-Desmedt, *Gentse Textielnijverheid*, p. 24. 1836-43—D. J. B. Mareska and J. Heyman, "Enquête sur le Travail et la Condition Physique et Morale des Ouvriers dans les Manufactures de Coton à Gand," in Ministère de l'Intérieur, *Enquête sur la Condition des Classes Ouvrières* (Brussels: Th. Lesigne, 1846), 3: 418. Corrected for years (which are erroneously specified in source). Birth rates calculated on the assumption that the birth rate of 0.032, which was the average for 1839-43, prevailed for 1836-43 as a whole.

mentions records of about 150 new immigrants to Ghent. Almost all of these immigrants came to town in order to work and many of them explicitly cited wage differentials as their prime motive.[51]

There are other arguments that strengthen the thesis that the Z-good sector was the principal source of labor supply to modern industry. First, if we take the cotton industry as a whole, the fact that weaving was still put out to the countryside means that labor from the Z-good was employed in the cotton industry. Secondly, there is no evidence that the number of paupers decreased considerably between 1801 and 1812, while the number of paupers did in fact grow in the first quarter of the nineteenth century. Moreover, the increase in the demand for labor in Ghent must have been larger than the rise in the labor force employed in cotton alone, since the incomes generated in this industry must have had multiplier effects which increased the demand for labor for construction, food production, services, etc. Therefore, even if it were completely dissolved into a hardworking industrial proletariat, Dhondt's reserve army of wretched vagabonds could not have been sufficient. Finally, there is some reason to believe that many of the paupers were to varying degrees involved with domestic industry prior to the emergence of modern industry as well as later on. Van Hogendorp reports from Ghent:

> In the poor house in Ghent, thirteen hundred inmates were all occupied in spinning and weaving. . . . all people in the countryside and *many urban dwellers as well* spin and weave flax.[52]

51. Coppejans-Desmedt, "Gentse Textielnijverheid," p. 26. Cf. also Fris, *Histoire de Gand*, p. 324.
52. Van Hogendorp, *Bijdragen*, 2: 232, 236 (emphasis added).

Where did the capital come from? The leading specialist on Ghent's cotton industry maintains that capital was the chief bottleneck in the rapid expansion of that industry.[53] The initial capital which the first entrepreneurs brought with them into the industry was insufficient even in the case of Lieven Bauwens, who was already a wealthy man in 1798. The available funds were still mostly in the hands of the nobility and the old-time financiers, who declined to meddle with modern industry and refused to lend their money to what seemed to them reckless adventurers. Consequently, the modern, capital-intensive firms financed their mechanization from "own means," that is, retained profits.[54]

Admittedly, the cotton industry of Ghent cannot be said to have been exclusively dependent on retained earnings for its investment outlays. For one thing, the confiscation of the possessions of the Catholic church enabled manufacturers to purchase buildings at very low prices which had previously been used as churches or monasteries.[55] Some of the new manufacturers seem to have been borrowing, mostly on a short-term basis. There is no evidence that credit for long-term investment was available. Bauwens, in many ways unrepresentative of the general conditions in the industry, seems to have been able to mobilize relatively large sums. His main creditor was, significantly enough, the French government. Bauwens enjoyed a special status with the government, and he shrewdly exploited his connections for his financial benefit. Napoleon thought highly of him and personally conferred upon him an officership in the Legion of Honor. The French prefect, Faipoult, intervened on his behalf to secure a government loan.[56] It is doubtful whether any of the other cotton manufacturers could have had access to Bauwen's sources of credit. Banks or other financial intermediaries had little to do with industry in the French as well as in the Dutch periods.[57]

The capital required by the rapidly expanding industry was not insubstantial. Rosseel's spinning mill, established in 1805, cost over 400,000 francs. Other firms were mostly in the order of 100,000 francs.[58] The initial investment came from relatives, friends, or inheritances, but there can be little doubt that sustained expansion was financed by means

53. Coppejans-Desmedt, "Gentse Textielnijverheid," pp. 256, 377.
54. Coppejans-Desmedt, "De Betekenis," pp. 20–24. For general statements along these lines, see Demoulin, *Guillaume Ier*, pp. 232–33. Briavoinne, *De l'Industrie*, 2: 372.
55. Dhondt, "L'Industrie Cotonnière," p. 277.
56. Leleux, *Liévin Bauwens*, pp. 246, 250.
57. B. S. Chlepner, *La Banque en Belgique* (Brussels: M. Lamertin, 1926), p. 22.
58. J. Voortman, *Les Débuts de l'Industrie Cotonnière Gantoise sous le Régime Français et le Régime Hollandais d'après les Archives de la Maison A. Voortman* (Ghent: L. van Melle, 1940), p. 66.

which originated in the "surplus" created by the machines with their higher productivity. Most of this "surplus" accrued to the entrepreneurs in the form of higher profits.[59] Faipoult, the observant prefect, noted in 1806:

> Previously all capital was, so to speak, almost exclusively absorbed in commerce. . . . If, therefore, so many new industries have emerged without damaging the old manufactures, it must have been with new capital generated by the ceaseless profits from earlier industry as well as savings.[60]

Contemporaries believed that for the period as a whole, profits had been extraordinarily high.[61] On the other hand, the standards of living of the entrepreneurs, although rising, did not become excessive as far as could be verified.[62]

In the Dutch period as well, firms continued to depend largely on self-finance and, in a few cases, on government assistance. Only a single case is cited in which a banker and an industrialist formed a *societé à commandité* in which the banker provided the capital and the industrialist the initiative and the technical know-how.[63] Movements of funds between firms in the same industry were less rare. The family, not the firm, was the central unit in the social structure of the Flemish cotton industry. Most mergers occurred through marriages, splittings occurred when a firm was equally divided among inheritors. Only in the late 1830s did joint-stock corporations make their appearance in Flanders, and even the joint-stock companies were financing most of their expansion out of retained profits. In this period, however, funds started to move from one segment of the modern textile sector in Flanders to the other. For instance, the two large linen spinning enterprises which were set up in the late 1830s as joint-stock corporations, La Lys and La Linière Gantoise, were financed by profits accumulated in the cotton industry.[64] The conclusion is that throughout the first half of the nineteenth century, the textile industry in Flanders was largely self-sufficient in investment funds. The same is true for the industries that produced the capital goods used as inputs in the textile industries. At times, when the need for investment

---

59. Coppejans-Desmedt, "Gentse Textielnijverheid," pp. 186–87. Leleux, *Liévin Bauwens*, p. 147.

60. Cited by Nève, *Gand sous la Domination*, pp. 168–69.

61. "Avanti," *Een Terugblik—Proeve eener Geschiedenis der Gentse Arbeidersbeweging gedurende de XIXe Eeuw* [History of the workers' movement in Ghent in the nineteenth century] (Ghent: Samenwerkende Volksdrukkerij, 1908), p. 22.

62. Leleux, *Liévin Bauwens*, p. 244, describes Bauwens's extravagant standards of living. Yet again Bauwens seems to be the exception rather than the rule.

63. Coppejans-Desmedt, "Gentse Textielnijverheid," p. 377.

64. J. Laureyssens, "Le Crédit Industriel et la Société Générale des Pays Bas Pendant le Régime Hollandais," *RBHC* 3, nos. 1–2 (1972): 123n.

funds became very severe, the capitalists turned to the government for help. The machine workshop of J. J. Huytten-Kerremans once turned to the Dutch government with the remarkable ultimatum of receiving a loan of 50,000 florins or turning the whole concern over to the government. Huytten-Kerremans ended up with a loan of 100,000 florins.[65]

The industrialization process in Flanders has been described in some detail because its essential character as a "big spurt" or "takeoff" is still sometimes denied.[66] Of course, the expansion of the modern cotton industry was not occurring uniformly at all times or in all places. West Flanders experienced relatively less industrialization than East Flanders, and the years 1813–20 and 1834–44 were periods of stagnation. This should not allow us to be mistaken about the basic fact that the cotton industry in East Flanders grew faster than in any other region on the Continent, except perhaps Alsace. The emergence of Ghent and its surroundings as a fully modernized cotton center stands as a remarkable example of economic modernization and should be investigated as such.

THE WOOLEN INDUSTRY

In the same year in which Lieven Bauwens smuggled his first spinning mule out of England, 1798,[67] the woolen industry in the Walloon provinces adopted its first mechanical devices. In the case of the woolen industry, the diffusion of technical change took a rather different form from the process in Flanders. An English mechanic, one William Cockerill, was hired by the leading firm of Biolley-Simonis in Verviers, and for the sum of 25,000 francs, Cockerill supplied the first *assortiment* of implements consisting of a carding machine, a card, a spinning machine for rough yarn, and four spinning machines for fine yarn.[68]

Cockerill's machines, primitive as they were, turned out to be a vast success. All the other woolen cloth manufacturers of the region displayed immense interest in the new devices. Cockerill had signed an exclusive contract with Biolley-Simonis and was not supposed to produce machines for his employer's competitors. The initial profits made by the first owners of the new equipment were, however, such that no contract could prevent the dissipation of the innovations to other manufacturers.[69]

65. Coppejans-Desmedt, "Incidenten," p. 176.
66. Mendels, "Agriculture and Peasant Industry," p. 23, states: "[Flemish] factory industrialization was very slow throughout the nineteenth century. This remains to be explained."
67. Lebrun, *L'Industrie de la Laine*, p. 234, argues that 1799 is probably the correct date.
68. Briavoinne, "Sur les Inventions," p. 89.
69. There are various and conflicting anecdotal details on this process. Cf. W. O. Henderson, *Britain and Industrial Europe* (Leicester: Leicester University Press, 1965), p. 109. Lebrun, *L'Industrie de la Laine*, pp. 235–38.

In the first decade and a half of the nineteenth century, the woolen industry underwent a profound transformation. By 1812 the number of machine makers had risen to a total of twenty-one for the province as a whole. In that year, output of capital goods included 3,062 spinning machines for fine yarn, 554 for rough yarn, 554 carding machines, 1,650 shearing machines and various other mechanical implements. The total value of the output of capital goods was estimated at more than five million francs. The 2,578 workers employed in the manufacturing of machines for the woolen industry earned an annual total wage of 1,658,700 francs.[70] The total assets invested in the firm of James Hodson, Cockerill's son-in-law and a leading machine maker, grew between 1810 and 1813 alone from 547,000 to 798,000 francs. His profits in 1811 amounted to 115,000 francs.[71]

The woolen goods produced consisted primarily of woolen cloth, as well as serges and kerseymeres. Thomassin tries to estimate the increase in productivity resulting from the introduction of machinery compared to unaided labor. A carding machine would do the work of 24 manual laborers. The wool-combing machine replaced 60 workers. The spinning machine could do the work of 24 spinners using spinning wheels, while the flying shuttle doubled the output of weavers.[72] Thomassin does not provide the number of workers operating each machine, so the exact increment in productivity cannot be calculated directly. The exception is spinning, for which we have Cockerill's testimony. According to this source, one *assortiment*, employing 11 persons of whom only two were male adults, could produce the same amount per day as 100 persons spinning by hand.[73] For the industry as a whole, however, we can use Thomassin's data to measure the increase in labor's (average) productivity. Thomassin compares the input of labor necessary to produce an annual 1,500 pieces of cloth before and after the introduction of machinery. The total labor input, not including weaving,[74] in the *ancienne fabrication* system was 297 workers,[75] whereas in the new system using two *assortiments*, the necessary input of labor was only 109 workers. Total expense on wages declined from 88,575 francs to 42,575 francs.[76]

70. Thomassin, *Mémoire Statistique*, p. 450.

71. Lebrun, *L'Industrie de la Laine*, p. 239.

72. Thomassin, *Mémoire Statistique*, p. 449.

73. Letter of W. Cockerill to the prefect of the *Département de l'Ourthe* (the province of Liège) of May 9, 1809. Cited in T. Gobert, "Conditions de l'Industrie du Tissage à la Fin de l'Ancien Régime—Les Cockerills à leur Début," *BIAL* 40 (1910): 180–82.

74. Weaving has not been included here since Thomassin ignores the effects of the flying shuttle.

75. Lebrun, *L'Industrie de la Laine*, p. 381, estimates that a representative eighteenth-century firm producing 1,000 pieces annually employed about 300 workers, including weavers.

76. Thomassin, *Mémoire Statistique*, p. 474.

Somewhat different increases in productivity are implied in the figures provided by Lebrun. The differences stem from the fact that Lebrun compares somewhat different periods and confines himself to the town of Verviers. Lebrun's findings are summarized in table 2.5.

In spite of the rapid growth of the modernized industry, it should be kept in mind that for a long period the new and the old industries coexisted. In 1812 only 6 out of 144 manufacturers in Verviers owned complete *assortiments*.[77] These six producers accounted, however, for half of the total output. Moreover, many manufacturers who did not own complete *assortiments* owned at least some machines. Certainly the flying shuttle, introduced by Cockerill, became widely used in the French period. It is

Table 2.5   Development of the Woolen Industry in Verviers

	1780–85	1805–10	1845–50
Fixed capital per worker (in constant prices)	286	857	3,286
Variable capital per worker (in constant prices)	914	1,443	2,014
Total capital per worker	1,200	2,300	5,300
Output per worker (pieces)	3.1	5.0	9.3
Fixed capital per piece (constant prices)	91	170	355
Variable capital per piece (constant prices)	295	287	215
Total capital per piece	386	457	570
Total output in Verviers (pieces)	22,500	36,000	70,000
Total output in the county (pieces)	n.a.	80,000	150,000
Number of firms	150	125	50
Number of workers[a]	7,000	7,000	7,000
Number of workers living in the city	2,000	2,500	4,500
Total amount of capital (current prices, 10^3 francs)	8,500	23,000	38,000
Total amount of capital (constant prices, 10^3 francs)	8,500	16,000	37,000

[a]The constancy of the number of workers is somewhat dubious in the short run. One source from 1816 claims that mechanization caused the number of workers to decline by a factor of three. Cf. N. Caulier-Mathy, *Statistiques de la Province de Liège sous le Régime Hollandais* (Louvain-Paris: Nauwelaerts, 1962), table I–3.
SOURCE: P. Lebrun, "L'Expérience de l'Industrie Drapière Verviétoise, 1750–1850," in *First International Conference of Economic History, Stockholm 1960, Contributions and Communications* (Paris-The Hague: Mouton et Cie., 1960), pp. 561–62.

77. In the first decade of the nineteenth century, one *assortiment* included: one carding machine of 2,400 francs, one preparing machine (*pour ouvrir la laine*) of 600 francs, one combing machine of 2,400 francs, one spinning machine of 500 francs, and four spinning machines of 400 francs each. Total value was about 7,500 francs. Cf. ibid., p. 449.

thus quite clear that the inventions in the woolen industry were labor saving in the Salterian sense, that is, the savings in the labor requirement for the unit output were larger than the savings in the capital requirements. While output increased rapidly, the number of workers employed by the industry remained more or less the same, although some shifts within the industry occurred.

Starting in the late eighteenth century, and increasingly pronounced in the first decade and a half of the nineteenth, the center of gravity of the woolen industry shifted from the countryside to the city. This process happened not only in spinning but also in weaving, which remained to a large extent a manual industry. There were several causes for the urbanization and centralization of the industry, in addition to mechanization. First, the flying shuttle, which doubled the productivity of a weaver, was four times as expensive as an older model loom.[78] Many weavers had to comply with the capitalists' demands for increased centralization simply because the latter could afford to purchase the new looms and they could not. The superior bargaining power of the capitalists enabled them to eliminate embezzlement and other disciplinary problems in the putting-out industry by concentrating the workers in workshops. Moreover, there were important economies of scale in the centralized workshops—and these were becoming more pronounced in the nineteenth century—in taxation, quality control, heating, lighting, and other overhead costs. Gradually, it seems, these factors began to outweigh the advantages of decentralization which had kept the Z-good sector alive for centuries.

Little information is available concerning the development of the woolen industry after 1812. It seems that the post-Waterloo crisis by which the Walloon industries were hit was less severe than is generally thought. The prohibition on imports imposed by France, though a heavy blow, did not destroy the woolen industry. Exports continued to Germany, Russia, the Ottoman Empire, Spain, Portugal, Italy, Switzerland, and the Scandinavian countries, as well as sales to the northern part of the United Kingdom of the Netherlands.[79] Output for the whole province, which was estimated at 169,102 pieces in 1812 by Thomassin, was put at 95,000 in 1815. Yet the number of workers in the province as a whole (probably excluding domestic workers) rose from 15,680 in 1812 to 16,447 in 1816.[80]

78. The price of a loom with a flying shuttle was 400 francs, equal to the gross annual earnings of an average weaver, cf. ibid., p. 450. An old loom cost only 80 florins de Liège or 98 francs. See J. S. Rénier, "Histoire de l'Industrie Drapière aux Pays de Liège," MSLEL, n.s. 6 (1881): 257.

79. N. Caulier-Mathy, Statistiques de la Province de Liège sous le Régime Hollandais (Louvain-Paris: Nauwelaerts, 1962), table I-3.

80. Thomassin, Mémoire Statistique, pp. 473–76. Caulier-Mathy, Statistiques, table I-3. It should be noted that Caulier-Mathy believes that the 1816 Statistiques were written and compiled by Thomassin.

The industrialists surveyed in 1816 complained bitterly about the corner-
ing of the raw material markets by England and about the difficulty of
keeping their skilled workers from emigrating, and asked for government
intervention to prevent emigration. Complaints of this nature are not
compatible with a severe demand-caused crisis. The following years were
probably harder, but still there is no reason to speak of a "collapse." The
survey of 1819 notes that "the large factories of Verviers have survived,
but smaller firms, totalling 124, including 41 spinning mills and 26 fulling
mills, have failed since 1815."[81] The decline in exports, though substantial, was not catastrophic; accounts based on reports made by manufacturers probably exaggerated the effects of the crisis. This can be
illustrated by the experience of van Hogendorp, who visited Verviers in
1817. Having been told in advance by an industrialist that the woolen
cloth factories were almost at a standstill, he paid special attention to the
question of demand. His conclusion was that the tariffs imposed by
various countries did constitute a severe difficulty. Nevertheless, says
van Hogendorp:

> New improvements are still introduced in the factories on a daily
> basis . . . the manufacturers wish nothing but to be left by themselves
> —they can easily manage on their own industriousness and the pro-
> tection of the laws. . . . even though the sales to France are largely
> foregone, demand will soon increase, the goods will be sold. . . . in
> the meantime the manufactures contract a little.[82]

After 1819 exports revived gradually, especially following the discovery
of the large market for woolen goods in the United States.[83] Another
stimulus to demand was the decision of the Dutch king to confine all
purchases for the army to domestically manufactured goods, an important
advantage to the producers of woolen military uniforms and blankets.[84]
By 1830 the ground lost in the years following the collapse of the Napoleonic Empire was almost recovered. The figures available are not reliable
enough to make inferences about the growth rate of woolen cloth output,
but it is clear that the Verviers area grew rather slowly, if at all, during
the Dutch period taken as a whole. Output in 1830 as well as in 1838 is
estimated at around 120,000, which is probably about the same as the

81. I. J. Brugmans, ed., *Statistieken van de Nederlandsche Nijverheid uit de Eerste Helft van de Negentiende Eeuw* [Statistics of Dutch industry from the first half of the nineteenth century], 2 vols., in *RGP* 98 and 99 (The Hague: Martinus Nijhoff, 1956), vol. 1: 322–23. Henceforth referred to as Brugmans, *Statistieken*, vols. 1 and 2.

82. Van Hogendorp, *Bijdragen*, 2: 268–69.

83. Demoulin, *Guillaume I*[er], p. 318.

84. E. Barlet, *Histoire du Commerce et de l'Industrie* (Liège: J. G. Lardinois, 1858), pp. 188–89.

average annual output in the last years of the First Empire.[85] The Dutch period was an age of slow transition rather than of discontinuously rapid expansion. Power looms were not yet introduced, though steam engines became of importance in spinning as well as in other stages of woolen cloth making. The constraint to expansion seems to have been, after all, on the demand side. France remained officially closed to Belgian woolen products, while the other markets expanded slowly and were of an uncertain nature. Colonial demand was probably negligible. At the same time, competition with England was severe. It is important to note, however, that the Belgian woolen industry was greatly feared by the English.[86]

For the period starting in 1831, foreign trade data are available. Since Belgium produced in large part for export and imported most of its raw wool, these two series can be used as an indication of the trend in the woolen industry.

Table 2.6 indicates a very slow rate of growth. It should be noted, however, that the last quinquennium is somewhat biased because of the worldwide disruption of trade in 1848. Imports in 1849–50 average 4,434 tons, which is considerably higher than for the preceding years. In addition, exports of finished woolen goods grew, in spite of everything, by almost 75 percent in 16 years, which means an annual rate of growth of 3.6 percent. In fact, however, output must have grown faster because of the rapid expansion of the domestic market which was noted above. (The

Table 2.6   Annual Trade in Raw Wool and Finished Cloth, 1833–50
(tons)

	Imports of Raw Wool	Exports of Finished Goods
1833–35	3,701	416
1836–40	3,729	554
1841–45	4,066	739
1846–50	3,916	769

SOURCE: *Statistique de la Belgique, Tableau Général*, passim.

85. Demoulin, *Guillaume I*^{er}, p. 322. Briavoinne, *De l'Industrie*, 2: 398. The quantitative evidence is extremely difficult to assess. According to a source from 1833, output in Verviers had tripled between 1812 and 1833 while that of Dison about quadrupled. This contradicts other evidence. What seems relatively certain is that between 1810 and 1850, output tripled in spite of many temporary setbacks. Cf. Lebrun, "La Rivoluzione Industriale," p. 606.

86. Henry Hughes, an English manufacturer of woolen goods, testified in 1833 before a Parliamentary Committee: "I have received the manufactures of that country [Belgium] with greater dread than any other on the continent of Europe, with regard to our own because they have labor cheaper and they have a wonderful means of manufacture." Great Britain, *Parliamentary Papers*, vol. 6 (*Report on Manufactures, Commerce and Shipping*), 1833, p. 69.

data for the first years of independence appeared unreliable and were consequently omitted.)[87]

In spite of the relative stagnation experienced during the Dutch period, the process of technical change continued unabated. Among the important innovations introduced were the shearing machine, imported at first, but after 1821 locally manufactured.[88] Teaseling machines were brought in somewhat earlier.[89] The first steam engine was introduced in 1816, but steam became widespread only from the mid-1820s on. Originally, steam seems to have used primarily as a means to remove the gloss from the wool and only later as a driving force.[90] Fulling mills made of metal were introduced in 1824 and diffused rapidly. All these innovations were constantly improved after their first application. In the 1830s, a substantial contribution to the art of designing patterns on the finished cloth was made by Lambert Bonjean, whose value to the Verviers woolen industry was esteemed so highly that in 1853 a railroad locomotive was named after him.[91] In other aspects of production, too, technological advance continued with undiminished momentum. It is noteworthy that by the early 1830s, virtually all machines were built in Belgium, and operated and maintained by Belgians. The technological dependence on England was over.

In similarity to the cotton industry, capital accumulation was a major force behind the transformation of the woolen industry in Belgium. Capital formation meant the purchase and accumulation of fixed goods

87. It appears from the statistics that in 1831–32 Belgian woolen exports reached a peak never to be achieved again until late in the nineteenth century: exports in 1831 are reported to equal 1,610 tons, and are still above 1,000 tons in 1832, dropping suddenly to 344 tons in 1833. Briavoinne, otherwise an extremely careful and scrupulous writer, takes these figures seriously and proceeds to explain them by a sharp drop in foreign demand caused by the establishment of the German Zollverein. This is highly unlikely, to say the least. If the Zollverein did have an immediate effect on the imports of nonmembers, English wool exports to Germany should have declined equally. This was by no means the case: the value of English woolen exports to Germany averaged 585,000 pounds in 1830–31, was still 566,000 pounds in 1834, and 581,000 pounds in 1836. (Great Britain, Parliamentary Papers, vol. 33 [Accounts and Papers Relating to Trade, etc.], 1833, pp. 636–39. Id., vol. 48 [Accounts and Papers Relating to Trade, etc.], 1835, p. 663. Id., vol. 47 [Tables of the Revenue, Population, Commerce, etc. of the U. K. and its Dependencies], 1837–38, p. 105.) It is equally clear that in the late 1830s Belgium still exported a considerable amount of woolen cloth to Prussia, the major partner in the Zollverein. In 1838 Prussia alone accounted for 8,756,000 francs out of a total export of 16,002,000 francs. (Statistique de la Belgique, Tableau Général du Commerce Avec des Pays Etrangères, 1838 [Brussels: Ministère de l'Intérieur, 1839], p. 257.) It is therefore plausible that the export statistics for the first years of independence are erroneous and that the trend was consequently up and not down.

88. Rénier, "Histoire de l'Industrie," p. 177.

89. Briavoinne, "Sur les Inventions," p. 90.

90. Ibid., pp. 91–93.

91. Biographie Nationale de Belgique (Brussels: H. Thiry van Buggenhoudt, 1868), vol. 2: 685. See also Rénier, "Histoire de l'Industrie," pp. 181 ff.

in which the new technology was embodied. In addition, capital formation involved buildings, supervisory personnel, and other costs incurred by centralization. Where did the capital come from? It is important to realize that, contrary to the cotton industry which emerged almost *ex nihilo*, the woolen industry could draw upon "original" or premodern accumulation. According to Lebrun, the circulating (or "working") capital, which was the predominant form of capital in the traditional industries, used by the woolen industry in the last years of the *ancien régime*, was about six million francs in Verviers alone.[92] Verviers accounted for somewhat less than a third of the total output.[93]

The fact that the woolen industry employed considerable amounts of capital prior to mechanization does not necessarily provide an answer to the question of how the process of accumulation after 1798 was brought about. The substitutability between circulating capital and fixed capital was probably very low or nil. The need for circulating capital arises from the nonsimultaneity of the production process and takes three major forms: the wages fund, intermediary inputs, and inventories. There seems to be no reason to suspect any a priori relation between the amount of circulating capital required and output per worker when fixed capital accumulation *cum* technological change takes place—the production process may become more or less "roundabout."

Could the availability of circulating capital prior to modernization have played a significant role in the accumulation of fixed capital? In principle, this could only have been the case if modernization reduced the absolute amount of circulating capital required. This was, as might be expected, by no means the case. The role of circulating capital can be illustrated as follows: let K_c be the stock of circulating capital; L, labor inputs per annum; w, the average wage rate; and Q, annual output. For a given technique and organizational set-up, the amount of circulating capital needed is:

$$K_c = \alpha w L + \beta Q \qquad (2.1)$$

where α and β are parameters. The parameter α is the average time lapse between the payment of wages and the completion of the sale of final output. β is the corresponding time lapse with respect to intermediary inputs, which can be supposed to be proportional to output. Thus the dimensions of α and β are in time units, since the dimensions of wL and Q are in terms of numéraire/time while the dimension of K_c is numéraire.

92. Lebrun, "L'Expérience de l'Industrie Drapière Verviétoise, 1750–1850," in *First International Conference of Economic History, Stockholm 1960, Contributions and Communications* (Paris-The Hague: Mouton et Cie., 1960), p. 561.

93. In 1812 Verviers accounted for 28 percent of the output of the whole area, and there is no reason to believe that this proportion was much different before 1798.

Assume that for any given technique, the output/labor ratio is constant.

$$Q = cL \qquad (2.2)$$

where c is the productivity of labor. From (2.1) and (2.2):

$$K_c = (\frac{\alpha w}{c} + \beta) Q \qquad (2.3)$$

The amount of circulating capital required is determined by the amount of total output, Q, the productivity of labor, c, and the simultaneity parameters α and β. The research of Professor Lebrun (see table 2.7) makes it possible to estimate these figures for Verviers, thus decomposing the demand for circulating capital.

The need for circulating capital can thus be seen to have increased, since the growth of output, compounded by a rise in β as well as in w, more than offset the fall in α. The latter probably was caused by the decline of the domestic industry and the concentration of production. On the other hand, the turnover of intermediate inputs slowed down somewhat.

The important conclusion for the present purpose is that the accumulation of fixed capital could hardly have been financed by the partial substitution of fixed capital for circulating capital.[94] In effect, the expansion that occurred after 1800 needed large amounts of *both* circulating and fixed capital, as can be verified from tables 2.5 and 2.7. This rapid accumulation was financed almost exclusively by the "own sources" of the entrepreneurs. Banks and other credit institutions played a negligible

Table 2.7 Decomposition of the Demand for Circulating
Capital in the Verviers Woolen Industry

			1780–89	1805–10	1845–50
K_c (current prices)			6,500,000	15,000,000	17,000,000
Q	"	"	6,000,000	17,000,000	21,000,000
L	"	"	7,000	7,000	7,000
w	"	"	266	461	510
c	"	"	857	2,428	3,000
α	"	"	1.58	1.17	1.0
β	"	"	0.53	0.68	0.68
$\frac{K_c}{Q} = \frac{\alpha w}{c} + \beta$			1.04	0.91	0.85

SOURCE: Computed from data in Lebrun, "L'Expérience de l'Industrie Drapière," pp. 561–65.

94. If it were possible to borrow at a nearly perfect capital market for purposes of merchant-credit, the constraint of self-finance would largely disappear. This is to some extent true for England, but much less so for Belgium where circulating capital, too, originated in retained earnings.

role in the process.[95] The main source was, as with the cotton industry, the plowed-back profits earned on previously accumulated capital goods. All the same, the dependence on retained current profits may have been somewhat less than in Flanders. After all, in the second half of the eighteenth century, the woolen industry had enjoyed a period of high profits and some entrepreneurs had accumulated substantial wealth. It is hardly possible that these assets played no role at all in the financing of the first stage of industrialization. Yet, a glance at a few portfolios of merchant-entrepreneurs in the eighteenth century is sufficient to show that the traditional industrialist had a high preference for riskless assets (real estate and securities). Much of their wealth, moreover, was in very illiquid form and could only with difficulty be transformed into working or fixed capital.[96] In any case, the wealth accumulated in the protoindustry seems sufficient to finance only the initial stages of capital formation. It is important to note that, unlike the cotton in Ghent or the heavy industry in the Walloon provinces, the woolen industry received almost no government loans or support.[97]

To summarize the development of the woolen industry in Belgium, it could be said that the initial period of qualitative transformation as well as quantitative expansion was short and intensive. After 1811–12, a contraction set in, which was reversed in the late 1810s. Henceforward, slow, more or less steady technological change started which lasted until the Belgian Revolution. For a few years, the trend was somewhat disrupted but moderate growth soon resumed and lasted, with one violent interruption in 1848, until the end of the 1840s. By that time the woolen industry of Belgium had become one of the technologically most advanced corners in Europe.

Some of the prominent characteristics of the Walloon woolen industry bear a remarkable resemblance to the cotton industry in Flanders. In both areas, an industry emerged by adopting technological advances developed in England.[98] Like the Flemish cotton industry, the export market was probably more important than domestic demand. Hence, output and employment were highly sensitive to political disturbances and temporary

95. Lebrun, "L'Experience de l'Industrie Drapière," p. 552.
96. Lebrun, *L'Industrie de la Laine*, pp. 470–83.
97. Demoulin, *Guillaume Ier*, p. 165.
98. In 1833 the above-mentioned Henry Hughes testified that Belgium possessed "almost all our [woolen manufacture machines]; through the great facility of getting into our manufactories in England they are sure to get and carry off our improvements." Great Britain, *Parliamentary Papers*, vol. 6 (1833), p. 69. Belgian dependence on English technology is summarized by a leading historian of the era as follows: "As is known, our ancestors [that is, the Belgians in the nineteenth century] achieved little or nothing in the field of technical innovations. Their success stemmed essentially from their being the first to realize the possibilities of the new inventions, and their ability to apply them here." Coppejans-Desmedt, "Incidenten," p. 164.

disruptions of trade. Yet it is remarkable to note that the process of capital investment and technological progress seem almost unaffected by the fluctuations in the level of sales and output. One nineteenth-century author writes:

> The woolen industry, despite the disturbing political events, has not ceased its progress .... from 1815 on, after the political upsets suddenly resulted in the loss of the French market for the Verviers industry, the able manufacturers of that area redoubled their efforts to produce high quality goods at low costs by means of the introduction of improved machinery.[99]

Finally, in both the cotton and the woolen industries, there was a very slow rise, if any, in the wage level, while profits rose rapidly, both in absolute value and as a proportion of total output.

THE METALLURGICAL AND HEAVY INDUSTRIES

As was noted in chapter 1, Belgium was already an important producer of iron in the eighteenth century (as well as before). The French conquest in 1795 united the two main competing regions, Liège and Charleroi. From then on, it is permissible to deal with a "Belgian" iron industry as a whole. It is convenient to divide the metallurgical industry into two principal parts: a primary section which consisted of the production and refinement of cast iron, and a secondary section which included the armament industries, the machinery industries, nail and cutlery manufacturing, and later on the railmaking and related railroad industries. The mining of coal and iron will not be described in detail.

Unlike the case of the textile industries, there were no technological breakthroughs in the iron industry during the French period (1795–1814). On the other hand, the growth of the textile machinery industry meant the rise of a wholly new part in the secondary section of the metallurgical industry.

In the primary section of the metallurgical industry, the new blast furnaces erected in the French period were not significantly different from the old, though they were larger and capable of producing greater heat. The new furnaces were up to twenty-five feet high instead of the seventeen feet of the ancient furnaces, and of a round rather than an octangular shape. Cylindrical forge bellows replaced the old leather bellows, and a new technique to remove the phosphorus from the ore came into use.[100]

---

99. Barlet, *Histoire du Commerce*, p. 28. Cf. also van Hogendorp, *Bijdragen*, 2: 268.
100. Briavoinne, "Sur les Inventions," pp. 122–23.

The French period was one of important, though not spectacular, quantitative expansion of the production of iron using more or less the same techniques. The number of blast furnaces grew from 63 in the period before 1795 to 83 in 1814. The new furnaces were, however, capable of producing up to 3,000 kg daily, three times the capacity of the old furnaces.[101] Most of this expansion took place in the Charleroi region, while production in the department *Ourthe* (province of Liège) grew much more slowly. One source claims that in 1804, regional output was exceeded by consumption of iron by a factor of ten, the rest brought in from Charleroi as well as from Luxembourg.[102] This figure seems exaggerated, but it is true that the Liège area became prominent in the production of iron only after the introduction of coke smelting in the Dutch period. The

Table 2.8   Iron Furnaces and Production in Four Belgian Provinces, 1789 and 1811

		Forêts (*Luxembourg*)	*Jemmapes* (*Hainault*)	*Ourthe* (*Liège*)	*Sambre et Meuse* (*Namur*)	*Total*
Number of blast furnaces	1789	20	3	13	23	59
	1811	38	5	17	27	87
Number of refineries	1789	47	43	26	51	167
	1811	98	46	37	71	252
Output of pig iron (tons)	1789	7,483	1,025	4,600	10,671	23,779
	1811	15,247	1,150	5,700	15,240	37,337
Output of cast iron (tons)	1789	n.a.	n.a.	n.a.	n.a.	n.a.
	1811	700	720	—	—	1,420
Output of wrought iron (tons)	1789	6,858	1,780	3,265	5,479	17,382
	1811	13,683	2,543	3,435	8,264	27,925
Number of workers	1811	8,762	4,900	6,100	6,525	26,286
Value of output (10³ francs)	1811	5,589	2,316	3,992	4,400	16,297

SOURCE: Montalivet, *Exposé de la Situation*, pp. 46–49.

101. Ibid., pp. 121, 124. The average growth in capacity of a blast furnace was probably closer to twofold. Cf. A. Wibail, "L'Évolution Économique de la Sidérurgie Belge de 1830 à 1913," *BISEL* 6, no. 1 (November 1933): 32.
102. Warzée, "Exposé . . . Liège," p. 458.

rates of change in four key provinces during the French period are presented in table 2.8, which was constructed from data assembled by Montalivet, the Minister of Interior of the French Empire. Inspection of table 2.8 reveals that these data are not very reliable. For example, the department of *Forêts* employed about twice the workers of *Jemmapes* and the values of the outputs in the respective provinces related to each other as 1 : 2.5. Yet, in physical terms, the output of iron in *Forêts* was seven times as large as in *Jemmapes*. A similar discrepancy is revealed by a comparison between *Ourthe* and *Sambre et Meuse*. The absolute values of Montalivet's data must therefore be treated with the utmost suspicion.[103] Yet, there can be little doubt that the picture presented by Montalivet's data is roughly correct: these four provinces account for a significant proportion of the total iron output of the French Empire. This is illustrated in table 2.9.

A second conclusion that can be drawn from Montalivet's data is that between 1789 and 1811, output grew by a factor of around 50 percent. It should be noted that the orders of magnitude of Montalivet's data are to some extent corroborated by a source from 1816. Eighteen sixteen was a severe crisis year, and output of iron was 65 million pounds (29 thousand metric tons).[104] Compared with the 1811 data for Hainault, Liège, and Namur (output in Limburg was negligible and Luxembourg seems omitted from the 1816 source), this is a decline of 28 percent, which appears not implausible in view of the crisis following the collapse of the

Table 2.9   Iron Production in Belgium and the French Empire in 1811

	Four Belgian Depts. (Forêts, Jemmapes, Ourthe, and Sambre et Meuse)	Total French Empire	Belgium as a Percentage of Total
Blast furnaces	87	487	17.9
Refineries	252	1,356	8.6
Pig iron output (tons)	37,337	143,720	26.0
Cast iron output (tons)	1,420	20,151	7.0
Wrought iron output (tons)	27,925	115,499	24.2
Workers in iron industry	26,286	160,000	16.4
Value of output (10^3 francs)	16,297	108,000	15.1
Population	1,251,618	42,738,377	2.9

SOURCE: Montalivet, *Exposé de la Situation*, pp. 46–49.

103. For some additional use of Montalivet's data, see Craeybeckx, "Les Débuts," pp. 128 ff.

104. "Mémoire sur les Houillères des Provinces de Hainaut, Namur, Liège et Limbourg" (Mons, 1816), cited by Warzée, "Exposé . . . Hainaut," p. 43.

First Empire. In general, it must be admitted that the statistics compiled by the officials of the First Empire are of such quality that they should not by used for anything but the crudest approximations. Perhaps very careful research will provide indications as to which of the conflicting and incompatible sources can be believed, but it seems unlikely.[105]

After the incorporation of the Belgian provinces in the Netherlands a period of decline set in. But already in the late 1810s, the Dutch government started to realize the tremendous potentialities in the metallurgical industry in eastern and southern Belgium.[106] In 1822, a young naval officer named G. M. Roentgen was commissioned to investigate the possibilities of large-scale iron production in the Walloon provinces.[107]

In his report, Roentgen argues that technological progress in the Walloon iron industry during French domination had been insignificant compared to England. Roentgen was in a position to know, because a year before he had investigated the English iron industry, also on royal orders. According to Roentgen, the two major innovations which had revolutionized the English iron industry, the use of coke for smelting and Cort's puddling and rolling process, were still unknown in Belgium. Many other defects were summed up by Roentgen, both technical and organizational. Nevertheless, Roentgen realized the possibilities that this region held with respect to the production of iron and recommended a government policy encouraging the usage of coke for smelting, the construction of modernized blast furnaces, and the use of limestone together with coal. In addition, Roentgen recommended the utilization of Cort's process in the production of wrought iron and proposed an active policy to encourage its adoption. If his plan was followed, Roentgen concluded, then:

> Within a few years our iron works will be elevated from the present condition of decay to a size hitherto unknown and exceeding any other country in Europe [i.e., the Continent] in the quality of iron as well as the low price at which it is sold. . . . everything necessary to make our

105. Two seemingly independent sources provide figures for the iron industry in two provinces which are irreconcilably different from Montalivet's. One is Thomassin in his *Mémoire Statistique*, p. 434, for the province of Liège. The other is for Hainault, reproduced in Warzée, "Exposé . . . Hainaut," pp. 37–42. A striking note of warning about the reliability of the statistics collected during the Consulate and the First Empire is sounded by Jean-Antoine Chaptal, minister of the interior 1799–1804. See John U. Nef, "The Industrial Revolution Reconsidered," in *War and Human Progress* (New York: Norton, 1968), p. 285. For a similar conclusion reached by a modern historian cf. R. Darquenne, "Histoire Économique du Département de Jemmapes," *MPSH* 79 (1965): 117–19.

106. M. G. de Boer, "Guillaume Ier et les Débuts de l'Industrie Métallurgique en Belgique," *RBPH* 3 (1924): 527–52.

107. G. M. Roentgen, "Berigt van den Toestand van de IJzerwerken in de Waalsche Provincien" [Report on the condition of the iron industry in the Walloon provinces], ed. M. G. de Boer, *EHJ* 9 (1921): 103–49.

country the capital of iron making is found right here, in the Walloon provinces.[108]

Indeed, Roentgen's bold prophecy was realized within a few years. Huart-Chapelle, an iron producer from Charleroi, is generally credited with the introduction of coke smelting in Belgium in 1824.[109] He was followed within a few years by Hannonet-Gendarme in Couvin, Fontaine-Spitaels in Hauchies, and others. The expansion of blast furnaces using coke was so rapid that in 1831, 4,600 tons of cast iron or 70 percent of total output was produced by coke furnaces in the *arrondissement* of Charleroi. Out of a total of sixteen blast furnaces in the province of Hainault in the same year, nine were using coke. Two years later, the province of Hainault as a whole was producing more than 20,000 tons of cast iron, of which 95 percent were produced by coke furnaces. In 1836, Belgium had altogether twenty-two coke furnaces in operation and twenty-five more under construction, about half in the Charleroi area.[110] The development of cast iron production is illustrated in table 2.10.

Table 2.10 reflects the enormous growth in output due to the shift from charcoal to coke furnaces as well as the somewhat surprising long life of the charcoal furnace. The coexistence of modern and obsolete methods lasted for a quarter of a century. Charcoal furnaces even experienced a revival in the late 1830s (when the price of coal rose temporarily). But, on the whole, there can be little doubt about the substitution of coke for charcoal, and the consequent shift of the center of gravity in iron production from the timber-intensive provinces of Luxembourg and Namur to Hainault and Liège. In 1845, Hainault accounts for about 45 percent of total iron production, Liège for about 36 percent, and Namur and Luxembourg together for only 11 percent.[111] This is a striking reversal from 1811, as can be verified from table 2.8, according to which Luxembourg and Namur produce more than 80 percent of pig iron and 79 percent of wrought iron.[112]

About the same time that coke smelting was being introduced, production of wrought iron by means of Cort's rolling and puddling process was becoming more widespread. The first who is known to have used this process in Belgium was Orban in Grivegnée in 1821. Orban also pioneered

108. Ibid., p. 149.
109. Briavoinne, "Sur les Inventions," p. 126.
110. Ibid.
111. *Exposé de la Situation*, pp. 117–18.
112. The comparison is very inexact, and not only because of the overall bad quality of the Imperial statistics. The province of Luxembourg before 1830 (as well as the French dept. of *Forêts*) included both the present Grand Duchy of Luxembourg and the Belgian province of the same name. However, the data from 1845 pertain only to the latter. The orders of magnitude involved are however such that this bias does not distort the basic picture.

Table 2.10   Iron Production in Hainault, 1829–51

	Active Furnaces		Output of Cast Iron (tons)			Value (in 10³ francs)	Hainault as a Percentage of Belgium
	Charcoal	Coke	Charcoal Furnaces	Coke Furnaces	Total		
1829	n.a.	n.a.	n.a.	n.a.	10,274	n.a.	n.a.
1830	n.a.	n.a.	2,200	5,760	7,960	1,035	n.a.
1831	3	4	2,000	4,600	6,600	858	7.3
1832	3	5	1,700	10,615	12,315	1,601	13.2
1833	n.a.	n.a.	1,150	19,180	20,330	2,643	21.4
1834	2	8	2,016	27,260	29,276	3,806	29.3
1835	n.a.	n.a.	2,016	29,420	31,436	4,714	27.3
1836	5	9	6,300	27,360	33,360	6,062	24.9
1837	n.a.	n.a.	n.a.	n.a.	n.a.	n.a.	n.a.
1838	5	9	n.a.	n.a.	n.a.	n.a.	n.a.
1839	4	11	n.a.	45,000	n.a.	n.a.	n.a.
1840	3	13	2,628	50,000	52,628	6,315	55.4
1841	3	13	2,462	n.a.	n.a.	n.a.	n.a.
1842	2	10	1,695	41,240	42,935	4,249	44.7
1843	n.a.	n.a.	n.a.	n.a.	n.a.	n.a.	n.a.
1844	2	10	1,995	41,956	43,951	3,905	41.1
1845	2	16	1,407	58,678	60,085	6,677	44.6
1846	3	22	2,183	99,619	101,802	13,749	53.8
1847	3	24	3,297	115,278	118,575	13,756	47.7
1848	2	18	1,163	68,724	69,887	6,196	43.2
1849	1	13	726	69,079	69,805	5,730	47.0
1850	1	12	696	62,125	62,821	4,702	43.5
1851	0	15	—	70,924	70,924	5,472	42.3
1860	0	25	—	183,910	183,910	15,420	57.5

SOURCES: Warzée, "Exposé...Hainault," pp. 61–62. Wibail, "L'Évolution Économique," p. 50.

the first rolling mill.[113] In 1822–23, a number of other entrepreneurs adopted the process simultaneously. Among the pioneers in Hainault were Huart-Henrard and Hannonet-Gendarme, while in Liège the famous John Cockerill seems to have been the first. Diffusion was rapid. In 1830, puddling ovens refined about 10,800 tons of wrought iron, about one-third of total output. At the same time, the number of charcoal using refining ovens fell from 206 to 150 in the Dutch period.[114] The output of wrought iron (fer affiné) in the province of Hainault increased especially after the revolution: output climbed from 7,220 tons in 1830 to 34,369 tons in 1850. The number of puddling hearths increased correspondingly.

113. J. Franquoy, "Mémoire sur l'Historique des Progrès de la Fabrication du Fer dans le Pays de Liège," MSLEL, n.s. 1 (1860): 429.
114. Demoulin, Guillaume Iᵉʳ, p. 314.

In 1850, there were about 200 of them in Belgium, half of them in Hainault and about one-third in Liège.[115] It is interesting to note that in this case, technological change confined itself to the transformation to a new process. Further improvement on the new system was slow. This can be inferred from the fact that the capacity of the average puddling oven did not change very much over time. A source from 1833 estimates the annual output of a puddling oven at 540 tons. In 1850, there were 97 ovens in Hainault, of which 65 were active. Output of wrought iron amounted to 34,369 tons, or 537 tons per oven.[116]

Some additional technological advances in the iron industry should be noted. An early development was the recovery of blast furnace gas, first used in 1815, twenty-five years before it was introduced in England.[117] The rolling mills (laminoirs) and sledge hammers used in slitting mills (fenderies et marteaux) were mechanized in the 1820s by the continuous application of steam power. In 1837, the Hainault iron industry employed 53 steam engines with a capacity of 1,857 HP, while the Liège industry employed 55 machines with 1,174 HP.[118] The difference between the two regions with respect to average capacity is a result of the fact that in Hainault the primary section of heavy industry was relatively more important, while in Liège, the secondary section, which used comparatively smaller engines, was predominant. Aggregate figures of the development of the use of steam power in the iron industry are presented in table 2.11.

The secondary section of the metallurgical industry included those

Table 2.11   Steam Power in the Metallurgical Industry, 1838–50

	1838		1844		1850	
	Number	HP	Number	HP	Number	HP
Blast furnaces	52	1,828	64	2,684	121	4,586
Metal working	45	1,165	61	1,381	73	1,694
Machine making	56	553	81	817	118	1,170
Armaments	7	68	8	111	13	175
Total metallurgy	160	3,614	214	4,993	325	7,625
Percentage of the iron industry of total steam power	15	14	15	13	16	15

SOURCE: Exposé de la Situation, p. 113.

115. Exposé de la Situation, p. 120.
116. Assuming that there was some more or less constant optimal capacity at which the mills were run, which seems not implausible since it was probably more efficient to curtail production by idling some mills altogether than to run them at less than full capacity.
117. Wibail, "L'Évolution Économique," p. 32.
118. Heuschling, Essai, 1st ed., pp. 154–57.

activities using iron as a direct input, as opposed to those for which iron was the principal output. The emergence of a machinery industry which served the textile industry in the French period was described in some detail above. Initially, this industry was small, although it grew rapidly. Out of 8,753 metal workers in the city of Liège, only 1,477 were engaged in the production of capital goods for the woolen industry, although the number for the whole province was more substantial.[119] The armament industry at the same time employed over 2,500 (mostly domestic) workers.[120] The cannon foundry, established in 1803, grew rapidly and soon became the largest single plant in the province of Liège.[121]

The machine industry continued its rise to prominence after 1815. The dominant figure during most of the period under discussion was John Cockerill, the youngest son of the man who first introduced mechanical spinning in the woolen industry of Belgium. The elder Cockerill had terminated his exclusive engagement with the firm of Biolley-Simonis in 1807 and settled in Liège, where he opened an independent workshop for the manufacturing of textile machinery. By 1809, Cockerill, according to himself, had produced ninety complete assortments at an average price of more than 10,000 francs per piece. His workshop employed 144 adults (blacksmiths, carpenters, etc.) and 100 children.[122] In 1810 Cockerill was awarded French citizenship and, together with another Englishman, William Douglas, received a prize for his outstanding inventive ability.[123] According to Thomassin, Cockerill's activities were spread over the entire province, and he employed 2,000 workers in 1812 who produced machines and tools at a value of over 2.5 million francs. More than half of that sum was paid in salaries.[124]

119. Lebrun, "La Rivoluzione Industriale," p. 613.

120. The armament industry did not expand as fast as might have been expected in a turbulent period like the first decade and a half of the nineteenth century. Instead of purchasing their weapons from the traditional local entrepreneurs, the French founded an "Imperial Manufacture" in the city which employed about 1,000 workers and produced annually 27,000 rifles. According to Briavoinne, the disappointed weapon manufacturers formed an association with the purpose of convincing the French authorities to purchase arms directly from the manufacturers. On one of his voyages the Emperor himself happened to pass through the city of Liège, and the arms manufacturers exploited this opportunity to present a petition in which they asked for fair competition in the orders of weapons for the French army. The petition was accompanied by an expensive rifle as a present for the Emperor. Napoleon, a soldier all his life, instinctively tried to load the rifle on the spot. Unfortunately, the bullet did not fit in the muzzle. His Majesty frowned, and the petition remained unanswered. See Briavoinne, De l'Industrie, 1: 273.

121. Franquoy, "Mémoire sur l'Historique," p. 383. Thomassin, Mémoire Statistique, pp. 435–39.

122. Letter of Cockerill to Thomassin, cited in Gobert, "Conditions de l'Industrie," p. 181.

123. Henderson, Britain and Industrial Europe, pp. 111–12.

124. Thomassin, Mémoire Statistique, p. 450. Cockerill employed 75 percent of all the workers in the machine industry in the province, and produced half of the machines. The latter figure seems a more realistic estimate of Cockerill's share in the industry.

Cockerill's youngest son, John, who took over his father's business in 1813 at the age of twenty-three, soon became the pivotal figure in the Belgian machine industry and indeed on the European continent as a whole.[125] The growth of Cockerill's machine factory was spectacular. In 1816, he was already producing hydraulic presses, steam engines, and pumps, in addition to textile equipment. At this time he already employed 4,500 workers in his various businesses, despite the overall slump in business.[126] A year later, he bought the Castle of Seraing from the Dutch king, and turned the site into an industrial plant. Seraing was admirably located in an area rich in coal and limestone on the river Meuse, and the sum of 45,000 francs was in fact so low that it can only be viewed as a subsidy extended by the king to Cockerill. At this occasion, William I is reported to have said to Cockerill: "Continue your grand enterprises without fear and remember that the king of the Netherlands always has money at industry's service."[127]

From this time on, Cockerill's enterprise expanded at a dazzling rate, both horizontally and vertically. The foundry at Seraing became one of the largest in Europe. In the early 1820s a puddling plant was installed; the first blast furnace operating on coke was built in 1823. In the mid-1820s steamship construction became a major occupation while in the early 1830s railway equipment, both rolling stock and tracks, became an important focus of activity. The array of products turned out by Cockerill was far wider, however. The huge cast iron lion, commemorating the battle of Waterloo, was made at Seraing, as well as a constant stream of steam engines of various sizes and for extremely diverse purposes. Output of steam engines (without capacity specification) averaged nine in the years 1818–23, rose to an average of twenty-six for the years 1824–30, and fell suddenly in the first years of independence. In 1831 only seven machines were produced; in 1832, five machines. But Cockerill soon recovered and in 1837, no less than fifty-four steam engines were turned out by the Cockerill plants, of which twenty-seven were locomotives. A considerable part of these machines were exported.[128]

In 1830, Seraing alone employed 2,000 workers, one of the largest plants on the Continent.[129] In addition, Cockerill had widespread interests in textile, machine, and metallurgical industries all over Europe. Among his many interests were a zinc mine near Aachen, a cotton mill in Bar-

125. For an excellent bibliography of Cockerill, cf. Henderson, *Britain and Industrial Europe*, p. 116n.

126. De Boer, "Guillaume Ier," p. 529.

127. Cited, among others, by Henderson, *Britain and Industrial Europe*, p. 124.

128. P. Jacquemin, *Notice sur les Etablissements de la Société Cockerill* (Liège: L. de Thier, 1880), p. 75.

129. Demoulin, *Guillaume Ier*, p. 282. Henderson (*Britain and Industrial Europe*, p. 124) puts the number at 2,500.

celona, a steam-driven sugar refinery in Dutch Guyana, and blast furnaces in southern France.[130] In the late 1830s, he even conceived of a grandiose plan involving the construction of a railroad network in Russia. He died in 1840 in Warsaw, no doubt the most prominent industrial tycoon of continental Europe.

Unfortunately, most of the business records of the central plant at Seraing have been destroyed by man and Providence alike on various occasions.[131] Therefore, good quantitative evidence is unavailable on the exact dimensions and development over time of Cockerill's establishment. In 1842 a joint-stock company, the "Société Cockerill," was founded to manage the Seraing works. The assets of this company should convey some idea of the size of the Seraing plant. These assets included, among others, a mine concession of 195 hectares, 39 coke furnaces, 2 large blast furnaces, 2 foundries, an ironworks with 35 puddling ovens, 5 rolling mills, a mechanical construction shop employing 144 blacksmiths, 280 lathes and drills, 200 machines for planing, grooving, mortising, and piercing, and steam engines with a total capacity of 920 HP. In 1846, the firm employed 2,200 workers and its annual sales amounted to 6.7 million francs.[132]

A complementary source of information on the Seraing factory is the descriptions of contemporaries. A Frenchman observed in 1835:

> The last Bishop of Liège who died a few years ago [the reference is to Count François of Méan who was deposed as Bishop of Liège by the French in 1795 but later appointed Archbishop of Mechelen] has lost his position as ruler of Liège to John Cockerill, a *Liègeois* of English descent better described as a tremendous mind without fatherland, a citizen of every country that will offer him a spot to put his machines on. His establishment in Seraing is the largest in Europe, but it is only his headquarters from which he spreads out his influence all over Europe . . . he is indeed the new prince-sovereign of Seraing with lieutenants all over the world. . . . Government officials sign his passport without suspecting that this quiet man is a revolutionary far more dangerous than a sharp-witted agitator filling their lands with pamphlets and manifests. . . . It is with good reason that the establishment at Seraing is widely regarded a model enterprise. All the different activities associated with metallurgy are concentrated under the same roof. . . . The most attention-attracting section in the

130. Demoulin, *Guillaume Ier*, p. 231.
131. E. Mahaim, "Les Débuts de l'Établissement John Cockerill à Seraing," *VSWG* 3 (1905): 627.
132. Jacquemin, *Notice sur les Établissements*, pp. 27–30.

magnificent plant at Seraing are the workshops in which machines are assembled. This workshop is divided into three vast sections: the boiler workshop, the locomotive manufacture and the steam engine construction shop. The latter especially has left me flabbergasted. . . . One becomes dizzy amidst thousands of spinning wheels, geared by the most diverse and seemingly contradictory gears, turning to all directions at all speeds.[133]

The second contemporary witness who visited the machine workshops in the Liège area was an Englishman, J. C. Symons, who reported in 1839 to the Parliamentary Commission on handloom weavers about industrial conditions on the Continent. Symons's impressions were quite different from Nisard's and are worth quoting:

One of the most ungainsayble evidences of the progress of manufacturing in a country is unquestionably that of the number of its machine making establishments. In these, for extent Belgium surpasses, in proportion to her size and population every nation in the world; whilst she can hardly be considered permanently second to England in mechanical perfection, when English engineers are at the head of all her establishments, English patents open to her immediate adoption, and English artisans in nearly all her *ateliers*. Of these establishments that of Mr. Cockerill of Liège is, if I am rightly informed, the second largest in the world. The number of workmen there varies from 2,000 to 2,300; and Mr. Cockerill has also an establishment at his residence at Liège, where he employs 700 more men—all these in the production of machines from spinning machines up to steam engines. It is difficult to name any large enterprise or manufacturing industry . . . with which Mr. Cockerill is unconnected. . . . When we consider that the machinery that he turns out is, after all, of secondary reputation for quality and extremely dear, we may form some idea of the natural advantages Belgium affords to the manufacture of machinery.[134]

The contradictions in this statement are obvious. As it seems, the conclusions of most Englishmen concerning the Belgian machine industry are a mixture of a wishful attempt to belittle the achievements of the latter with a genuine fear of a successful competitor. Symons, after having claimed that Belgian machine making was inferior to English both with respect to price and with respect to quality, went on to say that he saw

133. Nisard, "Souvenirs de Voyages, Le Pays de Liège," *Revue de Paris* 24 (1835): 130–46.
134. Great Britain, *Parliamentary Papers*, vol. 42 (*Report from the Assistant Hand-loom Weavers Commission*), 1839, p. 157.

"only one obstacle to the career of Belgium in her manufacturing progress of competition with England," which was the "fact" that Belgium seemed to be running out of coal and would become directly dependent on England. A similar attitude can be detected in the report of Grenville Withers, an English engineer, who wrote to a parliamentary commission:

> The quality of the work done at Seraing used to be the best on the Continent...the machines are exported to all parts of the world. They are inferior to English machines. . . . The models are made from machines brought from England for that purpose, but the copy is always *very, very* inferior to the model. . . . Cockerill's machines are the best that are made on the Continent but are very inferior to English made machines...when the English government permit the exportation of machines, foreign machine makers may have to shut up their establishments.[135]

A few years later, the same man testified before the House's Select Committee on the Exportation of Machinery that machine making in Belgium had improved greatly since 1838 and if it continued that trend, the repeal of the law which prohibited exports of machinery would be meaningless.[136] One of the members of that committee, J. Emerson-Tennent, had written a few years before that he considered De Phoenix machine works in Ghent to be "the most admirably arranged establishment that I ever saw—those of England not excepted."[137]

John Cockerill and De Phoenix did not monopolize the Belgian machine industry. Especially in Liège, there was stiff competition. D. Houguet in Hodimont, F. Spineux and the Poncelet Brothers in Liège, were some of the principal competitors. Similar to the histories of Cockerill and De Phoenix, these firms followed a path of remarkable expansion between 1819 and 1850, though their growth, too, fluctuated wildly with political events and later with the business cycle. In 1837 there were 235 steam engines in the province of Liège, 65 of which had been made by John Cockerill, 20 imported, and 150 manufactured by smaller local workshops. The average capacity of an engine made by Cockerill was, however, 145 HP, as compared to about 20 HP of the machines made by his competitors.[138] It is thus evident that a division of labor between Cockerill and his competitors existed in the Walloon machinery industry.

135. Ibid., p. 173. Emphasis in original.
136. Ibid., vol. 7 (*Report from the Select Committee into the Operation of the Existing Laws Affecting the Exportation of Machinery*), 1841, p. 43.
137. J. Emerson Tennent, *Belgium* (London: Richard Bentley, 1841), 1: 67.
138. M. Lévy-Leboyer, *Les Banques Européenes et l'Industrialisation Internationale dans la Première Moitié du XIXe Siècle* (Paris: Presses universitaires de France, 1964), p. 361, n. 89.

Table 2.12   The Development of Belgian Steam Power, 1831–50
(excluding railroads and shipping)

	Number of Steam Engines		Capacity in HP	
	Stock at End of Year	New Machines Installed	Stock at End of Year	New Machines Installed
1831	n.a.	7	n.a.	n.a.
1832	n.a.	26	n.a.	907
1833	n.a.	20	n.a.	162
1834	n.a.	27	n.a.	212
1835	n.a.	36	n.a.	422
1836	n.a.	43	n.a.	563
1837	n.a.	64	n.a.	742
1838	1,044	n.a.	25,312	n.a.
1839	n.a.	125	n.a.	4,417
1840	n.a.	97	n.a.	2,464
1841	n.a.	86	n.a.	1,716
1842	n.a.	106	n.a.	3,018
1843	n.a.	87	n.a.	1,589
1844	1,450	123	37,370	2,438
1845	1,514	159	39,230	2,701
1846	1,631	171	41,822	3,516
1847	1,730	180	44,727	4,428
1848	1,924	167	47,466	3,946
1849	1,974	167	50,731	4,206
1850	2,040	n.a.	51,055	n.a.

SOURCES: 1831–38—*Documents Statistiques Récueillis et Publiés par le Ministre de l'Intérieur du Royaume de Belgique* (Brussels: de Mat, about 1838), pp. 223–29. 1838–50—*Statistique de la Belgique: Mines, Usines*, 1 (1846): 48–51, 2 (1852): 104–15.

The overall significance of the Belgian machine industry can be assessed from the number of steam engines produced. Since imports of steam engines were insignificant and the data on exports of machines are available, new installments of steam engines are an acceptable proxy to the output of the machine industry. Some of these data are summarized in table 2.12. It is interesting to note that the stock of steam engines in 1830 was already fairly large and that accumulation was slow in the first eight years of independence. This impression is partly due to probable underreporting in the early 1830s as well as to the fact that in these years most steam engines were built for the use of railroads, which had to be excluded from the table. Secondly, it is remarkable how self-sufficient Belgium was with respect to machines: in 1844, only 4.3 percent of all machines, with 5.4 of total capacity, were of foreign make.[139] Self-suffi-

139. *Statistique de la Belgique, Mines, Usines Minéralurgiques, Machines à Vapeur* (Brussels: Ministère des Travaux Publics, 1846), vol. 1: 48.

ciency in this respect was not solely due to the miraculous efficiency of Belgian engineering. The export prohibition on machines, imposed by England, played an important role in helping Belgium to develop its own machine industry, as well as export substantial quantities of capital goods. Between 1841 and 1845, machines accounted for about 6 percent of industrial exports, falling to less than 5 percent in the subsequent quinquennium.[140] Thirdly, it is interesting to note that there is no clear-cut evidence that machines were becoming larger and/or more efficient between 1831 and 1850. The average capacity of the stock of steam engines in 1838 was almost exactly the same as in 1850, although the machines installed between 1831 and 1838 were clearly smaller than those installed after 1838. The explanation of this phenomenon has little to do with direct technological change, but centers on the distribution of steam engines over the various industries. Between 1831 and 1835, the price of coal was very low, so that mine owners had little incentive to buy new machines, while those industries which used coal as an input, on the other hand, had all the more reason to install new engines. Since the average capacity of a steam engine in mining was much larger than in manufacturing, and in view of the fact that the price movement of coal was reversed in 1836–37, this seems a satisfactory explanation.

In the case of metallurgical and heavy industries, perhaps even more than in the case of textile industries, the process of horizontal expansion accompanied by continuous technological change was wholly dependent on the constant formation of capital. Where did these funds come from? There can be little doubt that the absence of capital markets made retained earnings the main source of investment funds, similar to the textile industries. Since, however, expansion in the metallurgical industry was a less smooth process due to the indivisibilities in large plants, the role of outside sources of funds was more important here than in textile industries. During the Dutch period, most of these outside funds originated with the government, whereas later on the role of the banks became more important.

Some examples of the overall attitude of William I's government to industry were provided above. Following Roentgen's report, the Dutch government extended advances to those entrepreneurs who were modernizing their plants or who were thought to be capable of doing so. Cockerill received 300,000 florins, Hannonet-Gendarme, 150,000 florins, and Huart-Chapelle, 44,000 florins.[141] A special industrial fund, known as *Merlin Million*, was created in order to supply long-term credit to Belgian

140. See below, table 2.16.
141. Demoulin, *Guillaume Ier*, p. 162.

industry. The loans from this fund alone amounted to more than a million
florins. Other ways to channel funds to industry were used as well. In
1825, John Cockerill sold half of his firm to the Dutch government, in
order to secure his monopolistic position as well as to obtain badly needed
liquid funds.[142] The total sum lent to Cockerill by the Dutch government
and William I was about 1.5 million florins.[143]

The best known step taken by the Dutch government to assist heavy
industry in its needs for long-term credit was the founding of the famous
Société Générale (henceforth referred to as S.G.). The S.G. played a
relatively minor role as a capital market before 1830. Before the Belgian
Revolution, it managed its portfolio "like a good father of the family,"
that is to say, it held its assets in real estate, government securities, and
discounted bills rather than in long-term loans to industry. After 1832,
however, the S.G. started to play an increasingly important role in the
financing of heavy industry, in particular, collieries and metal works.
In 1835, a second investment bank was founded, the Banque de Belgique,
which competed with the S.G. The two banks underwrote large sums of
stocks, as many of the former family firms of partnerships transformed
themselves into joint-stock companies, often at the instigation of the
banks. In this fashion, the banks played an important role in the financing
of industry in Belgium, especially the Walloon heavy industry and mining,
twenty years before the establishment of the Crédit Mobilier.[144] On the
other hand, it appears exaggerated to say that the banks provided Belgium
with a capital market.[145] The Sociétés Anonymes, which proliferated in
Belgium in the late 1830s and 1840s, had access to a rather isolated and not
very reliable pool of mostly speculative capital. Moreover, the sectors
that could draw upon the help of the banks were mostly mines and metallurgical industries. The textile and the machine making industries were
slower to benefit from this smoothening in the operation of financial intermediaries. In the period 1851–72, the S.G. held 22.3 percent of its
securities in mining and metallurgy and only 9.4 percent in "miscel-
laneous," which included textiles and other light industries. The Banque
de Belgique held 11.1 percent of its assets in mining and metallurgy and
5.1 percent in textiles.[146] For the period before 1850, these figures were
probably smaller still.

Among the machine factories purchased partially or wholly by banks

142. De Boer, "Guillaume Ier," p. 545.

143. Lévy-Leboyer, *Les Banques Européenes*, p. 362.

144. B. S. Chlepner, "Les Débuts du Crédit Industriel Moderne," *RS* 9, no. 2 (April–June
1929): 314–16.

145. Chlepner, *La Banque en Belgique*, p. 284.

146. R. Cameron, *Banking in the Early Stages of Industrialization* (New York: Oxford
University Press, 1967), p. 147. Chlepner, *La Banque en Belgique*, p. 284.

between 1835 and 1840, special mention should be made of De Phoenix, the largest plant of this type in Flanders and the second largest in the country. De Phoenix was bought by the S.G. after the death of its founder. A second firm which was bought by the banks was the versatile hardware manufacturer, Poncelet, in Liège, whose firm was bought by the Banque de Belgique in 1835.

The two other major industries which are classified under the heading of metallurgy are the nail industry and the armaments industry. The nail industry, which was a typical Z-good industry, did not grow after 1814. Output of nails in the province of Liège was 2,250 tons in 1814, 2,445 tons in 1829, and 2,000 in 1830.[147] The main sources of trouble seem to have been the high price of raw materials and the severe English competition. Consequently, the wages earned in this industry fell, without raising the (already very small) profits of the putting-out entrepreneurs.

In the 1830s, the first mechanical devices for the production of nails were introduced, and the domestic industry started a long period of decline until the end of the nineteenth century. The process is well described by Génart:

> After 1830, the introduction of machines delivered a new blow to the ailing domestic nail industry. . . . At the places where the grand industry demanded less men, the ancient industry resisted the longest period. The years of general prosperity were the most destructive for the nail industry inasmuch when labor was in high demand and man power expensive, the nail maker leaves his domestic occupation which pays so little. It is here that one should look for an explanation of the fall in the number of nail makers. . . this applies equally to Hainault [and to Liège].[148]

The domestic nail industry thus provided the modern industry with cheap labor in a similar fashion to the textile Z-good sectors in Flanders and Liège, which provided the labor force for the mechanized textile industries. The introduction of machinery in the nail industry did not immediately eliminate the traditional sector. The old and the new continued to coexist for many decades.[149] In 1838 the nail industry employed more than 11,000 workers—5,000 in Liège and 6,000 in Hainault. One of the causes of the long persistence of the traditional industry was the imperfection of the new machines which could not compete with manual

---

147. Demoulin, *Guillaume Ier*, p. 316.
148. Génart, *L'Industrie Cloutière*, pp. 31–32. In the Charleroi area the modern metallurgical industry absorbed most of the Z-good labor force between 1820 and 1830. Cf. V. Tahon, "L'Industrie Cloutière au Pays de Charleroy," *DRSAC* 36 (1914–21): 61.
149. Génart, *L'Industrie Cloutière*, p. 50.

labor in the production of larger sizes of nails, though the smaller sizes of nails were soon fully taken over by modern methods.[150]

The weapons industry remained largely a domestic industry during the entire nineteenth century. High quality goods, such as expensive hunting rifles and pistols, were produced by skilled craftsmen at home. Standardized products, such as rifles and cannons for military uses, were produced by centralized establishments. The industry, both domestic and concentrated in plants, was controlled by a relatively small number of entrepreneurs.[151]

As was described above, the armaments industry performed somewhat disappointingly during the First Empire. After 1815, however, a rapid expansion occured, especially after the U.S. market was opened to Belgian small arms. The number of rifles produced increased from 107,000 in 1823 to 190,660 in 1829.[152] After the Belgian Revolution production continued to increase, peaking at 349,379 rifles in 1836.[153] After a decline in the late thirties, output picked up again in the 1840s, averaging 345,000 rifles between 1845 and 1850.[154] To these numbers a few rifles which were not officially approved by the inspectors (banc d'épreuves) should be added, as well as some loose parts that were sold separately. In 1838, a comparatively bad year for the weapons industry, total employment was 7,000–8,000 workers, producing more than four million francs worth of small arms.[155] The industry remained, to a large extent, a domestic industry. This can be inferred indirectly from the comparison of the industrial section of the 1846 survey with the population section. The industrial survey, which ignored domestic industry, listed only 1,742 persons employed in the manufacture of small arms. The survey of population lists a total of 7,538 persons whose profession was the manufacture of weapons, half of them in rural communities.[156] Wages in the armament industry were probably low,[157] though the comparatively high skills required in this industry tended to offset to some extent the general poverty of Belgian domestic industries in this particular case.

In the small arms industry, as in most other industries, the old domestic industry coexisted with the modernized concentrated factories. In the 1830s, a large workshop for small arms manufacture, in which workers

150. Franquoy, "Mémoire sur l'Historique," p. 436. Génart, L'Industrie Cloutière, passim.
151. M. Ansiaux, L'Industrie Armurière Liégeoise (Brussels: J. Lebègue, 1899), pp. 28–29.
152. Demoulin, Guillaume Ier, p. 316. Briavoinne, De l'Industrie, 1: 273.
153. Briavoinne, De l'Industrie, 2: 310.
154. Warzée, "Exposé...Liège," p. 522.
155. Briavoinne, De l'Industrie, 2: 308.
156. Statistique de la Belgique, Recensement Général 1846, "Industrie," p. 310, "Population," pp. 458–59.
157. This is the opinion of Briavoinne, De l'Industrie, 2: 309.

were assembled in one place without essentially altering the manual character of the production process, was organized by a leading entrepreneur, Malherbe de Goffontaine.[158] The attempt met with success, yet the centralized factory did not prevail in the small arms industry before the end of the nineteenth century. The chief cause for this was the extraordinarily high division of labor attained by the putting-out entrepreneurs in the small arms industry.[159]

The cannon foundry, established by the French in 1803, was a centralized plant. The foundry flourished under the Dutch regime and was very fast in adopting steam power in various applications and other engineering innovations. The moving spirits behind the cannon foundry were its directors, Colonel Huguenin and his nephew, Major Frederix, both of whom were highly qualified metallurgical engineers. Between 1840 and 1858 the cannon foundry exported 3,000 guns and 123,000 shells of various types.[160] The cannon foundry's success serves as an example of the high quality of Belgian industrial products, as well as of the profitability and competitiveness of Belgian manufacturing.

Belgium had other, less important, metallurgical industries as well. Among those, the cutlery industry should be mentioned, as well as a large and extremely diversified hardware industry which produced, among others, carpenters' tools, furnaces, balances, and scythes and other agricultural tools. None of these were of major importance by themselves, but in conjunction with the machine, nail, and armaments industries, they formed, no doubt, the most formidable metallurgical sector on the Continent in 1850.

THE LINEN INDUSTRY

The dynamic development of an ancient, traditionally oriented industry in a modernizing economy is an issue that has not received sufficient attention from economic historians. For this reason, the analysis of the problematics and significance of the decline of the linen industry, the "sick man" of Belgian industry, will be treated separately in chapter 7. At this stage, the overall development of the industry will be sketched summarily, in order to provide a more complete picture of Belgian industrial development as a whole.

As was shown in chapter 1, the linen industry occupied a central position in the Flemish rural economy by the end of the eighteenth

158. Briavoinne, "Sur les Inventions," p. 138.
159. A. Swaine, "Die Heimarbeit in der Gewehrindustrie von Lüttich und dessen Umgebung," *JNS* 67 (1896): 180–81, 219.
160. Warzée, "Exposé . . . Liège," pp. 525–26.

century. In the middle of the nineteenth century its overall importance can still be ascertained from the foreign trade figures, which will be presented below. Until 1840, at least, the export of linen cloth accounted for one-third of the total industrial exports. As to the number of workers employed in this industry, some confusion arises from the fact that the 1846 industrial survey omitted most of the domestic workers. The population survey, which also provided a list of professions, indicated a total of 66,937 weavers in Belgium, of which almost 80 percent were in the countryside. Not all these weavers were occupied in the linen industry, but the correct figure is probably closer to this than to the figures provided by the industrial survey. As to spinners, the situation is even more difficult, since the population census subsumed the rural spinners under "workers without determined profession," of which there were no less than 389,049 in rural communities, in addition to 347,394 persons classified as "agriculturists."[161]

Fortunately, a wealth of information is available from the grand "*Enquête Linière*" undertaken in 1841.[162] The *Enquête Linière* lacks the scope and the professionality of the national surveys of 1846, but as was indicated above, the latter is unusable for the Flemish linen industry. Subsequent to the *Enquête Linière*, other surveys were held to investigate this crisis-ridden industry. Most of these data are summed up conveniently in G. Jacquemyns's classic on the Flemish linen industry.[163] Using this information, it is possible to get a clear picture of the developments in this sector.

The structure of employment in the linen industry at around 1840 is summarized in table 2.13. In 1840 the total number of spinners and weavers in Flanders was 277,759. In 1843 this figure was no more than 216,855.[164] As was shown in chapter 1, the corresponding figure for the end of the eighteenth century was about 250,000. It may thus be seen that in the first half of the nineteenth century the linen industry grew by at most 10 percent, while population in Flanders increased at the same time by 35 percent. The conclusion is thus inescapable: the relative size of the traditional sector was diminishing. This is consistent with the hypothesis that the Z-good sector was the main source of labor supply to the modern sector. The population of Ghent, the principal industrial center of Flanders, increased by 96 percent in the same period.

161. *Statistique de la Belgique, Recensement Général 1846*, "Population," p. 477.
162. Commission d'Enquête de l'Industrie Linière, *Enquête sur l'Industrie Linière*, 2 vols., vol. 2 (*Rapports de la Commission*) (Brussels: Ministère de l'Intérieur, 1841). Henceforth referred to as *Enquête Linière*.
163. G. Jacquemyns, "Histoire de la Crise Économique des Flanders (1845–50)," *ARBM* 26, no. 1 (1929): 1–472.
164. Ibid., p. 52.

Table 2.13   Employment in the Belgian Linen Industry, 1840

	W. Flanders	E. Flanders	Other Provinces	Belgium
Spinners	98,385	122,226	59,785	280,396
Weavers	24,430	32,718	17,552	74,700
Others	23,967[a]	46,705[a]	27,483[b]	98,155[b]
Total	146,782	201,649	104,820	453,251

[a]1843

[b]Computed on the assumption that the share of Flanders in the production of hackled flax was 72 percent. Cf. *Exposé de la Situation*, p. 49.

SOURCES: Spinners, Weavers—*Statistique de la Belgique, Enquête Linière*, annex 14. Others—Jacquemyns, "Histoire de la Crise," p. 43.

The decline of the linen industry in Flanders between 1800 and 1850 was anything but continuous. The French period was an era of relative prosperity, as booming demand drove up prices. True, the maritime and continental blockades resulted in the loss of the traditional markets for linen goods in Spain and South America. But the French market more than compensated for this. The increase in the price of finished linen goods, by definition, resulted in a rise in the (implicit) wages of the workers in the Z-good sector. In the French period, as one writer puts it, for the first time the weaver and the spinner could "eat whenever they were hungry."[165] The income of weavers in the first years rose by about 40 percent, although purchasing power increased by less. In 1812 the average price of a piece of linen cloth sold on the Ghent market had risen to 160 francs per piece,[166] which constitutes roughly a doubling of the price.[167] Since the price of final output reflected both the returns to labor and the costs of intermediary inputs (raw flax), the elasticity of wages with respect to price was greater than unity so that wages must have more than doubled. In view of this prosperity in the Z-good sector, it is not surprising that the newly emerging cotton industry initially ran into rising wages.[168] The rise of wages is to be seen as the combined effect of a shift along a positively sloped short-run supply curve of labor, and a shift upward of an elastic long-run supply curve due to a rise in the opportunity cost of labor.

It is important to note the boom of the Flemish linen industry despite its transitory nature during the French period because of the misconceptions that still exist concerning the history of the industry. One modern writer asserts that:

165. Varlez, *Les Salaires*, 2: xxvi.

166. From 0.63–0.72 francs in 1767 to 1.00–1.10 francs in the early 1800s. Cf. ibid., pp. xix–xx; p. xxviii.

167. Cf. above, p. 15.

168. Dhondt, "L'Industrie Cotonnière," p. 277. Varlez, *Les Salaires*, 1: 30.

...the most important casualty [of the maritime and continental blockades] was the linen industry, which had been very widespread in several Continental countries, especially in Western France, Flanders. ... The linen industry was an archaic industry, doomed anyway...still there is no doubt that its decline and decay were greatly accelerated by the loss of the overseas markets.[169]

It is unclear what is meant by an "archaic industry, doomed anyway." As will be shown below, the linen industry was by no means unamenable to technological progress. There seems to be no evidence, moreover, that the net effect of the disruption of international trade on the Flemish linen industry was negative. Crouzet wholly ignores the close substitutability between cotton and linen, which caused the demand for linen to rise with the price of cotton goods.

After 1815, a process of slow decline set in that accelerated abruptly in the late 1830s when mechanized flax spinning was introduced in Flanders. From that time on the Z-good sector declined at a rapid pace. The export

Table 2.14 Exports of Belgian Linen Goods, 1834–50

	Quantities (thousands kg.)	Value[a] (thousands francs)
1834	3,802	28,152
1835	4,572	33,087
1836	4,612	34,143
1837	3,977	29,634
1838	4,831	36,079
1839	3,115	23,535
1840	3,371	25,376
1841	3,520	26,421
1842	2,846	21,389
1843	2,755	19,853
1844	2,966	21,587
1845	2,969	21,540
1846	2,677	19,385
1847	2,207	16,166
1848	1,503	11,453
1849	2,208	16,548
1850	2,071	15,838

[a]Fixed prices. The varying proportion between value and prices is due to changing quality of exports.
SOURCE: *Statistique de la Belgique: Tableau Général du Commerce*, 1838 and subsequent issues, passim.

169. Crouzet, "Wars, Blockades and Economic Change," pp. 571–72. See also Dhondt and Bruwier, *The Industrial Revolution*, p. 26.

of linen goods to France did not terminate after the collapse of the First Empire, but gradually the French heightened the tariff barrier protecting their own linen industry. The two most important tariffs were those of 1826 and 1841, both of which hit the Flemish hard. The other mortal threat to the Flemish protoindustrial sector was the ever-sharpening competition with the English and Scottish linen industries, which based themselves on mechanically spun yarn, with Leeds and Dundee their main centers. The crisis became especially severe in 1839, the same year in which mechanical spinning was introduced in Flanders itself. The extent of the crisis can be seen from examining the figures on foreign trade reproduced in table 2.14.[170]

The chain of technological breakthroughs had left the Flemish linen industry almost untouched until the late 1830s. A major cause of this was the relative difficulty in constructing devices for mechanical flax spinning. Lieven Bauwens devoted considerable effort to various attempts to construct a workable mechanized flax spinner. In 1808 he wrote:

> In the mechanical spinning of flax there are still many difficulties to be resolved. I have tried to spin flax both wet and dry...I have invested considerable sums in it, but the resulting yarn cannot compete effectively with the cheap yarn produced by the rural spinners.[171]

The stimulus for the development of a mechanical flax spinner was increased by the prize of one million francs promised by the French Imperial government to the inventor of such a device. In spite of the apparent success of one J. B. Kruckx, an employee of Bauwens's,[172] the prize was not awarded and mechanical flax spinning did not get off the ground.[173]

The invention that eventually made mechanical flax spinning feasible was made in 1810 by Philippe de Girard.[174] Nevertheless, mechanical flax spinning was not successful in Belgium until the late 1830s, despite attempts by Lieven Bauwens, John Cockerill, and Mme. Biolley, three of

170. For a more detailed discussion, see below, chapter 7.

171. Letter of L. Bauwens to F. De Neufchâteau, cited by J. Lewiński, *L'Évolution Industrielle de la Belgique* (Brussels: Misch and Thron, 1911), p. 77n.

172. Briavoinne, "Sur les Inventions," p. 100. Kruckx's invention preceded the promise of the reward by four years. This strengthens the suspicion that Kruckx's system did not provide a solution to the main bottleneck, which was the efficient spinning of flax tow.

173. In 1811–12 there is evidence of an experimental plant of some sort in which flax was spun by mechanical means. This firm did not survive the crash of 1813–15. Probably there were still too many technical bugs in the process. Varlez, *Les Salaires*, vol. 2, annexe 1: 4–5.

174. De Girard never received the reward either. His invention was perfected in 1825 by James Kay who developed the maceration process. From then on "wet spinning" increased rapidly in Leeds and Dundee.

the leading entrepreneurs of the era.[175] It is somewhat surprising that there was such a long lag in the diffusion of mechanical flax spinning to Belgium. After all, by the mid-1820s, Leeds could boast of seventeen big flax spinning mills with 50,000 spindles.[176] There is no evidence that ignorance of the opportunities was a factor in this respect—quite the contrary, as may be learned from the remark of a contemporary writer who predicted in 1834: "whichever city will establish within its limits a mill like the English can expect a prosperous future."[177] Nor is there marked absence of inventive effort in Belgium. Apart from the efforts to improve flax spinning noted above, other technological improvements in the linen industry were taking place continuously in the 1820s and 1830s. For example, the process of the retting of the raw flax in water was greatly improved by one d'Hont d'Arcy, an inventor from Ghent. It should be noted, however, that the adoption of the new process was tedious due to the "attachment of the peasants to custom and habit."[178]

Why, then, did it take so long until mechanized flax spinning was dissipated in Flanders? The most frequently stated explanation centers around the careful guarding of the secret by the English.[179] This argument is unsatisfactory. De Girard's invention was stolen from him by two associates who sold it to England. But the inventor himself remained on the Continent and sold his machines to the Austrian government. Soon, flax spinning mills were scattered all over Bohemia and Moravia and spread from there to Russia, where a whole village devoted to linen spinning was appropriately named Girardow. It is thus clearly unacceptable that the technology was inaccessible. Furthermore, the English prohibition on the export of machinery was not very effective. James G. Marshall, a son of the great Leeds flax spinner, testified before the House's select committee on machinery export that "foreigners have both imported considerable quantities of prohibited machinery and have made considerable progress in the manufacture of machinery themselves."[180]

The more plausible reason for the lag in the adoption of mechanized spinning in Flanders appears to have been that the initial amounts of

175. Demoulin, *Guillaume Ier*, p. 257. A. Beaucourt, *La Filature Méchanique de Lin en Belgique* (Paris: Librairie Nouvelle de Droit et de Jurisprudence, 1914), p. 15.

176. W. G. Rimmer, *Marshalls of Leeds, Flax Spinners 1788–1886* (Cambridge: At the University Press, 1960), p. 125.

177. F. de Pouhon, cited by Jacquemyns, "Histoire de la Crise," p. 76.

178. P. van Griethuizen, "Iets over de Nederlandsche Vlasteelt" [Something on the flax cultivation in the Netherlands], in *Mengelingen* (Amsterdam: 1826–27), pp. 30–31. Briavoinne, "Sur les Inventions," p. 100.

179. Beaucourt, *La Filature Méchanique*, p. 18.

180. Great Britain, *Parliamentary Papers*, vol. 7, 1841, p. 186.

capital required in an optimally sized plant using De Girard's gill frames were very large, and probably prohibitive in a country critically poor in long term investment funds. In 1821, a contemporary noted that "gill machines are chiefly confined to the largest mills."[181] The Leeds flax spinning industry was dominated by a few large firms and the initial outlay formed a formidable barrier to entry. The new firm of Benyons and Hives made an initial investment of over £50,000, which is not surprising in view of the fact that the firm ran about 10,000 spindles at a price of 4 pounds a spindle. Marshall spent £99,000 on new machinery between 1825–36 alone.[182] Moreover, the output per spindle ratio fell with the quality (fineness) of the yarn, and since Belgium had traditionally exported fine linen goods, initial investments were a severe bottleneck in the absence of a properly functioning capital market.

The source of the initial capital that eventually helped to establish the modern linen industry was within the modern sector itself, namely the cotton industry.[183] This is indicative of one of the most interesting elements of the industrialization process in Belgium. Each industry within the modern sector was basically self-propelled into sustained expansion by means of the reinvestment of retained earnings. Only when profits fell in one industry would capital flow to finance projects in other segments of the modern industrial sector. This made the large and discontinuous outlays, which were increasingly necessary as time elapsed, possible. In addition, as was shown above, after 1835 capital markets improved somewhat in Belgium, thus facilitating the flow of funds from one industry to another. There was, as yet, little investment in the modern industry from private sources outside the modern industrial sector.

The three principal firms in the mechanized linen industry were the Linière Gantoise, the Société de la Lys, and the Société St. Léonard. In 1838 these three companies controlled 27,000 spindles out of a total of 47,000. The initial capital outlays of these three joint-stock companies averaged between 2.2–2.5 million francs each.[184] Their expansion was rapid: by 1847 their spindlage had doubled and their share in total spindlage in the industry had increased as well. The effect of the rapid mechanization on the traditional sector has been termed the *lutte des techniques* (struggle of techniques). Obviously, the question had profound social and political aspects, which complicates its full understanding as an economic phenomenon. For this reason, the problem of the interaction of the new technique on the old and vice versa will be dealt with in some detail in chapter 7.

181. Cited by Rimmer, *Marshalls of Leeds*, p. 129.
182. Ibid., pp. 125–26, 196.
183. See above, p. 40.
184. *Enquête Linière*, p. 220. Jacquemyns, "Histoire de la Crise," p. 77.

OTHER MODERN INDUSTRIES: SUMMARY

By limiting the discussion thus far to textile and metallurgical industries, two other parts of the modern sector have been undeservedly ignored. One is the mining sector, of major importance in this mineral-rich country. Quite arbitrarily, mining has been omitted from the present study, especially since some recent high-quality work has been done on this activity.[185] Secondly, a host of smaller industries which modernized in the first half of the nineteenth century should be mentioned. None of these industries is of major importance by itself, but together they present an impressive record of economic growth. Among the more prominent of these were the paper industry, the sugar refineries, the tapestry industry, and glass and crystal works.

Paper

Until the late 1820s, Belgium was a large importer of paper, mostly from France. In spite of tariff protection as well as high transport costs, the local paper industry remained insignificant until the closing years of the Dutch period. In the early twenties, the first steam driven paper mill was introduced by one Hennessy, rapidly followed by Cockerill. By 1836 six fully equipped paper mills existed in Belgium,[186] rising to fourteen in 1839.[187] In 1838 the number of steam engines in the paper industry was fourteen with 153 HP, rising to twenty-five steam engines with a capacity of 357 HP in 1846. In this industry too, however, the old and the new coexisted for a long period. Out of 142 paper makers surveyed in 1846, 75 firms still used water mills and 7 used windmills.[188]

The foreign trade statistics shed some light on the remarkable expansion of the Belgian paper industry. While in 1836–38, Belgium was still a net importer of paper products, it became a net exporter in the early 1840s, while in the late 1840s, exports already exceeded imports by a factor of six.[189] In the heavily tariff-encumbered world of international trade in the 1840s, this was an impressive achievement.

Sugar Refining

The modernized sugar refining industry was another development of the second quarter of the nineteenth century, although many of the firms that led in the innovations movement were in existence already at least

185. N. Caulier-Mathy, *La Modernisation des Charbonnages Liégeois pendant la Première Moitié du 19ᵉ Siècle* (Paris: Société d'Édition les Belles Lettres, 1971).

186. Briavoinne, "Sur les Inventions," pp. 110–12.

187. E. H. Perrot, *Revue de l'Exposition des Produits de l'Industrie Nationale en 1841* (Brussels: at the author's, 1841), p. 310.

188. *Statistique de la Belgique, Recensement Général 1846*, pp. x, xv.

189. *Statistique de la Belgique, Tableau Général de Commerce*, various issues, passim.

as early as 1816. The most important innovations were imported from England: Howard heating pans (1829), the Philip Taylor process (1829), and the Roth process, which created a vacuum in which the syrup was boiled with the help of steam engines (1835). New filters, an important part of the production, were also introduced in this period.[190] The number of steam engines in sugar refining grew from zero in 1828 to forty with a capacity of 463 HP in 1838. From then on, growth slowed down, and in 1850, the number of steam engines in sugar refining was fifty-one with a capacity of 641 HP.[191] Exports of refined sugar grew from an average of 4,189 tons (of a thousand kilograms each) annually for the period 1831–35 to 10,780 tons for 1846–50. In the late 1840s, the value of exports of refined sugar was about equal to the value of imported raw sugar, so that Belgium can in some sense be regarded as "self-sufficient" in this basically exotic product. The output of beet sugar, though growing, remained important mainly for local consumption. Output of beet sugar was about 2,000 tons in 1842,[192] while exports of refined cane sugar amounted to 10,177 tons in the same year. For the sake of comparison, it is meaningful to note that total French exports of sugar in the same period (1840–44) averaged 8,800 tons.[193]

Tapestry

The main center of the tapestry industry was in the city of Tournay (province of Hainault). The largest firm was that of Piat Lefebvre, founded in 1781. This firm, and the industry in general, maintained its decentralized character throughout the first half of the nineteenth century. Most activity was carried out by rural workers at their homes.[194] The absence of dramatic technological breakthroughs as well as the relatively limited market for this high income elasticity product may have retarded expansion of this industry. Within the limits of the traditional sector, however, some technological improvements occurred, especially in weaving. Enhanced labor productivity was the main factor behind the rise of the weekly wage paid to the workers in this industry from about six to nine francs in the French period to fifteen francs in the late 1830s.[195] In 1838, the tapestry industry employed 1,600 workers, who produced 120,000 square meters of tapestry, of which 88 percent was exported.[196]

190. Briavoinne, "Sur les Inventions," pp. 156–59.
191. *Exposé de la Situation*, p. 113.
192. Heuschling, *Essai*, p. 109. Lévy-Leboyer, *Les Banques Européenes*, p. 265.
193. Lévy-Leboyer, *Les Banques Européenes*, p. 259, n. 27.
194. Briavoinne, *De l'Industrie*, 2: 409.
195. Ibid.
196. Heuschling, *Essai*, p. 93.

Glass

The modern glass and crystal industry in Belgium was launched in 1803 by a Frenchman named Aimé d'Artigues, who founded a large glass works in Vonêche (province of Namur) and soon became the leading glass manufacturer in the French Empire.[197] One of the most important innovations introduced in this period was the usage of artificial sodas. The techniques used by d'Artigues were soon emulated by other entrepreneurs and the more traditional producers soon found themselves in difficulties. After 1815 the glass industry, like the rest of the modern sector in Belgium, suffered through some hard times without actually collapsing, and by 1823 recovery was complete. A simple device, the "lanceman," which greatly facilitated the production of window glass, dates from this period. In 1825, two of d'Artigues's close collaborators founded a new and modern glass works in Val St. Lambert, near Seraing (province of Liège). The dynamic director of the Val St. Lambert works, F. Kemlin, was the first to get a patent for a revolutionary oven using coal, built with the help of English engineers.[198] Other new devices such as pistons and presses used in the inflation of crystals were imported from France and the U.S.[199]

The Val St. Lambert survived with relative ease the events of 1830 and soon emerged as the largest plant of its kind in Belgium. In 1836 the Société Nationale pour Entreprises Commerciales et Industrielles, a daughter company of the S.G., formed the Société Anonyme des Manufactures de Glaces, Verres à Vitres, Cristaux et Gobeleteries which acquired not only the Val St. Lambert works but most other glass makers as well, including the works at St. Marie d'Oignies near Charleroi, which was also at the forefront of glass technology of the period.[200] The exports of glass grew at a dazzling rate: from an average of 820,000 francs annually in 1831–35, exports of glass products grew to 13,698,000 francs per annum in 1846–50.[201] Technological change continued at a rapid pace in the 1840s, both in crystals and other luxury products and in window glass, bottles, and mirror manufacturing.[202] By 1850, Belgium was the leading producer of glass products on the Continent.

The picture emerging from these and similar industries is basically

---

197. R. Chambon, *L'Histoire de la Verrerie en Belgique du IIme Siècle à nos Jours* (Brussels: Editions de la Librairie Encyclopedique S.P.R.L., 1955), p. 285.

198. Chambon, *L'Histoire de la Verrerie*, pp. 169–70.

199. Briavoinne, "Sur les Inventions," pp. 171–72.

200. Heuschling, *Essai*, p. 107. *Exposé de la Situation*, p. 140. Chambon, *L'Histoire de la Verrerie*, p. 172.

201. *Statistique de la Belgique, Tableau Général du Commerce*, various issues, passim.

202. Chambon, *L'Histoire de la Verrerie*, pp. 174–75.

the same as that in the textile and metallurgical industries. A rapid process of accumulation accompanied by concentration took place, with technological progress largely embodied in a variety of new capital goods. A heavy reliance on foreign markets can be observed in almost all modern industries. Furthermore, there can be little doubt that the modernizing industries drew their labor power from the traditional Z-good sectors, although it is difficult to produce direct evidence on this issue. The modern industries clustered around the centers of protoindustry: East Flanders, the area around Charleroi, and the old centers in eastern Belgium in the Vesdre valley and around the city of Liège. Moreover, it is a common characteristic to most of the modern industries in Belgium that they existed side by side with remnants of the traditional manual sector, which resisted modernization for many decades. The Flemish linen industry is the most prominent but by no means the only example of this phenomenon.

A summary of the structure of the modern sector in Belgium is presented in tables 2.15–2.21, which include figures on the input of labor

Table 2.15   Exports of Industrial Products from Belgium, 1831–50
(in thousands of francs)

	1831–35	1836–40	1841–45	1846–50
Iron (pig and wrought)	564	1,084	5,233	10,645
Machines	1,572	3,847	5,043	4,686
Nails	1,919	2,618	3,057	5,620
Armaments	2,505	2,781	2,782	5,064
Total metal	6,560	10,330	16,115	26,015
Linen cloth, lace	30,619[a]	29,753	22,158	15,878
Woolen cloth	8,477[b]	11,884	16,337	16,989
Cotton cloth	6,747	5,779	6,584	9,805
Total principal textiles	45,843	47,416	45,079	42,672
Glass	820	2,955	7,158	13,698
Sugar	5,027	12,222	9,945	12,936
Paper	176	317	403	1,067
Others[c]	—[d]	7,475	6,393	2,005
Total industrial[e]	74,430[f]	80,715	85,093	98,393
Total exports	128,289	141,751	162,403	211,959

[a]1834–35 only.
[b]1833–35 only.
[c]Residual.
[d]Omitted, since it could not be computed meaningfully.
[e]Calculated by adding sugar (originally classified under "foods") to the number given for total exports of manufacturing.
[f]1834–35 only, adjusted for consistency.
SOURCES: *Statistique de la Belgique, Tableau Général du Commerce*, 1838 and subsequent issues, passim.

Table 2.16   Composition of Belgian Exports, 1831–50
(in percentages)

	1831–35	*1836–40*	*1841–45*	*1846–50*
Iron (pig and wrought)	0.75	1.34	6.15	10.82
Machines	2.11	4.77	5.93	4.76
Nails	2.58	3.24	3.59	5.71
Armaments	3.37	3.45	3.27	5.15
Total metal	8.81	12.80	18.94	26.44
Linen cloth, lace	41.14	36.86	26.04	16.14
Woolen cloth	11.39	14.72	19.20	17.27
Cotton cloth	9.06	7.16	7.74	9.97
Total principal textiles	61.59	58.74	52.98	43.37
Glass	1.10	3.67	8.41	13.92
Sugar	6.75	15.14	11.69	13.15
Paper	0.23	0.39	0.47	1.08
Others	—	9.26	7.51	2.04
Total industrial	100.00	100.00	100.00	100.00
Industrial exports as a percentage of total exports	58.01	56.94	52.40	46.42

SOURCES: *Statistique de la Belgique, Tableau Général du Commerce*, 1838 and subsequent issues, passim.

and machines in the modern sector as well as the contribution of industry to Belgian exports.

Tables 2.15 and 2.16 demonstrate the transformation of Belgium's exports in the period between 1831 and 1850. While industrial exports continued to account for roughly 50 percent of total exports throughout the period (the slightly declining trend of this ratio is explained by the rapidly increasing amounts of coal sold to France as well as by the increase in raw flax sold to England), the share of textiles declined, while that of heavy industry, glass and sugar rose. The reason for this was the internal crisis in the linen industry, which was contracting faster than the modern textile industries were expanding.

Table 2.17 presents a cross section view of the structure of employment in Belgian industry as reflected by the returns of the survey of 1846. There are considerable difficulties in the interpretation of these data. To start with, as has been shown in various instances above, the industrial survey of 1846 did not cover the rural-domestic workers and therefore under-represents the linen industry, as well as other branches in which Z-good production had not vanished. Moreover, the figures for the urban industries include many firms referred to as "artisans," by which are meant a host of bakers, cobblers, blacksmiths, carpenters, tailors, as well as a part of the weavers in the Z-good sector. Since in these industries the

Table 2.17   Composition of the Belgian Industrial Labor Force, 1846
(including mining and artisans)

	Male	Female	Children under 16	Total Employment	Firms	Total	Percentage of Total
Coal mining	31,742	4,105	10,339	46,186	202	46,388	10.80
Metal	35,598	1,659	5,032	42,289	14,447	56,736	13.21
Quarries, potteries	25,945	1,265	4,555	31,765	8,399	40,164	9.35
Cotton	7,552	3,129	3,999	14,680	393	15,073	3.51
Wool	10,134	4,686	3,333	18,153	768	18,921	4.40
Linen, hemp, lace[a]	18,565	17,413	24,045	60,023	21,133	81,156	18.89
Other textiles	7,694	3,374	3,674	14,742	11,137	25,879	6.02
Glass	2,953	319	687	3,959	530	4,489	1.04
Paper	3,236	924	1,216	5,376	753	6,129	1.43
Foodstuffs	24,742	2,491	2,628	29,861	16,362	46,223	10.76
Leather	10,331	398	2,422	13,151	12,809	25,960	6.04
Wood	18,484	222	2,251	20,957	21,668	42,625	9.92
Others	10,808	688	2,204	13,700	6,150	19,850	4.62
Total	207,784	40,673	66,385	314,842	114,751	429,593	100.00

[a]See text concerning the significance of this row.
SOURCE: *Statistique de la Belgique, Recensement Général 1846*, "Industrie," pp. x–xi.

Table 2.18   Composition of the Belgian Industrial Labor Force, 1846
(excluding coal mining and artisans)

	Male	Female	Children	Total Employment	Firms	Employment per Firm	Percentage of Employment
Metal	22,138	1,536	2,604	26,278	2,419	10.86	16.68
Quarries, potteries	15,249	1,118	3,609	19,976	1,613	12.38	12.68
Cotton	7,551	3,029	3,738	14,318	350	40.91	9.09
Wool	10,134	4,686	3,333	18,153	768	23.64	11.52
Linen, hemp, lace	7,006	6,585	3,638	17,229	2,401	7.18	10.93
Other textiles	7,694	3,374	3,674	14,742	11,137	1.32	9.36
Glass	2,718	318	658	3,694	35	105.54	2.34
Paper	1,202	914	565	2,671	142	18.81	1.69
Foodstuffs	18,451	2,057	1,896	22,404	8,434	2.66	14.22
Leather	2,292	180	220	2,692	968	2.78	1.70
Wood	1,524	53	145	1,722	1,032	1.67	1.09
Others	10,808	688	2,204	13,700	6,150	2.23	8.69
Total	106,767	24,528	26,284	157,579	35,449	4.45	100.00

SOURCE: *Statistique de la Belgique, Recensement Général 1846*, "Industrie," pp. x–xi.

vast majority of masters worked along with their assistants, the number of firms should be added to the number of employees if one is interested in calculating the size of the labor force. Even though inadequately covered, the linen industry emerges as the largest industrial employer.

In table 2.18 only the modern industry is covered: "artisans," as well as mining, have been omitted. Nevertheless, the row "other textiles," which includes a heterogeneous mass of different industries, probably includes to some extent industries which should be regarded as part of the "traditional sector." In spite of many shortcomings, the data presented in tables 2.17 and 2.18 provide an indispensable insight into the structure of the Belgian economy at the end of almost five decades of industrial modernization.

Tables 2.19, 2.20, and 2.21 present figures concerning the distribution of steam engines over the modern sector. Needless to say, steam engines constituted only one component of the stock of capital goods, but unfortunately, there are no time series for other types of capital goods available, so that steam engines must serve as a proxy for the capital stock as a whole. The accumulation of capital goods can be viewed alternatively in terms of the number of machines or in terms of capacity. In principle, one needs a series of prices of steam engines in order to choose which series correctly represents the accumulation of capital goods. If the price per engine remained constant, while the capacity per unit rose, the number of machines represents the "effort" devoted to capital accumulation, while the difference between the growth in capacity and the growth in the number of machines represents embodied technological progress. If, on the other hand, the price of a steam engine increased proportionately

Table 2.19   Distribution of Steam Engines, 1838–50

	1838		1844		1850	
	Number of Engines	HP	Number of Engines	HP	Number of Engines	HP
Coal mining	376	15,604	503	23,003	612	28,700
Metal	167	3,708	228	5,287	363	8,850
Cotton	106	1,562	106	1,722	116	1,994
Wool	100	871	126	1,442	151	1,864
Linen	5	73	20	519	32	1,164
Other textiles	6	68	14	143	26	241
Glass, potteries	9	103	16	263	23	376
Paper	16	161	28	369	35	557
Foodstuffs	164	2,032	234	2,829	439	4,658
Others	95	1,130	173	1,795	243	2,651
Total	1,044	25,312	1,448	37,372	2,040	51,055

SOURCE: Exposé de la Situation, p. 113.

Table 2.20   Distribution of Steam Engines, 1838–50
(percentages)

	1838		1844		1850	
	Number of Engines	HP	Number of Engines	HP	Number of Engines	HP
Coal mining	36.01	61.65	34.74	61.55	30.00	56.21
Metal	16.00	14.65	15.75	14.15	17.79	17.33
Textiles	20.79	10.17	18.37	10.24	15.93	10.31
Glass, paper, and foodstuffs	18.10	9.07	19.20	9.26	24.36	10.95
Others	9.10	4.46	11.95	4.80	11.91	5.19
Total	100.00	100.00	100.00	100.00	100.00	100.00

SOURCE: *Exposé de la Situation*, p. 113

Table 2.21   Steam Engines, 1838–50, Annual Rates of Growth
(percentages)

	1838–44		1844–50	
	Number of Engines	HP	Number of Engines	HP
Coal mining	4.85	6.47	3.26	3.69
Metal	5.19	5.91	7.75	8.59
Textiles	3.39	6.61	3.34	5.31
Glass, paper, and foodstuffs	6.43	6.84	10.53	7.99
Others	9.99	7.71	5.66	6.50
Total	5.45	6.49	5.71	5.20

SOURCE: *Exposé de la Situation*, p. 113.

with the capacity per machine, the series for HP are the correct measure of capital accumulation. Since no prices for steam engines are available, both series are presented in tables 2.19–21.

Both the exports and the steam engine statistics show that the two decades following the 1830 revolution were a period of continued growth in Belgium. This sustained expansion is to be attributed in part to the effects of the construction of a railway network. Yet, as tables 2.15 and 2.16 demonstrate, exports were still a dominant element in the demand for Belgian industrial products. A decline in the relative importance of textiles can be observed, and consequently the center of gravity of the Belgian modern industrial sector starts to shift from Ghent and Verviers to Liège and Hainault. Nevertheless, in 1846, textiles are still by far the largest industrial employer in the country.

3 STAGNATION IN THE NETHERLANDS, 1795–1850

Whether we fly high or low, we Dutchmen are all bourgeois—lawyer and poet, baron and laborer alike. Our national culture is bourgeois in every sense you can legitimately attach to the word. The bourgeois conception of life is shared by all classes or groups of our people— urban and rural, property owning or not. . . . It was a bourgeois atmosphere that was responsible for our unmartial spirit and our commercial propensities. Bourgeois life explains the lack of revolutionary passion in our people and why the even tenor of our national life remained almost unruffled by the high winds of great ideas. . . . Our bourgeois ways were, moreover, responsible for the gradual decline in our national life in the eighteenth century and the slowness of its reawakening in the nineteenth.

Johan Huizinga, 1935

The economic processes that took place in the Netherlands[1] in the first half of the nineteenth century contrast sharply with the developments in Belgium in the same period. As was seen in chapter 1, the Netherlands started the period with a considerable industrial sector located in densely populated and highly urbanized areas. What is to be explained is why this area never managed to get on the bandwagon of the "first" industrial revolution. The present consensus is that industrialization in the Netherlands did not attain significant dimensions until the "second" industrial revolution, that is, the wave of innovations and investments centered around chemical and electrical engineering, open hearth steel making, and consumer durables. The timing of the beginning of this process in the Netherlands is pinpointed at about 1890.[2]

---

1. The term "Netherlands" as used here applies to the territory within the present boundaries, while the term "United Kingdom of the Netherlands" will be reserved for the area in the 1814–30 boundaries, including Belgium.
2. J. A. de Jonge, "Industrial Growth in the Netherlands, 1850–1914," *AHN* 5 (1971): 198. Id., *De Industrializatie in Nederland tussen 1850 en 1914* [The industrialization in the Netherlands, 1850–1914] (Amsterdam: Scheltema en Holkema, 1968), pp. 343ff.

The present chapter is not concerned primarily with the explanation of Dutch retardation, which will be attempted in chapter 5. Rather, it is intended to be a descriptive summary of the nonevent of economic stagnation. Unfortunately, it is impossible to produce quantitative evidence comparable to the material available for Belgium, so the comparison between the two countries must be somewhat lopsided. The absence of statistical material on the Dutch economy for the first half of the nineteenth century is explained largely by the Dutch government's increasing indifference to economic affairs after the Belgian Revolution. This indifference, often blended with blatant incompetence, was masked as a return to seventeenth-century free trade conceptions which had, in fact, been rejected previously by William I.[3] It is noteworthy in this context that most of the statistical material pertaining to the United Kingdom of the Netherlands was compiled by Belgians.[4]

The absence of reliable quantitative material for the period after 1815 is compounded by the unhappy coincidence that the Dutch provinces were not annexed to the French Empire until as late as 1810. For this reason, such useful *Mémoires Statistiques* as were compiled by Faipoult for East Flanders and Thomassin for Liège are absent for the Netherlands. The material collected by Dutchmen during the era of the so-called "Batavic Republic" (1795–1806), mainly by J. Goldberg, is largely of a nonquantitative nature.[5] A partial substitute is the survey compiled by d'Alphonse, to which reference will be made below. For the period 1830–50 especially, in contrast to Belgium, there is an almost complete absence of statistics on the Dutch economy.

Dutch industry can be treated under three headings: the urban industries in the maritime provinces, the rural industries in the Twente area in the East (province of Overijssel), and the rural and urban industries in the South (province of North Brabant and Limburg). In the present chapter, the three regions will be described in some detail. The periodization is more or less similar to that for Belgium: three major events—the revolution of 1795, the collapse of the French Empire in 1814, and the Belgian Revolution in 1830—serve as convenient dividers.

3. See I. J. Brugmans, "Koning Willem I als Neo-mercantilist" [King William I as a neomercantilist], in *Welvaart en Historie* (The Hague: Martinus Nijhoff, 1950), pp. 38–50. C. Terlinden, "La Politique Économique de Guillaume Ier," *RH* 139 (January–April 1922): 1–39.

4. E. Smits, *Statistique Nationale*. A. Quetelet, *Recherches Statistiques sur le Royaume des Pays Bas* (Brussels: M. Hayez, 1829).

5. J. Goldberg, "Journaal der Reize van den Agent van Nationale Economie der Bataafsche Republiek, 1800" [Journal of the agent for the national economy of his journey through the Batavic republic], *TSS* 18 (1859) and 19 (1860): passim.

THE MARITIME PROVINCES

The Dutch "traffic" industries were described to some extent in chapter 1, where it was emphasized how vulnerable these industries were to disruptions in the flow of international trade. Such disruptions were the salient characteristic of the French period. The effects can be discerned as early as 1800. The Dutch colonies were gradually lost to England after 1795, and the supply of colonial raw materials (sugar, tobacco, furs, etc.) greatly diminished. France erected a high tariff barrier against imports which closed not only the French market to Dutch products but also the Belgian provinces and parts of Germany and Italy annexed to the rapidly expanding republic. In 1799, a contemporary observer states that

> For five years there has been a formal prohibition on the imports of Dutch products to France, or a tariff which is equivalent to a total prohibition. The normal course of commerce cannot tolerate the tariffs which are at present levied on Dutch goods ... Dutch manufactures have fallen into a state of total ruin and enfeeblement.[6]

The writer of these lines was French, not Dutch.

The most reliable and comprehensive source on the state of the Dutch economy in this period is the report written by the "agent of the national economy," Johannes Goldberg.[7] Goldberg traveled throughout the whole country in 1800, and compiled extensive notes on the state of the economy. Although there is no attempt systematically to present statistical material (as for example, there is among the French prefects in the Belgian provinces), Goldberg's report reflects the mounting difficulties resulting from the deteriorating political situation, and the many traffic industries were in great trouble. The distilleries of Schiedam (near Rotterdam) experienced "a remarkable reduction in sales due to the obstruction of imports into France and Belgium and to the circumstances of the war."[8] "The sales of salt to Germany have been arrested since the conquest of the Rhineland by the French, shipping is considerably encumbered by taxes." "The city of Enkhuizen [province of North Holland] is declining

6. Report of T. Lubbert to the French Minister of Finance, April 1799, in *Gedenkstukken der Algemene Geschiedenis van Nederland* [Documents on the general history of the Netherlands], ed. H. T. Colenbrander (The Hague: Martinus Nijhoff, 1907), vol. 3, *RGP* 3: 49.
7. Goldberg, "Journaal der Reize." For details on the man and his work, cf. L. van Nierop, "Een Enquête in 1800" [A survey in 1800], *De Gids* 77, no. 3 (1913): 71–106, 293–323. W. M. Zappey, *De Economische en Politieke Werkzaamheid van Johannes Goldberg* [The economic and political activity of Johannes Goldberg] (Alphen on the Rhine-Brussels: N. Samson, 1967).
8. Goldberg, "Journaal der Reize," *TSS* 18: 198.

and impoverished since the [East Indian] Company has been paralyzed by the war.'' The fisheries suffered severely from the insecurity on the seas.[9] The so-called *Goldberg enquête*, in which manufacturers were required to fill out forms with details on the current state of their business, is flooded with hundreds of requests for peace and unhampered trade, and most manufacturers complain bitterly about the many disruptions and dislocations caused by the war.[10]

As time elapsed, the situation became considerably worse. In 1806 the Continental Blockade was declared by Napoleon, and Dutch shipping, fishing, and commerce were further impeded. The activity of Dutch industry was reduced to a fraction. This is evident from the figures compiled by d'Alphonse.[11] D'Alphonse was Intendant de l'Intérieur of the seven *départements* formed by the former Batavic Republic after the annexation of the country to France in 1810. His essay is rich in quantitative detail, although some doubts can be cast on its reliability.[12]

The overall diagnosis of Dutch industry by d'Alphonse is straightforward:

> Almost twenty years of war have dealt Dutch industry a decisive blow. . . . The interruption of shipping has deprived it of its raw materials as well as of its markets . . . fishing and shipping are inactive, as are the industries associated with them. . . . Dutch industry could never have resisted such destructive forces.[13]

The description refers to the period 1810–12. In addition, d'Alphonse supplies a wealth of data on employment and output of various industries for 1806 and 1811, a sample of which is presented in table 3.1. As noted above, the data are of dubious quality; yet they serve as an indicator of the steep decline of Dutch industry after 1806, already an unnaturally depressed year. Such typical traffic industries as sugar, tobacco, silk, alcoholic beverages, and shipyards, as well as the herring fisheries, all but ceased their activities entirely. One of the few products which did not contract was beer brewing, which is explained by d'Alphonse as resulting

9. Ibid., p. 202; ibid., *TSS* 19: 254–57.
10. Dutch National Archives, The Hague, Collection Goldberg, files 37, 38, 50.
11. F. J. B. d'Alphonse, *Aperçu sur la Hollande* (1811), published by the Dutch Central Bureau of Statistics (The Hague: Belinfante Bros., 1900).
12. For example, d'Alphonse repeatedly provides figures pertaining to various industries for 1806 and 1811. Yet, some of the *départements* referred to were created by the administrative division of 1810. Before that, the administrative division was quite different (and in fact altered repeatedly between 1803 and 1810), which begs the question of how we can trust data pertaining to nonexisting provinces. It is therefore preferable to look at the aggregated data, in which mistakes due to changing geographical units would be washed out.
13. D'Alphonse, *Aperçu*, p. 226.

Table 3.1   The Decline of Dutch Industry, 1806–11

Industry	Area Included	Units	Production 1806	Production 1811	Employment 1806	Employment 1811
Cane sugar	EC	10^3 tons	41.7	0.3	1,408	133
Tobacco	NH, F, O, G	tons	5,573	1,031	2,125	376
Silk	Towns of Haarlem and Utrecht	pieces	1,700	600	700	225
Paper	NH, SH, U, F, G	10^3 reams	113.4	54.4	661	453
Potteries	SH, F	10^3 pieces	6,127	4,884	378	268
Oils	EC	10^6 pints	9.3	6.3	n.a.	n.a.
Tapestry	City of Hilversum	10^3 ells	130[b] 300[b]	40 150	140	80
Distilleries	SH	10^6 litres	46	22	n.a.	n.a.
Breweries	EC	10^3 tons	325	370	900	900
Shipyards	NH, U	—	n.a.	n.a.	3,000	387
Sailcloth	NH, U	pieces	19,768	5,800	106	48
Herring fisheries	EC	10^3 tons	36.4	12.8[c]	1274	448

[a] NH = North Holland; SH = South Holland; F = Friesland; O = Overijssel; U = Utrecht; G = Groningen; EC = entire country.

[b] First figure refers to high quality products, second figure to a lower quality.

[c] 1810.

SOURCE: d'Alphonse, *Aperçu*, pp. 223–351.

from the severe decline in the imports of wine and by the fact that beer was probably an inferior good.[14]

The tariff barrier that separated the Dutch provinces from the rest of the Empire was an important element in the plight of the Dutch provinces while other parts of the Continent (with Belgium at the forefront) thrived. The tariff was removed only two years after the formal incorporation of the Netherlands in the Empire (decree of Smolensk, 1 October 1812). By that time the Empire was in a process of dissolution, and no beneficial effect could be expected from the annexation.[15] In any case, one might

14. Ibid., p. 261.

15. I. J. Brugmans, *Paardenkracht en Mensenmacht, Sociaal Economische Geschiedenis van Nederland* [Horsepower and human might, a social and economic history of the Netherlands, 1795–1940] (The Hague: Martinus Nijhoff, 1961), p. 46.

doubt that even if the tariff had been removed earlier, the Dutch would have performed significantly better. After all, Dutch industry was to a large extent oriented towards the maritime sector, and it seems unlikely that in a relatively short time Dutch industry would have been able to transform itself from its orientation on overseas markets and sources of raw materials to a more continentally oriented economy.

The British maritime blockade was the most baleful element in the series of economic disasters that befell the Dutch in this period. It is important to realize that the economic war between Britain and the French Empire with its satellites (including the Batavic Republic) did not exclude trade with the adversary. In fact, the share of the "enemy" in total British exports fell only from 15.5 percent in 1792 to 12 percent in 1800, in spite of incessant war.[16] The main purpose behind the maritime blockade was to disrupt forcefully the trade of enemy nations with third nations (neutrals, other enemy nations, or their own colonies) in order to usurp for Britain the benefits of this trade. Consequently the maritime routes between the Netherlands and France (by far the cheapest) were greatly hindered, so that trade between the Netherlands and the more remote parts of the French Empire would have been difficult even without the tariff. In any event, most of Dutch trade was not with either England or France but with the Baltic areas, the Mediterranean regions, the Levant, and the "Indies," both West and East. It was this trade that was most severely hit by the British blockade, and the result was simultaneous loss of markets and raw materials supplies. The Continental System introduced in 1806 aggravated a problem that had already been plaguing the Dutch for a dozen years. Moreover, the overall effectiveness of the Continental System in this area was far from impressive. Louis Napoleon (the Emperor's brother and king of the Netherlands between 1806 and 1810) repeatedly complained that it was physically impossible for the Dutch to endure the closing of the harbors and that smuggling was inevitable. The smuggling was largely in British goods, however, because the British navy was the only factor which had the power to prevent smuggling.

In short, the British maritime blockade, not the French tariff barrier or the Continental Blockade, seems the central element in the economic catastrophes which hit the Dutch in the French period, although the latter two were no doubt contributing factors. England was the chief beneficiary of the commercial war (at least as far as the Netherlands was concerned), and thanks to its control of the oceans, it managed to gain control of most Dutch commerce, colonial as well as noncolonial.[17]

16. E. F. Heckscher, *The Continental System, an Economic Interpretation* (1922; reprint ed., Gloucester, Mass.: Peter Smith, 1964), p. 42.

17. Heckscher, *The Continental System*, p. 327. Brugmans, *Paardenkracht*, p. 37.

The only industries in the Netherlands that fared relatively well during the French period were the rural textile industries, which will be dealt with in some detail below, and the substitute industries, which produced surrogates for colonial goods. The most important of the substitute industries were the beet sugar mills and the production of chicory, a surrogate for coffee. The former disappeared promptly with the restoration of normal trade, while the latter was reduced to a fraction of its size, although it did not disappear altogether.[18] There is no trace of the emergence of new, mechanized industries like the ones in Verviers, Ghent, and many other areas on the Continent.

An example of the inability of the Dutch to innovate may be found in the calico printing industry. As was shown in chapter 1, this branch had been declining in the eighteenth century. The French period presumably provided an excellent opportunity for the cotton printers to recover, due to the removal (albeit partial) of British competition. No such recovery occurred—the calico printing plants in Amsterdam and Rotterdam all but vanished.[19] This was caused not so much by a lack of demand or raw materials as by what appears to be a lack of technological knowhow. The Dutch printers were able to print only white calicoes woven in the East Indies. The calicoes produced in Belgium or the Rhineland could not be used, since the Dutch were unable to remove the grease from the texture to allow the dyes to become permanent.[20] The many other technological breakthroughs which spread to the Continent in this period passed the Netherlands by.

The restoration of 1813 and the disintegration of the First Empire ostensibly removed most of the causes for the depression of the Dutch industries in the maritime provinces. The blockades were lifted, the Dutch received their colonies back and were awarded Belgium to form the United Kingdom of the Netherlands. But in spite of the high expectations, the traffic industries failed to return to their eighteenth-century levels. The difficulty in any precise assessment of the degree of recovery of the sector is in the absence of any kind of quantitative evidence which might have been compared to the figures provided by d'Alphonse. Only a few scattered observations form the basis of the foregoing statement. Nevertheless, for the traffics as a whole the conclusion is quite inevitable:

18. Brugmans, *Paardenkracht*, pp. 47, 150.
19. D'Alphonse, *Aperçu*, pp. 255–56.
20. Van Hogendorp, *Bijdragen*, 1: 130. W. L. D. van den Brink, *Bijdrage tot de Kennis van den Economischen Toestand van Nederland in de Jaren 1813–1816* [A contribution to the knowledge of the economic situation of the Netherlands in 1813–1816] (Amsterdam: H. J. Paris, 1916), p. 164. On the relative obsolescence of the calico printing industry, see also W. M. F. Mansvelt, *Geschiedenis van de Nederlandsche Handelsmaatschappij* [History of the Dutch Commercial Company] (Haarlem: Joh. Enschedé en Zonen), 1: 151.

industries which managed to attain their past glories would not have escaped the attention of both contemporaries and historians. The hard reality was that Dutch commerce and maritime power had definitively lost the last traces of the status attained in the seventeenth century, and the industries that were dependent on the carrying trade declined with it. In addition, many of the products that had constituted the backbone of Dutch industry were being produced increasingly by foreigners, primarily of course England and Belgium. In chapter 2, the process of the gradual mechanization of cotton printing, papermaking, sugar refining, glass and crystal manufacturing, etc., in Belgium was described in some detail. The industrial revolution focused initially on industries that were un-important in the Netherlands (textiles, metals), but soon the new tech-niques spread inexorably to branches that competed with the Dutch traffic industries. The long-run consequences for the latter were lethal.

In the maritime provinces of the Netherlands, the old urban centers clung desperately to their traditional techniques, slowly and reluctantly giving up markets to better and cheaper products made by capital inten-sive, mechanized techniques. The crucial question is not why the ancient industries failed to recover, but why they were not abandoned altogether and why they failed to transform themselves and adopt the new techniques.

A case in point is the paper industry. The Dutch paper manufacturers in the Zaan area (North Holland) were world famous in the eighteenth century for the quality of their paper. The French period was catastrophic for the industry. A contributing factor, besides the general hardships of the times, was the mounting difficulty in obtaining supplies of rags, an essential raw material in paper production. Many countries imposed export prohibitions on rags. Furthermore, the decline of shipping and fishing reduced the supply of rags (from old ropes and sails) which these branches had traditionally supplied to the paper industry.[21] It was therefore particularly unfortunate that some crucial technological break-throughs in the industry occurred precisely in this period. The main innovation was the mechanical paper mill invented by N. L. Robert in 1798. Chlorine bleaching and the resin process should also be mentioned as new techniques that revolutionized the industry in this period, thereby making the old techniques increasingly obsolete. Yet the real problem is why the new techniques failed to be introduced after peace was restored. One writer puts it succinctly:

> It was quite obvious that in the French period nobody even contem-plated the application of the paper machines. That was hardly to be expected, after all. Possibly the new inventions were not even

21. B. W. de Vries, *De Nederlandse Papiernijverheid*, p. 91.

known in the Netherlands. But after 1815, too, it took many years until these machines are mentioned at all in our country. . . . The Dutch paper manufacturers could not keep up with the new times which were starting for the paper industry, as they did for other industries. It seems as if the hardships of the past half century had paralyzed the Dutch paper manufacturers and chained them to their traditional methods.[22]

Between 1815 and 1850 the paper industry in the Zaan area continued its decline. The old mills closed one after the other, unable to compete with the cheaper and superior products of countries which had adopted the new technology.[23] In 1854 there were only seventeen mills left in this region, employing 500 workers. This constitutes a decline of 50 percent compared to 1819.[24] In 1846 exports of paper were less than a quarter of Belgian exports.[25] One can thus safely conclude that the paper industry was subject to continuous decline throughout the first half of the nineteenth century. The dislocations of the French period should be regarded as a transitory disturbance compounding structural weaknesses which eventually destroyed the industry. As noted above, the central symptom of this structural weakness was the failure to adopt the inventions which revolutionized the papermaking industries abroad: the first mechanical paper mill which proved a success was founded in the maritime region as late as 1845.[26]

Somewhat more successful was the sugar industry, another typical traffic. The sugar industry was particularly hard hit in the French period: in 1813 only three out of eighty-six refineries in Amsterdam were still operating.[27] By 1816 the fluctuations in the supply of raw cane sugar had leveled off and it might have been expected that the sugar refineries would recover. But revival was only slow and partial. Contemporaries attributed the slowness of recovery to the tariff of 1816, but this hardly seems likely since the tariff was only 0.60 florins on 100 kg. of raw sugar. It is more plausible to ascribe the difficulties encountered by the industry to the "general hardships of the times," mainly of course the rapid technological progress among the main competitors of the Netherlands.

22. Ibid., pp. 87, 190.
23. In order to keep their prices competitive, the Dutch resorted to quality adulteration—obviously without much success.
24. B. W. de Vries, *De Nederlandse Papiernijverheid*, pp. 106, 193.
25. D. Buddingh, *Algemeene Statistiek voor Handel en Nijverheid* [General statistics for commerce and industry] (Haarlem: A. C. Kruseman, 1846), 1: 327.
26. J. C. A. Everwijn, *Beschrijving van Handel en Nijverheid in Nederland* [Description of commerce and industry in the Netherlands] (The Hague: N. V. Boekhandel, 1912), p. 398.
27. J. J. Reesse, *De Suikerhandel van Amsterdam, 1813–1894* [The sugar trade of Amsterdam, 1813–1894] (The Hague: Martinus Nijhoff, 1911), p. 75.

Even in this "dark period," as one author calls it (the reference is to 1815–30, not to 1795–1814), sugar kept its dominant position among the many declining export goods, although its absolute value was much reduced. In 1819 total output for the whole United Kingdom of the Netherlands was estimated at 60 million kg. and thus probably was less than in 1806.[28] In 1828 the Amsterdam Chamber of Commerce noted: "With regard to industry: nothing favorable is reported. The sugar refineries, the most important branch of industry, are in a state of decay, which can be learned from the fact that their number diminishes every year."[29]

The use of steam power in the Dutch sugar industry dates from after 1830. Initially, the rate of diffusion of steam engines in the refineries was very slow, and only after 1843 did the new technique definitively establish itself. Belgium had passed that stage in the 1830s. Nonetheless, the application of steam power in the Dutch sugar industry, though belated, is the one advanced enclave in a generally stagnant industrial sector in the maritime province and should be recognized as such.

The shipbuilding industry, which had occupied a central part in the maritime economy of the Dutch provinces in the seventeenth and eighteenth centuries, was in a state of total disrepair in 1816. The decline of shipping started relatively abruptly in 1792, since shipbuilding had managed to hold its own during most of the eighteenth century. The two decades of French domination were totally destructive to the industry.[30] Of the twenty large shipyards still active in the Zaan area by the end of the eighteenth century, only one still operated in 1816.[31] A consequence of the destruction of the shipyards was that the Dutch merchant marine became more dependent on foreign-built ships, a phenomenon that would have been unthinkable in the seventeenth century. An indication in this direction can be seen in the structure of the merchant fleet registered in Amsterdam in 1824 (see table 3.2).

For the entire seaworthy fleet, including fishing boats, the proportion of foreign-built ships was only about one-third, but even that was considered "a disgrace for a country like the Netherlands which at previous times had supplied half of Europe with ships and had grown by being a seafaring nation."[32] This attitude explains the fact that in shipping, in contrast to most other traffic industries or other associated maritime industries, the Dutch government felt an urgent need to come to the help

---

28. Ibid., p. 18. Cf. table 3.1. The output of 41.7 million kg. pertains to about a third of the population of the United Kingdom of the Netherlands.
29. Cited by Reesse, *De Suikerhandel*, pp. 78–79.
30. Everwijn, *Beschrijving van Handel en Nijverheid*, p. 71.
31. Mansvelt, *Geschiedenis van de N.H.M.*, 1: 144.
32. Ibid., 1: 146.

Table 3.2   Composition of the Dutch Merchant Marine by Origin of Ship, 1824

Country of Construction	Number of Ships	Weight in 10^3 Lasts[a]
The Netherlands	6	1,490
Baltic Area	11	2,800
United States	11	1,790
England	4	860
Total	32	6,940

[a] 1 Last = 4.763 kgs.
SOURCE: Mansvelt, *Geschiedenis van de N. H. M.*, 1: 144.

of the ailing branch. In 1819, William I ordered no issuance of new Dutch registrations to ships built abroad, unless explicit royal permission was obtained. Such exceptions were, however, made quite frequently. A few years later (1823–25), a complicated system of subsidies was devised in order to support the shipyards. These subsidies reduced average costs by about 10 percent.[33] Both measures were not very successful and were abandoned in 1830. The establishment of the Dutch Commercial Company (N.H.M.), which was mentioned above in connection with the Flemish cotton industry, was of more consequence. The N.H.M. was obliged to use locally built ships, and its rapidly increasing role in Dutch colonial trade provided a considerable boost to Dutch shipbuilding. Between 1823 and 1827, 182 ships were built, weighing 30,000 *lasts*. Especially the construction of small ships was flourishing, since the *Fluytschip*, the famous Dutch ship which had helped Holland to dominate the seas in the seventeenth century, was being replaced by the *Kolfschip* and the *Smak*.[34] These ships were particularly suited to serve the harbors of Amsterdam and Rotterdam, which suffered from continuous silting. The larger ships were still built abroad as can be seen from table 3.3.

Table 3.3   Ships Registered in the Netherlands, 1826 and 1829

	Built in the Netherlands			Built Abroad		
	Number	Tonnage	Average Size	Number	Tonnage	Average Size
1826	978	240,374	246	198	115,387	583
1829	1,166	327,917	281	180	100,291	557

SOURCE: Everwijn, *Beschrijving van Handel en Nijverheid*, p. 76.

33. Everwijn, *Beschrijving van Handel en Nijverheid*, pp. 72–73.
34. Mansvelt, *Geschiedenis van de N.H.M.*, 1: 227.

After 1830, the protection of the shipbuilding industry continued undiminished. The total number of ships built annually between 1830 and
1850 increased by 85 percent, with total tonnage increasing during the
same period by 160 percent.[35] Nevertheless, the Dutch shipbuilding
industry could not be considered fully recovered by 1850. Sales of ships
built in the Netherlands to other countries were negligible. The policies
of subsidies resulted in a distortion toward the building of ships of smaller
than optimal size, as well as sailing ships instead of steamships.[36] The
subsidies also caused gluts in the market from time to time, as happened
for example in the early 1840s.[37]

Most other traffics never fully recovered. Examples are the tobacco
industry[38] and the distilleries of jenever, the Dutch gin, which centered
around Schiedam. Rotterdam, previously a major center of the traffic
industries, became in the nineteenth century a transit harbor which had
no place in it for the former traffic industries. Everywhere the ancient
industries were contracting without, however, losing their essential features.[39]

The textile industries in the maritime provinces did not revive either
after 1815, which is not surprising, since these were already in deep
decay by the end of the eighteenth century. In the French period production came to almost a complete halt, woolen cloth being the good which,
according to d'Alphonse, suffered the most.[40] Goldberg, perhaps the
leading expert on manufacturing in the Netherlands in this period, noted
in 1816 that while in 1802 the Netherlands was still a net exporter of cloth,
in 1814 its imports of cloth exceeded exports by a factor of five. In other
woolen fabrics, too, Goldberg stressed the loss of competitive ability on
the part of the Netherlands, especially in comparison with Belgium.[41]
In the period between 1815 and 1830, no sign of recovery can be discerned
in the textile industry in the maritime provinces.

After the Belgian Revolution of 1830, however, the trend was reversed,
at least temporarily. A number of prominent Belgian manufacturers
decided for political or economic reasons to move to the North. The
N.H.M. encouraged some of them to settle in the old centers of Dutch

35. Everwijn, *Beschrijving van Handel en Nijverheid*, p. 78.
36. Brugmans, *Paardenkracht*, p. 91.
37. Mansvelt, *Geschiedenis van de N.H.M.*, 2: 130, 235.
38. E. Baasch, *Holländische Wirtschaftsgeschichte* (Jena: Gustav Fischer, 1927), p. 480.
39. Z. W. Sneller, *De Ontwikkeling der Nederlandsche Exportindustrie* [Development of
the Dutch export industry] (Haarlem: H. D. Tjeenk-Willink, 1925), p. 16.
40. D'Alphonse, *Aperçu*, p. 286.
41. J. Goldberg, "Memorie over de Nederlandsche Fabrieken van Manufactuurwaaren"
(1816) [Memorandum concerning Dutch manufactures], ed. N. W. Posthumus; reprinted in
Bijdragen tot de Economische Geschiedenis van Nederland (The Hague: Martinus Nijhoff, 1916),
pp. 155, 158.

textile industry, Haarlem and Leyden. The most important of these entrepreneurs were Thomas Wilson, a cotton weaver from Brussels, Theo Prévinaire, a cotton printer from Brussels, and the firm of Poelman fils and Fervaecke from Ghent, who all settled in Haarlem, and de Heyder, from the town of Lier (province of Antwerp) which settled in Leyden. With the help of the N.H.M. and the energetic Dutch minister of colonies, J. van den Bosch, a short-lived revival of the textile industries in the traditional centers of Holland set in. In the 1830s these industries were expanding rapidly. In 1836 the three firms in Haarlem employed 1,146 workers (population of the city was about 20,000). Prévinaire especially met with initial success and within a few years became the leading industrialist in the Netherlands.[42]

Nevertheless, it seems necessary to qualify some rash evaluations concerning the "revival" of the textile industries in Holland. Brugmans's flat statement that Haarlem was becoming a "Dutch Manchester" seems an exaggeration.[43] To start with, an important contingent of the workers as well as the capital operating in the new firms was foreign. Initially, Prévinaire employed only 14 foreigners but this number soon rose to 54. Poelman employed in 1836 100 foreigners out of a total of 523 workers.[44] The equipment used was largely brought over from Belgium or purchased anew there or in England. Secondly, the continued expansion of the textile industries in the western parts of the country led the entrepreneurs away from the urban centers of Holland to the cheaper labor force on the countryside. In 1840 Prévinaire employed 2,587 persons of which only 600 were in Haarlem and the rest in the rural South and East. Especially for the purpose of weaving, the new manufacturers turned increasingly to Twente and North Brabant.[45] Thirdly, and most seriously, Brugmans completely ignored the ultimate failure of the cotton industry in the maritime provinces. The downturn started in the late 1830s. Spinning was the first activity to collapse. Poelman failed totally and was discharged from his firm, De Phoenix (not to be confused with the famous Ghent machine maker), which from then on continued to exist solely at the mercy of the N.H.M., finally closing in 1848.[46] As to calico printing: this activity had become increasingly concentrated in the hands of Prévinaire and Wilson, whose chief customer, the N.H.M., was constantly complaining about overproduction on their part. With the decline in the flow of orders the two firms contracted; their importance after 1845 was minimal.

42. Mansvelt, *Geschiedenis van de N.H.M.*, 1: 314, 316.
43. Brugmans, *Paardenkracht*, p. 75.
44. Mansvelt, *Geschiedenis van de N.H.M.*, 1: 314–15.
45. Ibid., pp. 308, 316.
46. Ibid., 1: 322; 2: 106, 114.

Wilson went bankrupt ultimately, while Prévinaire's plant continued a stagnant and insignificant existence. Mansvelt's conclusion that "the huge efforts in Haarlem were an utter waste . . . the Provinces of Holland were infertile soil for the cotton industry"[47] summarizes the situation. No Manchester was to be established in this area in the nineteenth century.

The only modern industries founded in the maritime provinces as early as the 1820s were the machine workshops in Amsterdam and Rotterdam. The dimensions of this industry in Holland were of an entirely different order of magnitude than in Belgium and its expansion much less spectacular. The Rotterdam firm was founded in 1823 by G. M. Roentgen, the same who had investigated the Walloon iron industry in 1822.[48] Initially the firm started as a shipping company, using steamships, named the Nederlandsche Stoomboot Maatschappij (Dutch Steamship Company), and although it soon started to produce its own steam engines, its main occupation was in shipping, not heavy industry.[49] The principal customer of the company was the Dutch government, which at the same time was the major creditor of the firm. In spite of the efforts of the Dutch government to help it, the firm did not prosper. The shipping business was consistently disappointing and the attempt to construct machinery for other industries in the late 1830s was abandoned after a while.[50] It is not altogether clear what caused the lack of success of this firm: Roentgen was a superb engineer (he was considered a coinventor of the compound steam engine), and the help of the government should be regarded as a partial compensation at least for the general hardships of the times. Moreover, many of the difficulties into which Roentgen ran (such as the chronic lack of working capital) were equally encountered by his more successful competitors in Belgium.

Roentgen's counterpart in Amsterdam was Paul van Vlissingen, who founded a machine workshop in 1827. Very little is known about this firm, since its records were destroyed by fire. It can be concluded, however, that the firm was virtually dependent on government orders and credit, as well as on the orders of Dutch colonies, primarily from Surinam (Dutch Guyana). Only in the early 1840s, with the increase in the demand for steam engines for railroads and sugar refineries, did this firm attain a significant position. Its sales tripled between 1844 and 1847 from less than 500,000 florins to 1.33 million, and employment reached 800 persons in 1846.[51]

47. Ibid., 2: 280.

48. See above, pp. 54–55

49. M. G. de Boer, *Leven en Bedrijf van G. M. Roentgen* [Life and enterprises of G. M. Roentgen] (Groningen: P. Noordhoff, 1923), p. 48.

50. Ibid., pp. 122–23.

51. M. G. de Boer, *Honderd Jaar Machine Industrie op Oosterburg, Amsterdam* [A hundred years of machine industry in Amsterdam] (Amsterdam: Bussy, 1927), p. 27.

Roentgen and van Vlissingen were exceptions, not the rule, and they were, moreover, kept artificially alive by frequent government help. In spite of this help, the Dutch did not develop a machine industry of major importance before mid-century. As Everwijn summarizes: "In the first half of the nineteenth century, most machines were still imported, steam-engines for steamships excepted. . . . Only very gradually did the most energetic pioneers manage to conquer for themselves markets in the industries which were starting to apply mechanized techniques."[52] Not only demand problems plagued the Dutch machinery industry: often they were unable to produce capital goods which were qualitatively adequate. The sugar mills in the Dutch colonies in the West Indies, for example, which purchased their machines from Roentgen and van Vlissingen, were dissatisfied with the quality of the devices supplied.[53]

The Dutch iron industry was mainly an appendage of the iron-using industries and consequently did not attain much significance in the first half of the nineteenth century.[54] The most important foundries were those attached to van Vlissingen's and Roentgen's machine workshops. The raw materials were partly brought over from the small iron ore mines in the eastern part of the country (province of Gelderland) and partly imported. After 1835 the use of scrap iron as a raw material became more widespread.[55] The need to import coal remained an obstacle to the expansion of the Dutch iron industry, compounding the general factors affecting the rate of industrialization in the Netherlands. A specialized and somewhat more successful branch of the industry was the production of sheet iron, which had been a rather successful traffic industry in the eighteenth century and recovered after 1815. However, the transformation of this activity into a large-scale, modern industry did not begin before the 1860s.[56]

To summarize: keeping in mind a few exceptions, it can be concluded that, in general, industrialization in the Dutch maritime provinces was absent. The ancient industries, remnants of a glorious era in which the Dutch had dominated the seas, were wiped out by the economic warfare of the Revolutionary and Napoleonic wars. In these very same years new and revolutionary production technologies were diffused throughout the Continent, bypassing the Netherlands, which was isolated from overseas by a blockade and from the Continent by a tariff barrier. After the

52. Everwijn, *Beschrijving van Handel en Nijverheid*, pp. 52–53.
53. Mansvelt, *Geschiedenis van de N.H.M.*, 2: 234n.
54. J. C. Westermann, *Geschiedenis van de IJzer en Staalgieterij in Nederland* [History of the iron and steel foundries in the Netherlands] (Utrecht: Demka, 1948).
55. Ibid., pp. 42–46.
56. J. C. Westermann, *Blik in het Verleden, Geschiedenis van de Nederlandsche Blikindustrie in hare Opkomst* [History of the rise of the Dutch sheet-iron industry] (Amsterdam: Vereenigde Blikfabrieken, 1939), pp. 121–48.

settling of the war dust in 1815, the Dutch discovered to their dismay that the world of manufacturing had changed and would never be the same again. The maritime provinces, mainly Holland and Utrecht, failed, however, to learn a lesson from this. The new technologies were diffused at a very slow rate, with the result that industry stagnated. It is important to note that most of the new processes and techniques were not wholly unknown in the Netherlands. Van der Boon Mesch, a contemporary political economist, presents a long list of innovations supposedly introduced in Dutch industry, including improvements in the chemical and glass industries, the Jacquard loom, and improvements in windmill construction and instrument making.[57] The issue is, however, not so much whether a given technology was wholly unknown, but rather at which rate its application was being diffused among industries. In this respect van der Boon Mesch's optimistic account is flatly contradicted by all other sources.[58]

After the secession of the Belgian provinces, there was a conscious attempt by the government and the N.H.M. to reestablish textile industries in the urban centers of provinces of Holland. The hopes were apparently to create a source of supply for the textile market in the Dutch East Indies while at the same time to provide employment for the unemployed and paupers in the decaying towns. In spite of the imports of human and nonhuman capital, as well as entrepreneurship, the attempts failed. In 1850, the western parts of the Netherlands, once its economic center of gravity, did not possess any modern industry. The contrast with Belgium is consequently quite striking, but it was obvious that the Netherlands was in fact falling behind the entire western Continent. One contemporary notes:

> Those who failed to realize the tremendous powers of the steam-engine were crushed by its gigantic gears. Our country, chained to the habits of the previous century, its mind dominated by fear and disgust of anything novel, was entirely overwhelmed by the industrial revolution which was taking place everywhere around. Gradually Holland was becoming incapable of participating in this movement which was growing everywhere in gigantic proportions.[59]

Needless to say, the author's notion of the dimensions of the progress

57. A. H. van der Boon Mesch, "Over het Nederlandsche Fabrijkswezen" [Essay on Dutch manufacturing], *TBN* 7, pt. 4 (1843): 550–64.

58. See, for example, E. H. von Baumhauer, *Voorlezingen over de Nederlandsche Nijverheid en de Middelen om haar te Ontwikkelen* [Readings on Dutch manufacturing and the ways to improve it] (Haarlem: A. C. Kruseman, 1856), p. 40.

59. H. J. Koenen, *Voorlezingen over de Geschiedenis der Nijverheid in Nederland* [Readings on the history of manufacturing in the Netherlands] (Haarlem: A. C. Kruseman, 1856), p. 140.

achieved "everywhere else" is exaggerated, but this only underlines the awareness of Dutch "relative backwardness" that pervades his thought.

THE TEXTILE INDUSTRIES IN THE TWENTE AREA

The Twente area, located in the eastern part of the province of Overijssel, was one of the few areas in the Netherlands in which protoindustry was important. Located in a comparatively isolated corner of the Republic, it played a modest role in the "maritime economy" of the eighteenth century. Precisely for this reason, this Z-good type industry was spared the devastating crisis of the French period.

The resemblance of the Twente area to Flanders was conspicuous and did not fail to draw the attention of intelligent contemporaries. Van Hogendorp, who visited the area in 1819, was struck by the similarity and wondered what prevented Twente from following the footsteps of Flanders in establishing a modern industry.[60] Twente in the eighteenth century was producing fustians and cotton goods exclusively for domestic consumption. The techniques used were the ancient, manual methods, except for small spinning jennies which were introduced before 1795.[61] The linen industry was being replaced gradually in the second half of the eighteenth century by fustian (linen warp with cotton weft) or pure cotton goods. The decline of the linen industry in Twente accelerated in the French period, but this was probably compensated by the growth of fustian as well as cotton production. The overall situation in Twente during the French period was not nearly as bad as in the rest of the country. This fact is illustrated by the figures provided by d'Alphonse —see table 3.4.

Table 3.4   Growth of the Textile Industry in Overijssel, 1806 and 1811

Category	1806	1811
Number of cotton-weaving manufactures	53	65
Employed by these	4,093	4,700
Output of these (in thousands of pieces)	103	107
Number of cotton spinning manufactures	30	39
Employed by these	649	738
Output of these (in hundreds of kgs.)	4,738	5,587

SOURCE: d'Alphonse, Aperçu, pp. 254–57.

60. Van Hogendorp, Bijdragen, 5: 166–68.
61. J. A. P. G. Boot, De Twentsche Katoennijverheid, 1830–1873 [The cotton industry in Twente, 1830–1873] (Amsterdam: H. J. Paris, 1935), p. 18. Goldberg, "Journaal der Reize," TSS 18: 457.

The period 1815–30 was one of little change in the Twente textile industry. The shift from linen to cotton continued, especially in the erst-while linen center of Almelo. But the cotton industry remained a rather primitive protoindustry. No technological progress of any consequence nor any significant accumulation of fixed capital can be observed. The industry remained a peasant occupation producing for the domestic market, while the exports to the Dutch Indies, organized by the N.H.M., were based in Flanders. One or two cases excepted, the entrepreneurs (that is, the "putters-out") seemed disinterested in and ignorant of technological improvements introduced abroad. The first mechanized spinning mill, operating on steam, was established as late as 1830 by Hofkes in Almelo.[62] But still in 1832, a very well informed contemporary writes about the Twente textile industry as follows:

> Among about twenty manufacturers of textiles [which I visited in Twente], I have noted with few exceptions, not precisely ignorance, but certainly far less industrial knowledge than might have been expected. . . . I dare to add that an improvement in the tools and raw materials used could trigger a notable saving in the inputs as well as [increase] the output itself.[63]

A rather abrupt and unexpected change in the fate of Twente and its textile industry came about as a result of the Belgian Revolution. The N.H.M., under the pressure of the minister of colonies, J. van den Bosch, had decided not to resort to imports for the supply of cotton goods to the Dutch East Indies, after the formal prohibition imposed on goods from "those parts of the Realm which are in rebellion." Instead, it was decided to establish a cotton industry in the Netherlands itself. As was shown above, part of the efforts were directed to renovate the textile industry in the maritime provinces. The conditions in Twente were not unknown, thanks possibly to van Hogendorp's detailed account of the area. The N.H.M. decided to send its director and acting secretary, W. de Clercq, to the area in the summer of 1832, with the assignment to examine "whether and to which extent Twente can be expected to replace those

62. Boot, *Twentsche Katoennijverheid*, p. 29.

63. E. C. van der Meersch, "Report on Industry in Twente," manuscript, Dutch National Archives, Kabinet des Konings, 17 February 1834, no. 62, pp. 2–3. The writer is the same author quoted above, p. 30. He was a specialist on cotton industry from Ghent, who defected to the North after the revolution of 1830 and was hired by the N.H.M. to investigate the Twente textile industry. See also J. A. P. G. Boot and A. Blonk, *Van Smiet-tot Snelspoel, de Opkomst van de Twents-Gelderse Textielindustrie in het Begin van de 19ᵉ Eeuw* [The rise of the textile industry in Twente in the beginning of the nineteenth century] (Hengelo: Stichting Textielgeschiedenis, 1957), pp. 104–12.

export products which have been lost for the N.H.M. by the secession of the Belgian provinces."[64]

In fact, there is little reason to believe that the Dutch authorities were unfamiliar with the potentialities of a textile industry in Twente. Earlier in 1832, a Belgian manufacturer of colored cotton goods, Charles de Maere, proposed to William I to move his plant from St. Nikolaas to the Northern Kingdom. The minister of industry, Netscher, advised him to settle in the village of Hengelo in Twente, which was the only place which produced such goods in the Netherlands. The N.H.M. assured him of the necessary orders, whereupon de Maere moved to Hengelo. He discovered that the flying shuttle was unknown in Twente and his first efforts were concentrated on the purchase and construction of flying shuttles and on teaching the local peasantry to use them.[65]

De Clercq's mission to Twente probably consisted of inspecting the advances made by de Maere. He found that the latter's enterprise was still extremely limited in size, although "the flying shuttle clearly reduces the labor."[66] Otherwise, de Maere was a simple putting-out entrepreneur, with no fixed plant of his own to speak of.[67] While in Hengelo, however, de Clercq met an employee of de Maere's by the name of Thomas Ainsworth. This meeting proved of considerable historical importance and has been the subject of various anecdotes. Ainsworth was the son of an English cotton manufacturer who went bankrupt, whereupon his son moved to France. From 1827 to 1830, he worked for John Cockerill, but he was forced to leave Seraing in 1830 for unclear reasons. His technical proficiency was versatile: in previous years he had been active in helping a paper manufacturer produce colored paper, and had been employed by the Almelo manufacturer, Hofkes, in the setting up of a chemical bleaching plant. In 1832 he was working for de Maere in a similar occupation.

Ainsworth convinced de Clercq of the vast possibilities that a cotton industry would have in Twente and promised him to formulate his ideas more precisely. His memorandum included a recommendation to replace the old-fashioned looms by flying shuttles (which was, in fact, already being put into effect by de Maere for colored cottons, though not for

64. Cited by Mansvelt, *Geschiedenis van de N.H.M.*, 1: 267.

65. B. C. Sluijk, "Charles de Maere en de Verniêuwing van de Handweverij in Twente" [Charles de Maere and the renovation of manual weaving in Twente], *Overijssel, Jaarboek voor Cultuur en Historie* (1957), pp. 11–14. See also Boot, *Twentsche Katoennijverheid*, pp. 35–36.

66. Report of de Clercq to N.H.M., reprinted in "Bijdragen tot de Geschiedenis der Nederlandsche Grootindustrie," [Contributions to the history of Dutch large scale industry], pt. 2, *EHJ* 11 (1925): 184.

67. Mansvelt, *Geschiedenis van de N.H.M.*, 1: 269.

calicoes). Ainsworth argued that handloom weaving seemed the optimal technique in the production of calicoes "not only because a mass of people would thereby be employed, but as the cheapest system, whereas in this country labour is cheap. . . . To establish power looms, where labour is low as in this country would be an undeniable absurdity."[68] Ainsworth provided a detailed estimate of the cost of converting the weaving population of Twente to the use of flying shuttles, while realizing the need to spend some time in teaching the new technique. With regard to spinning, Ainsworth was more vague: he recommended the establishment of local spinning mills but his reasoning was based on the need to secure a stable supply of yarn rather than on an efficiency argument.

On the basis of de Clercq's impressions in Twente, and Ainsworth's memorandum, the N.H.M. submitted to the Dutch government a plan which included, among others, the establishment of a weaving school in Twente and the widespread application of weaving using looms equipped with flying shuttles, as well as the extension of a loan of 40,000 florins to Hofkes for the completion of his spinning mill.[69] After some hesitation, the plan was accepted.

In the summer of 1833, Ainsworth opened his weaving school in the village of Goor in the southern part of Twente. A few English workmen instructed the Twente workers and children how to operate flying shuttles. The weaving school was a spectacular success, and soon many competing schools emerged, founded by entrepreneurs who hoped to switch their production to calicoes. The orders placed by the N.H.M. were very large in the first years, and traditional techniques were initially unable to meet the demand. The flying shuttle increased the productivity of workers, measured by the number of times per minute the shuttle was thrown from side to side, by a factor of three.[70] At the same time, however, the calicoes were generally of a finer composure than the old fustians or rough cottons, which means that the increase in productivity measured in pieces of cloth was smaller. In any event, within two years most of the work of the weaving schools was accomplished, and by 1838 most of them had closed.

In addition to the rapid diffusion of the flying shuttle in Twente (a century after its invention, to be sure), a few other technological improvements were introduced by Ainsworth. One of the most important innovations was the introduction of the sizing machine which strengthened the yarn before the weaving. The yarn itself was still largely imported from

68. Reprinted in Posthumus, *Bijdragen*, pt. 2, pp. 175–79. The question of the choice of an optimal technique will be discussed below.
69. Reprinted in Posthumus, *Bijdragen*, pt. 2, pp. 195–208. Boot, *Twentsche Katoennij-verheid*, p. 52.
70. Boot, *Twentsche Katoennijverheid*, p. 55.

England. In addition, Ainsworth attempted to found an experimental weaving factory where new types of cotton fabrics could be tried, as well as a flax spinning mill and linen goods manufacture in which he tried to introduce Jacquard looms. None of these plans had any success, however, and Ainsworth had to be bailed out by his employer, the N.H.M. He died in 1841.

Ainsworth's principal achievement was the foundation of an industry which could supply the Dutch East Indies with cotton goods and thus save the notorious "Culture System" which the Dutch had introduced in their colonies. This system was based on a more or less compulsory barter exchange between the homeland and the colonies. After 1830 it seemed that the main product which the Dutch had been exporting to the East Indies, calicoes, would have to be purchased by them from the Belgian rebels or the English archrivals, none of which seemed politically very attractive. Ainsworth managed to avert this menace as can be verified from tables 3.5 and 3.6.

It can be ascertained that Dutch cotton products managed to take over more than half of the market in the Dutch Indies. But tables 3.5 and 3.6 also reveal a basic weakness of the industrialization process in Twente: its complete reliance on the market in the East Indies with the monopolistic intermediary, the N.H.M., in between. The precise shape of the demand curve facing the Dutch textiles depended on various exogenous factors such as the size of the harvests on Java, the world price of coffee and other exotic products, and the price at which competing calico manufacturers (mainly English) offered their goods. It seems clear, however, that the Netherlands was facing a downward sloping demand which included an inelastic portion at its lower end. Dutch exports to Java and Madura peaked around 1840, after which the absolute value of their export as well as their share in the total declined, as can be observed from table 3.6.

The tariff system which enabled Twente to compete in the Java market

Table 3.5   Exports of Some Textiles from Twente to the
Dutch Indies, 1834–40
(in pieces[a])

	1834	1839	1840
Calicoes	13,200	460,767	678,222
Other white cottons	—	10,909	7,926
Colored cottons	5,775	11,070	11,949
Linen cloth	1,070	300	84

[a]Since the pieces are not of uniform length, the columns are not summed up.
SOURCE: Boot, *Twentsche Katoennijverheid*, p. 71.

Table 3.6   Imports of Cotton Goods in Java and Madura, 1830–48
(in millions of florins)

	Foreign Products	Dutch Products	Total	Percentage of Dutch
1830	1.51	2.37[a]	3.88	61
1831	1.55	1.39[a]	2.94	47
1832	1.89	0.07	1.96	3
1833	3.89	0.09	3.98	2
1834	4.12	0.33	4.45	7
1835	2.58	1.55	4.13	37
1836	2.90	3.28	6.18	53
1837	3.46	3.68	7.14	51
1838	3.97	5.78	9.75	59
1839	3.23	7.30	10.53	69
1840	4.27	8.83	13.10	67
1841	2.72	4.97	7.69	65
1842	3.57	7.29	10.86	67
1843	3.62	3.54	7.16	49
1844	4.10	4.77	8.87	54
1845	5.61	5.32	10.93	49
1846	5.93	6.54	12.47	52
1847	4.61	5.46	10.07	54
1848	3.84	4.60	8.44	55

[a]Includes Belgian products.
SOURCE: Muller, *Nederlandsche Katoennijverheid*, pp. 26–27.

was introduced in 1824 to support the Flemish exports of calicoes to the Dutch Indies.[71] The tariff was reduced to 12.5 percent in 1831, but reinstated in 1832, after the Dutch made the basic decision to start a cotton industry on their own. The weakening of the international position of the Netherlands after the Belgian Revolution tempted the English government to exert increasing pressure on the Dutch to restore the lower tariff of 12.5 percent. The Dutch government succumbed to the pressure, but evaded the agreement by subsidizing the N.H.M.'s exports with a secret 12 percent ad valorem premium. This arrangement is known as the "secret cotton contracts," according to which the N.H.M. promised to export given quantities of cotton to Java while the Dutch government provided the company with a guarantee against losses of up to 24.5 percent. Later on, the form of the subsidy was changed to a favorable foreign exchange settlement.[72] This arrangement offset the concession extorted

71. See above, p. 32.
72. N. W. Posthumus, ed., "De Geheime Lijnwaadcontracten der N.H.M. (1835–1854)" [The secret cotton contracts of the N.H.M.], *EHJ* 2 (1916): 3–207. Mansvelt, *Geschiedenis van de N.H.M.*, 1: 284 ff. A. de Vries, *Geschiedenis van de Handelspolitiek Betrekkingen tusschen Nederland en Engeland* [History of the commercial relations between England and the Netherlands] (Amsterdam: Martinus Nijhoff, 1931), pp. 75–95.

by the English but had the undesirable side effect of strengthening the
N.H.M. as a monopolistic intermediary between the protected industries
in the homeland and the markets in the colonies. It is quite obvious,
however, that this protection was a *sine qua non* for the growth of the
textile industry in Twente.[73]

How did the expansion of the Twente textile industries and the
conversion to the weaving of calicoes with flying shuttles affect the
economic structure of the area? The transformation of the Z-good sector
in this area can hardly be considered an "industrial revolution." The
amount of fixed capital remained negligible. No large, centralized plants
were set up and no economies of scale realized. The Twente cotton
industry remained a classical Z-good industry. The raw materials were
largely imported, the finished products sold at a foreign market with the
prices given to each entrepreneur (but not determined at the world
market as much as by the decisions of the N.H.M.). Capital inputs
remained small. Ainsworth estimated the cost of a loom with a flying
shuttle at 24 florins.[74] The actual price was initially 30 florins, later falling
to 12–15 florins.[75] This was probably not more expensive than the old
looms.[76] No investment in buildings was required since the industry
remained almost wholly domestic. Mechanized spinning mills were still
of minor importance. The first mill, opened by Hofkes in Almelo in 1830,
ran into many difficulties, including the refusal of the Dutch government
to raise the tariff on yarn.[77] A second firm, in the city of Enschede, was
founded by an Englishman by the name of Dixon. Little progress was
recorded by this firm in the 1830s, while in the following decade, the
number of spindles stagnated at about 10,000.[78] The capacity of steam
engines in Twente was growing very slowly over the whole period, as
indicated in table 3.7. The first power looms were introduced as late as
1846, and it was not until the mid-1850s that power weaving or spinning
attained any importance, even at the modest scale of the relatively small
area of Twente.

To summarize, the first decades of "industrialization" in the Twente
area should thus be regarded as a period of improvement within the limits
of the traditional sector, rather than a period in which the industrial sector
was switching to techniques which were radically new. The flying shuttle

73. Boot, *Twentsche Katoennijverheid*, pp. 72, 192–96, 347.
74. Posthumus, *Bijdragen*, pt. 2, p. 178.
75. C. T. Stork, *De Twentsche Katoennijverheid, hare Vestiging en Uitbreiding* [The establishment and expansion of the Twente cotton industry] (Enschede: M. J. van der Loeff, 1888), p. 25.
76. Boot, *Twentsche Katoennijverheid*, p. 54n.
77. Ibid., pp. 125–29.
78. A. Blonk, *Fabrieken en Menschen, een Sociografie van Enschede* [Factories and people, a sociography of Enschede] (Enschede: M. J. van der Loeff, 1929), p. 74.

Table 3.7   The Growth of Steam Power in the Twente Textile Industry, 1830–59

Year	HP	Year	HP	Year	HP
1830	18	1840	90	1850	220
1831	18	1841	90	1851	220
1832	18	1842	90	1852	240
1833	18	1843	90	1853	328
1834	18	1844	110	1854	336
1835	42	1845	110	1855	343
1836	42	1846	122	1856	352
1837	50	1847	147	1857	421
1838	90	1848	147	1858	459
1839	90	1849	152	1859	530

SOURCE: Boot, *Twentsche Katoennijverheid*, appendix 2.

did not create a "modern" sector in any sense. Total capital invested was small, the archaic putting-out system still dominant.

It may be worthwhile to examine in some detail what may be called "the economic consequences of Mr. Ainsworth." The introduction of the flying shuttle was basically a labor-augmenting technological change that made every worker equivalent to two or three "old" workers by a rather minor alteration in his equipment. If the "putters out" were competitive, and if the price of output did not fall with the increase in output, the wages per unit of time earned by labor should have increased proportionately to the growth in productivity. Unfortunately, there was no basis whatsoever for these assumptions. The vast increase in output (by a factor larger than the gain in productivity, since the labor force employed increased considerably between 1830 and 1850)[79] was possible only because the industry switched from fustians and rough cotton fabrics to calicoes. Was the price of a piece of calico the same as the price of a piece of fustian or rough cotton? The kind of data that would be necessary to answer this question is not available at the present state of research. The indirect evidence suggests that the price of a piece of calico produced was substantially lower. Van der Meersch observed that at the pre-1832 wages, it was impossible to weave calicoes at a competing price.[80] This implies that the world price for calicoes was lower than for a piece of fustian of equal size which took two to three times longer to produce. One cannot be sure by how much if, as seems likely, the cost price of Dutch calicoes was not higher than the world price. The switching to calico

79. J. A. P. G. Boot, "Gebrek aan Handwevers in Twente na 1850" [A scarcity of weavers in Twente after 1850], *THB* 10 (1968): 18.
80. Van der Meersch, "Report on Industry in Twente," pp. 3–4.

production, therefore, increased the marginal physical product of labor but reduced the price of the product multiplying it, so that the rise in the wage level was more moderate than the rise in productivity. The hypothesis that the price received per unit of output was considerably lower for calicoes is supported by the fact that wages per unit of output (piece wages) fell drastically in 1834.[81] Still, the argument that the piece wage fell instantaneously by a factor of three leaving wages per unit of time basically unchanged[82] appears exaggerated and is, in fact, not consistent with Boot's own figures. There is, in addition, some evidence indicating a marked rise in the standards of living in the Twente area in the decade following 1832. Mansvelt describes the effects of the introduction of the flying shuttle as follows:

> In Twente the poor disappeared as if by magic...the calico weaving manufactures cleaned up the paupers and the beggars as if by a vacuum cleaner. Unemployment was replaced by a scarcity of man power. [A source from 1841 says] "many of our villages are beginning to acquire a new look...thousands of florins are earned by the lower classes which have substituted the flying shuttle for the beggar's staff."[83]

As far as can be ascertained, there seems to have been tight competition for labor between the putters-out, driving up the wage level in the late 1830s.[84]

How large was the Twente cotton industry? Exact data are absent, but from table 3.6 it can be seen that exports to the Indies did not exceed 9 million florins and averaged less than 6 million for the period 1838–48. Production for the local market was roughly equal to exports,[85] so that an estimate of 12 million florins total gross product per annum is not far from the mark. Value added was at most 25 percent of this sum, since the bulk of the yarn was imported and yarn constituted 75–80 percent of the production costs.[86] A total value added of about 3 million florins seems, therefore, a reasonable estimate for average annual net output in the period following the introduction of the flying shuttle. This figure is

---

81. Boot, *Twentsche Katoennijverheid*, p. 55.
82. In general, it will be expected that the piece wage will be proportional to the price of output and independent of the productivity of labor.
83. Mansvelt, *Geschiedenis van de N.H.M.*, 1: 337.
84. R. A. Burgers, *100 Jaar G. en H. Salomonson, Kooplieden, Entrepreneurs, Fabrikanten en Directeuren van de Koninklijke Stoomweverij te Nijverdal* [History of the firm of the brothers Salomonson in Nijverdal] (Leyden: Stenfert Kroese, 1954), pp. 62–63.
85. Boot, "Gebrek aan Handwevers," p. 16.
86. Burgers, *100 Jaar Salomonson*, p. 84.

confirmed by data provided by the N.H.M., which show that wage payments in 1840 (a peak year) amounted to 3.5 million florins.[87] Inputs of capital were negligible and profits were low, so that total income originating did not exceed 4 million florins. Exports declined by about a third in the decade following 1840, so that the estimate of 3 million seems realistic. The value added in the Flemish cotton industry in 1838 was estimated at 13.2 million Dutch florins.[88] Belgian textile production was much larger than the Flemish cotton industry alone, but the foregoing suffices to illustrate the minor significance of the Twente industry, compared to truly modern textile sectors.

A characteristic of the Twente cotton industry was the rather curious mixture of motivation among its key figures. Most of the entrepreneurs who were actually organizing production were simply trying to maximize profits, or at least followed satisficing behavior from their own point of view. But the existence of the N.H.M. introduced an element of philanthropy into the Twente cotton industry, which should be regarded as a fundamental cause of the particular course followed by this industry. The N.H.M. exerted pressure on their clients to engage in unprofitable but socially "desirable" activities. For example, the calico manufacturers of G. and H. Salomonson from Almelo founded weaving shops in various cities in the maritime provinces, including Zeeland, at the request of the N.H.M. Such unprofitable endeavors were undertaken only due to some arm twisting on the part of the N.H.M., which controlled the sales to the colonies.[89]

The philanthropic elements in the N.H.M.'s policy were related to the particular functions that the N.H.M. was supposed to fulfill. Its main function was, of course, to provide the products brought to Java as part of the "Culture System." The men who dominated the N.H.M. in the first two decades following the Belgian Revolution believed that the main function of industry was to supply employment for the paupers and the unemployed in the Netherlands. The dominant figure in the Dutch government who supported this view was the above-mentioned van den Bosch. According to him:

> The colonies have to import...many commodities which were formerly supplied by Belgium. We can meet their needs by our own means, and by doing so redress our once-flourishing industries from their deep decay and provide many needy people with the means to recover their former prosperity.[90]

87. Mansvelt, *Geschiedenis van de N.H.M.*, 1: 340.
88. Briavoinne, *De L'Industrie*, 2: 376–77. The official exchange rate was used.
89. Burgers, *100 Jaar Salomonson*, p. 65. The weaving manufactures in Zeeland were kept alive artifically for thirty years.
90. Cited by Boot, *Twentsche Katoennijverheid,* p. 343.

Willem de Clercq, the director of the N.H.M., was even more explicit. He believed that the chief task of industrial activity was to reduce poverty through the creation of employment opportunities. Therefore, the most efficient employers should not be supported by the N.H.M. (that is, receive orders for calicoes), but rather those who were deserving in some way.[91] This was the reason why he seemed to favor particularly small-scale producers, with the expected result that technological improvements associated with large size and the realization of economies of scale were discouraged. Moreover, there was no incentive whatsoever to increase efficiency, since lower prices had no effect anyway on the buying policy of the N.H.M. The profit maximizing or satisficing behavior of the Twente textile entrepreneurs was distorted into a policy that tried to maximize profits for a given quantity of output rather than overall profits.[92]

In 1844, de Clercq died, and the policy of fixed orders was gradually abandoned in favor of a more rational system of auctioning orders and awarding them to the lowest bidder. The transition was completed around 1848, and from then on the process of modernization took off. Whether this was a coincidence or not is a problem to which local historians have failed to address themselves, but which seems interesting enough to ponder.

The humanitarian-motivated policies of the N.H.M. made Ainsworth's basically fallacious advice—to shift the Twente textile industry to a flying shuttle-employing protoindustry while keeping its traditional structure intact—look as if it were the correct step. It is important to realize that the handloom, with the flying shuttle or without it, was fighting a losing battle all over Europe, regardless of whether it was in high-wage Lancastershire or low-wage Flanders. It is likely that the power loom technique was more efficient than the handloom technique at any feasible wage rate. But even if it were not,[93] wages in Twente were soon bid up to the level at which the power loom became the more efficient technique. This is illustrated in figure 3.1.

Panel a in figure 3.1 reflects the labor market. On the vertical axis the wage level is depicted in terms of agricultural goods. In the present model, it will be assumed that the price of agricultural goods is constant. Panel b

91. For example, one Mr. Fabius from Amsterdam was warmly recommended by de Clercq because "his aim is humanitarian and it is imperative to attract men of his type to manufacturing, since they can be expected to refrain from the gross selfishness displayed so often by the manufacturers of Overijssel." Cited by Mansvelt, *Geschiedenis van de N.H.M.*, I : 298.

92. A statement in this spirit is given in ibid., p. 340.

93. It can be proven that if no capital is employed in converting traditional looms into flying shuttle looms, while it requires some capital to produce power looms, there must exist a wage level (which could be very low, of course) at which handlooms are more efficient than power looms.

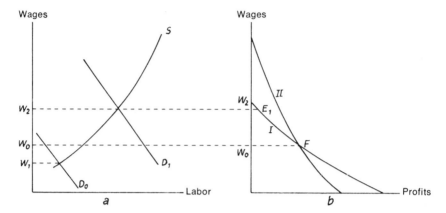

Figure 3.1   The Labor Market and Choice of Technique in the Textile Industry in Twente

presents the two techniques, the handloom opposed to the "mechanized" technique, in a factor-price-frontier diagram. Curve I represents the manual technique, while curve II stands for the mechanized technique.[94] The wage level, w_0, is what may be called the "equiprofitability wage." At wages lower than w_0, the handloom technique is more profitable (curve I is higher than curve II) whereas at wages higher than w_0, the efficiency conditions require the economy to shift to the mechanized technique.

In the absence of precise information on the location of w_0, it may at least be questioned whether Ainsworth did, as he claimed, observe in Twente wages lower than w_0. It could be argued that he was not fully up to date on technological developments in the English cotton industry (having been away from England for years), so that his evaluation of the location of curve II was inaccurate. But even supposing that his initial assessment was accurate, Ainsworth failed to realize that his recommendation that the N.H.M. order large quantities of calico from Twente would cause a shift in the demand for labor, driving up wages (from w_1, the initial wage level). If the new demand curve, holding prices of output constant for the moment, was located at around D_1, so that the new wage level would be $w_2 > w_0$, the economy of the Twente area would inevitably end up at a point like E_1. The inefficiency implied by the location of the economy at E_1 persisted for almost two decades, due to the policies pursued by de Clercq and his colleagues. Moreover, a fall in the price of calicoes that would admittedly bring down the demand for labor again (and with it, ostensibly, the wage level) will not change this result—as will be shown below.

94. Note that it is assumed here that the traditional manual techniques employ *some* capital.

Is there evidence of rising wages in the Twente area in the period between 1832 and 1850? The above-mentioned evidence of a rising standard of living could be due to the elimination of pockets of unemployment, at a constant wage level. There is no continuous time series on wages for this period. The big industrial survey of 1819 provides wage data for a large sample of industrial workers in the United Kingdom of the Netherlands. According to the figures computed from this survey, the wages of adults in the textile industries in the province of Overijssel (almost all of them in Twente) were 45.2 cents, while children earned on the average 36.6 cents.[95] For the wages in the post-1832 period, only scattered observations are available. A report of the N.H.M., which was cited already above, claimed that a total of 3.5 million florins were paid in wages to a labor force totaling 14,600 workers.[96] This is equivalent to a daily wage of 80 cents on the assumption that workers were employed in the textile industry 300 days per year, which is unlikely. Possibly the report underestimates the number of workers, but even if this was the case, the figures for employment would have to be fantastically high if the above sum was paid to workers earning their pre-1832 wages.

A second source on wages in this period is the sample collected by a survey organized by the Dutch Ministry of the Interior in 1841.[97] The purpose of the survey was to collect information on child labor and working conditions. Adult wages were only a byproduct of the process of data gathering, and consequently the data are in almost unusable form. In any case, the average adult wage in 1841 was according to the Gorter and de Vries data 61.0 cents per day, while that for children was 32.1 cents. This indicates a rise of 30 percent for adults with a slight decline in children's wages. The latter can probably be attributed to inconsistent age classifications.

Impressionistic estimates of reasonably well informed contemporaries strengthen the hypothesis that wages did rise as a result of Ainsworth's and the N.H.M.'s activities. Ainsworth himself estimated in 1832 that wages in Twente were a quarter of English wages.[98] A source from 1857 (referring probably to a somewhat earlier period) puts the ratio at 1 : 2.[99] Since wages in England went up between 1832 and 1850, it follows that wages in Twente must have at least doubled in the same period.

95. Brugmans, *Statistieken*, 1: 247–417.
96. Mansvelt, *Geschiedenis van de N.H.M.*, 1: 340.
97. R. A. Gorter and C. W. de Vries, eds., "Gegevens omtrent den Kinderarbeid in Nederland volgens de Enquêtes van 1841 en 1860," [Data on child labor in the Netherlands according to the surveys of 1841 and 1860], *EHJ* 8 (1922): 95–99.
98. Posthumus, *Bijdragen*, pt. 2, p. 179.
99. Cited in H. Smissaert, *Geschiedenis der Ontwikkeling van de Twentsche Katoennijverheid* [History of the development of the cotton industry in Twente] (The Hague: Mouton and Co., 1906), p. 104.

A shift in the demand for labor manifests itself not only in higher wages but also in increased employment (unless the supply of labor was perverse). Using van der Meersch's data, Boot and Blonk estimated the total number of weavers in 1832 at 8,000 working on the average 100 days a year in weaving. In addition, 12,000 persons were occupied in auxiliary activities in the cotton industry.[100] This number grew considerably: in 1840 the N.H.M. reported employing 14,600 persons altogether, and since employment in calico production was about equal to employment in the production for local markets,[101] it follows that employment grew between 1832 and 1840 by at least 50 percent. In fact, the input of labor probably grew faster than the number of persons employed, through an increase in the number of hours worked annually.

The evidence on wages is suggestive, but by no means decisive. There are, however, other indications concerning the decline of the profitability of the manual technique. One significant fact is the increasing employment of qualitatively inferior weavers. At a given homogeneous wage level, the employment of inferior workers is equivalent to a rise in wages. Boot has stressed the "scarcity" of reliable and qualified workers for the period after 1850, but his claim that there was no evidence of a scarcity of workers before that year [102] is not compatible with other evidence. Mansvelt claims explicitly that there was a scarcity of labor in the 1830s.[103] A letter from 1832 written by the directors of the N.H.M. recommended to "increase the number of weavers as to prevent a possible rise in wages as a result of the introduction of the new manufacturing."[104] It is likely, however, that this scarcity worsened after 1850.

Will a falling price of output, causing the curve D_1 in figure 3.1 to shift back to the left, change the above conclusions? It was pointed out that it seems likely that the conversion from fustians and rough cottons to calicoes by itself may have been tantamount to a fall in output prices. Boot provides figures for the piece wage rate which reflect the output price.[105] These figures show an unambiguous decline between 1832 and 1850. It seems highly likely, then, that prices of output were declining. It can be shown, however, that this will, in general, not change the foregoing conclusion that the manual technique was becoming increasingly unprofitable. Consider, for example, figure 3.1, and assume for simplicity that the wage level is constant. The two factor price frontiers in panel b

---

100. Boot and Blonk, *Van Smiet-tot Snelspoel*, p. 110.
101. Boot, "Gebrek aan Handwevers," p. 16.
102. Ibid.
103. Mansvelt, *Geschiedenis van de N.H.M.*, 1: 308.
104. Cited in Posthumus, *Bijdragen*, pt. 2, p. 215.
105. Boot, *Twentsche Katoennijverheid*, p. 292.

are defined for a given set of prices of output. A decline in the output price will cause both frontiers to shift inwards, to the left. Suppose now that Ainsworth observed a wage lower than the wage level w_1 and that labor supply was infinitely elastic at that wage level. It is still possible, and indeed very likely, that the mechanized technique becomes more profitable after a while. The reason is that when the two factor price frontiers shift inwards, the point of equiprofitability, F, falls and will sooner or later fall beyond w_0.[106] The reason for the switching of techniques is that with prices of the final output falling, the real wage from the point of view of the employer is falling, although the real wage in terms of goods consumed by the workers may have remained unchanged.

To summarize, Ainsworth's argument that the manual technique was the optimal choice in a country where wages were as low as in Twente was fallacious, and its influence on the men who carried out the policies of N.H.M. in this region is basically to blame for the failure of the Dutch to develop a modern industry in this area. Ainsworth was mistaken on at least three accounts. First, there is considerable doubt whether the wage he observed in Twente was, in reality, lower than the equiprofitability point F in figure 3.1. As will still be seen, wages in Flanders were in the same order of magnitude in this period, yet the number of power looms, spinning mills, and other mechanical production goods increased very rapidly, while the handloom disappeared, at least in cotton. Second, even if we suppose for the sake of argument that wages in Twente in 1832 were so low as to make the handloom technique the correct choice of techniques, he failed to realize that his own recommendation could invalidate the assumptions on which it rested. The adoption of the calico weaving was self-defeating in the sense that the increased demand for labor was in itself a factor that drove up wages. Third, to the extent that Ainsworth's advice resulted in increased employment in addition to higher wages (the exact path of the labor market obviously depended on the elasticity of the supply of labor), it caused prices of the final output to fall and therefore the equiprofitability point F in figure 3.1 shifted downwards. The available evidence, albeit of a scattered nature, suggests that the supply of labor as well as the demand for calicoes had finite elasticities, so that the rise in the wage level and the fall in the price of output reinforced each other. The N.H.M., by deliberately preventing the shift to the mechanized techniques out of humanitarian motives, sentenced the Twente industry to long-term inefficiency and thereby postponed the emergence of a modern textile sector in this region.

106. This will occur unless the parameters of the production function have bizarre values. For a mathematical proof, see Joel Mokyr, "Industrial Growth and Stagnation in the Low Countries, 1800–1850" (Ph.D. diss., Yale University, 1974), pp. 300–05.

To the extent that the activities of Ainsworth resulted in a higher wage (per unit of time), their significance was deeper than the effects stemming from a temporary efficiency. The pseudoindustrialization of Twente between 1832 and 1850 delayed the start of the transition of manufacturing in this area to a modern technology. But its primary importance was that it caused this transition, after it started, to take place at a much slower rate than would have occurred otherwise. The rationale for this relationship will be expounded in chapter 4.

INDUSTRIAL DEVELOPMENT IN NORTH BRABANT AND LIMBURG

As was noted in chapter 1, there were considerable similarities between the economic structure of Twente and North Brabant. In both areas the diluvial soils were far less fertile than elsewhere in the country, and a Z-good sector developed as a response to population pressure on the soil. Goldberg described North Brabant in 1800 as a region of poor, sandy soils in which even the most prosperous peasants seldom owned more than ten head of cattle, the majority much less than that. The people are described as poor, dwelling in unattractive clay cottages. One reason cited by Goldberg for this poverty is the fragmentation of farms due to equal share inheritance. In other parts of the province, large areas were uncultivated due to the poor quality of the soil.[107] In many villages, every housewife was spinning linen, and wool was probably equally important. An entrepreneur in s'Hertogenbosch (Bois-le-Duc) engaged in yarn twining was reported to employ 2,000 workers, probably domestic workers spread all over the province. Much rural manufacturing of woolen goods was observed by Goldberg, most of it organized on a putting-out basis. Unfortunately, no quantitative data are available, except for the almost uniformly low wage level.[108]

The period 1795–1809 was, on the whole, a period of depression for the textile industry in this area. The linen industry seems to have gone through especially hard times. In Eindhoven, the number of entrepreneurs declined from nine in 1800 to two in 1808.[109] In Helmond, the chief linen center, the situation was equally bad.[110] The cause for this depression was not so much the lack of demand which plagued the rest of the country, as much as the scarcity of raw flax, of which export from Flanders was

107. Goldberg, "Journaal der Reize," *TSS* 18: 320–21.
108. Ibid., pp. 321–31.
109. F. B. A. M. Verhagen, "De Linnen- en Katoenindustrie in de Bataafse en Franse Tijd" [The linen and cotton industries in North Brabant in the Batavic and French periods] in *Land van mijn Hart*, Festschrift presented to Prof. J. A. J. Goossens (Tilburg: Drukkerij Henri Bergmans, 1952), p. 124.
110. Harkx, *Helmondse Textielnijverheid*, p. 71.

prohibited by the French. In 1810, the tariff line was moved to the Rhine, thus making North Brabant a part of the French Empire for tariff purposes. The removal of the tariff barrier provided a boost to the textile industries in this area. Employment in the linen and hybrid linen industries in Eindhoven and Helmond approximately doubled.[111] The woolen industry centered around Tilburg enjoyed a sudden expansion due to a large order from the French army. On the other hand, the cotton industry all but collapsed under the sudden exposure to competition from the Ghent factories.

Modernization in North Brabant came first to wool. This is not surprising, since the technological breakthroughs in linen took place later, while cotton was of minor importance in this area. Hence, it was Tilburg, the wool center, where the first signs of transformation in the production occurred. In 1809 the first mechanical wool-spinning mill was established, consisting of two *assortiments* purchased from Cockerill.[112] The number of firms employing such mills grew to five between 1810 and 1812. By 1813 domestic spinning had declined considerably, though weaving was to remain a domestic activity until the end of the nineteenth century.[113] At this time Tilburg should be regarded as the only place in the Netherlands in which modern industry had succeeded in making a little headway.

The revolution of 1813 and the consequent establishment of the United Kingdom of the Netherlands meant a severe blow to the Tilburg woolen industry. As can be verified from table 3.8, the output of woolen cloth declined disastrously between 1812 and 1817. It should be kept in mind, however, that production in the last years of the Empire was unnaturally high due to the large orders from the French army.

In spite of the fact that it faced within the same border a competitor far more advanced technically, and in spite of the severe competition of English manufactures, the Tilburg woolen industry managed to survive. Moreover, it succeeded in conquering an important bridgehead in the heart of the territory of its most severe rival: the revival of the Tilburg woolen industry in the early 1820s was largely a result of increased sales to the Belgian provinces.[114] This success was a result of specialization in coarser woolen fabrics, mainly baize and flannel. By 1830, 75 percent of the products of Tilburg were sold to the Belgian provinces of the kingdom.

111. Verhagen, "De Linnen-en Katoenindustrie," p. 126.
112. Ibid., pp. 127–28.
113. A. W. M. Keune, "De Industriële Ontwikkeling Gedurende de 19ᵉ Eeuw" [Industrial development in Tilburg during the nineteenth century] in *De Opkomst van Tilburg als een Industriestad*, ed. H. F. J. M. van den Eerenbeemt and H. J. A. M. Schurink (Nijmegen: N. V. Centrale Drukkerij, 1959), pp. 14–16.
114. Keune, "Industriële Ontwikkeling," p. 24.

Table 3.8   Output of Woolen and Cotton Fabrics in Tilburg, 1810–30
(in pieces)

Year	Woolen Fabrics	Cotton Fabrics	Year	Woolen Fabrics	Cotton Fabrics
1810	10,210	1,750	1821	4,963	1,223
1811	9,645	750	1822	5,661	1,189
1812	10,579	310	1823	4,250	1,152
1813	6,906[a]	68[a]	1824	5,805	1,108
1814	n.a.	n.a.	1825	10,214	1,135
1815	n.a.	1,462	1826	14,254	1,204
1816	n.a.	1,620	1827	14,732	1,135
1817	3,471	1,142	1828	15,580	878
1818	1,975	929	1829	21,689	694
1819	2,326	1,136	1830	21,646	691
1820	3,922	1,017			

[a]Computed on the assumption that production in the last two quarters of 1813 was the same.
SOURCE: Keune, "Industriële Ontwikkeling," pp. 14, 15, 17.

On the other hand, the colonial market never attained much significance for Tilburg, since there was no demand for woolen goods in the tropical areas. The only demand from this direction came from the Dutch army in the East Indies, after a royal order explicitly prohibited the purchase of textiles for government uses from foreign suppliers. Government orders were, in fact, of some importance before the royal order. In 1818, van Hogendorp noted that "In Tilburg, I have seen large woolen manufacturers which had diminished in the past years, but lately have been recovering thanks to the introduction of machineries and deliveries to the army... amounting to 300,000 florins."[115]

The Belgian Revolution resulted in the loss of the Belgian market, which was offset however by a sharply increased demand for military uniforms, not only because of the increased military activity but also because of the termination of all government purchases from the rebellious provinces. The resulting boom lasted until 1838.

The technological progress achieved by the Tilburg woolen industry between 1820 and 1838 was remarkable compared to the rest of the Netherlands, although of modest proportions compared to Belgium. The first steam engine introduced in the Dutch textile industry was bought by Pieter van Dooren in Tilburg (1827). In 1836 the city could boast 10 steam engines, of which 8 were active in the woolen industry. By 1839 this number had been augmented by two more, of which one was used in the production and maintenance of other steam engines. The new building of the firm of Diepen, Jellinghaus, and Co., constructed after the previous

115. Van Hogendorp, Bijdragen, 3: 5.

one was destroyed by fire, is described as "a beautiful and expensive construction which exceeds in beauty, solidity, and splendor any other building in this town [Tilburg] and probably in the entire kingdom."[116]

The expansion of the woolen industry in Tilburg was checked after 1838 due to the decline in demand. The local manufacturers complained continuously about the unfavorable situation of the industry. While most continental countries surrounded themselves by tariff barriers, the Dutch had maintained low tariffs on woolen manufactures. Accumulation of capital remained slow until the late 1840s. In 1845 out of 52 firms, 13 used steam engines. Output started to recover in the late 1840s, however, and with the general recovery accumulation picked up as well. In 1857 the number of firms had grown to 88, with 27 of them using steam.[117]

An indicator of the degree of modernization of the woolen industry is the proportion of the workers employed by the industry who worked at their homes. In 1817 only 25 percent of the workers worked *in situ*; the rest were still domestic workers. By 1825 the proportion of domestic workers had fallen to about half. As late as 1870, 29 percent of the labor force in the Tilburg woolen industry were domestic workers.[118]

The second center of the textile industry in North Brabant was Helmond. Quite a lot of quantitative information is available on the Helmond industry.[119] Unfortunately, Helmond was the center of the linen industry in this area, and linen was the last of the three main branches of textiles to undergo a technological transformation. The relative importance of linen as opposed to cotton is illustrated in table 3.9, which also demonstrates the relative stagnation of Helmond during the period 1815–30. The distribution of the three major textile industries over North Brabant in 1829 is presented in table 3.10. There was clearly a division of labor between the two main centers of textiles: Tilburg specialized in woolen products while Helmond was the center of linen and cotton production.

The transition of Helmond from linen to cotton production accelerated after 1830. While in 1812 only 18 percent of the weavers were employed in the cotton industry, this proportion rose to about 50 percent in 1838. Most of this switch occurred in the years following the Belgian Revolution.[120] Yet even after the transition to cotton and the diffusion of technological improvements in linen and flax, Helmond remained

116. Keune, "Industriële Ontwikkeling," pp. 31, 32.

117. Ibid., p. 37.

118. G. F. A. de Jong, "Enige Sociale Aspecten van de Arbeid in de Textielindustrie Gedurende de 19ᵉ Eeuw" [Some social aspects of labor in the textile industry in Tilburg in the nineteenth century] in *De Opkomst van Tilburg*, pp. 171–72.

119. Most of the data were collected by three governors of the province of North Brabant who served between 1814 and 1842 and collected a wealth of information on the textile industry. Parts of their statistics are reproduced by Harkx, *Helmondse Textielnijverheid*.

120. Ibid., pp. 117, 170.

Table 3.9   Production of Linen and Cotton Cloth in Helmond, 1810–30
(in thousands of pieces)

Year	Linen or Half Linen	Cotton	Year	Linen or Half Linen	Cotton
1810	9.8	n.a.	1821	38.9	1.3
1811	19.2	n.a.	1822	39.0	1.3
1812	24.3	n.a.	1823	39.0	1.5
1813	22.8[a]	n.a.	1824	39.0	1.6
1814	n.a.	n.a.	1825	39.1	1.6
1815	32.6	1.1	1826	37.8	1.5
1816	37.7	0.9	1827	38.6	1.7
1817	39.2	1.3	1828	54.5[b]	3.2[b]
1818	38.8	1.2	1829	54.0	3.6
1819	38.7	1.1	1830	50.5	3.7
1820	38.4	1.2			

[a]Computed on the assumption that output in the two last quarters of 1813 was the same.
[b]From 1828 the figures include the surrounding countryside.
SOURCE: Harkx, *Helmondse Textielnijverheid*, pp. 122–23.

Table 3.10   Textile Production in North Brabant, 1829
(in thousands of ells)[a]

	Tilburg	Helmond	Eindhoven	Others	Total
Wool	715.7	—	28.0	128.6	872.3
Cotton	45.1	231.1	—	83.2	359.4
Linen and half linen	—	1,514.0	400.4	—	1,914.4
Total	760.8	1,745.1	428.4	211.8	3,146.1

[a]One ell = 0.69 meter. The table is computed under the assumption that a piece of woolen cloth equals 33 ells, a piece of linen or half linen 28 ells, and a piece of cotton 65 ells.
SOURCE: Harkx, *Helmondse Textielnijverheid*, pp. 124–25.

basically a traditional industry center, with its industry organized on a putting-out basis using archaic, manual techniques. The first steam engine was introduced in Helmond as late as 1846, while power looms appeared only in 1870.[121] Even the flying shuttle was introduced in Helmond only in 1838, later than in Twente. In short, Helmond, in contrast to Tilburg, was a case in which the Z-good sector utterly failed to transform itself into a modern industry. The failure was even more complete than in Twente, while at the same time it cannot be explained, as in the Twente case, by the distorting influence of institutions like the N.H.M. The latter did little business with North Brabant.

121. Ibid., pp. 161, 188.

The question of Helmond's retardation is not insoluble. Although Helmond seems to have had an important linen weaving industry, spinning never attained proportional importance. The linen and cotton yarns used in Helmond were largely purchased from Belgium and Germany. After 1815 linen spinning declined fast; while in 1816–17 the number of spinners was still 80 percent of the number of weavers, it declined to 3 percent in 1830.[122] Since the main technological breakthroughs in linen occurred in the spinning and preparation of yarn, it is not surprising that there was little progress in the Helmond linen industry.

It still remains to be explained why Helmond failed to switch from linen, a "traditional" good, to the production of cotton which was more amenable to technological change. Cotton spinning, in spite of a misquote from Hogendorp by Brugmans unduly emphasized by Harkx, never got off the ground in Helmond.[123] Of a total of 770 workers in the village itself in the textile industry in 1840, only eleven were spinners.[124] Weaving switched to the use of the flying shuttle, but otherwise remained traditionally organized until the mid-1850s.

Part of the explanation of Helmond's disappointing performance is to be found in its small dimensions. Helmond was, no doubt, a classical model of a Z-good sector. But it was, after all, a miniature model. The population of Helmond in 1840 was 4,587, compared to 13,348 in Tilburg and over 71,000 in Twente. It is true that the population in Helmond grew from 1795 to 1869 by 158.6 percent, faster than any other area in North Brabant. Still, with such a small absolute population, some of the economies of scale which operated in Ghent and to some extent even in Twente failed to make themselves felt in Helmond. Harkx argues that the firms in Helmond were too small to introduce spinning profitably.[125] It was, however, not so much the inability of firms to reach their optimal scale that prevented Helmond from becoming a second Ghent (at a smaller scale), as the absence of phenomena that would be classified as economies of scale to the region or external economies among the firms. Two of the most important of these were the development of marketing agencies and the creation of a pool of technical know-how embodied in a class of engineers and technicians.

The main, and for some time, almost only marketing organization of

122. Ibid., appendix II.
123. Ibid., p. 91. A check in the source reveals, contrary to what Harkx asserts, that van Hogendorp had not seen spinning jennies in Helmond. Cf. van Hogendorp, *Bijdragen*, 3: 14. I. J. Brugmans, *De Arbeidende Klasse in de 19ᵉ Eeuw* [The working class in the Netherlands in the nineteenth century] (Utrecht-Antwerp: Het Spectrum, 1971, originally published in 1925), p. 43.
124. Harkx, *Helmondse Textielnijverheid*, p. 213.
125. Ibid., p. 102.

the Dutch textile industry was the N.H.M. The N.H.M. was, however, unequivocal about its preference of Twente over North Brabant. The motives behind this preference were first that North Brabant was too close to the southern border and therefore too vulnerable in case of a war with France and/or Belgium. Secondly, the proximity of North Brabant to the Belgian cotton centers seemed a disadvantage because of the (not unrealistic) fear that local manufacturers would pass off smuggled Belgian calicoes as their own and enjoy the subsidy-inflated prices offered by the N.H.M.[126] Consequently, except for a short interval in 1838–40, the N.H.M. ignored the Helmond cotton industry.

In view of the above critique on the policies of the N.H.M. it may seem as if Helmond might have been better off without the N.H.M. meddling in its affairs. This was, however, not the case. For one thing, it is possible that by subsidizing exported Twente products the N.H.M. made it more difficult for Helmond to compete against Twente on the local market, for which Helmond produced exclusively. More serious, perhaps, was that the Dutch government and the N.H.M. diverted the influx of Belgian and Anglo-Belgian entrepreneurs to areas where it was thought they would be needed most, Holland and Twente. North Brabant was thus deprived of the entrepreneurial talent and technological know-how of its competitors. With its characteristic need for learning and "infant-industry" protection the cotton industry consequently suffered.

More than anything else, Helmond just was too small to develop by its own means the technical infrastructure and marketing channels necessary to develop a viable cotton industry. These entry costs had risen considerably between 1800 and 1830. The later a region started with the conversion of its Z-good industry to a modern industry, the higher the initial barrier they had to overcome. Helmond was too late and too small. In addition, the "imported" and subsidized entrepreneurs in Holland may have had an unfavorable influence in that they put out much work to North Brabant.[127] The result was that Helmond manufacturers had to bid up wages paid to their weavers.[128] The consequent rise in wages may have been detrimental to the modernization of the Helmond cotton industry.

A comparison between North Brabant and Twente is not really meaningful, since the latter specialized in calicoes while in the former the modernizing sector was woolen manufactures. In any case, it can safely be said that in the period 1830–50, the foundations for a modern textile industry were laid in the Netherlands. In spite of the fact that, especially in Twente, the road followed to "modernity" was not always the shortest,

126. Mansvelt, *Geschiedenis van de N.H.M.*, 1: 266.
127. Ibid., p. 308.
128. Harkx, *Helmondse Textielnijverheid*, p. 137.

it did eventually lead to the emergence of a mechanized textile industry. However, in 1850 both Twente and North Brabant were still quite far from the target. An attempt to analyze why it was in these areas that the first enclaves of modern industry were formed will be presented in chapter 5.

Finally, no account of Dutch industry in the first half of the nineteenth century would be complete without mention of one of the most impressive and successful entrepreneurs in Dutch history, Petrus Regout. A recent biography has shed considerable light on this fascinating case of "entrepreneurial history."[129] The city of Maastricht, in which Regout was active all his life, was in more than one sense a part of Belgium rather than of the Netherlands. In the eighteenth century, it had been a garrison city and was annexed to France as early as 1795, together with the Belgian provinces. No dramatic economic changes occurred in it during the French occupation, except for the emergence of some "hothouse" industries, which vanished again after 1815. In the Dutch period (1815–30), the garrison was gradually liquidated, but the economic effects of this on the city were offset by the opening of the Zuid Willemsvaart, a canal connecting the Meuse with the Rhine in 1826, causing an increasing amount of goods to be transported on the Meuse.

The Belgian Revolution put a temporary end to the transit of goods from Belgium through Maastricht, after the Dutch imposed a prohibition on imports from the rebellious provinces. What happened was that the influx of Belgian goods was not stopped effectively, but shifted to illegitimate smuggling routes, most of them via Germany. The official transit route through Maastricht was closed down, with disastrous effects on the town. Moreover, since Maastricht was considered (probably justly) sympathetic to the rebels, the importation of goods manufactured there was equally prohibited. The town was declared under state of siege, implying that all movement to and from the city required special permits. The Meuse was blocked and the Zuid Willemsvaart sabotaged by the Belgians.

In 1833, quite unexpectedly, the desperate situation was diametrically reversed. The Dutch authorities allowed the restoration of trade between Maastricht and the rest of the Netherlands, provided the goods traded were not of Belgian origin. This ordinance was complemented in 1834 by an order permitting the import of Belgian raw materials or semifinished products into Maastricht, provided these goods served as inputs for industries located within the city.[130]

---

129. A. J. F. Maenen, *Petrus Regout, 1801–1878, een Bijdrage tot de Sociaal-Economische Geschiedenis van Maastricht* [Petrus Regout, 1801–1878, a contribution to the social-economic history of Maastricht] (Nijmegen: N. V. Centrale Drukkerij, 1959).

130. Ibid., p. 19.

As Maenen stresses, it is difficult to overestimate the importance of the latter decree for the future development of industry in Maastricht. It clearly placed the city at an advantage relative to the rest of the Netherlands, which had no access to Belgian-made intermediate inputs or at least had to pay a smuggling premium for them. The same is true, *mutatis mutandis*, for the relative position of Maastricht vis à vis Belgium. For a few years, Maastricht enjoyed an exceptionally advantageous position, and it was in precisely these years that Maastricht's industry was consolidated.

It should be emphasized that in addition to the "institutional windfall" of the 1833–34 ordinances, Maastricht enjoyed some structural advantages which accounted for its overall successful development, at least when compared to the maritime provinces. These advantages are well summed up by Maenen:

> It is obvious why the modern economic spirit emerged so much earlier in Maastricht than in North-Netherlands. The orientation of Maastricht on Belgium and in particular on the industrial area of Liège [the distance between the two cities is only 15 miles], created in Maastricht a different race of manufacturers, manufacturers who were able to keep up to date on the most modern production methods. Technical know-how as well as raw materials and semifinished products were imported from Belgium. . . . There was no lack of potential factory workers: due to the decline of handicrafts and commerce the army of paupers had grown enormously and these impoverished people had to find in industry a means of subsistence.[131]

The first argument in this quote seems unassailable. But the second raises some difficulties: armies of impoverished urban paupers existed in much larger numbers in the maritime provinces. One wonders why this factor, if it was so important, failed to operate in Holland and Utrecht while successful in Maastricht. In any event, Maenen's view of the modern factory system in Maastricht as basically successful as compared with the rest of the country seems appropriate. The development of this industry was led by a single pioneer, Petrus Regout.

Regout was an ambitious and dynamic entrepreneur, fully aware of the need to keep up to date with both technology and consumers' tastes. He traveled extensively, visited international exhibitions, and maintained commercial relations with many countries. Regout started off as a merchant and remained one all his life. His most important industrial endeavor was the manufacture of glass. Before 1830 he had been a merchant in glasswares, maintaining a small workshop in which a few workmen were

131. Ibid., p. 29.

employed in polishing. Initially, the polishing of glass was, however, wholly subordinate to the trade, and in this respect he had a typical "traffic" business. The events of 1833–34 made it profitable to import large quantities of unpolished glass from the Val St. Lambert works and to have it polished in Maastricht. The factory was opened in 1834, with 80 workers operating 80 polishing machines moved by an 8 HP steam engine.[132] The directors of the Val St. Lambert works feared that Regout's glass polishing plant might endanger their market in the Netherlands (until 1835, they exported glassware to the Netherlands through Germany, with Belgian glass presented as of German origin). As a warning, they cut off supplies of unpolished glass to Regout. The latter managed, however, to find an alternative source of supplies in Namur. As the gigantic Société Anonyme des Manufactures de Glaces, which owned the Val St. Lambert, continued to purchase glass works throughout Belgium in the late 1830s, Regout lost his sources of supply once again. This induced him to take up glassblowing himself in 1839.

By the decision to produce the whole product rather than refining semifinished products, Regout's traffic was transformed into a full-fledged industry. The initial capital was provided in part by a loan of 30,000 florins from William I, while the skilled labor was largely imported from Belgium. In the same year, 1839, the final settlement of the Dutch-Belgian conflict was signed, and the prohibition on Belgian imports to the Netherlands was lifted. The Belgian glass industry had suffered some setbacks between 1834 and 1839[133] and dumped large quantities of finished products on the Dutch market. Yet, in spite of the advantages which protectionist Belgium may have provided over free trade Nether-lands,[134] Regout's new plant withstood the competition successfully and expanded continuously, becoming by 1850 one of the very few truly modern industrial concerns in the Netherlands.

Regout's earthenware factory was equally successful. The European market for pottery had been flooded by high quality British manufactures in the decades following 1815. Consequently, continental producers shifted to the production of cheap pottery, intended for low income consumers. Maastricht was well-located for the manufacture of earthenware, since both the fuel and earth needed as raw materials were found relatively nearby. Regout's products were qualitatively inferior to English goods,

132. Ibid., p. 185.
133. The extent of the crisis in the Belgian glass industry following the revolution of 1830 is overstated by Maenen, *Petrus Regout*, pp. 202–03. Cf. Chambon, *L'Histoire de la Verrerie*, pp. 171, 174.
134. The tariff on 100 kgs. polished crystal was 5.17 florins in the Netherlands and 53.33 florins in Belgium. For unpolished crystal the tariffs were, respectively, 3.94 and 23.18 florins.

but were on the average 40–50 percent cheaper.[135] In 1845 however, Regout hired an Englishman, William Crisp, as a technical adviser to his earthenware factory, and by 1850, his products were, according to contemporary specialists, qualitatively equivalent to the English products. Regout's earthenware was well on its way to becoming "one of the largest enterprises in this area in Europe, making Maastricht world famous."[136] On the other hand, Regout's attempts to produce substitutes for the Belgian iron industry, such as his nail factory and his armaments plant, failed.

The exceptional development of Maastricht should not be too puzzling. Geographically, and to a large extent ethnically, the city should be considered a part of Belgium. In addition, the city enjoyed exceptionally favorable political circumstances. Moreover, Regout had unusually good political connections. The favorable royal order of 1834 as well as the loan received in 1839 and other favors were obtained through the intermediation of the special commissary for Limburg, Gericke van Herwijnen.

Maastricht, then, occupied an exceptional position in the Netherlands and Regout occupied an exceptional position in Maastricht. There was more modern industry, however, in Dutch Limburg. The paper industry in Maastricht and Roermond had by 1850 overtaken the traditional paper mills in the Zaan area, both in size and in technological progress.[137] It is clear that "traditional" Netherlands, unlike Dutch Limburg, was unable to capitalize on the spillovers of Belgian industrialization, magnified by favorable policies of the Dutch government and Petrus Regout's entrepreneurial talents.

CONCLUDING REMARKS

It has been shown above in some detail that the Netherlands failed to undergo the process of industrialization, in the sense of adopting new, capital intensive, and mechanized techniques in manufacturing. In some industries, notably metallurgy and machinery, modernization was almost entirely absent or quantitatively insignificant. In textiles, no doubt the most rapidly modernizing consumers' good in England and Belgium, expansion in the Netherlands occurred largely *within* the traditional sector rather than side by side with it. Consequently, the old-fashioned, manual techniques were not replaced by more efficient, modern techniques. A few enclaves of modernity have been pointed out, such as the

135. Maenen, *Petrus Regout*, p. 227.
136. Everwijn, *Beschrijving van Handel en Nijverheid*, p. 147.
137. Brugmans, *Arbeidende Klasse*, p. 38. B. W. de Vries, *Nederlandse Papiernijverheid*, pp. 205–08.

woolen industry in Tilburg, Regout's glass and earthenware works in Maastricht, the sugar refining and shipbuilding industries in the West, but these were too small and too scattered to change the overall picture significantly.

The contrast with developments in Belgium, as sketched in chapter 2, is thus striking. Nevertheless, it is imperative to conduct the comparison between the two countries on a more rigorous, that is, quantitative, basis. The need for such a comparison is logical: it has been shown that Belgium had a higher *rate* of industrialization but also that the Netherlands started from a higher basis, being more industrialized and technologically more advanced in 1795. The net result is not a priori obvious, since without being able to parametrize the two paths of growth, the relative positions of the two countries in the subsequent period is indeterminate.

The absence of comparable statistics is almost unsurmountable here. GNP figures, or anything which could be used as a proxy for them, do not become available before the twentieth century. An index for Belgian industrial production starting in 1831 has been compiled,[138] but since none exists for the Netherlands, it could not be used for comparative purposes. Some quantitative information is available on foreign trade, the number and capacity of steam engines in operation, patent registrations, and the performance of the two countries at international industrial exhibitions. In the present section, an attempt will be made to present some very crude, indirect comparative estimates to indicate the orders of magnitude involved.

The quality of the Belgian statistics after 1830 is unmatched by the Dutch, and foreign trade statistics are no exception to this rule. Immediately following the revolution, detailed data on Belgian foreign trade became available, rapidly improving in quality.[139] The first detailed tables on Dutch foreign trade appeared in 1847.[140] The quality of the early Dutch foreign trade statistics can hardly be underestimated. For one thing, the figures are all in current prices, that is to say, in values as given on the merchants declarations. This would subject the data to biases of indeterminate size and direction. The tables differentiate in principle between "general commerce" (including also goods in transit) and "special commerce" (consisting only of imports for domestic consumption and exports of domestically produced goods), but in practice, the distinction cannot

138. J. Gadisseur, "L'Indice de la Production Industrielle en Belgique de 1830 à 1913," 2 vols., mimeographed (Liège: 1971).

139. *Statistique de la Belgique, Tableau Général du Commerce* 1832, and subsequent issues.

140. *Statistiek van de Handel en de Scheepvaart van het Koninkrijk der Nederlanden* 1846 and subsequent years [Statistics of the trade and shipping of the kingdom of the Netherlands] (The Hague: Giunta d'Albani for the Department of Finance, 1847 and subsequent years).

be said to have been carried out meticulously. For example, the series of exports "from the free traffic," that is, exports of Dutch products, includes every year a few million florins worth of raw cotton. The figures for the flows of bullion are, by the compilers' own admission, wholly erroneous.[141] Finally, the classification of commodities into various groups is not wholly consistent. The comparison between the two countries based on foreign trade statistics can thus not be assigned excessive significance. Nonetheless, the differences in structure are marked enough to survive even large cumulative errors and most other imaginable quibbles on the quality of the data. The results are presented in tables 3.11 and 3.12.

The absolute foreign trade values mean little, since the Dutch data are in current prices, while the Belgian data are in constant prices. The proportions presented in tables 3.11 and 3.12, however, show clearly

Table 3.11   Percentage Composition of Dutch and Belgian Foreign Trade, 1846–50

		Exports		Imports	
	Class	Belgium	Netherlands	Belgium	Netherlands
1846	Food	7.69	61.09	48.59	34.24
	Manufactures	44.87	18.52	15.37	26.39
	Raw materials	47.44	20.39	36.04	39.37
	Total	100.00	100.00	100.00	100.00
1847	Food	11.52	65.56	48.89	38.36
	Manufactures	40.10	16.11	14.65	24.22
	Raw materials	48.38	18.33	36.46	37.42
	Total	100.00	100.00	100.00	100.00
1848	Food	18.88	65.89	51.82	34.52
	Manufactures	40.47	15.76	11.93	25.70
	Raw materials	40.65	18.35	36.25	39.78
	Total	100.00	100.00	100.00	100.00
1849	Food	18.76	62.43	39.06	34.18
	Manufactures	38.50	14.69	14.93	25.47
	Raw materials	42.74	22.87	46.01	40.35
	Total	100.00	100.00	100.00	100.00
1850	Food	17.00	62.22	41.28	32.46
	Manufactures	38.75	15.66	16.34	26.65
	Raw materials	44.25	22.12	42.38	40.89
	Total	100.00	100.00	100.00	100.00

SOURCES: Computed from *Statistique de la Belgique*, *Tableau Général du Commerce*, passim; *Statistiek van den Handel*, passim.

141. For a long list of defects, see ibid., vol. 1 (1846): iv–vii. One cannot help being reminded of the ancient Hebrew saying "It is a poor dough which the baker proclaims bad."

Table 3.12   Export-Import Ratios for Belgium and the Netherlands, 1846–50

	Class	Belgium	The Netherlands
1846	Food	0.13	1.27
	Manufactures	2.47	0.50
	Raw materials	1.11	0.37
	Total	0.85	0.71
1847	Food	0.21	1.23
	Manufactures	2.42	0.48
	Raw materials	1.17	0.35
	Total	0.89	0.72
1848	Food	0.30	1.39
	Manufactures	2.78	0.45
	Raw materials	0.92	0.34
	Total	0.82	0.73
1849	Food	0.46	1.30
	Manufactures	2.45	0.41
	Raw materials	0.88	0.40
	Total	0.95	0.71
1850	Food	0.46	1.42
	Manufactures	2.64	0.43
	Raw materials	1.16	0.40
	Total	1.11	0.74

SOURCES: *Statistique de la Belgique, Tableau Général du Commerce*, passim; *Statistiek van den Handel*, passim.

that by the end of the 1840s, the Netherlands exported largely agricultural goods and imported most of its consumption of industrial products. Belgium, on the other hand, had become a net importer of food, paying for its imports by the exports of finished manufactures and raw materials. Belgian manufactured exports exceed imports by a factor of two and a half, while its food imports exceed its exports by a factor of more than two throughout the 1830s and 1840s, and by much more than that during the crop failures of the mid-forties. In the Netherlands the export-import ratios are closer to unity which seemingly indicates less specialization, but in reality was a result of specialization in some agricultural goods while others were imported. The deficit on current account (proportional to the overall export-import ratio) is a result of the exports of the service sector and interest payments, which were still of importance in this period.

A second indicator of the size of the gap that had formed between the two countries is the industrial capital stock, on which the number and capacity of the steam engines employed in industry furnish some evidence. Unfortunately, the data for the Netherlands are not available in a degree of detail which can be compared to the Belgian figures presented in chapter 2.[142] In 1837 the total number of steam engines, excluding ships and locomotives, in the Netherlands was 73, with a total capacity of 1,120 HP. In 1853 the number of machines had risen to 392 with a total capacity of 7,193.25 HP.[143] In Belgium the total number of steam engines in 1850 was 2,040, with a capacity of 51,055 HP. Subtracting the steam engines employed in the coal mines leaves 1,428 machines with a capacity of 22,355 HP. The ratio of Dutch to Belgian industry was thus 1 : 5.2 with respect to the number of machines and 1 : 3.1 with respect to capacity. The heavier capacity of Dutch steam engines is explained by the greater proportion of steam engines employed in corn and oil mills and sugar refineries in the Netherlands. The distribution of steam power over the various Dutch industries can be computed from a document from 1857 which provides raw data on capacity of industrial steam engines.[144] A summary computed from this source is presented in table 3.13 juxtaposed with the Belgian data.

The significance of the steam engine figures will be clear if it is remembered that the population of the Netherlands in 1857 was about 3.2 million, as compared with Belgium's 4.4 million in 1850. The quantitative gap reflected by the figures in table 3.13 is compounded by a structural difference. A relatively large proportion of Dutch steam power is employed in food production, whereas the steam power in metallurgy, including the production of capital goods and steam engines, is far smaller, even on a relative basis, than in Belgium.

Another indication of the different stages of development reached by the two countries is the proportion of the labor force employed in manufacturing. Needless to say, this measure has many pitfalls which should warn the reader not to rely on it except as corroborating evidence. In addition, the data that can be used for this comparison contain grave inconsistencies and merely indicate orders of magnitude. Still, it is striking that the proportion of the Belgian labor force employed in manufactures in 1846 was one and a half times as large as in the Nether-

142. See above, pp. 81–82.
143. *Staatkundig en Staathuishoudkundig Jaarboekje* [Yearbook of politics and political economy], 7 (1855): 69. No additional information can be gained from the time series presented by J. H. van Stuijvenberg, "Economische Groei in Nederland in de 19ᶜ Eeuw: Een Terreinverkenning" [Economic growth in the Netherlands in the nineteenth century: A Reconnaissance] in *Bedrijf en Samenleving*, Festschrift presented to I. J. Brugmans (Alphen on the Rhine-Brussels: N. Samson, 1967), p. 223, since his continuous series is based on geometrical interpolations.
144. *Staat van de Nederlandsche Fabrieken volgens de Verslagen der Gemeenten, Uitgegeven door de Nederlandsche Maatschappij ter Bevordering van Nijverheid* [Table of the Dutch factories, according to the reports of the municipalities, published by the Dutch society for the advancement of industry] (Haarlem: de Erven Loosjes, 1859).

Table 3.13   Steam Engine Capacity in Industry in the
Netherlands (1857) and Belgium (1850)

Activity	Capacity in HP		Percentage	
	Belgium	Netherlands	Belgium	Netherlands
Metallurgy	8,850	1,099.5	39.6	16.6
Cotton	1,994	512	8.9	7.7
Wool	1,864	570	8.3	8.6
Linen	1,164	45	5.2	0.7
Unclassified and other textiles	241	189	1.1	2.8
Glass, pottery	376	299	1.7	4.5
Paper	557	258	2.5	3.9
Foodstuffs	4,658	2,538.5	20.8	38.3
Others	2,651	1,122	11.9	16.9
Total	22,355	6,633	100.0	100.0

SOURCES: Netherlands—computed from *Staat van de Nederlandsche Fabrieken*, passim. Belgium—table 2.19.

lands: about 32 percent in Belgium as opposed to about 22 percent in the Netherlands.[145]

A fourth measure of the gap emerging between the two countries relates to the difference in innovative activity. An indicator of this activity is found in the patents granted to inventors and importers of new equipment from abroad.[146] In general, international comparisons of the number of patents are meaningless, because different patent laws, or even different attitudes to patents by different bureaucracies, were likely to result in different numbers of patents issued.

Fortunately, Belgium and the Netherlands formed one country between 1814 and 1830, and for that period it is possible to compare the intensity of the processes of technological change in the two parts of the kingdom, by using the registration figures at the patent office in The Hague. Patents were granted both for new inventions and for the adoption of foreign

145. The figures are summarized in Simon Kuznets, *Economic Growth of Nations, Total Output and Production Structure* (Cambridge: Harvard University Press, 1971), pp. 262–63. The figures for Belgium are based on the census of 1846, while the Dutch data come from the 1849 population census. The problems involved in using the 1846 Belgian census for estimating the number of workers employed in manufacturing, especially the domestic industry, are discussed in chap. 2. As for the Dutch data, see the critique in J. A. de Jonge, *De Industrializatie in Nederland tussen 1850 en 1914* [The industrialization in the Netherlands between 1850 and 1914] (Amsterdam: Scheltema en Holkema, 1968), pp. 8–9, 19.

146. The use of patent statistics as an index of inventive activity is not new and has culminated in the work of Jacob Schmookler. For a summary of the merits and pitfalls of this source of information, see A. E. Musson, ed., *Science, Technology and Economic Growth in the Eighteenth Century* (London: Methuen, 1972), pp. 24–27, 49–52.

inventions. It is open to doubt, perhaps, whether all inventions were in fact wholly new or whether some were merely adaptations, minor improvements on foreign inventions, or at times outright thefts of foreign (mostly English and French) inventions. At any rate, the number of patents should reflect the overall propensity of industries and regions to engage in innovations and to adopt new techniques to the production process.

Dutch patent statistics up to the abolition of the Dutch patent law (1869) have been compiled with annotations by G. Doorman.[147] Doorman's lists provide not only the nature of the invention but also the residence of the person applying. It is therefore possible to classify the patents issued between 1817 and 1830 by sector according to industry and according to whether the applicant was Belgian or Dutch. The results demonstrate quite clearly that most of the technological change was concentrated in Belgium. Of the total number of patents, only 27.6 percent were issued to the Dutch. Moreover, in those activities in which technological change had the most economic significance, the Belgian domination was even more clear-cut. In textiles, 85.7 percent of all patents were granted to Belgians; in metallurgy their share was 94.7 percent. The Belgian provinces accounted for 76.3 percent of all patents in the capital goods industry (construction, tools, machinery). Not much better was the Dutch performance in food and distilling industries (21.3 percent) and the paper and printing industries (18.2 percent). Only in chemicals (32.3 percent) and shipping (51.9 percent) did the Netherlands account for a respectable share.[148] Crude as the patent statistics may be as indices of innovative activity, these gaps clearly demonstrate that the *absolute size* of the modernizing sector in Belgium was much larger than that in the Netherlands.

A final comparative indicator is the overall performance of the two countries in the various international industrial exhibitions in which both participated.[149] The results, in terms of medals and distinctions awarded, provide at least a prima facie indicator of the degree of technological advancement attained by the participating countries. Technology is extremely difficult to quantify, and naturally many criticisms can be put forward against the use of exhibition data. For one thing, performance at the exhibitions is an imperfect measure of industrialization. In general,

147. G. Doorman, *Het Nederlandsch Octrooiwezen en de Techniek der 19ᶜ Eeuw* [The Dutch patent system and nineteenth century technology] (The Hague: Martinus Nijhoff, 1947).

148. All figures computed from ibid., pp. 115–76.

149. The significance as well as the limitations of exhibition data as a source of historical information have not yet fully been recognized by economic historians. A pioneering study in this respect is H. Baudet, "De Dadels van Hassan en de Start der Nederlandse Industrialiteit" [The beginning of Dutch industrialism] in *Bedrijf en Samenleving*, pp. 1–15. See also von Baumhauer, *Voorlezingen*, pp. 1–38.

exhibitions tended to reward quality, not quantity, although in some instances there was an emphasis not only on quality per se but also on low
prices, that is, technical efficiency. Moreover, countries with a thin, highly
specialized luxury industry tended to outperform countries concentrating
on cheap, mass-produced consumer goods. Countries which were more
diversified in their industrial production tended to do better in exhibitions
than countries that exhibited in a single branch in which they had a comparative advantage. Success in industrial exhibitions also reflected the
ability and desire to exhibit. It is likely that technological competence and
motivation to exhibit were positively correlated, but unless this correlation
was very strong, performance in exhibitions would not be an unbiased
indicator of their technological level. Equally serious was the bias created
by the uneven composition of juries; the awarding of medals involved
much "wheeling and dealing," and efforts on the part of governments to
put as many of its nationals as possible on juries could affect a country's
performance positively.

Table 3.14   Scores on Industrial Exhibitions by Dutch and Belgian Participants

	Haarlem, 1825		London, 1851		Paris, 1855[a]	
	Belgium	Netherlands	Belgium	Netherlands	Belgium	Netherlands
Mining	—	—	35	0	90	0
Engineering, machines	234	119	54	10	186	30
Metallurgy			26	7	59	8
Cotton	225	23	3	0	33	2
Wool	102	68	9	3	59	7
Linen, hemp	275	102	23	2	150	6
Other textiles	104	136	76	2	59	13
Paper	73	99	8	4	9	3
Glass, pottery	63	34	3	2	29	2
Chemicals	58	78	6	4	78	20
Foodstuffs, agriculture	—	—	44	10	53	19
Others	105	103	48	6	87	38
Total	1,239	762	335	50	892	148

[a]Includes only the awards won by exhibits, not the distinctions won by individual co-
opérateurs.
SOURCES: 1825—*Rapport der Hoofdcommissie ter Beoordeling der Voorwerpen van Nationale
Nijverheid, tentoongesteld te Haarlem in de Maanden Juli en Augustus 1825* [Report of the
commission judging the entries in the industrial exhibition in Haarlem in July and August
1825] (The Hague, 1825), pp. 252–87. 1851—*Exhibition of the Works of Industry of all Nations,
Reports by the Juries* (London: Spicer Brothers, 1852), pp. xxxv–cxx. 1855—*Exposition
Universelle de 1855, Rapports du Jury Mixte Internationale* (Paris: Imprimerie Impériale,
1856), 2 vols., passim.

All in all, the use of exhibition results as a yardstick for the relative levels of industrial technology in Belgium and the Netherlands seems permissible as long as we restrict the analysis to exhibitions in which the two countries competed under similar conditions. Three exhibitions were chosen: the Haarlem exhibition of 1825, which was on a national basis, before the division of the United Kingdom of the Netherlands into two states, and the two great international exhibitions of London (1851) and Paris (1855). To make the figures comparable, the awards were converted into scores by the simple procedure of assigning a score of one to the lowest distinction, a score of two for the second lowest, etc. The results are reproduced in table 3.14.

It can be verified from table 3.14 that the gap between the two countries was still relatively small in 1825. At this period, as was shown above, Belgium had completed a quarter century of rapid, though erratic, technological progress, while the Netherlands had just begun to recover from a severe crisis which had lasted for more than two decades. Still, the difference in the *absolute levels* of industrial technology was as yet of modest proportions in the 1820s. At the given difference in the rate of accumulation of capital goods and the technology they embodied, twenty-five more years created a very large gap in industrial technology. In both the London and the Paris exhibitions, Belgium outscored the Netherlands by a ratio of better than 6 : 1. This is not to say that this ratio reflects a cardinal measurement of technological progress—but as an ordinal measure, it seems not entirely without significance. Clearly, by the mid-nineteenth century, a large technological gap between the two countries had emerged.

4 A MODEL OF EARLY EUROPEAN INDUSTRIALIZATION

It is easy enough to make models on stated assumptions. The difficulty
is to find the assumptions that are relevant to reality. The art is to
set up a scheme that simplifies the problem so as to make it manageable
without eliminating the essential character of the actual situation
on which it is intended to throw light.

Joan Robinson

At this stage, it may be useful to restate the "stylized," that is, essentially true historical development described in chapters 1–3. These stylized facts are a condensed summary of the chief elements in the industrialization process in the Low Countries, as well as in some other European regions and countries to varying degrees. Any model that purports to formalize the course of modernization in the first half of the nineteenth century will have to be able to reproduce them.

The industrial revolution was, as John Hicks noted, the rise of modern industry, not of industry as such.[1] But what is it that distinguishes modern from ancient industry? For the present purposes, it seems convenient to adopt Hicks's definition and to define the discontinuous element in the industrial revolution as the becoming available of new techniques which made it possible to produce consumer goods by means of a combination of fixed capital and labor rather than by labor alone.[2] From this, it follows that the process we are dealing with is a *transition* between two production

---

1. John R. Hicks, *A Theory of Economic History* (Oxford: Oxford University Press, 1969), p. 141.
2. Ibid., pp. 142–43. See also John C. H. Fei and Gustav Ranis, "Economic Development in Historical Perspective," *AER* 39, no. 2 (May 1969): 395–97. Capital in the preindustrial "epoch" was largely circulating capital not directly involved in the production process and thus of an entirely different character than fixed capital, the accumulation of which forms the focus of the following discussion. Needless to say, other definitions of the industrial revolution exist, but for the present purposes, the above seems the most useful.

techniques, a manual and a mechanized technique. Such a transition implies ipso facto that for some period of time the two techniques coexisted side by side. The coexistence of the "old" with the "new" seems to have been a pivotal element in the European economies in the period under discussion. What is at stake, then, is the speed at which the transition occurs and the time span of the transition period.

In general, it may be incorrect to assume that technology emerged independently of initial economic conditions. With regard to continental Europe between 1795 and 1850, however, it seems more justifiable to speak of a process of emulation than a process of innovation. Europe tried to imitate the techniques developed in England, while its own contribution to the technological improvements which transformed industry was comparatively modest. In France, this may have been less true than for the Low Countries or Germany. At any rate, in the following model, technology will be treated as exogenously given.[3]

The absence of capital markets and the consequent reliance on self-finance for the accumulation of capital constitutes an essential element of the model. Two basic variants of such a model can be distinguished: a rigid reinvestment model in which each firm in the modern sector is confined to its previous profits for the finance of investment, or a less rigid model permitting capital flows among firms within the modern sector. The latter form of the model became more significant as time passed. Capital flows to the modern sector from extrasectoral savings were empirically insignificant and will not be allowed for in the model.[4] Nor is there any indication of large amounts of savings generated by industrial workers, who were formally part of the modern sector.[5]

The labor for modern industry came essentially from workers previously employed in the traditional sector.[6] This is almost a tautology, but it is important to realize that traditional sectors might be—and Belgium and some parts of the Netherlands certainly were—already industrialized to a great extent. As will be shown below, it is immaterial whether the workers who became the urban industrial proletariat came originally from

    3. Cf. above, p. 50. This is not to say that no diffusion lags occurred.
    4. Cf. above, pp. 39–41, 50, 64. Similar arguments have been made for France and England. See, e.g., D. Landes, *The Unbound Prometheus* (Cambridge: At the University Press, 1969), pp. 130, 131n. François Crouzet, "Capital Formation in Great Britain during the Industrial Revolution," in *Capital Formation in the Industrial Revolution*, ed. François Crouzet (London: Methuen, 1972), p. 188.
    5. G. Arrivabene, *Sur la Condition des Laboureurs et des Ouvriers Belges* (Brussels: Méline, Cans et Cie., 1845), p. 10.
    6. It is frequently argued that population growth was the source of the labor for modern industry. Incremental population, born with a pair of hands but no capital, is for the purpose of our model a part of the traditional, manual labor sector which determines its opportunity cost in other uses.

the rural-industrial ("Z-good") sector or were mostly active in agriculture. The central contention here is that it was through the supply of manpower that the interaction between the traditional and the modern sector took place.[7]

The process of accumulation of capital and the concomitant rise in the overall capital-labor ratio did not result in a rise in the wage level.[8] The "surplus" created by the increased productivity of labor accrued mostly to capitalists who consumed part of it and reinvested the remainder. The rest of the surplus was transferred to consumers in the form of lower prices for industrial goods.

The European economies in the first half of the nineteenth century were basically open economies and a large segment of their industrial product of both the traditional and the modern industry was exported and sold at the world market.[9] Since the two countries dealt with specifically were relatively small, it can be assumed that their overall impact on world prices was small. This assumption can, however, be relaxed without altering the basic structure of the model and its basic conclusions.

A direct corollary of the above is that the ability of the agricultural sector to generate an increasing surplus of food products, which has often been regarded as a necessary condition for industrialization, may have been of less importance than has been thought. In the eighteenth century a process of interregional and international specialization was taking place.[10] Some areas that were more amenable to technological progress in agriculture specialized in agrarian activities, while other areas for a variety of reasons specialized in Z-goods. The latter complemented their deficits in food production by imports which were paid for with Z-goods. The transformation of Z-good sectors into modern industries required in principle no transfer of workers from agriculture to industry. It is therefore not clear whether industrialization reduced supply of agricultural goods. Nor did urbanization and concentration of workers in large-scale, capital-intensive industry imply necessarily an increased demand for food if the wages earned by labor did not rise significantly. The industrialization process can thus be viewed as an internal change which occurred within a composite industrial sector. At least for a small region or country, it may be assumed that the terms of trade at which goods were exchanged between

7. Cf. above, pp. 36–38, 66.

8. The evidence for this will be presented in chapter 5. For the similarity of the case of England to the pattern described here, cf. P. Deane, *The First Industrial Revolution* (Cambridge: At the University Press, 1969), p. 138.

9. For a recent reemphasis of the "openness" of the European economy, see S. Pollard, "Industrialization and the European Economy," *EHR* 26, no. 4 (November 1973): 636–48.

10. E. L. Jones, "Agricultural Origins of Industry," *P and P* 40 (July 1968): 58–71. Reprinted in *Agriculture and the Industrial Revolution* (Oxford: Blackwell's, 1974), pp. 128–42.

the "industrial" and the "agricultural" sector were determined in the world market and unaffected by anything that happened to the internal balance between the two sectors.

In spite of the concentration of the model on long-term, structural changes, it is important to note that the rate of capital accumulation is relatively independent of short-term fluctuations in world demand. A naive model of a small, open economy would postulate that the rate of accumulation varies directly with the level of foreign demand and the world price level. This seems to be less than correct for the case of Belgium.[11]

Which characteristics would be required from a model that was to reproduce the above stylized facts and in addition provide a plausible explanation of Belgium's success in industrialization in contrast to the failure of the Netherlands? Perhaps the most important point to keep in mind is that steady state properties, which figure so prominently in modern growth theory, are not particularly relevant here, since the industrial revolution was not a process of steady state growth. Rather, it seems that the industrial revolution should be regarded as what Hicks calls the "traverse" or movement from one steady state to another. An illuminating view of the process of rapid and discontinuous industrialization is presented by Bensusan-Butt, who looks upon economic growth as the transition between a steady state characterized by a very low capital-labor ratio to one in which a much higher capital-labor ratio prevails.[12]

It follows that the main dynamic force in the development of the economy is the accumulation of capital and the concomitant rise of the capital-labor ratio. It will be useful to take as the starting point an economy in which the amount of capital is zero. That this is an oversimplification in a historical context is evident, but for the present purposes of little importance as long as it is assumed that the initial state is much less capital-intensive than the final. What should be emphasized is that the present model is focused upon the transition period between two stationary states. Indeed, the final stationary state need never be reached—as long as technological change and/or population growth continues, the capital-labor ratio, or even its rate of growth, need never become constant.

The reason for the necessity to deal with non-steady-state models in this context is rather obvious. As was argued above, the industrial revolution was a process that radically altered the structure and sectoral balance in the economies involved, in addition to its, equally crucial, quantitative

11. See above, pp. 33, 51.

12. D. M. Bensusan-Butt, *On Economic Growth, An Essay in Pure Theory*, reprint ed. (Oxford: Oxford University Press, 1963). The indebtedness of the following to this magnificent little book will be evident.

aspects. Steady states deal exclusively with the latter. They have been defined as processes in which "all elements . . . are growing at the same (constant) rate—so that, although there is an absolute expansion, every element remains in the same proportion to every other."[13] The following model could be termed a model of *growing up* rather than a model of growth, since the entire structure of the economy alters in the process.

Ideally, one might desire a highly disaggregated multisectoral model that would accurately reflect the diversity of the old and the new. But such models are very cumbersome. On the other hand, it is necessary to preserve the essential distinction between capital and consumption goods. The model will therefore have two main sectors, a traditional and a modern.[14] The traditional sector consists of the Z-good industry and agriculture. The modern sector consists of a consumption good industry and a capital good industry. In the background there is a third sector, the "rest of the world" sector which purchases industrial goods (produced either in the Z-good or in the modern consumption industry) and supplies the necessary agricultural goods in return.

The presentation below explores the dynamic properties of the path followed by the economy in the growing up process. The discussion is in general terms rather than addressed directly to the two countries with which the rest of this study deals. Since the level of abstraction in the present chapter is higher than in the rest of this study, the application of some of the results of the model to the economy of the Low Countries is deferred to chapter 5. In order to facilitate reading, the text will be accompanied only by diagrams. For an algebraic presentation and some proofs of verbal statements the reader is referred to my dissertation.[15]

THE TRADITIONAL SECTOR

The central macroeconomic relations governing population and consumption per capita were outlined in chapter 1. As was demonstrated there, the Z-good sector, under the assumption of an exogenous world price, removes the constraint imposed by diminishing returns. The emergence of a Z-good sector has a somewhat different long-run impact than technological progress in agriculture. The latter moves the constraint

13. John R. Hicks, *Capital and Growth* (Oxford: Oxford University Press, 1965), p. 133. The stationary state is clearly a special case of the steady state, in which the rate of growth at which all elements are growing is zero.
14. This duality is the dominating feature of many models of economic development inspired by the work of W. Arthur Lewis.
15. Mokyr, "Industrial Growth," pp. 275–304.

on population outwards so that the "trap" prevails at a higher level of population. A protoindustrial sector, on the other hand, could remove the constraint altogether and allow population to grow without limit. A downward sloping demand curve for Z-goods is equivalent to pecuniary diminishing returns, as can be seen from figure 1.1.

In any case, while the assumption of given relative prices may be debatable with respect to the whole economy, it is unassailable at the level of the individual producer. The single peasant, owning or cultivating a given amount of land, faces diminishing returns to labor (measured in manhours) in agriculture but constant returns to labor in Z-good production. At this stage, it will be assumed that no Z-goods are consumed by the peasants and that the entire output of the Z-good industry is exchanged for food, a simplification that does not change the central argument.

The typical peasant's equilibrium is depicted in figure 4.1. The curve MP_A represents the marginal product of labor in agriculture and is downward sloping due to diminishing returns to labor when land is fixed. The line ZZ' depicts the productivity of labor in Z-good production. Its exact height is fully determined by the productivity of labor in Z-good

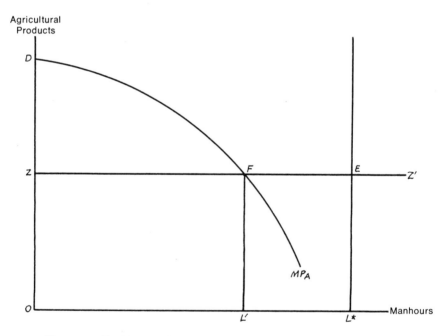

Figure 4.1   Equilibrium of an Individual Peasant in the Traditional Sector

production (marginal and average productivity are identical in a one-factor activity with constant returns to scale) and the relative price of Z-goods in terms of agricultural goods.

Suppose the amount of labor performed annually by each worker is given by L^*. It can clearly be seen that the amount worked is divided between OL', which is allocated to agricultural production, and $L'L^*$, which is allocated to Z-good production. The model is wholly independent of a work-leisure choice, which definitely is not a major issue here.[16] Consider figure 4.1. The diagram has been drawn under the assumption of a fixed labor supply of L^* (for example, a 6-days-a-week, dawn-to-dusk work ethic). However, it will immediately be realized that an upward sloping, downward sloping, or backward bending labor supply can equally be reconciled with the model without changing any of the conclusions. The only difference that a dependence of the labor supply on the "wage" will make is that the actual amount of hours worked will change with relative prices or productivity. A more remote possibility is that the stability of the system may be jeopardized if the labor supply is negatively sloped.

The simple model presented in figure 4.1 suggests a few hypotheses that, in general, are borne out by the facts. First, a rise in the relative price of Z-goods will result in an increase in the amount of labor spent on Z-good production.[17] Second, in areas in which labor productivity in agriculture was low, either because of a high labor-land ratio or because of the poor quality of the soil, Z-goods played a more prominent role in the economy.[18] From this, it immediately follows that technological progress in agriculture would increase the labor time allocated to agriculture in the areas where the change could be applied, while at the same time increasing the Z-good activities in areas which, for whatever reason, did not adopt the new techniques in agriculture. The mechanism which assures this is a rise in the relative price of Z-goods.

The points above are rather transparent, but it is important to stress them because the basic mechanisms of labor allocation and income determination are often misunderstood. It is frequently argued, for instance, that the reason why industrial wages in the countryside were

16. The labor-leisure trade-off is emphasized by Mendels, "Industrialization and Population Pressure," pp. 240–43.

17. Jones stresses the fact that protoindustry in England grew especially between 1650 and 1750, when agricultural prices were depressed. Cf. Jones, "Agricultural Origins," pp. 59–64.

18. H. Kellenbenz, "Industries Rurales en Occident de la Fin du Moyen Age au XVIIIe Siècle," *Annales* 18, no. 15 (September-October 1963): 875. Jones, "Agricultural Origins," p. 64.

low was because the peasants had *some* income from agriculture, to which the Z-good was only a supplement.[19] This argument cannot withstand close scrutiny; it implies that for very low incomes, the marginal utility of leisure is zero whereas the marginal utility of income is positive for some range but at some given level ("subsistence") falls off to zero. In this fashion, presumably, the peasant "shoots" for some level of total annual income. Since most of this "desired" income is earned in agriculture anyway, the residual is then presumably spread over many hours of Z-good production, the opportunity cost of which is zero. The absurdity of the assumptions behind this model is apparent. In addition, it is contradicted by the fact that Z-good production was, in general, associated with low productivity agriculture. In the present model, the marginal utility of leisure and income can take any value—they will only influence the total amount worked, but not the allocation mechanism of labor between agriculture and Z-good production and not the implicit wage per unit of time paid in the Z-good sector.

A slight modification of this result would be obtained if it is assumed that there is imperfect competition in the labor market. Assume that the peasant faces a monopsonistic entrepreneur. In that case he receives a wage which is smaller than his marginal (= average) product. To be precise, the wage he receives is equal to his marginal product, discounted by one plus the reciprocal of the elasticity of his labor supply function to the Z-good entrepreneur. The latter is defined as the difference between his overall supply function of labor and the marginal product of labor in agriculture. The difference between the actual wage received by the peasant for his nonagricultural activities and his marginal product depends on the elasticity of his nonagricultural labor supply. The less elastic this supply, the greater the difference. The elasticity of the single peasant's nonagricultural labor supply will be smaller the more rapidly his marginal product in agriculture diminishes and the less leisure and income can be substituted for each other in the peasant's utility function. One may, however, question the appropriateness of a monopsonistic model to describe the operation of the protoindustrial sectors of premodern Europe, since there is abundant evidence of competitiveness and mobility among the "putters-out."

For all peasants active in the Z-good industry the opportunity cost of a unit of labor is given by the height OZ in figure 4.1. The same is true for peasants who buy rather than sell Z-goods, as long as they are somewhat active in their production. Consider again figure 4.1. Total output per annum is given by the rectangle $FEL'L^{\star}$ (Z-goods) plus the area $DFOL'$

19. Jones, "Agricultural Origins," p. 61. Brugmans, *Arbeidende Klasse*, p. 120.

(A-goods). The latter is composed of the rectangle $ZFOL'$ which represents the contribution of labor to agricultural output and the area DFZ which is the share of land in agricultural product. Obviously the hourly wage (explicit or implicit) is the total annual earnings of labor $OZEL^\star$ divided by the number of hours worked per annum $OL^\star$, OZ. This is the wage any outside employer will have to pay in order to bid away labor from the traditional sector.[20] It is thus immaterial whether the worker bid away from the traditional sector worked exclusively in the Z-good sector or whether he worked only a very small number of hours in the Z-good industry—in both cases his opportunity cost is determined by his marginal productivity in Z-good activity.

The conclusion that the actual proportion of labor devoted to Z-good production does not matter as long as it is positive may have to be revised when seasonality in agriculture is introduced. It has been argued that the highly seasonal nature of agrarian activity was a major factor behind the emergence of the protoindustrial sector altogether.[21] As was shown above, it is perfectly possible to achieve a complete understanding of the economics of Z-good production without resorting to the notion of "labor surplus" in the slack season. In some sense, seasonality could be regarded as a special case of diminishing returns to labor. In principle, it is possible to order the days of the year by their marginal productivity and get a curve similar to the MP_A curve in figure 4.1. Those portions of the curve that fall below the line ZZ' will be defined as the slack season; that is, in those periods in which the marginal productivity of labor in agricultural production falls below that in Z-good production (not necessarily to zero), the peasant will engage in Z-good production.

The full implications of seasonality are, however, somewhat more complex. The reason is that it is impossible to transfer labor from one season to the other. Therefore, each season is defined by the fact that the basic activity in it is of a uniform nature (harvesting, sowing, plowing, threshing, etc.). Within each season, then, the peasant faces diminishing marginal productivity. This idea is presented in figure 4.2.[22] For simplicity, it is assumed that the year consists of three seasons of equal length, each $L^\star/3$ workhours long. It is also assumed that the Z-good sector is completely independent of seasonality.

20. As W. A. Lewis has noted, it is likely that some constant will have to be added to this wage in order to compensate for the psychic costs of alienation, urbanization, etc. This complication will be abstracted from at present. Cf. W. Arthur Lewis, "Economic Development with Unlimited Supplies of Labor," reprinted in *The Economics of Underemployment*, ed. A. N. Agarwala and S. P. Singh (Oxford: Oxford University Press, 1963), pp. 410–11.

21. Mendels, "Protoindustrialization," p. 254.

22. I should like to acknowledge my debt to Dr. Yoav Kislev of Hebrew University for his insightful comments which resulted in the present presentation.

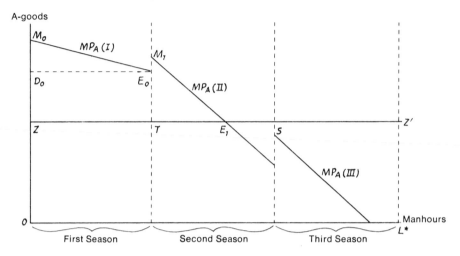

Figure 4.2   Seasonality and Z-good Production in the Traditional Sector

As can be observed from figure 4.2, the first season is wholly devoted to agricultural activity, the second season is split between the two activities, while in the third season ("wintertime") the Z-good is the sole occupation. The allocation of total annual labor between Z-goods and A-goods is still uniquely determined by the distance OZ. The annual income of labor is, however, higher than the rectangle $ZZ'OL^\star$—it is equal to $ZZ'OL^\star$ plus the rectangle ZD_0E_0T. The latter rectangle will be called the Seasonal Agricultural Surplus (SAS). Total earnings of the land are given by the sum of the two triangles $M_0D_0E_0$ and M_1TE_1.

The existence of the SAS has two important implications. The first is related to the concept of subsistence consumption. Assume that there is some level of annual consumption of agricultural goods that is the "biological minimum of subsistence." It is debatable whether it is possible to provide an unambiguous definition of this concept, but these difficulties will be ignored at present. Suppose that it so happens that this critical level of annual consumption is larger than the rectangle $ZZ'OL^\star$ but smaller than or equal to the sum of the latter *plus* the SAS. In this case, the Z-good sector is in some sense supported by the agricultural sector. It still would be false to say that the Z-good sector paid low wages since it was anyway only supplemental to agricultural earnings. It would, however, be correct to state that the wages in the Z-good sector were very low because the productivity of labor in Z-good production was very low, and that the only reason the peasants did not starve was that in some seasons their earnings in agriculture exceeded their marginal productivity in Z-good production. It is likely, moreover, that the SAS was positively correlated to the amount of land owned by the peasant. This would have the result that Z-good production would attain prominence in areas in which equal share inheritance was the rule rather than primogeniture.[23] In other words, a peasant would be unable to maintain himself or herself exclusively on Z-good production, but a relatively small holding (free- or copyheld), though inadequate to maintain a peasant by itself, would provide a sufficient SAS to supplement earnings from Z-good activity.

The second implication of the existence of the SAS is more pertinent to the issue at stake here. Consider an outside employer attempting to bid workers away from the traditional sector. The foregone earnings of the peasant which will have to be compensated for are given by OZ *plus* the daily equivalent of the SAS given by the rectangle ZD_0E_0T divided by the length of $OL^\star$.[24]

A somewhat similar effect results from imperfect land markets. Suppose that through absenteeism, transactions costs in the actual enforcement of contracts, unfamiliarity with conditions on the fields, customary rents, etcetera, landlords are not able to extract the full marginal product of the land. Thus the peasant earns not only the rectangle $ZEOL^\star$ (figure 4.1) but also some part of the area DZF. The latter will be called the Land Market Imperfection Surplus (LIS). It seems likely that the LIS was positive over widespread areas in Europe. If such were the case, peasants bid away from the traditional sector would have to be offered the "going wage" (given by OZ) plus compensation for the loss of the LIS on the part of the peasant moving to the modern sector. A similar result obtains even if there are no landlords and the traditional sector consists exclusively of freeholders. In this case, the peasant earns annually the entire area $ODFEL^\star$ in figure 4.1. If he leaves the land and moves to the city, he can sell or rent the land, so that he still receives the annual rent, given by the area DZF. The opportunity cost of labor is therefore still OZ. If there are, however, imperfections in the land market or very high transactions costs on the alienation of land, the peasant is likely to receive less than the area DZF. The difference is another form of the LIS, and its effect on the wage that an outside employer has to pay is the same.

The essential significance of the SAS and the LIS stems from the fact that both are, in some way, positively associated with the amount of land

23. As has been observed by Joan Thirsk, "Industries in the Countryside," in *Essays in the Economic and Social History of Tudor and Stuart England in Honor of R. H. Tawney*, ed. F. J. Fisher (Cambridge: At the University Press, 1961), pp. 77–78.

24. It is not excluded that the urban employer will be able to operate on a seasonal basis, in which case he can hire workers from the traditional sector in the second and third season, but release them in the first ("harvest") season. To the extent that this is possible, the seasonality modification can be ignored.

per peasant. The net result of seasonality and imperfect land markets is therefore not only that the wage which the outside employer has to pay is higher than the productivity of the peasants in Z-good production, but also that this wage will be rising over time. Continuous hiring of workers from the traditional sector by outside employers will raise the land-labor ratio above the level it would otherwise reach with a growing population and therefore increase the SAS and the LIS for each remaining worker. The implications of rising wages will be dealt with in detail below.

THE MODERN SECTOR

The essential characteristics of the modern sector are the production of consumption goods by labor aided by capital goods and the production of these capital goods themselves. The essential feature of the modern sector is that in it the productivity of labor in making consumption goods exceeds that of the traditional sector. In addition, simplifying assumptions will be made to keep the model manageable. Some of these assumptions will be relaxed at a later stage.

First, it is assumed that the consumption good produced in the modern sector ("textiles") is identical to the good produced in the Z-good sector and that hence the two goods have the same price. Second, it is assumed that the two industries in the modern sector have fixed coefficient (Leontief) production functions.[25] None of the conclusions below depend, however, on this particular form since the model makes heavy use of the Factor Price Frontier (henceforth referred to as FPF) which is the dual of a perfectly general production function. Third, at this stage it will be assumed that machines are perfectly malleable, that is, the capital goods can be shifted costlessly and effortlessly from consumption good production to the production of other capital goods. Machines cannot be consumed, there is no depreciation, and at this stage no technological obsolescence. Furthermore, it is assumed that in the modern sector, as in the Z-good sector, workers consume only agricultural goods. Hence, the entire output of textiles is "exported" to food surplus regions (some of which could conceivably be within the same political boundaries) in exchange for agricultural goods. Fifth, as stressed above, the only source of finance is retained profits. At this stage it will be assumed that the capitalists reinvest a constant proportion of their profits. Finally, population is assumed constant and there is no further technological progress in the modern sector after the initial introduction of the new techniques. Both assumptions are patently unhistorical and will be relaxed in the next section.

25. See Hicks, *Capital and Growth*, chapters 12–16, to which the following is indebted.

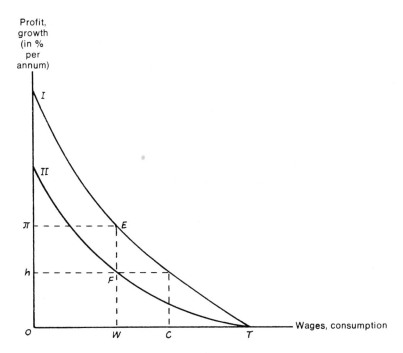

Figure 4.3   Distribution and Accumulation in the Modern Sector

The basic operation of the model is demonstrated in figure 4.3. The diagram makes use of the result that the trade-off between growth and consumption in simple two sector models is mathematically identical to the FPF.[26] This relation is embodied in curve *I* in figure 4.3. The basic saving behavior is given by curve *II*, termed the Kaldor line. In the case in which workers do not save the Kaldor line is proportional to the FPF, the factor of proportionality being equal to the average propensity of capitalists to reinvest. In the special von Neumann-Joan Robinson case in which all profits are reinvested, the two curves will be identical.

In figure 4.3 it can readily be verified that once one of the distribution parameters is exogenously given, the whole system is fully determinate. Suppose for instance that the modern sector can hire workers from the traditional sector at the "going wage," *W*. From the FPF the profit rate π can be read off. From point *E*, the rate of growth, *h*, equal to the rate of profit times the reinvestment propensity of capitalists, can be read off. Every relevant variable can thus be seen to be determined in figure 4.3. The wage rate and workers' consumption are given by *OW*, consumption

26. Michael Bruno, "Fundamental Duality Relations in the Pure Theory of Capital and Growth," *ReStud* 36, no. 1 (January 1969): 39–53.

of capitalists is proportional to WC, and investment is proportional to CT. The rate of profit on capital is given by $O\pi$, the rate of expansion of the economy by Oh.

What determines the location of the FPF? The FPF is uniquely determined for every set of productivity parameters and relative prices.[27] An increase in the productivity of either labor or capital in the production of either "textiles" or machines will shift the FPF outward. Similarly, a rise in the relative price of industrial consumption goods in terms of agricultural goods will shift the FPF outward and vice versa. In addition, the FPF is independent of scale. Therefore, two countries with access to the same technology and the same world market would face essentially the same trade-off between profits and growth on the one hand and wages and consumption on the other. Suppose it was observed that one country consistently experienced a higher rate of expansion than a second. In principle this could be attributed to two different factors: first, the two countries differed in their initial income distributions, so that they would be on different locations along the FPF; second, the two countries could be facing different Kaldor lines due to different savings behavior, so that for the same point E a different point F would obtain. A combination of the two causes is of course possible.

The history of the transformation of the traditional economy into a modern economy can now be traced. Suppose a given mechanized technique becomes suddenly available (say, imported from abroad). There is a minor logical difficulty here. Since it was assumed that there was no capital in the traditional sector and there are no transfers of capital from nonindustrial sources, it is unclear how the very first investments are to be financed. Other writers, dealing with similar models, have encountered the same difficulty and proposed different solutions. Marx argues that:

> The whole movement seems to turn in a vicious circle out of which we can only get by supposing a primitive accumulation...which precedes capitalistic accumulation; an accumulation not the result of the capitalistic mode of production but its starting point.[28]

Others view the initial discontinuity in a less dramatic fashion:

> To get things moving, any kind of appropriate incident...can be imagined....it seems right that the event is small and occurs to a few people only. ... Its exact nature does not much matter. It will be quickly submerged in past history.[29]

27. See Mokyr, "Industrial Growth," p. 277. C. E. Ferguson, *The Neoclassical Theory of Production and Distribution* (Cambridge: At the University Press), pp. 261–62.

28. Karl Marx, *Capital* (New York: International Publishers, 1967), 1: 713.

29. Bensusan-Butt, *On Economic Growth*, p. 16.

After the initial investment has been made, the system expands continuously at a steady pace. The sustained growth is self-propelled by the reinvestment of profits, the "engine" of growth. For any given capital stock, the fixed coefficients production functions determine a unique number of workers employed in the modern sector.[30] The value of output of these workers is known since prices are exogenously given. On the other hand, the wage bill is determined by the number of workers times the "going wage." The difference between revenue and wages is in part reinvested in the business, thus determining the capital stock in the next period.

It is important to realize that profits are the pivotal dynamic element in the present model. Yet the nature of profits as used here has little in common with the neoclassical "parables" concerning the marginal productivity of capital. It can be shown that the rate of profit in the present model will diverge in general from the marginal productivity of capital.[31] The emergence of profits is a result of the fact that there are two techniques to produce "textiles": a relatively inefficient technique ("Z-good"), and a more efficient technique ("modern sector"). The coexistence of the two techniques implies that the more efficient technique earns a quasi rent, as long as the wage paid to labor is the same in both sectors. These quasi rents are reinvested, and thus a continuous process of accumulation is generated. It also must be noted that the rate of profit in this model, contrary to standard neoclassical growth models, will not fall with the rise in the aggregate capital-labor ratio. The reasons are succinctly pointed out by Lewis, who is working with a similar model:

> . . . in this system the rate of profit cannot fall. As Ricardo pointed out, however big the increase in capital may be, it can always be matched by a proportionate increase in the employment of labour. With given technology and unlimited labor at constant wages, no "deepening" of capital takes place; only "widening." So the rate of profit on capital is constant. . . [it] could only fall if wages were rising.[32]

At this stage it can be seen why the absence of good capital markets was of crucial importance in determining the nature of the growing up process in the West. Had there been good capital markets, the modern

30. The allocation of capital goods between the consumption and the capital good industry is uniquely determined by the productivity parameters and the reinvestment propensity. See below, p. 150.
31. A. Bhaduri, "On the Significance of Recent Controversies on Capital Theory," *EJ* 79 (1969): 532–39. For an adaptation of Bhaduri's conclusion, see Mokyr, "Industrial Growth," pp. 291–92.
32. W. Arthur Lewis, "Unlimited Labour: Further Notes," *The Manchester School* 26, no. 1 (January 1958): 18.

sector would have been able to borrow large amounts from nonindustrial savings as long as there were high quasi rents to be earned. In the extreme case, the transition from the traditional to the modern technique would have been instantaneous, at least in small countries and regions whose impact on capital markets would have been small. Capital would have been invested until the rate of return equaled "the" rate of interest. As it happened, the growing up process was spread over a long time span, due to a bottleneck in investment. More precisely: the rate of growing up, given by the rate of accumulation, was constrained by the quasi rents earned in the modern sector, i.e., the rate of profit. The higher the latter, the more rapid the growing up process.

The complete dynamic process of growing up is summarized in figure 4.4. The northeastern quadrant presents the expansion path (i.e., capital-labor ratio) of the modern sector, the line OM. There is no particular reason for this line to be straight over its entire range, and it is likely to bend upwards or downwards at its upper part.[33] The exact form of this line is unimportant, however, as long as it is uniquely defined and monotonic. The northwestern quadrant shows the supply of labor as a function of the wage rate w (which is the real wage since it is specified in agricultural goods, the only good consumed by workers). As long as the Z-good sector exists and ignoring for the moment the complications implied by a positive SAS or LIS, the supply of labor will be perfectly elastic at the "going wage," which is determined in the manner described earlier. Only as the Z-good sector is depleted will the labor supply curve bend upwards. The southwestern quadrant reproduces the FPF and Kaldor line from figure 4.3, while the southeastern quadrant transforms a *rate* of growth, h, into actual (physical) capital goods, by means of a set of auxiliary lines like $K_1 N_1$, $K_2 N_2$, etc. These lines have been constructed in such a way that they connect any point on the K-axis, say K_1, with an imaginary point in the southeastern quadrant for which $h = 100$ percent and $K = 2K_1$. Hence, the lines will map any point K, given a rate of growth h, into a point $K \cdot (1 + h)$.

Consider any positive capital stock, say K_1. From K_1 and the expansion path OM, the labor force in the modern sector can be read off on the northern axis. Total nonagricultural labor is OL', which is divided between OL_1 in the modern sector and $L_1 L'$ in the Z-good sector. As long as the reservoir of labor in the Z-good sector is not exhausted, the wage level will be fixed at w_0, determining the rate of accumulation h. In the next period the amount of capital is $K_2 = K_1(1 + h)$, and the cycle is repeated.

33. The expansion path will be a straight line throughout if and only if both industries in the modern sector are strictly one-technique industries and have in addition identical capital-labor ratios.

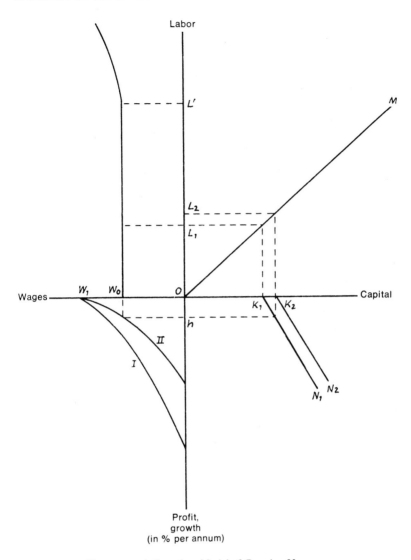

Figure 4.4   A Complete Model of Growing Up

After the Z-good sector is depleted, the wage that the modern sector has to pay rises, since then it is bidding away workers from agriculture. At some stage, the wage w_1 is reached when profit and accumulation have fallen to zero. The "classical stationary state" prevails from then on. The stationary state is the only true equilibrium in this model; the growing up process is basically a disequilibrium.

The affinity of the present model with the labor-surplus model developed by Lewis and Fei and Ranis will by now be apparent. It is worth stressing, however, that in the present model there is no "surplus" labor in any sense—all labor is employed and none is superabundant. The wage level is fully determinate in terms of technological and economic parameters, and it is not necessary to resort to an institutionally determined wage—a somewhat vague concept.[34] For this reason, the present model could aptly be called a pseudo labor-surplus model.

One issue still to be settled is the allocation of labor and capital between the two industries in the modern sector. Since during the process of growing up there is enough labor for both industries, it is only the allocation of capital between them that matters. The issue is illustrated in figure 4.5.

At any given point in time, the modern sector faces two constraints: the capital constraint given by lines like $S_0 T_0$ and the labor constraint given by $X_0 Y_0$. Consider any point in time during which the labor constraint has not yet been reached (so that the reservoir of pseudo labor-surplus is not yet exhausted) and the capital stock is given, say, by the

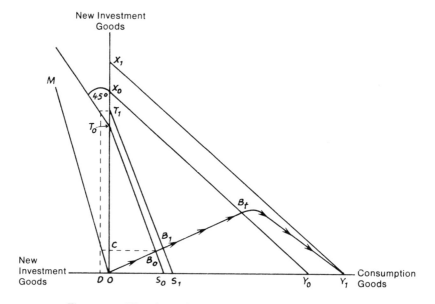

Figure 4.5   Allocation and Accumulation in the Modern Sector

34. "... the institutionally determined wage level is set, *usually not far* from caloric subsistence and *related more or less* to the average productivity of agricultural labor." J. C. H. Fei and G. Ranis, *Development of the Labor Surplus Economy* (Homewood, Ill.: Richard D. Irwin, 1964), p. 22. Emphasis added.

constraint $S_0 T_0$. The slope of the constraint ST is given by the ratio of the productivities of capital in the two industries. The modern sector could employ all its capital in consumers' goods and be at point S_0, or be at T_0 and produce only capital goods, or be at any point in between. The exact point on the line $S_0 T_0$ where the economy will be is determined by the intersection of the capital constraint with the line OB_t, which will be termed the Equilibrium Growing Up Path (EGP). The EGP is fully determinate in terms of the four productivity parameters and the reinvestment coefficient.

The capital constraint and the EGP intersect at point B_0, where OC new capital goods are produced. The maximum amount of new machines which OC machines can make is given by OD (the slope of OM in the western quadrant represents the productivity of machines in reproducing themselves). The capital constraint in the next period can be derived by adding the distance OD to OT_0 and then drawing the line $T_1 S_1$ parallel to $T_0 S_0$. The modern sector will thus be at B_1, and the process will repeat itself in similar fashion until the labor constraint is hit at B_t. At this stage the reservoir of pseudo surplus-labor in the Z-good sector is exhausted, wages will start to rise and profits consequently to decline. The decline of investment will result in a higher proportion of output devoted to consumption goods, so that the EGP will bend in the fashion depicted in figure 4.5. As wages rise, the supply of labor increases, so that the labor constraint shifts to the right. At the wage level that eliminates profits, the system will come to a rest—at Y_1 the stationary state is reached, since the constraint $X_1 Y_1$ is defined for a wage equal to the average product of labor in the consumption good industry in the modern sector. The adjustment process from B_t to Y_1 could be instantaneous if the machine industry is more capital-intensive than the consumption good industry, and the supply of labor is rather inelastic after the turning point B_t.

PRICES, PROGRESS, AND POPULATION

It was seen above how the growing up process terminates after the modern sector has accumulated sufficient capital to employ the entire labor force previously employed in Z-good production. The mechanism operating here is the rise in the wage level that gradually eliminates the profits earned by the capitalists. It is in this sense that profits in the present model should be viewed as quasi rents. It could be argued, however, that the "quasiness" of the profits could have another cause. In most standard economic models, quasi rents earned by the person who introduces a new technique disappear after a while because the diffusion of the technique increases supply and therefore reduces output prices.

A process of this type was explicitly ruled out in the present model since prices were fixed by assumption. Suppose now that the economy as a whole faces a downward sloping demand curve. As a matter of logical consistency, such an assumption is almost inevitable: perfect price takers are small compared to the rest of the world, yet we are dealing here with an economy undergoing rapid output growth, presumably at a faster rate than the rest of the world. Thus, its relative "smallness" cannot be maintained forever, and the demand curve faced by the economy will have a downward sloping segment in it. Since growing up implies an increase in total output of "textiles,"[35] the economy can reasonably expect to slide down the demand curve. Can declining prices cause the rate of accumulation to slow down?

The answer is negative. Under the present assumptions, the rate of accumulation (and the rate of profit on capital) can be shown to be independent of the terms of trade between industrial and agricultural goods.[36] The intuitive reasoning is as follows. The decline of the price of "textiles" will affect both the modern sector and the traditional sector. The fall in the price of Z-goods reduces the opportunity cost of labor and therefore the wages. The revenue of the capitalist is therefore reduced by the fall in prices but so is the wage bill. Nonetheless, actual profit, in terms of the numéraire, falls. But the wage level has fallen throughout the economy and consequently the price of new machines falls too. The smaller profits still buy the same number of (cheaper) machines. The crucial assumptions on which this conclusion is based are admittedly restrictive: the homogeneity of the labor force and the identity of the textiles produced in the traditional and modern sectors. Nevertheless, this conclusion provides a theoretical basis to the observation that accumulation in Belgium seemed surprisingly little affected by the changing fortunes of the world market.

The difficulty with the argument above is, in addition to the strong assumptions noted, that it cannot be taken for granted that wages in the modern sector were perfectly flexible downward. It is likely that there exists some floor beneath which the wage paid to factory workers cannot fall. After this wage is reached, additional price declines will have to be absorbed by profits, and accumulation will slow down and eventually come to a complete halt, even if the supply of pseudo surplus-labor from the Z-good sector is not exhausted. As will be shown in chapter 7, the results of this "dismal stationary state" can be disastrous for the traditional sector.

35. It might be thought that growing up could result in an actual decline in the total output of consumption goods if many workers are diverted from Z-good production to the production of capital goods. It can be proven unambiguously that along the EGP this cannot occur.
36. For a proof, see Mokyr, "Industrial Growth," p. 279.

At this stage it may legitimately be asked what factors eventually prevented the stationary state from occurring altogether. After all, it is quite obvious that stationary states with zero accumulation and profits were not a general characteristic of European economies in the nineteenth century. The principal factors that prevented the stationary state were technological progress and population growth. There has been a tendency in modern growth theory to treat these two elements in similar terms. Technological progress is viewed as an increase in the effective labor force, and it is the sum of labor augmenting technological progress and population growth which makes the difference between the stationary and the steady state. Since the present model focuses, however, on non-steady-state properties of economic growth and accumulation, the role played by technological progress is quite different from the role of population growth.[37]

Suppose now that additional technological change takes place after the initial emergence of the new technique. There are two distinct ways to handle this problem. The first is to assume that additional goods start to lend themselves to capital-intensive, mechanized techniques. One can then form an array of goods that become mechanized one after the other. This is the approach taken by Bensusan-Butt.[38] Alternatively, one might consider a world in which only one consumption good exists, but new and more efficient techniques to produce this good are becoming available over time. The latter approach will be adopted at present. It should be noted that by "more efficient" is meant that the FPF moves outward at the constant wage rate. This does not necessarily imply that the new technique is more efficient at *all* possible income distributions. As long as the economy is in a pseudo labor-surplus situation and the wage rate is constant, no problems of choice of technique arise, not to mention such complications as double switching.

The central assumption of the present model of technological change is that there is no ordinary "disembodied" technological change. Labor is assumed homogeneous and of constant quality, and capital goods have fixed *ex post* productivities. It follows that changes in productivity can occur only due to the introduction of new capital goods of a better "vintage." If technological progress of this type has been going on for some time different qualities of machines of different vintages will be operating simultaneously.

Analytically, two types of technological change can be distinguished.

37. The difference in the role of population growth in the present model and neoclassical models is not related to the impact of population growth on demand. Both types of models are supply-oriented and assume relative prices as given in addition to full employment.
38. Bensusan-Butt, *On Economic Growth*, pp. 15–33.

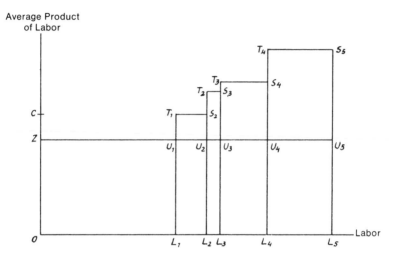

Figure 4.6   Distribution in a Model with Embodied Technological Progress

One type makes labor and capital more efficient in the production of new machines, while the other type raises the productivities of the factors of production in the consumption good industry. Although the two types of technological progress affect different parameters, their effect is the same: they will cause the FPF to shift outward.[39] The *actual* FPF facing the modern sector is a weighted average of the various frontiers corresponding with the various techniques, where the weights are the relative amounts of machines used of each vintage. Therefore, even if technological change is discontinuous, the FPF will shift out in a gradual fashion, since the rate at which the new, best practice technique is adopted is constrained by the rate of accumulation.[40]

The operation of the modern sector in a model with embodied technological change is illustrated in figure 4.6.[41] The height of the rectangles $L_1 T_1 L_2 S_2$, $L_2 T_2 L_3 S_3$, etcetera, is determined by the average productivity of labor in the various vintages, while the length of the respective bases

39. If labor is measured in efficiency units rather than in physical units, technological change of the embodied type will cause the FPF to shift inwards rather than outwards. For the present purpose, it is preferable to deal with labor measured in conventional units. Cf. David Levhari and Eythan Sheshinski, "The Factor Price Frontier with Embodied Technical Progress," *AER* 60, no. 5 (December 1970): 807–13.

40. W. E. G. Salter, *Productivity and Technical Change*, 2d ed. (Cambridge: At the University Press, 1969), pp. 48–65.

41. The diagram has been adapted from Salter, *Productivity and Technical Change*, p.53. See also R. M. Solow, *Growth Theory, an Exposition* (Oxford: Oxford University Press, 1970), p. 46.

is equal to the number of machines available of each vintage, multiplied by the corresponding labor-capital ratios. The rectangle OZU_1L_1 represents the traditional Z-good sector. Except for the fact that the technique employed in this sector uses no fixed capital at all and can therefore pick up the entire residual nonagricultural labor force, the Z-good is not inherently different from any mechanized vintage. The wage level in this model, like any standard vintage model, is determined by the average product of labor employed in the least efficient technique, while all other capital goods earn a quasi rent equal to the sum of the rectangles $T_1U_1S_2U_2 + T_2U_2S_3U_3 + \ldots$. The conclusion reached earlier is thus generalized.

One result of this model is that different qualities of machines yielding different rates of profit can coexist for a long period. The coexistence of the traditional sector using manual labor only and yielding no profits with a mechanized sector is nothing but a special case of this general property of vintage models. As accumulation proceeds, the polygon $U_1T_1U_5S_5$ expands to the left, "pushing" the lower rectangles toward the vertical axis. Eventually the rectangle $T_1U_1S_2U_2$ will hit the axis, at which point the labor reservoir in the Z-good sector is exhausted. From that moment on, wages start to rise. If the modern sector consists of just one technique, as was assumed above, the stationary state will be reached when wages equal $OC = L_1T_1$. However, if additional technological progress has been made in the modern techniques since their first adoption, wages can continue to rise. The first mechanized vintage will be scrapped when the wage level exceeds OC and so on. It has been shown that the neoclassical steady state properties can be reached by this model, but that exercise lies outside the scope of the present model. What is important to realize is that it is really technological progress that makes the engine of growth run. After all, it is technological progress that creates quasi rents on recent vintages of capital and thus provides the fuel for the traverse. Additional technological progress may result in the perpetuation of an intrinsically ephemeral phenomenon.[42]

To summarize: the existence of high profits in an economy in the early stages of industrialization can be explained, in addition to various market and other imperfections, by the fact that the economy is in the process of shifting to a best practice technique. During the transition period (which may last forever if the process of technological change is sustained) the different techniques coexist and the better practice techniques earn a

---

42. The view that the earnings of existing capital goods are essentially quasi rents was propounded by Marshall. Cf. A. Marshall, *Principles of Economics*, 9th ed., ed. C. W. Guillebaud (New York: Macmillan, 1961), pp. 412, 593. For an excellent exposition, see Salter, *Productivity and Technical Change*, pp. 61–65.

quasi rent. The higher this quasi rent, the more rapid the rate of accumulation and the faster the transition period will burn itself out if no additional technological progress takes place.

Turning finally to population growth, the role of population growth in this model is quite simple. Every baby is born without any capital but with a pair of hands that qualifies one in principle for the Z-good sector. Therefore, population growth will replenish the labor absorbed from the Z-good sector and postpone the exhaustion of the pseudo labor-surplus reservoir and the subsequent rise in wages. Equally important, growing population may endanger the success of the growing up process altogether.[43] Basically, three cases can be distinguished. The first is the case in which the traditional sector actually shrinks in absolute size despite its population growth; thus, success is assured. The second case is the case in which workers born in the modern sector migrate back to the traditional sector. In this situation the relative size of the modern sector moves back asymptotically to zero after having jumped initially to some positive fraction. The third case is the case in which there is a net influx of labor from the traditional to the modern sector, but the growth of the capital stock is insufficient to absorb all incremental population in the traditional sector. In this case, thus, the labor forces in both sectors are growing. The last case is unstable and will ultimately transform itself into either the successful or the unsuccessful case.

A GENERALIZED PSEUDO LABOR-SURPLUS MODEL

As was indicated earlier, it is not really likely that the wage paid to the workers hired by the modern sector remains equal to the productivity of labor in Z-good production. The latter is clearly a lower boundary to the wage in the modern sector. As long as a simple constant is added to this wage, in the fashion envisioned by Lewis, the operation of the model is unaffected. However, as was argued above, the SAS and the LIS cause a more complicated divergence of the wage rate from the Z-good productivity. Peasants bid away from the traditional sector will demand a markup on their Z-good productivity. The difficulty is that this markup will be rising as the relative size of the modern sector grows.

To simplify matters, assume that population is constant, and that there is no technological progress in the modern sector. As accumulation pro-

43. The definition of success here is the ultimate absorption of the nonagricultural traditional sector in the modern sector. Cf. Fei and Ranis, *Development of the Labor Surplus Economy*, pp. 111–24. The possibility of the failure of the labor surplus economy to develop has been emphasized by Lloyd G. Reynolds, "Economic Development with Surplus Labour: Some Complications," *OEP* 21, no. 7 (March 1969): 97–98. A complete algebraic presentation of a model with population growth can be found in Mokyr, "Industrial Growth," pp. 297–300.

ceeds, the number of workers in the traditional sector declines, implying a rise in the land-labor ratio. As was argued above, the SAS and the LIS will be proportional (or at least positively correlated) to the land-labor ratio, and consequently wages will rise. A further complication is that land is unequally distributed among the peasants. Some peasants may have been completely landless (i.e., agricultural laborers), but even for them the SAS could be positive (though the LIS, by definition, is zero for them). At any rate, an unequal distribution of land implies that as the modern sector expands, it has to bid away peasants owning increasingly more land, and unless both the LIS and the SAS are zero, wages will rise. The various possible time patterns of the wage level under different assumptions are demonstrated in figure 4.7.

The path ZKG describes the simple pseudo labor-surplus model, presented in length above. Wages are constant and equal to OZ until time t_1 at which point the Z-good sector is exhausted. From t_1 on, the wage equals the marginal productivity of labor in agriculture, and will thus be rising until it hits the ceiling OC. The path ZKM depicts a situation in which there is a landless proletariat which earns neither LIS nor SAS and can thus be bid away at the wage OZ. At time t_1' the first layer of pseudo surplus-labor is exhausted and wages start to rise. The process of growing

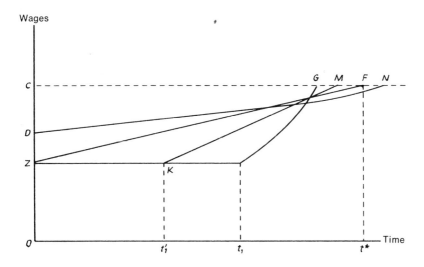

Figure 4.7   Movement of Wages Over Time in a Generalized Pseudo Labor-Surplus Model

up here lasts longer than in the economy following the path ZKG, since the rate of accumulation is lower for the whole period in which the path KM is above KG. A third variant is depicted by DN, which assumes that the wage which the modern sector has to pay is higher from the beginning than the productivity in Z-good production.

In this section, it will be assumed for simplicity that the economy follows a path which looks like *ZF* in figure 4.7. The wage starts at *OZ* but rises from the very beginning in a continuous fashion until it hits the ceiling *OC*. It is thus possible to define a variable λ which is equal to zero at time *o* and to unity at $t^\star$, and makes wages a function exclusively of λ. A good candidate for λ is the ratio of workers in the modern sector to total industrial workers (Z-goods plus modern industry).[44]

In the growing up process, the wage level is always between the productivity of labor in the traditional sector and the productivity of labor in the modern sector. The wage level can be expressed as a weighted average of these two parameters, with the weights changing with λ.[45] The

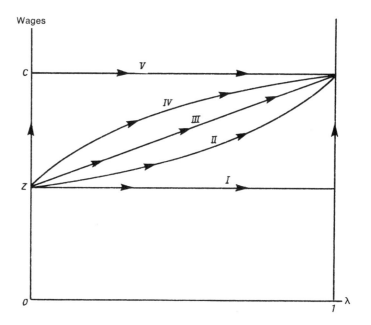

Figure 4.8   Various Paths of Wages for Different Values of the LAC

44. There are some fairly minor difficulties with the above definition. For example, in the case that the SAS and the LIS are of importance, the Z-good may not be entirely eliminated when the rate of profit has fallen to zero and the stationary state has been attained. This complication requires some modification in the proper definition of λ.

45. The wage equation is given by $w = \lambda^\alpha \cdot c + (1 - \lambda^\alpha) b$ where w is the wage paid by the modern sector, b and c are the productivities of labor in the traditional and modern sector respectively, λ is as defined in the text, and α is the LAC.

possible paths followed by the economy as λ moves from zero to unity are depicted in figure 4.8. The exact path followed is determined by a parameter termed the Labor Availability Coefficient (LAC). Path *III* in figure 4.8 represents a situation in which the LAC happens to equal exactly unity, while paths *II* and *IV* depict situations in which the LAC is respectively larger and smaller than unity. The "pure" pseudo labor-surplus situation is the economy in which the LAC is very large or infinite so that the wage is constant and equal to OZ until the Z-sector is completely exhausted, at which point the wage level leaps discontinuously to OC. This case is represented by path *I*. Finally, path *V* is described under the rather unlikely assumption that the LAC is very small or zero. More complex models could be constructed to take into account the more gradual rise of the wage level after λ has reached unity. It will be realized that in this simple model the LAC occupies a pivotal function since it determines the wage level for every λ, and the wage level determines, as was demonstrated above, the dynamic properties of the model.

The relationship between the growing up process and the LAC can be worked out algebraically. The following propositions can be shown to hold.

1. Wages will rise continuously with λ. If the LAC is greater than unity, wages will rise with λ at an increasing rate. If the LAC is smaller than unity, wages will rise at a falling rate. In the special case in which the LAC happens to be exactly unity, wages will rise proportionately to λ, the factor of proportionality equal to the difference in the productivity of labor in the two sectors.

2. The higher the value of the LAC, the higher the rate of profit and the rate of accumulation, hence the shorter the length of the period of growing up. For any given λ, wages are lower, the higher the LAC.

3. The rates of profit and accumulation will be falling continuously over time. If the LAC is greater than unity, the rates of profit and accumulation will be falling at a rate that is either increasing throughout or is at first decreasing and becomes increasing during the process. If the LAC is smaller than unity, these rates will be falling at a rate that is either decreasing throughout or becomes so during the process.

4. Total profits will rise at first and then start to decline, ending at zero. If the LAC happens to equal unity, the peak of total profits will coincide with $\lambda = \frac{1}{2}$. If the LAC is greater than unity, this will occur at $\lambda > \frac{1}{2}$ and vice versa.

As to the factors determining the LAC, the degree of complexity is such as to make the rigorous derivation impossible. Rather than trying to isolate with precision the various elements embodied in the LAC, the

LAC should be considered as a basically heuristic parameter. Some of its possible determinants are listed below, but it cannot be shown with rigor how they jointly determine its exact value.

1. The LAC will be higher, the higher the initial proportion of labor devoted to Z-good production in the traditional sector.

2. The LAC will be higher, the less marked the seasonal differences in agricultural productivity and the more the modern sector can operate on a seasonal basis. The former condition implies that the SAS is small, while the latter implies that the SAS is not necessarily lost due to modernization.

3. The LAC will be higher, the more perfect land markets are, i.e., the less the significance of the LIS.

4. If the LIS is positive, the LAC will be higher, the more unequal the distribution of land ownership.

5. The LAC will be higher, the more rapid population growth.

6. The LAC will be higher, the more perfect the labor market, the more mobile the labor force, and the less the psychic, transactions, and other costs involved in moving from the traditional to the modern sector.

In conclusion, it can be seen that the "fixwage" model, in which the wage level determines all other variables in the model, can be replaced by a "flexwage" model, in which the wage level is a function of the degree to which the transition has been completed. The LAC measures the extent to which the economy is a pseudo labor-surplus economy, that is, the LAC measures the speed at which wages rise as the modern sector expands. Additional complications, such as technological progress in the modern sector, population growth, changes in the terms of trade, etc., could be dealt with in this model, but would greatly complicate the mathematics without fundamentally changing the main conclusions.

SOME OTHER RAMIFICATIONS

One of the fundamental assumptions of the model presented above has been that the proportion of profits plowed back into the firm (reinvestment coefficient) is constant. Yet it will be immediately recognized that a lower reinvestment coefficient would have effects that are perfectly symmetrical to a lower profit rate. It is therefore appropriate to go into some detail in describing the properties of this central parameter and its possible determinants.

For one thing, it should be clear that the reinvestment coefficient is not necessarily identical to the capitalists' average propensity to save. The reason for this is that, even though it was assumed that capitalists cannot borrow in the capital markets, this does not imply necessarily that they cannot lend to extrasectoral borrowers such as the government. In addition, capitalists can of course always hoard money. Therefore the average propensity to save of the capitalists is the upper bound of the reinvestment coefficient, and the latter is thus determined by factors involving both the present versus future consumption trade-off and the allocation of wealth among the various assets held in the portfolios of capitalists. There should be no illusion among economists that they will be able to fully uncover the factors that make capitalists accumulate. In the words of one writer:

> . . . savings are the sole motive force of the model and the speed and shape of its progress naturally depend upon their relationship to income and the rate of profit. If the model is to exhibit an economic history of an interesting kind the savings habits of its inhabitants have to be restricted to the range of the reasonably sensible. It is far from easy to do this. Saving is one of the most irrational, conventional, and socially motivated of economic activities and consorts ill with rational, narrowly mechanical, selfish, and sensual behaviour which one can use as the image of normal human nature in examining other kinds of economic decision.[46]

Economic factors played only a partial role in the process of accumulation. Lust for power, "achievism," social prestige, and possibly even religious considerations played roles with which the economist may be uncomfortable but which will have nevertheless to be faced by the historian. In a celebrated passage, Marx described the capitalist as a vehicle of forces stronger than himself:

> Except as personified capital, the capitalist has no historical value and no right to . . . historical existence. . . . Fanatically bent on making value expand itself . . . [he] forces the development of the productive powers of society, and creates those material conditions, which alone can form the real basis of a higher form of society. . . . [The capitalist] shares with the miser the passion for wealth as wealth. But that which in the miser is a mere idiosyncrasy, is, in the capitalist, the effect of a social mechanism, of which he is but one of the wheels. Moreover, the development of capitalist production makes it constantly necessary to keep increasing the amount of the capital laid out in a given industrial undertaking, and competition makes the immanent laws of capitalist production to be felt by each individual, as external coercive laws. It compels him to keep constantly extending his capital in order to preserve it, but expand it he cannot except by means of progressive

46. Bensusan-Butt, *On Economic Growth*, pp. 34–35.

accumulation. . . . Accumulate, accumulate! That is Moses and the prophets![47]

The view that takes the "animal spirits" (the term is Keynes's) as the driving force behind the reinvestment coefficient is consistent with a constant proportion of profits plowed back into the firm, possibly equal to unity as is assumed in the von Neumann-Joan Robinson models. It is, however, possible to argue that the reinvestment coefficient is a function of various variables in the system. The most obvious candidate for such a variable is the rate of profit itself.

The introduction of the rate of profit as a determinant of the reinvestment coefficient does not necessarily alter our previous conclusions. As long as the two are positively related, the previous model is reinforced, since now low wages lead not only to high profits but also to a higher proportion of these profits being reinvested in the firm. Such a positive relationship can be derived from three different types of models. The first is a model in which the savings rate of the capitalists is given, but the composition of his portfolio depends on the rate of return on the risky asset (capital) as compared to the rates of return on the comparatively safe assets (bonds and money). In such a model the relation between the rate of profit and the reinvestment is definitely positive. A second type of model bases the investment decision on the expectations of the entrepreneurs with respect to the future rate of profits. Here, too, it is difficult to imagine that a present high rate of profit would imply anything but optimistic expectations with regard to the future. More ambiguous are models that focus on the trade-off between present and future consumption, what Marx has called the "Faustian conflict between the passion for accumulation and the desire for enjoyment." In a simple Fisherian model a higher rate of profit could imply a higher savings rate (and therefore *ceteris paribus* a higher reinvestment coefficient) if the substitution effect outweighs the income effect. If the converse obtains, or if saving is of the "life time cycle" type (not a plausible assumption for nonwage income), a higher profit rate may imply a lower savings rate. Even then, however, it is not certain that lower wages will imply a slower rate of accumulation. For this result to obtain, it is necessary that the elasticity of the reinvestment coefficient with respect to the rate of profit is not only negative but smaller than minus one. This seems unlikely.

It is of some interest to examine the model under the assumption that there is a capital market for relatively safe securities such as government bonds, at which capitalists can lend but not borrow. Such a model seems not unrealistic for early nineteenth-century Europe, especially for the

47. Marx, *Capital*, 1: 592–95.

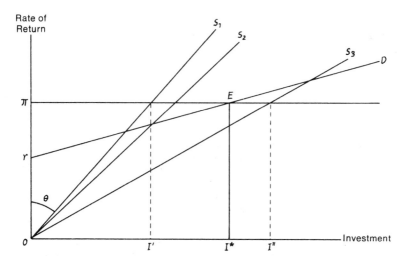

Figure 4.9   Accumulation and Portfolio Choice

Low Countries. Assume, as seems reasonable, that capitalists are risk averse. The risky asset will therefore have to yield a higher rate of return than the safe asset if it is to be held at all.

The process of accumulation and portfolio choice in such a world is illustrated in figure 4.9.[48] It is assumed that the rate of profit earned on investment by each entrepreneur is independent of his capital stock or changes therein; perfect competition and constant returns to scale under conditions of pseudo labor-surplus assure this. Although there is no market for investment funds and the supply and demand decisions are simultaneously made by the same person, it is still possible to make an analytic distinction between the supply of funds and the decision to actually reinvest them in the firm. For simplicity, the savings decision is assumed exogenously given, and the only choice faced by the capitalist is whether to reinvest in his business or to invest in the safe asset.

In figure 4.9 the "supply" of investment funds is given by straight lines like OS_1. It is simply determined by the total amount of previously invested capital given by the angle θ and the rate of profit given by the distance $O\pi$. The maximum amount that can be reinvested, given the impossibility of borrowing, is therefore the rate of profit multiplied by the amount of capital (in value terms), given by OI'. The line rD shows the amount of capital that the entrepreneur wishes to invest in his firm as a

48. The following is inspired by J. Tobin, "Liquidity Preference as Behavior Towards Risk," *ReStud* 25 (February 1958): 65–86.

function of the profit rate (existing at present and expected to last). Investment in the firm is zero if the rate of profit is equal to or smaller than the "safe" rate Or. Suppose the amount of capital is given by θ and the rate of profit is given by $O\pi$. The amount of incremental capital desired is $OI^\star$, yet the maximum investment is only OI'—the desire for the difference is simply frustrated. The capitalist wishes to invest more but cannot, since he is limited to self-finance. The next period the amount OI' is added to his capital, so that the "supply" of capital becomes OS_2 and so on. Finally, an investment supply line will obtain that intersects with the rate of profit at a point to the right of E. For example, at the capital stock that implies a "supply" curve OS_3, total funds available for investment (accruing from the firm and ignoring earnings on other assets) are I'', of which only $OI^\star$ is reinvested in the firm, while the rest, given by $I^\star I''$, is invested in the safe asset. Obviously, the crucial parameter in this process is the slope of the line rD, which is determined by the risk averseness of the entrepreneur. For example, if the entrepreneurs are risk neutral, the line rD will be horizontal and an infinitesimal differential in the rates of return will assure a continuous maximal effort to accumulate capital.

5 THE MODEL APPLIED: INCOME DISTRIBUTION AND INDUSTRIALIZATION IN THE LOW COUNTRIES

To attempt to account for what makes the propensity to accumulate high or low, we must look into the historical, political and psychological characteristics of an economy. . . . It seems plausible, however, to say that, given the general characteristics of an economy, to sustain a higher rate of accumulation requires a higher level of profits, both because it offers more favourable odds in the gamble and because it makes finance more readily available.

Joan Robinson

The usefulness of the model presented in chapter 4 for the understanding of the particular process of uneven development in the Low Countries is that it focuses attention upon a few crucial variables that may have been of major importance in determining the rate of capital accumulation in the modern industrial sector. As was demonstrated in detail in chapter 4, a priori considerations indicate that income distribution parameters should be considered as central in this respect. The present chapter will summarize the evidence on income distribution in the two countries and will make an attempt to explain why the distributions were so different. Other possible explanations for Belgium's success and the Netherlands' sluggishness in industrialization will be examined in chapter 6.

As was pointed out above,[1] there is reason to expect that the modern sector in low-wage-high-profit economies will grow faster than in high wage economies. A generalized version of the same conclusion states that an economy in which wages are initially at a low level *and* rise slowly would industrialize at a faster rate than a country in which labor was either

---

1. See above, chapter 4.

expensive (elastically supplied at a high price) or in inelastic supply, so that wages rise rapidly as the modern sector bids away workers from the traditional sector.

It is obvious that such statements are only strictly true *ceteris paribus*. Specifically, the assumption is that both technology (in the form of the productivity parameters) and the terms of trade between industrial and agricultural goods are given to the two countries. For Europe as a whole, such assumptions seem unwarranted: the wage level in southern Italy, for example, was probably one of the lowest in Europe, but it is hard to argue that southern Italy had as easy an access to English industrial technology in the first half of the nineteenth century as the Netherlands or Belgium. In addition, the more remote a country from the main trade routes, the more the relative prices in that country could deviate from the international terms of trade. For the Low Countries, however, the assumptions above seem not unreasonable.

Before examining some data for the Low Countries, it seems worthwhile to prevent a possible misunderstanding.[2] It has been argued widely that high wages, rather than being a hindrance to capital accumulation, provide a positive incentive to substitute capital for labor and therefore enhance the adoption of mechanized (i.e., more capital-intensive) techniques. The simplest version of this argument is based on a static choice of technique argument and is not really applicable here. Under some assumptions, an economy in which low wages prevail will choose a more capital-intensive technique. But this says nothing about the *rate* at which the new technique is adopted.

Consider figure 5.1, another adaptation of the Factor Price Frontier diagram used in chapter 4. The traditional technique is presented by FPF $\pi_0 w_0$. As can be seen, the old technique is fully dominated by the new techniques, that is, at every factor price combination the new techniques are more profitable than the old ones. The process of "growing up" consists of gradually moving from the traditional technology (technique $\pi_0 w_0$) to the new technology (either technique $\pi_1 w_1$ or technique $\pi_2 w_2$). The *speed* at which the economy moves to the new technique, that is, the rate at which it accumulates the capital goods in which the new technique is embodied, does not depend on whether the economy moves to FPF $\pi_1 w_1$ or to FPF $\pi_2 w_2$. If the economy was initially at point E_0, and if wages remained constant (or rose little), technique $\pi_1 w_1$ will be chosen. Otherwise, it would choose the technique described by FPF $\pi_2 w_2$. A path such as $E_0 E_2'$ may not involve necessarily much more capital accumulation

2. The following, as well as some other parts of the present chapter, is adapted from J. Mokyr, "The Industrial Revolution in the Low Countries in the First Half of the Nineteenth Century: A Comparative Case Study," *JEH* 34, no. 2 (June 1974): 365–91.

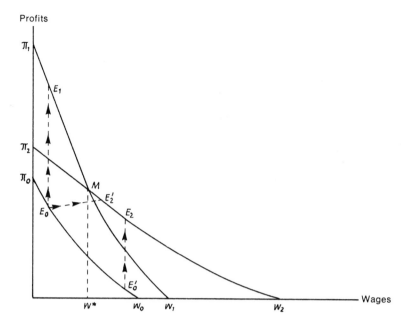

Figure 5.1   "Growing Up" and the Choice of Technique

than E_0E_1, but it will take more time since the rate of accumulation slows down as profits decline and wages rise. The same is true if we compare the two "fixwage" paths $E_0'E_2$ and E_0E_1. The choice of technique issue is thus seen to be a separate problem and not directly related to the dynamic questions at stake here, in which the fundamental relationship between income distribution and capital accumulation is analyzed.

Moreover, it could be argued that if there is a choice of techniques in modern technology, such as is depicted in figure 5.1, a high wage economy will tend to adopt a more capital-intensive technique so that the traverse will not only take place at a lower speed, but also cover a larger distance. If this is the case, the negative relationship between wages and accumulation would be reinforced. However, it is not invariably true that the economy facing a higher wage rate will adopt a more capital-intensive technique. Consider figure 5.1. Economies with a wage higher than $w*$ will choose the technique given by FPF π_2w_2, since for any given wage rate profits will be higher if this technique is used. On the other hand, low wage economies, in which the wage level is lower than $w*$, will choose the first technique, given by π_1w_1. But it is not possible to say unambiguously that π_2w_2 represents *necessarily* a more capital-intensive technique than π_1w_1. All we can say with certainty about the two techniques represented by the frontiers $\pi_1 w_1$ and $\pi_2 w_2$ in figure 5.1 is that the average product of labor in manufacturing consumption goods is higher in the second technique, while the average product of capital in reproducing itself (i.e., producing new capital goods) is higher in the first technique. The capital-labor ratio in consumption goods is, oddly enough, irrelevant here. Hence it cannot be said unambiguously that the technique represented by $\pi_2 w_2$ is more capital-intensive than the one represented by $\pi_1 w_1$.

A more sophisticated model linking income distribution to the industrialization process has been proposed by Habakkuk.[3] In Habakkuk's model high wages stimulate the development of labor saving inventions. In other words, technology itself is made a function of factor prices and not only the choice between the various feasible techniques in a technology. Such an approach raises various theoretical difficulties.[4] Moreover, since it was shown above that technology was largely exogenously given to the two economies under consideration, local inventive activity cannot be regarded as a central factor, even if such activity were guided by relative factor prices.[5]

Having established the causal link between income distribution and capital accumulation at a theoretical level, it now becomes necessary to show that wages in Belgium were in fact lower than in the Netherlands during the period under discussion.

WAGES IN THE NETHERLANDS AND BELGIUM COMPARED

It was shown in some detail in chapter 1 that the wage level in the traditional protoindustrial ("Z-good") sector in Belgium was extremely low and that contemporaries in the eighteenth century were aware of the fact that wages in Belgium were much lower than in the Netherlands.[6] Moreover, it appears that wages in the Netherlands in the eighteenth century were higher than in most countries.[7] A statement to this effect can be found in no less an authority than Adam Smith: "The wages of labour are said to be higher in Holland than in England, and the Dutch, it is well

3. H. J. Habakkuk, *American and British Technology in the Nineteenth Century* (Cambridge: At the University Press, 1962).
4. Salter, *Productivity and Technical Change*, pp. 43–44. P. Temin, "Labor Scarcity and the Problem of American Industrial Efficiency in the 1850s," *JEH* 26, no. 3 (September 1966): 277–95.
5. See above, p. 134.
6. Cf. the quote cited on p. 20 above.
7. See Joh. de Vries, *Economische Achteruitgang*, p. 107. According to de Vries, Dutch wages in the poor diluvial provinces where protoindustry was of some importance were lower than in the maritime provinces, but still higher than abroad. Cf. also van Dillen, *Van Rijkdom en Regenten*, p. 553.

known, trade upon lower profits than any people in Europe."[8] The same
opinion is expounded by E. Luzac, a Dutch political economist and a
contemporary of Adam Smith. Luzac writes:

> In order to prevent the worker from quitting and in order to counter
> the disadvantages thereof, there has been no other way than to raise
> the daily wages. The elevation of wages has resulted of course in a
> rise in the prices of our manufactures. Consequently, other peoples
> have been our competitors ... and eventually defeated us so that
> most of our manufactures are sold today domestically, and little
> export takes place.[9]

Luzac's opinion is worth noting, since his book is largely an improved
and annotated translation of a book by a French author, Jacques Accarias
de Sérionne, which equally emphasizes the high wages in the Netherlands.[10] His opinion is the more valuable because as a foreigner his
standards of comparison were probably better founded. Sérionne (1709–
92) was an extremely well-read and widely-traveled man, who wrote many
comparative economic studies on Europe.[11]

High wages were one of the most frequent complaints in the response
to the Goldberg survey of 1801. Dutch wages were repeatedly reported
to be higher than elsewhere. Among the specific areas in which wages were
supposed to be lower, the Wuppertal and Flanders figure prominently.[12]
An anonymous memorandum on the situation of Dutch industry, written
in 1810, equally emphasized the high wage level as a severe hardship on
Dutch manufactures.[13] It is thus evident that wages in the Netherlands
failed to decline even in a period of severe economic depression. Certainly
they remained higher than Belgian wages, and not only in the Flemish
provinces. G. M. Roentgen, one of the best informed men of his time,
stressed the comparatively low wages in the Walloon provinces and viewed
them as an important advantage in the development of the iron industry
there.[14] As late as in 1843 a Dutch political economist cited the high wages

8. Adam Smith, *The Wealth of Nations*, ed. Andrew Skinner (Harmondsworth: Penguin Books, 1970), p. 194.

9. Luzac, *Hollands Rijkdom*, 4: 84–85.

10. Jacques Accarias de Sérionne, *La Richesse de la Hollande*, 2 vols. (Londond: Aux dépens de la Compagnie, 1778), 2: 37.

11. *Biographie Universelle* (Paris: L. G. Michaud, 1825), vol. 42: 74.

12. Dutch National Archives, The Hague, Goldberg Coll., file 37, nos. 204, 239, 241; file 50, nos. 44, 71, 73, 150, 205.

13. "Memorie over de Fabrieken en Trafieken in het Voormalig Koninkrijk Holland" [Memorandum on the manufactures and "traffics" in the former kingdom of Holland], manuscript, Dutch National Archives, Binnenlandse Zaken 1796–1813, no. 783.

14. Roentgen, "Berigt van den Toestand," p. 149.

"without which it is impossible to get the laborers to work" as one of the causes for the decline of manufacturing in the Netherlands.[15]

Three points must now be established. First, is there more than anecdotal and fragmentary evidence concerning the wage differential between the Netherlands and Belgium? Second, did Belgian wages remain more or less constant in spite of the growth of modern industry? Third, did wages in the Netherlands remain comparatively high in spite of the stagnation of the Dutch economy in the first half of the nineteenth century?

The first question can fortunately be given an affirmative answer. The crucial piece of evidence here is the large industrial survey conducted by the Dutch government in 1819, in which wages were recorded for all nineteen provinces of the United Kingdom of the Netherlands.[16] A meaningful comparison of the wage level between the ten Dutch provinces and the nine Belgian provinces could thus be carried out. Before presenting the results, a few details on the survey itself are in order.

The 1819 industrial survey (actually undertaken in 1820) was a repetition of an earlier, unsuccessful survey made in 1816. The latter survey was carried out by the municipal authorities and seems to have been confined deliberately to "large enterprises and manufactures" rather than industry as a whole, so that handicraft workers and artisans were largely excluded. The principal reason that caused authorities to decide to repeat the survey was the "uneven, incomplete, and often inefficient response of the municipalities, while others failed entirely to reply."[17] The same letter ordered a new survey undertaken and included specific instructions as to how to carry it out. The minister recommended that the provincial authorities "invite business experts to assist the officials in charge of collecting the data and to contribute to the success of the survey with their experience and insights." It was emphasized that the survey explicitly aimed at completeness and that no establishment should be omitted.

How the data were actually collected on the firm level is difficult to say. Brugmans mentions in his introduction that in Flushing the chamber of commerce participated, in Nijmegen the provincial authorities sent delegates to the larger industrialists, whereas the artisans and small entrepreneurs were summoned to city hall for questioning. In Delft, on the other hand, the forms were distributed and filled out by the entrepreneurs. Needless to say, the survey was not anywhere close to modern standards or even to the standards set by the grand *Recensement Général* carried out by Quetelet and Heuschling in Belgium in 1846. Yet compared to other

15. Van der Boon Mesch, "Over het Nederlandsche Fabrijkswezen," p. 374.
16. Brugmans, *Statistieken*.
17. Letter of the Minister of Education, Industry, and Colonies to the provincial authorities, cited in ibid., 1 : xvii.

censuses and surveys carried out on the Continent in this period, the Dutch
Industrial Survey of 1819 is probably still one of the more reliable sources.
It is significant to note in this context that a letter written by the Dutch
minister of the interior in 1843 criticized the 1819 survey and called for
a new survey. However, the reason for the criticism of the 1819 survey
was not the way in which the data were collected, but rather the setup of
the survey as a whole, which presumably double counted people with
double professions. The attempt to avoid double counting caused the
1843 survey to become, in Brugmans's words, a list of industrial professions rather than of industries.[18] In any case, the 1843 survey includes
no wage data and is therefore useless for the present purposes.

Most of the manuscript returns of the 1819 survey have been lost; what
is left over today is the aggregation compiled by the ministry of industry
for the country as a whole, plus some scattered, more detailed returns for
two provinces and sixteen cities (all northern). The tables were recovered
and eventually published by Brugmans after having remained obscure for
more than a century. It is amazing that the Dutch government, after
having gone to considerable pain and expense to collect these data, made
virtually no use of them. The returns of the 1819 survey seem to have sunk
into oblivion almost as soon as they were compiled.

The aggregate returns of the 1819 survey are summarized in 525 tables,
each referring to one industrial activity. Some of the tables are, however,
empty, leaving about 450 usable. The classification into the various classes
of activities was not based upon the actual returns but prepared before-
hand. The ambiguities in the list probably vexed the compilers as much as
the historian. Many activities are ill-defined and overlap with others. The
information contained in each table includes the number of firms in each
province, the number of adult and children workers employed by these
firms, the average daily wage paid to these workers (in Dutch cents), the
location of the markets respective before and after December 31, 1813
(typical entries: local, domestic, foreign), and the "state of business"
respectively before 1814, 1814–16, 1817–19, and on December 31, 1819
(typical entries: declining, medium, good). Many tables include some
extratabular remarks and recommendations, such as demands for protection, reduction of taxes, reinstatement of the guilds, and other requests
that might be expected from businessmen addressing their government.

The most important question for the present study is the quality of the
wage data. Since all wage figures are averages over all firms in a given
activity in each province, the weighting of the averages is of some importance. As to the averaging over all workers in each individual firm,

18. Ibid., 1: xxx.

there are hints that the correct procedure was used, namely dividing the total wage bill by the number of workers.[19] However, the calculation of the provincial average wage was performed by assigning each firm the same weight rather than a weight proportional to its employment. This is confirmed by a comparison between the aggregate returns and the returns on the provincial and local level, as far as they were available. Additional evidence pointing in this direction can be seen from the fact that the arithmetic of averages was not carefully observed in the aggregate tables themselves: the two *national* wage averages in each table over all provinces were given as a simple average between the highest and the lowest entry and a simple *unweighted* average over all provinces. In this case, the error could be corrected since the number of workers in each activity for every province is given in the table itself, but it indicates that weighted averaging was not a common procedure among the compilers of the survey.

There are two significant drawbacks to this procedure. The first is that if there is a correlation between firm size and wage, the wage figures will be biased in a direction opposite to the sign of the correlation. Suppose the correlation is positive, so that large firms pay higher wages. In that case, calculating unweighted means would give smaller and lower wage firms a larger than appropriate weight, thus biasing the overall average downward.[20] Second, even if the estimates are unbiased, their standard error will, in general, be larger if unweighted averages are computed.[21] While it is useless to worry about the increased variance in the estimates due to the erroneous weighting, the bias introduced due to possible correlation between firm size and wage could lead to serious error. Unfortunately no data whatsoever were available on the firm level, so that it was impossible to estimate whether large firms in a given industry and province paid higher or lower wages than smaller firms in the same industry and province.

19. Ibid., 1 : 192; 2 : 712. Here by mistake the total wage bill for all workers is entered rather than the quotient of the total wage bill to the number of workers, from which it could be concluded that the total wage bill for each firm was available.

20. Assume that there are for a given activity in a given province n firms, each firm employing m_j workers, $j = 1,\ldots,n$. Let $\alpha_j = \dfrac{m_j}{\sum_j m_j}$ with $\Sigma \alpha_j = 1$, $0 < \alpha_j < 1$. The true average wage is therefore: $w^\star = \Sigma \alpha_j w_j$, while what was actually computed was: $\bar{w} = \dfrac{1}{n} \Sigma w_j$. Now:

$$E(w^\star) = E\Sigma(\alpha_j w_j) = \Sigma E(\alpha_j) \cdot E(w_j) + cov(\alpha,w) = \frac{1}{n} \Sigma E w_j + cov(\alpha,w) \text{ since } E(\alpha_j) = \frac{1}{n}$$

$E(\bar{w}) = \dfrac{1}{n} \Sigma E w_j$. Hence $\bar{w}$ is unbiased only if α and w are uncorrelated.

21. The problem is analogous to problems that come up in stratified sampling. Cf. e.g., William G. Cochran, *Sampling Techniques*, 2d ed. (New York: John Wiley and Sons, 1963), pp. 116–18.

However, some detailed figures were available for two provinces, Friesland and Drenthe. For these provinces data on the level of villages and townships were available, so that it was possible to calculate the correlation between firm size and wage under the assumption that in each village all firms were of the same size. Taking only industries for which at least seven observations (villages in Friesland and Drenthe in which the activity occurred) were available, a total of forty-three regression equations could be estimated. The test performed was whether the correlation between firm size and wage was significantly different from zero. The results were as follows:

Correlation Coefficient	Frequency	Correlation Coefficient	Frequency
< −.4	4	> .4	4[a]
−.4 − −.35	2	.4 − .35	3
−.35 − −.3	2	.35 − .3	1
−.3 − −.25	2	.3 − .25	1
−.25 − −.2	1	.25 − .2	2
−.2 − −.15	1	.2 − .15	3
−.15 − −.1	2	.15 − .1	2
< −.1	7	< .1	6
	21		22

[a]One of these was significant at the 1 percent level and one at the 5 percent level. None of the negative coefficients was significant.

The fact that the number of positive correlation coefficients is equal to the number of negative coefficients, and that half of all the coefficients were smaller in absolute value than .2 while only two were statistically significant, lends support to the assumption that firm size and wage were not significantly correlated, so that no serious bias was introduced because of the failure to weight the averages by firm size. The test performed is, however, too weak to draw any stronger conclusions.

There are other problems with the use of the 1819 wage data, which underline the caution with which the results should be handled. One problem is that wages were sometimes paid in kind. It seems that this custom had become relatively rare in these highly monetized economies, the only exception being that in some activities workers received board and room. The compilers of the survey seem to have been aware of this and attempted to correct for payment in kind. In the municipal returns of the city of Groningen, it is mentioned that pastry bakers pay their adult workers 15 cents plus board, while children earn nothing but board.[22]

22. Brugmans, *Statistieken*, 2:656.

In the aggregate returns for the province as a whole (in which all pastry bakers are from the city of Groningen), the same adults and children are reported to earn 55 cents and 25 cents respectively.[23]

A second problem is the seasonality of work. Many firms operated only part time for various reasons. Seasonality per se does not constitute a problem since the wages recorded were daily, not annual wages. It seems likely that some workers were employed by different firms in different seasons. The difficulty is that the length of the working day may have varied over the year, and the wages of firms sensitive to seasonal fluctuations may be subject to various biases as a result.

Finally, there is the problem of piece wages. Piece wages were widespread, especially in the textile industries (both putting-out and centralized). The reason why piece wages constitute a problem is that it is difficult to know what the daily wage was, since the length of the working day may have varied considerably, especially in the domestic industry. Therefore it is not easy to assess the reliability of the wage estimates for those industries. In some cases there are indications that the firms reporting piece wages were simply jettisoned for the purpose of wage calculation, though the firms themselves were included in the overall figures. This procedure is equivalent to attributing the wages of workers employed on a daily basis to workers on a piecewage basis, and is somewhat questionable in the case of the Z-good industries. Fortunately, there is independent information on the earnings of the Belgian (especially Flemish) proto-industry, which seems to corroborate the orders of magnitude reported in the 1819 survey. In other industries piece wages may have been of comparatively minor significance.[24]

In most other respects the data appear relatively reliable. By comparing the provincial returns of the provinces of Friesland and Drenthe with the entries for these provinces in the aggregate tables, it could be ascertained that the compilation and editing of the returns was carried out with scrutiny. Some doubtful cases remain, however. Sometimes the errors were manifest and could be corrected (such as those cases mentioned above in which the weekly wage instead of the daily wage was reported). In most doubtful cases, it was preferred to jettison the observations rather than to perform speculative corrections on them.[25] The two most notable excep-

23. Ibid., 1: 316.

24. It is interesting to note that Roentgen reported in 1823 that Belgian workers, in contrast to English workers, were generally paid on a daily rather than a piece wage basis. Cf. Roentgen, "Berigt van den Toestand," p. 114.

25. Wherever the number of adult workers was given but not their wage, the observations were left out in order to prevent the computer from counting their wages as zero. No such policy was adopted for children, since it is possible that in many cases apprentices received negligible or zero wages.

tions were the flax spinning industry of East Flanders and the overall record of North Holland. As to the former, only 2 firms were reported, employing 52,824 workers, while the neighboring province of West Flanders reported 36,194 firms with 39,037 workers. Since this was obviously a copying error and since omitting the observation would have implied a considerable loss of information, the number of firms in East Flanders was estimated by using average firm sizes from other provinces. In the case of North Holland, the returns are singularly incomplete. It is quite impossible that this relatively wealthy province was completely devoid of, among others, cornmills, tailors, blacksmiths, glassworks, brick-makers, and cobblers. By comparing the 1819 returns with the 1816 returns (which have survived for North Holland), it can be seen that the authorities in North Holland included only those industries surveyed in 1816, omitting most artisans and small workshops. The number of workers in North Holland was estimated under the assumption that the ratio of industrial workers to urban population in North Holland was the same as in South Holland. The estimated wage figure for North Holland was not revised: if there was no strong correlation between firm size and wages, the fact that only large firms were included should not bias the estimated wage.

Otherwise, the coverage of the industrial sector in the Low Countries seems to be quite impressive, although no claim for completeness should be made. Still, a deliberate attempt in this direction was made. One example will suffice: originally, the returns for the city of Utrecht, the municipal returns of which were preserved, were of a very low quality. About half of all the entries read "unanswered." Yet the entries for the province of the same name as they appear in the aggregated tables are corrected to a considerable extent. For instance, the two vinegar makers and the four (out of five) printers, who had declined to send in their forms to the municipal authorities, appear in the aggregated tables.[26] What probably happened was that the city officials sent out forms to the various enterprises in the hope that these would be filled out and returned. The provincial (or perhaps central) government, dissatisfied with the way the city had conducted the collection of the data, had the results revised and enlarged by forcing the surveyors to visit the establishments in person and collect the data directly.

Before examining the wage data, the total number of workers for the kingdom as a whole are presented in table 5.1. While it cannot be denied that underreporting was severe, it still seems believable that the variability in underreporting from province to province was not of such dimensions

26. Brugmans, *Statistieken*, 1: 251, 265; 2: 668, 670.

Table 5.1   Number of Firms, Employment, and Average Firm Size
in the Low Countries, 1819

Province	Firms (F)	Adults (A)	Children (K)	A/F	K/F	(A + K)/F
N. Brabant	8,659	12,716	2,400	1.47	0.28	1.75
Gelderland	5,130	6,692	1,267	1.30	0.25	1.55
S. Holland	6,764	20,446	1,739	3.02	0.26	3.28
N. Holland[a]	8,493	25,674	2,184	3.02	0.26	3.28
Zeeland	3,094	3,653	621	1.18	0.20	1.38
Utrecht	3,126	8,169	2,438	2.61	0.78	3.39
Friesland	4,991	8,785	1,384	1.76	0.28	2.04
Overijssel	4,636	12,209	3,261	2.63	0.70	3.33
Groningen	4,606	6,606	852	1.43	0.18	1.62
Drenthe	1,234	1,967	n.a.	1.59	n.a.	1.59
Total North	50,733	106,917	16,146	2.11	0.32	2.43
S. Brabant	6,732	13,608	538	2.02	0.08	2.10
Limburg	6,770	6,371	236	0.94	0.03	0.97
Liège	5,482	27,911	4,018	5.09	0.73	5.82
E. Flanders	37,288[a]	101,601	10,780	2.72	0.29	3.01
W. Flanders	59,336	74,675	3,806	1.26	0.06	1.32
Hainault	8,415	32,893	2,591	3.91	0.31	4.22
Namur	2,712	6,915	163	2.55	0.06	2.61
Antwerp	7,192	23,167	1,391	3.22	0.19	3.41
Luxembourg	8,395	12,295	273	1.46	0.03	1.49
Total South	142,184	299,436	23,796	2.10	0.12	2.22
Total	193,055	406,353	39,942	2.11	0.21	2.31

[a] Estimated, see text.
SOURCE: Computed from Brugmans, *Statistieken*, 1: 247–417.

that no inference can be made concerning the geographical distribution of industry. It should be realized that the numbers in table 5.1 pertain to at least four distinct types of industrial enterprises and industrial workers. First, there is the modern industry, mostly urban, large scale, and mechanized, concentrated in Flanders, Hainault, and Liège. Second, there is the protoindustry, largely (though not exclusively) rural, rudimentary, and small scale. Third, there are the traffic industries, mostly located in the Dutch maritime provinces.[27] Finally, there is a large contingent of small artisans producing for a localized market that had been the industrial backbone of Europe since medieval times: the village miller, baker, blacksmith, cobbler, carpenter, and so on.

Turning now to the wage figures, the aggregates are summarized in table 5.2. It can be verified that the fundamental argument presented to explain the differential development of the Netherlands and Belgium is upheld by the data. The average wage paid in the northern provinces was 56.5 percent higher than in the southern provinces. Wages were

27. For a definition, see chapter 1.

Table 5.2   Wages of Adults and Children and Their Ratio, by Province
(in cents)

Province	Adult Wage W_a	Child Wage W_k	W_k/W_a
N. Brabant	55.2	16.5	0.30
Gelderland	62.7	18.2	0.29
S. Holland	86.0	25.8	0.30
N. Holland	94.2	20.2	0.21
Zeeland	82.5	19.0	0.23
Utrecht	82.0	21.2	0.26
Friesland	76.5	13.6	0.18
Overijssel	58.2	32.6	0.56
Groningen	76.0	22.3	0.29
Drenthe	73.4	—	—
Total North	74.8	22.4	0.30
S. Brabant	59.8	9.5	0.16
Limburg	52.4	19.6	0.37
Liège	65.6	23.9	0.36
E. Flanders	40.3	17.5	0.43
W. Flanders	32.3	12.8	0.40
Hainault	77.1	29.0	0.38
Namur	70.6	30.6	0.43
Antwerp	48.6	24.1	0.50
Luxembourg	54.5	23.6	0.43
Total South	47.8	19.5	0.41
Total	54.1	20.6	0.38

SOURCE: Computed from Brugmans, *Statistieken*, 1: 247–417.

particularly high in the maritime provinces of North and South Holland, Zeeland, and Utrecht. On the other hand, wages in the Dutch Z-good provinces, Overijssel and North Brabant, were considerably lower than average. As to the Belgian provinces, wages in Flanders were very low, while wages in Liège were higher but still 15 percent below the northern average. More problematic are Hainault and Namur, where wages were relatively high. Here, however, it should be remembered that the mining industry was an important employer and that mining paid traditionally higher wages because of the unpleasant and risky nature of the work. In addition, the figure for Hainault is probably biased upward due to the abnormally and probably erroneously high wages reported by the two large tapestry firms in the town of Tournay.[28]

Interestingly enough, the differences in children's wages are much

28. The wage reported was 100 cents daily for more than 3,000 workers, virtually all of them domestic workers employed on a putting-out basis. Since no children were reported, it seems likely that the high wage was, in fact, per family. Assuming the "typical" family consisted of two adults and two children, the wage level in this industry can be seen to be in the same order of magnitude as the Flemish protoindustry. Cf. Brugmans, *Statistieken*, 1: 382.

smaller than in adults' wages. One possible cause of this fact is that training was of more importance in the traffic industries than in either the Z-good industries or the "modern industries," so that the children's wages included a tuition premium in the Netherlands but not (or less so) in Belgium. Also the Belgian wage data for children are probably biased because of the underreporting of child labor in the protoindustry in Flanders. It seems highly unlikely that the 60,000 "firms" in West Flanders, which employed about 75,000 adult workers, so that the number of adults active in industry was at least 135,000, employed only 3,806 children. This does not imply that the wage of 12.8 cents per diem reported for children was necessarily biased, but it certainly means that the weight given to this figure in calculating the average children's wage for Belgium is too small.

Table 5.3 Employment, Location, Firm Size, and Wages, by Industrial Class

Industry	Total Employed[a]	Percent of Total	Percent Located in South	Firm Size[b]	Adult Wage	Child Wage
Linen, flax	253,631	41.7	96.0	2.20	32.3	15.0
Cotton	32,228	5.1	60.7	9.73	58.5	26.7
Wool	36,216	6.0	70.0	10.57	52.3	21.2
Leather	28,514	4.7	58.5	1.16	60.0	16.5
Tapestry	4,678	0.8	65.2	30.19	93.2	20.6
Apparel	24,252	3.9	64.7	1.34	57.7	12.8
Luxury textiles	939	0.1	39.4	10.45	100.7	22.8
Textiles for sailing and fishing	3,868	0.6	20.8	4.45	53.8	16.3
Unclassified textiles	1,212	0.2	41.7	1.35	72.9	8.9
Paper	5,806	1.0	44.9	5.46	78.6	21.1
Shipbuilding	3,087	0.5	33.0	2.78	90.1	22.0
Furniture	19,667	3.2	47.5	1.56	75.0	16.5
Breweries	17,779	3.0	81.9	1.42	74.7	18.2
Potteries, glass	11,037	1.8	51.0	3.05	65.4	27.8
Foodstuffs	43,766	7.2	56.6	1.08	66.9	27.8
Unclassified consumption goods	331	0.1	75.5	1.51	95.6	—
Instruments	13,057	2.1	72.9	1.41	75.4	21.8
Construction	23,873	3.9	60.9	3.40	80.2	31.3
Metallurgy	31,020	5.1	68.8	2.01	69.8	16.4
Mining	33,361	5.5	55.5	10.29	86.5	35.4
Chemicals	20,883	3.4	66.7	1.91	75.3	22.8
Total	608,193	100.0	75.8	3.31	54.1	20.6

[a]Defined as the number of adults and children hired plus the number of firms under the assumption that the owner in most cases worked in the enterprise.
[b]Defined as total employed per firm.
SOURCE: Brugmans, *Statistieken*, 1: 247–417.

Table 5.4   Adult Wages in Four Selected Industries
(in cents)

Province	Textiles	Foodstuffs	Capital Goods	Paper
N. Brabant	52.5	68.6	50.7	57.9
Gelderland	58.3	71.1	60.4	56.9
S. Holland	72.8	96.5	69.3	84.3
N. Holland	76.8	116.6	121.7	118.0
Zeeland	55.8	90.6	78.7	98.9
Utrecht	52.5	77.7	76.7	73.6
Friesland	60.9	75.1	63.3	66.4
Overijssel	45.2	64.8	57.3	59.9
Groningen	62.0	88.8	64.8	61.0
Drenthe	50.1	59.9	47.5	60.0
Total North	55.0	83.7	72.7	91.8
S. Brabant	53.6	71.7	48.4	59.0
Limburg	47.6	54.0	51.0	74.2
Liège	70.1	64.0	63.3	78.5
E. Flanders	37.4	67.3	54.8	68.8
W. Flanders	27.0	70.4	50.2	82.3
Hainault	35.6	87.6	86.2	71.2
Namur	59.1	76.5	68.9	48.4
Antwerp	34.8	67.3	76.0	82.0
Luxembourg	45.2	66.1	54.9	61.2
Total South	36.0	70.9	62.3	64.7
Total	37.9	74.9	66.9	78.6
Ratio North/South	1.528	1.182	1.151	1.419

SOURCE: Brugmans, *Statistieken*, 1:247–417.

The distribution of wages among the various industries is illustrated in tables 5.3 and 5.4. Table 5.3 presents the twenty-one classes in which the 450 tables were grouped together. Efforts were made to make the classification as consistent and as logical as possible, but it is hard to say if all pitfalls were avoided successfully. Almost all classes contain combinations of "new" and "old" industries. For example, the cotton industry includes both the mechanized spinning mills of Ghent, the rudimentary home weaving in the Twente and Flemish countryside, and the Amsterdam cotton printers. The iron industry includes thousands of village blacksmiths, as well as the Cockerill iron works and the nail and cutlery industries in the Walloon countryside.

Table 5.4 presents the wages in a few key industries. The four industries selected were textiles (cotton, linen, and wool), capital goods (construction, metallurgy, and instrument making), foodstuffs (largely a small-scale artisan industry), and paper (a relatively capital-intensive industry in the process of being mechanized in Belgium while stagnating in the Netherlands).[29] As can be verified from table 5.4, the North-South differential was particularly pronounced in textiles and paper, while smaller in foodstuffs and capital goods. The reason for that may have been that textiles and paper could more readily draw upon the reserves of labor in the Z-good sector, whereas in the capital goods and foodstuffs industries skills and other barriers to free entry of labor kept the wage level in Belgium relatively higher. It is not entirely clear whether the capital goods needed more skills than the textile industry, but it may be conjectured that it needed *different* skills—skills that were less readily available in the traditional sector. At any rate the wage differential seems a consistent feature in virtually all sections of the industrial sectors in the two countries.

It is thus clear that the 1819 industrial survey, the one body of comparatively systematic and uniform evidence available on wages, tends to corroborate the hypothesis put forward in the present study, namely that labor in Belgium was cheaper than in the Netherlands. The 1819 data do not demonstrate whether labor in Belgium was more elastically supplied than in the Netherlands. The test of that hypothesis is whether Belgian wages rose as industrialization proceeded. A related question is whether high wages in the Netherlands were maintained through the three decades following the 1819 survey. The answer to both questions jointly determines whether the wage gap between the two countries was maintained. There is no coherent comparative material for the period after 1819, and the only way to show that the wage gap did not diminish is by looking at time paths of the wages in the two countries separately.

As to the Netherlands, the evidence from which the behavior of wages for the period subsequent to the 1819 survey could be inferred is scant indeed. The state of stagnation and inertia to which the Dutch economy was subject seemed to manifest itself into relatively stable wages. Thorbecke, a leading liberal politician, noted in 1855 that the constancy of wages in the Netherlands was remarkable.[30] One source notes that wages in a Dutch papermill in 1846 were virtually the same as the wages paid in the same mill for the same type of labor in 1751.[31] Some of the rather fragmentary evidence collected by Brugmans is presented in table 5.5. The evidence is neither comprehensive nor consistent enough to draw conclusions stronger than saying that there is no evidence for a decline in wages.

Brugmans concludes, on the basis of this evidence, that nominal wages rose an average of 10 percent between 1819 and 1853. Since, Brugmans argues, prices rose by 50 percent (here the period of reference is 1820-70),

29. See above, pp. 75, 90-91.
30. Cited in Brugmans, *Arbeidende Klasse*, p. 140.
31. B. W. de Vries, *Nederlandse Papiernijverheid*, p. 310.

Table 5.5   Changes in Dutch Wages, 1819–Midcentury
(1819 = 100)

Activity	Province	Year of Comparison	Wage Index
Carpenter	Groningen	1848	151.5
"	Overijssel	"	114.1
"	Utrecht	"	120.1
"	S. Holland	"	113.1
"	Zeeland	"	127.4
"	N. Brabant	"	180.0
Shoemaker	N. Brabant	1853	114.4
Tanner	"	"	125.8
Gin distiller	S. Holland	"	145.8
Madder refiner	Zeeland	"	147.6
Rope maker	S. Holland	"	101.3
Oil mill worker	N. Holland	"	106.7
Paper mill worker	"	"	48.6
Blacksmith	Gelderland	"	111.8

SOURCE: Brugmans, *Arbeidende Klasse*, pp. 128, 132.

real wages declined in the first half of the nineteenth century.[32] The price data used by Brugmans are highly questionable, and a secular rise in prices of necessities between 1820 and 1870 (or 1850 for that matter) flies directly in the face of the information for similar trends in France, Germany, England, and Belgium, in none of which a long term price rise was observed (though the price level fluctuated considerably, of course).

As to Belgian wages, the question is somewhat more complicated. In contrast with the Netherlands, the Belgian economy grew and transformed itself into an industrialized economy in the period under discussion, so that the Principle of Insufficient Reason cannot be appealed to in order to explain why wages remained constant.[33] What happened to wages in Belgium was determined by the long-run labor supply facing the modern sector. In terms of the framework presented in chapter 4, the question centers around the Labor Availability Coefficient. A low value of the LAC would indicate that even if wages rose somewhat, the economy was still basically a pseudo labor-surplus economy, and could benefit from the advantages thereof with respect to industrialization.

What happened to Belgian wages during the process of industrialization in the first half of the nineteenth century? The caveats in making long term comparisons in a developing economy are many: the composition of

32. Brugmans, *Arbeidende Klasse*, pp. 128, 138.
33. In other words, in an economy which is basically stationary, it could be argued that wages should on the whole remain constant since there is no strong reason to expect them either to rise or to fall.

Table 5.6   Wages in the Flemish Cotton Industry, 1829–49
(1849 = 100)

Year	Carding	General Overhead	Year	Carding	General Overhead
1829	102.9	n.a.	1840	102.9	121.7
1830	101.0[a]	n.a.	1841	95.1	116.2
1831	n.a.	n.a.	1842	88.2	118.6
1832	84.3[b]	n.a.	1843	90.2	115.0
1833	n.a.	n.a.	1844	92.2	107.1
1834	n.a.	n.a.	1845	99.0	107.9
1835	101.0[c]	119.0[c]	1846	97.1	103.6
1836	107.8	124.1	1847	98.0	103.1
1837	96.1	118.6	1848	100.0	100.0
1838	92.2	n.a.	1849	100.0	100.0
1839	84.3[d]	n.a.			

[a] February, May, and August only.
[b] November only.
[c] August and November only.
[d] May, August, and November only.
SOURCE: Municipal Archives, Ghent, Fonds Voortman, files 333–44.

the labor force changed both functionally and qualitatively. The homogeneity of the labor force probably declined and the inequality in the
distribution of wages was likely to rise. There is also a difficulty in choosing
the proper deflator. Since there were no clear-cut trends in prices, there is
some justification in looking at nominal wages.

An important source of wage data is firm records. In this field the
present study has barely scratched the surface of an enormous pile of
records collected by H. Coppejans-Desmedt at the municipal archives
in Ghent. These records are assembled in two collections of accounts and
other firm records, the Fonds Voortman and the Fonds de Hemptinne.[34]
The only consecutive time series which was not marred by a changing
composition of labor and which paid on a time (rather than a piece) basis,
were the wages paid in the *carderie* and to the overhead personnel in the
firm of Jean Baptiste Voortman. These data are summarized in table 5.6.
The table was constructed by calculating averages from the weekly data,
choosing samples from the weeks around the 20th of February, May,
August, and November. Since the records provided figures for the whole
wage sum, the number of workers receiving this sum jointly, and the
average number of days worked by these workers, the daily wage estimates
should be unbiased. It should be kept in mind that Voortman was in some

34. H. Coppejans-Desmedt, *Bedrijfsarchieven op het Stadsarchief van Gent* [Business
archives at the Ghent municipal archives] (Leuven: Nauwelaerts, 1971).

Table 5.7   Costs and Profits as a Percentage of Sales in the Walloon Woolen Industry

	1	2	3	4	5
Date of reference	1780–89	1805–10	1812	1838	1845–50
Area of reference	Verviers	Verviers	Sample	Belgium	Verviers
Raw wool			56	50	
Dyes	53	54.5	1	10[b]	54.5
Other intermediary inputs			5	10[b]	
Labor	31	19	16	20	17
Taxes	−3[a]	7.5	2	—	4.5
Gross profits	19	19	20	10	24
	100	100	100	100	100

[a]Includes a "statistical adjustment."
[b]Overestimates, see text.
SOURCES: Cols. 1, 2, 5, Lebrun, "L'Industrie Drapière," p. 565. Col. 3, Thomassin, *Mémoire Statistique*, pp. 475–76. Col. 4, Briavoinne, *De l'Industrie*, 2:393.

ways an exceptional firm, being originally a cotton printer who took up spinning relatively late (1827). The firm was highly integrated horizontally, and its spinning and weaving activities seem somewhat peripheral to its main activity, printing. Nevertheless, there seems to be no reason why the overall trend in the wages paid to the workers in Voortman's firm should be different from the pattern followed by Flanders as a whole. Table 5.6 shows clearly that there is no evidence for rising wages in this period.

The conclusion of stable and low wages in the Ghent cotton industry in this period is corroborated by Mareska and Heyman, two social researchers who performed a careful examination of the Ghent working class in 1843. Certainly wages fluctuated severely with the cycle and with politically-caused perturbations in prosperity, but the movements appear trendless.[35]

A similar pattern of wage stability is observed in the woolen industry in the Walloon provinces. The breakdown of production costs in this industry is presented in table 5.7. As can be verified, the share of labor in total net value added (labor, profits, and taxes) falls from 66 percent during the ancient regime to 37.6 percent in 1845–50. Briavoinne's estimate for 1838 (column 4) is consistent with this trend. Obviously, his calculation overestimates intermediary inputs. If we assume that dyes and other intermediary inputs amounted only to 5 percent (as seems warranted

35. D. de Weerdt, "Loon- en Levensvoorwaarden van de Fabrieksarbeiders, 1789–1850" [Wages and standards of living of the factory workers, 1789–1850], in *Geschiedenis van de Socialistische Arbeidersbeweging in België*, ed. J. Dhondt (Antwerp: Ontwikkeling, 1960), pp. 75–76.

in view of the other observations) and impute the residual to profits, Briavoinne's figures fit the overall picture. The fall in the share of labor is a direct consequence of the constancy of wages during a rise in labor productivity due to mechanization. The share of profits rises over the whole period, which is to be expected. What the *rate* of profit was is difficult to assess, because of insurmountable difficulties in evaluating capital, as well as the lack of appropriate data about the depreciation of capital. Using Lebrun's estimates for the capital-labor ratios, the rate of profit (gross) was virtually stable around 13 percent. This would indicate a relatively low reinvestment coefficient, since the rate of growth of the capital stock was about 2.4 percent a year.[36] The true value of the reinvestment coefficient can be estimated only after the rate of depreciation is known.

As to the wage rate, the picture is somewhat clearer. Lebrun maintains that wages averaged about .90 francs a day in 1780–85, and about 1.50 francs in both 1805–10 and 1845–50. The initial discontinuous rise in wages is explained by the change in the composition of the labor force, e.g., less domestic spinners and more mechanics. Lebrun's data, based on firm records, are corroborated by evidence from other sources. Thomassin's data indicate an average wage of 1.20 francs in the "old industry" and 1.80 francs in the "new factories."[37] The 1819 survey yields an average wage of 1.49 francs for adults employed in the woolen industry in the province of Liège and 1.32 francs if children are included. Briavoinne cites a wage of 1.18–1.33 francs for 1838.[38] The 1846 survey gives an average adult wage of 1.36 francs in the woolen industry.[39]

The failure of wages to rise during a prolonged period of technological progress and capital accumulation is a striking phenomenon indeed, and did not fail to raise the attention of contemporaries. Van Hogendorp, insightful as usual, observed in 1817:

> In Verviers I noted the wealth of the manufacturers and the poverty of the workers. Whenever business booms and machines are being introduced so that goods can be produced at a lower cost than the market price, the workers continue to receive the same wages, while the manufacturers gain thousands.[40]

36. See above, table 2.5.
37. Thomassin, *Mémoire Statistique*, p. 474.
38. Briavoinne, *De L'Industrie*, 2: 393. Obtained by dividing the annual wage sum by the estimated number of workers, assuming 300 working days per annum.
39. *Statistique de la Belgique, Recensement Général 1846*, "Industrie," pp. xviii, xx–xxii. This figure is slightly biased downwards, see below.
40. Van Hogendorp, *Bijdragen*, 2: 269.

Table 5.8   Wages in Belgium, 1831–50, Selected Industries
(1850 = 100)

	Coal Mines	Zinc Mines	Cotton (piece)[a]	Cotton (hourly)
1831	77.7	n.a.	149.1	n.a.
1832	71.3	n.a.	142.6	n.a.
1833	80.9	n.a.	145.7	n.a.
1834	87.5	n.a.	95.2	n.a.
1835	97.1	n.a.	112.5	n.a.
1836	110.0	n.a.	108.7	n.a.
1837	123.0	74.5	110.5	n.a.
1838	129.4	74.5	101.1	n.a.
1839	124.3	75.6	105.3	n.a.
1840	118.4	75.2	109.5	n.a.
1841	113.2	76.2	125.8	92.5
1842	111.3	75.9	94.2	92.5
1843	103.7	76.7	93.5	91.6
1844	104.2	76.3	86.4	93.3
1845	113.5	79.1	75.9	94.8
1846	115.7	81.8	76.3	95.4
1847	113.0	80.0	102.9	95.6
1848	99.5	89.6	83.7	95.6
1849	97.3	102.2	77.7	100.0
1850	100.0	100.0	100.0	100.0

[a] Measured per week, regardless of number of hours worked or piece rate.
SOURCE: Peeters, "L'Évolution des Salaires," pp. 415, 417.

Some important research on Belgian wages has been carried out by Peeters, but unfortunately he includes no observations for the period prior to 1831, while the evidence for the years 1831–50 is scant.[41] Table 5.8 presents his findings as far as they pertain to the period under discussion. The picture is somewhat uneven. Wages in the coal mines were at an unnatural low following the confusion and disruption of the Belgian Revolution of 1830. After recovery, wages rose steeply between 1833 and 1838 but then slowly tapered off until 1850 with a brief surge in 1845–46, which reflects the steeply rising prices in the hungry forties. No such fluctuation is observed for the cotton industry or the zinc mines, in both of which a slow but steady long-term trend upward is observed. Whether this rising trend represents a genuine increase in wages or a catching-up phenomenon after the slump of the mid-1830s is hard to tell. Comparison with table 5.6 suggests that the latter is quite likely. It is also clear from table 5.8 that the piece wage in the cotton industry fluctuates much more

41. M. Peeters, "L'Évolution des Salaires en Belgique de 1831 à 1913," *BISEL* 10, no. 4 (August 1939): 389–420.

Table 5.9   Belgian Prices, 1832–50, Five-year Moving Averages
(1850 = 100)

	Retail Food	All Retail	Agricultural Wholesale
1832	96.7	n.a.	n.a.
1833	97.4	n.a.	n.a.
1834	97.6	n.a.	n.a.
1835	100.0	n.a.	n.a.
1836	101.3	n.a.	n.a.
1837	104.4	104.1	98.3
1838	107.9	105.8	102.9
1839	108.2	106.3	105.6
1840	110.8	108.4	108.8
1841	111.0	106.0	109.0
1842	107.5	103.9	106.6
1843	106.4	103.0	106.1
1844	109.3	102.4	112.2
1845	110.6	102.2	118.1
1846	110.2	103.7	117.9
1847	111.7	105.0	118.6
1848	109.1	104.1	114.7
1849	104.0	102.4	106.9
1850	100.0	100.0	100.0

SOURCE: Computed from F. Michotte, "L'Évolution des Prix de Détail en Belgique de 1830 à 1913," *BISEL* 8, no. 3 (May 1937): 353.

violently than the hourly wage, indicating irregular working hours. This underlines the fact that the piece wage is not a reliable indicator of the behavior of wages.

In order to justify the use of nominal wages, some price data are presented in table 5.9. By inspection, it can be ascertained that prices show a rather insignificant rise between 1832 and 1850.[42] It seems therefore excluded that the constant nominal wage could be interpreted as a rising real wage due to falling prices.

A more long-run and complete view of the behavior of Belgian wages is obtained by comparing the returns of the 1819 and 1846 industrial surveys, which are the only sources for industrial wages for more than a few isolated industries. The caveats in carrying out this comparison are many and should be underlined in order to stress the approximate nature of the conclusions. The most damaging defect of the 1846 survey was, as noted above, the omission of the Z-good industry.[43] The omission of these

42. The least square estimates of the trends of prices are not significant, except for the retail food prices, which have a positive trend which is significant at the 5 percent level ($t = 2.20, n = 19$).
43. See above, p. 69.

workers is particularly damaging for the linen industry, but for the woolen and metallurgical industries as well, since the 1819 survey includes no doubt many thousands of protoindustrial workers in these industries. Furthermore, a bias in the average wage level as computed by the compilers of the 1846 survey had to be corrected.[44]

In addition to these major problems, a host of less severe difficulties complicates the comparison between the wage figures from the 1819 survey and those from the 1846 one. The most important of these are listed below. (1) The 1819 figures for Belgium include the entire provinces of Limburg and Luxembourg, while the figures for 1846 pertain only to those parts of these two provinces which became part of Belgium by the settlement of 1839. (2) If the degree of monetization of the economy increased with its development, so that a larger share of wages was paid in kind in 1819 than in 1846, the 1819 figures are downward biased, unless the compilers of the 1846 survey succeeded fully in correcting for the payment in kind bias. (3) In the 1846 survey, adults are defined as workers beyond the age of sixteen, while the distinction in the 1819 survey is unclear. (4) Since the breakdown between men and women was given for the 1846 survey but not for the 1819 survey, it was impossible to distinguish pure changes in adult wages from changes in the aggregate wage due to changes of the sex proportions in the labor force. The wage level of women was approximately 50 percent of that of men. (5) The classification of goods and activities into classes was carried out by the compilers, but for the 1819 survey no classification was provided, and had to be made especially for the present study. Hence certain inconsistencies in the definition of classes of industries may have entered the calculation, although these are probably not of major importance. (6) Both surveys were taken at relatively unrepresentative moments: the 1819 survey during the recovery from the post-Napoleonic trough and the 1846 survey during the severe famine of the 1840s.

In spite of these shortcomings, the comparison of the 1819 and 1846 data, presented in table 5.10, can be seen to show that the available evidence points in the direction of more or less constant wages. The only industries in which significant wage rises were registered were metallurgy and mining. The reservoir of Z-good labor available to these industries

44. The survey does not provide average wage data but rather the number of workers earning less than 50 centimes, between 50 centimes and 1.00 francs, etc. In computing the averages, the compilers simply took the midpoints in each range, which is correct only if the wage distribution is uniform in each range. At least for the low ranges, this assumption is highly questionable. It is likely that most adults in the lowest range, for example, were clustered around the 50 centimes level rather than uniformly distributed over the range. The estimate of 0.25 francs for the range 0 to 0.50 has therefore been replaced by 0.50 francs, which hopefully corrects also for the analogous bias in the 0.50 to 1.00 range.

Table 5.10   Adult Daily Wages in Belgium, 1819 and 1846
(in francs)

Industry	1819	1846	Percentage Change
Linen	0.65	0.76	+ 16.9
Cotton	1.30	1.42	+ 9.2
Wool	1.10	1.38	+ 25.4
Leather	1.24	1.10	− 11.3
Apparel	1.22	1.06	− 13.1
Paper	1.37	1.53	+ 11.7
Wood	1.45	1.27	− 12.4
Potteries, glass	1.58	1.59	+ 0.6
Foodstuffs	1.32	1.17	− 11.4
Metallurgy	1.39	2.01	+ 44.6
Mining	1.64	1.32	+ 17.1
Chemicals	1.50	1.46	− 2.6
Total	1.01	1.38	+ 36.6
Total, excluding linen	1.45	1.49	+ 2.8

SOURCES: 1819—computed from Brugmans, *Statistieken*, 1: 247–417, and converted to francs by using the gold exchange rate 1 : 2.12. 1846—computed from *Statistique de la Belgique, Recensement Général 1846*, "Industrie," pp. xix–xxiii, corrected for linear averaging in lowest ranges (see text).

was clearly smaller than that available to textiles. On the other hand, the figure for metallurgy in 1846 is biased upward because of the omission of thousands of rural nailmakers from the survey. A similar bias, though probably of smaller proportions, exists in the woolen industry. The average wage without linen constitutes a more consistent comparison, since most of the linen workers were omitted from the 1846 survey, but included in the 1819 survey. The rise in Belgian wages was by no means large enough to close the gap in the income distributions of the two countries.

It is time to summarize the argument. It was shown in chapter 4 that the adoption of the modern technology depended on the "going wage" faced by the modern sector in two ways. First, only if the wage level is lower than the average productivity of labor in the production of consumption goods will the new technique be adopted at all. Second, the rate of accumulation is an inverse function of the wage level, so that even if in both countries conditions were such that the new technique was profitable, the low wage economy would switch to the new technique at a faster rate, i.e., in a shorter time span. In addition, it should be recognized that if the supply of labor was inelastic, the transition would be thwarted in its early stages. As was shown in this chapter, the historical evidence suggests that

Dutch wages were considered high in the eighteenth century, that these wages remained high during the French domination, and were considerably higher than Belgian wages in 1819. Furthermore, the available evidence suggests that Belgian wages failed to rise significantly between 1819 and the mid-century, in spite of the rise in labor productivity that accompanied the process of industrialization described in chapter 2.

Moreover, there is no evidence that Dutch wages fell before 1850. In fact, the policies of the N.H.M. and the Dutch government may well have contributed to counteract whatever tendencies there were in the Netherlands toward a lowering of the wage level. This seems to be true in both the maritime and the protoindustrial provinces. The issue that will have to be faced now is what were the possible determinants of the income distributions in the two countries, which indirectly determined the properties of the "growing up" paths in the two countries.

THE DETERMINANTS OF WAGES

The model presented in chapter 4 provides a unique and unambiguous mode of determination of the wage level faced by the modern sector. The productivity coefficient of labor in the Z-good sector, a technologically determined parameter, and the price of Z-goods, given by the international terms of trade, jointly determine the "going wage." The question of whether the labor hired by the modern sector was in fact at one time employed in the Z-good sector is irrelevant, since even if it were not, the Z-good activity would still determine the opportunity cost of labor.

Belgium had a large Z-good sector, and it is therefore likely that in its case the income distribution was determined in the fashion outlined above.[45] For a country that is a perfect price taker, there is no a priori reason why the wage which is "dictated" to the modern sector by the Z-good sector should be particularly low or high. At a lower level of abstraction, however, one can think of at least three reasons why the wage rate determined in the Z-good sector would tend to be low, so low in fact that the spectre of starvation loomed over the Belgian protoindustry throughout most of the period under discussion.[46]

First, the assumption that the terms of trade were wholly independent of the output of the economy clearly is an oversimplification. If the economy does face a downward sloping demand curve for its output, the increase in population within the protoindustrial sector will result in

45. See above, pp. 148–49.
46. See above, pp. 16, 70, and below, chapter 7.

pecuniary diminishing returns. Second, even if Belgium was facing a perfectly elastic demand curve for its Z-goods, there may have been other forces which consistently pressed this price down. The most important of these forces was the expansion of textile production in England, both in linen and in cotton. Especially the spectacular growth in cotton, which was a close substitute for linen, had adverse effects on the linen price. Although exogenous to the Belgian economy, these tendencies cannot have failed to make their impact felt. Third, the question of raw materials in the linen industry comes up. Raw materials have been ignored thus far but as a matter of fact the output of Z should be regarded as "net" output or value added. Now, if the raw materials such as flax were produced under conditions of diminishing returns, another form of diminishing returns is introduced in the economy. Thus the traditional economy may still be riding the population growth vehicle to the Malthusian trap at a point like E_1 in figure 1.2. For the woolen industry, the argument is analogous. Here the raw materials were imported, so that if the supply curve of raw wool was upward sloping, a similar effect would occur. There were other fixed factors as well in wool, such as water supply, power, and other locational advantages in the finishing processes, which would rationalize a process of diminishing marginal productivity of labor as population was growing.

It is therefore not difficult to see the causes for the low wage level in Belgium at the beginning of the industrialization period. The question of high wages in the Netherlands is somewhat more complicated. It is of course true that the very absence of a Z-good sector in most of the Netherlands could be put forward as an explanation of the high wages. But it is not clear if such an argument provides a full and satisfactory answer. For one thing, the Dutch economy at the end of the eighteenth and the first half of the nineteenth century was far too complex and varied to be analyzed in terms of a single phenomenon. More important, the absence of a protoindustrial sector may have been a result rather than a cause of the special characteristics of the Dutch economy. It is to these that we turn now.

Theory tells us that a major factor influencing the level of nominal wages is the price level of the goods consumed by the workers.[47] The most frequent explanation of the height of Dutch wages was that the price level of the necessities of life in the Netherlands was higher than elsewhere. The high excise taxes levied on consumption goods are often cited as

47. In an economy in which the goods produced are not the same as the goods consumed by workers, the term "real wage" is ambiguous.

the reason for this level of prices. Contemporaries were no doubt aware of the impact of the excise taxes on the nominal wage level. Luzac writes:

> As soon as it becomes clear that taxes on the food consumption of the common man raise the cost of living of the workers, and that therefore a worker has to earn more than otherwise, it will be clear also that the taxes are the cause of the high wages and any damages to the economy caused by the high wages should be considered a consequence of taxation.[48]

Ricardo, in an interesting footnote to his chapter on the "Effects of Accumulation on Profits and Interest," replies to Adam Smith's contention that the low rate of interest in Holland was because of an abundance of capital. According to Ricardo, the low profits in Holland were a result of the fact that "Holland was obliged to import almost all the corn which she consumed, and by imposing heavy taxes on the necessaries of the labourer, she further raised the wages of labour."[49] The same theme is reiterated by modern historians, notably Charles Wilson.[50]

To be sure, there can be no doubt that the argument in principle is sound. The Dutch had accumulated an enormous national debt during the incessant expensive wars it fought against England and France between 1651 and 1714. The interest and principal on these debts, as well as the need to maintain a large navy to protect its commercial interests and colonial empire, made the United Provinces of the Netherlands the heaviest taxed country in Europe in the eighteenth century. As early as 1695, Gregory King estimated that the tax burden per capita in Holland was more than double the burden in England and France.[51] This burden did not decline during the entire eighteenth century and the first decades of the nineteenth, although the tax burden per capita in other countries may have risen. At any rate, since the taxes were in part levied on the necessities of life (mainly milling and brewing duties), they did raise the prices of consumption goods and thus reduced the real wage. In the

48. Luzac, *Hollands Rijkdom*, 4: 82.

49. David Ricardo, *Principles of Political Economy and Taxation*, ed. R. H. Hartwell (Harmondsworth: Penguin Books, 1971), p. 291n. Ricardo's first argument, that prices were high because corn was largely imported, cannot withstand scrutiny. If the Dutch imported wheat, that must have meant, according to Ricardo's own theory of international trade, that the Dutch were relatively more efficient in producing those agricultural products which they exported (dairy products) than cereals, in which case the latter should be cheaper than if it were locally grown. In any case, the *proportion* of imported wheat should not be indicative of the price.

50. Wilson, "Taxation and the Decline of Empires, an Unfashionable Theme," in *Economic History and the Historians*, pp. 114–27.

51. Ibid., p. 120.

absence of long-run money illusion, this should cause the nominal wage to rise.

It is important to keep in mind, however, that an ad valorem tax of x percent will in general result in a less than proportional rise in the nominal wage. The reason for this is that a tax of x percent will only in part be borne by consumers, unless the elasticities of demand and supply have extreme values. Thus the price of the taxed good will rise only by y percent, where $y < x$. A rise in the price of the wage good by y percent will result again in a *less than* proportional rise in the nominal wage rate unless, again, the elasticities of supply and demand for labor are extreme.

There is some evidence which suggests that the impact of taxes on nominal wages was less important than was generally thought. In 1790 the Dutch politician, van de Spiegel, pointed out that nominal wages in Zeeland were similar to those in Holland and Utrecht, although indirect taxes in the latter two were substantially higher.[52] Moreover, the fact that the potato, which was a good substitute for the heavily taxed cereals, was not taxed[53] probably reduced the impact of the milling tax on the price of food since the availability of a substitute tended to make demand for cereals more elastic. It is noteworthy that in 1821 van Hogendorp discounted as trivial the impact of the excise tax on the Dutch economy as a whole and on the wage level in manufacturing in particular.[54]

A crude criterion of the impact of the indirect taxes on wages is the proportion of total wage income that ended up in the treasury through the excise tax. Theoretically, this criterion is not entirely satisfactory, but it suffices as an indicator of the orders of magnitude involved. Total income of the state from taxes around 1795 was estimated at 30 million florins. Of this, some 20 million came from indirect taxes on consumption, and of these, about 11 million were levied on luxury consumption and 9 million florins on necessities.[55] In the two decades that followed, the political and fiscal structure of the country underwent many transformations. Yet in 1826 total income from excise taxes in the northern provinces of the

52. L. P. van de Spiegel, *Over de Armoede en de Bedelaary, met Betrekkinge tot de Provintie van Zeeland* [On the poverty and mendicity, with reference to the province of Zeeland] (Goes: Huisman, 1780), pp. 21–23.

53. Luzac, *Hollands Rijkdom*, 4: 82.

54. Van Hogendorp, *Bijdragen*, 6: 306, 333. For a recent attempt to revive the fiscal explanation of high wages in the Dutch maritime provinces, see Richard T. Griffiths, "Iets meer over de Haarlemse Katoenfabrieken" [Some more on the cotton factories of Haarlem], *THB* 15 (1974): 53. While Griffiths's evidence points in the right direction, his figures do not prove that taxes were the only or principal factor in explaining wage differentials.

55. F. A. Sickenga, *Bijdrage tot de Geschiedenis der Belastingen in Nederland* [A contribution to the history of taxation in the Netherlands] (Leyden: P. Engels, 1864), p. 327.

kingdom was 9,730,000.[56] Between these dates, during the French domination, indirect taxes were somewhat higher: in 1806 and 1807, the figure stood around 14.5 million florins.[57]

Total income from labor in this period cannot even be approximated. Yet it is possible to estimate a lower boundary. At the beginning of the nineteenth century, total population in the Netherlands was about two million, which grew to about three million by 1850. Taking the lower figure and dividing by four, we obtain the minimum number of breadwinners at 500,000. The real number of workers must have been somewhat higher since many women and children worked as well. The average nominal daily wage of an adult worker in Dutch industry was about 0.75 florin.[58] If we assume that the average wages in other sectors, explicit or implicit, were at least as high as in industry,[59] it turns out that the lower bound of labor income in the Netherlands in this period was 112,500,000 florins. Whether the actual sum was one and a half times or six times as high is impossible to say. Yet if we cling to our assumption that all labor income was consumed, it can be said with reasonable certainty that the share of excise taxes on necessities was 10 percent *or less* out of total expenditures of workers.[60] This is by no means a small proportion. Still, it does not seem impressive enough to explain the entire wage differential between the Netherlands and its neighbors. After all, wages in the provinces of Holland were twice the wages in Belgium.

Taxation alone will not do as an explanation for high wages in the Netherlands. A second type of argument centers around the widespread poor relief in the Netherlands, both outdoor and indoor, and its impact on the labor market. Theoretically the point is transparent enough: comparing two societies otherwise the same, in only one of which extensive poor relief is practiced, it is likely that in the first economy the supply curve of labor lies to the left of that in the second economy, and hence wages are higher. Intuitively this is quite obvious—if potential workers

56. Quetelet, *Recherches Statistiques*, p. 41 and annex table 4.

57. I. J. A. Gogel, *Memoriën en Correspondentiën Betrekkelijk den Staat van s'Rijks Geldmiddelen* [Memoranda and correspondence relating to the financial resources of the state] (Amsterdam: J. Müller, 1844), pp. 510–11, 520–21.

58. See above, table 5.2.

59. This seems a plausible assumption for agriculture, which prospered in this period (see below). For other sectors information is even more scarce. In shipping, however, wages were considerably higher than in industry, cf. Brugmans, *Arbeidende Klasse*, p. 134.

60. In Dutch National Archives, Goldberg Coll., file 50, no. 208, the owners of the peeling mills in the Zaan area estimate the total of indirect taxes paid by their workers at 50 florins annually, which amounts to 15 percent of total wages. However, as stated, the French period was a time of extraordinary high taxes.

are paid for idleness, they will demand a higher wage for actual labor than if the income associated with idleness were zero.[61]

The importance of philanthropy and almsgiving in Dutch society in the eighteenth and nineteenth centuries seems evident, although it is far from easy to assign clear quantitative significance to charity as an economic phenomenon. One author writes, referring to the eighteenth century:

> Philanthropy was among the major luxury expenditures in this country [the Netherlands]. Charity was fashionable among the many rich *rentiers* and merchants, who contributed lavishly to alms, poor houses and so on. Especially the foundation of almshouses in which a group of paupers were gathered and which was often called after the founder, yielded considerable social prestige and flattered the vanity of the upper classes.[62]

Charity and poor relief remained of major importance until at least the mid-nineteenth century.[63] The main conclusion to be drawn from this is that the large number of unemployed, which were reported to be teeming in the Dutch cities, may have been to a large extent voluntary rather than involuntary unemployment. As early as 1778, a Dutch periodical complains:

> The workers are unemployed and going idle...it seems almost as if they prefer the austere living that they can make from alms to a richer existence they could enjoy if they had been willing to work.... In the midst of a large, poverty stricken community, one runs into com-

---

61. Sometimes the opposite argument is made, for example, Brugmans, *Arbeidende Klasse*, pp. 140–41 and J. de Bosch Kemper, *Geschiedkundig Onderzoek naar de Armoede in ons Vaderland* [A historical inquiry into the causes of poverty in our country] (Haarlem: de Erven Loosjes, 1860), p. 206. The reasoning seems to be that as far as the poor relief came out of taxes paid by the manufacturers, the latter viewed the relief payments as a form of wages and accordingly reduced the wages they offered to their workers. This may have been the case in small communities in which the employer could verify which part of his taxes was used to support his workers. But then there is no real analytic difference between direct wages and indirect wages in the form of poor relief. To the extent that poor relief was financed out of nonindustrial sources, it is difficult to imagine any reason why the *demand* for labor should be affected at all. It is possible to rescue the argument by postulating that the supply curve of labor was negatively sloped and flatter than the demand curve, since then a shift to the left of the supply curve will result in lower wages. Such a situation is implausible (since the labor market will be unstable) and it is not surprising that there is no evidence for the claim that poor laws tended to reduce wages. Cf. M. Blaug, "The Myth of the Old Poor Law and the Making of the New," *JEH* 23 (June 1963): 151–84. For an excellent treatment of this subject along similar lines, see D. McCloskey, "New Perspectives on the Old Poor Law," *EEH* 10 (Summer 1973): 419–36.

62. Henriette Roland-Holst, *Kapitaal en Arbeid in Nederland* [Capital and labor in the Netherlands], 4th ed. (Rotterdam: Brusse, 1932), 1: 34.

63. Brugmans, *Paardenkracht*, pp. 63, 195.

plaints about the scarcity of man power. Even with money it has become impossible to induce them to work.[64]

Another indicator of the same phenomenon is the fact that Dutch industry, in the eighteenth as well as in the first half of the nineteenth century, employed a large number of foreigners, mainly Belgians, Swiss, and Germans.[65] No doubt they were attracted by the high wages paid in the Netherlands. Brugmans argues that these foreigners were hired because they were far more skilled than Dutch workers, but this argument is not convincing, since it was exactly in the Dutch urban areas, with their long tradition of traffic industries, where one would expect to find skilled labor. It is far more likely that the bulk of the Dutch unemployed were unemployed because they did not want to work at the going wage and preferred leisure. One writer notes in 1853:

> Overpopulation and unemployment are often cited as causes of poverty. Yet much of the hard labor in the peat-bogs in this province [Utrecht] is carried out by about 2,000 Germans. The same is true for the harvesting of the grass and other heavy tasks in other provinces. The question arises whether the Dutch are unable to perform these jobs themselves. Experience indicates that the answer to this question is negative, because in recent years they have successfully engaged in these activities. The reason why in previous years this work was largely carried out by foreigners is that in the rich provinces of Holland [i.e., the maritime provinces] it was formerly much easier to earn a generous living with little effort, so that the heavy work could be carried out by foreigners.[66]

It is hence our conclusion that the Dutch workers were *on* their supply curve of labor, and the paradox of the long-run coexistence of high wages and urban unemployment is satisfactorily resolved. As de Bosch Kemper notes correctly, a large number of paupers subsisting on charity does not imply a low level of aggregate income but quite the contrary.[67] Only a rich society is able to spend large sums to support its poor and unemployed in a systematic fashion. In spite of its stagnation and recurrent crises, Dutch society was rich and remained so (to an ever decreasing extent, to be sure) until the mid-nineteenth century.

64. Cited by Roland-Holst, *Kapitaal en Arbeid*, 1: 36–37.
65. Brugmans, *Arbeidende Klasse*, pp. 89–91.
66. F. H. C. Drieling, "Verslag over den Toestand der Arbeidende Klasse, Vooral ten Plattenlande in de Provincie Utrecht" [Report on the state of the working class, especially in the countryside of the province of Utrecht], *TSS* 8 (1853): 439.
67. De Bosch Kemper, *Geschiedkundig Onderzoek*, p. 30.

What was the overall quantitative importance of poor relief in the Netherlands? Numbers will tell us little, unless a standard of comparison is found, and Belgium once again provides a suitable yardstick. The results are reported in table 5.11. It can be verified that poor relief per capita in the northern provinces was almost twice as high as in Belgium while the number of people receiving some form of relief was relatively higher in the South (13.4 percent of total population as compared to 8.3 percent in the North). Consequently the expenditures per person on relief were more than three times higher in the North than in the South.

Table 5.11   Population and Poor Relief in the Early 1820s

Province	Total Population (1824)	Persons on Relief (1822)	Total Expenses (thousands of florins, 1822)	Expenses per Client (florins)	Expenses per Capita (florins)
N. Brabant	326,617	22,457	303	13.49	0.93
Gelderland	284,363	19,831	421	21.23	1.48
S. Holland[a]	438,202	42,854	1,924	44.90	4.49
N. Holland[a]	393,916	62,697	1,427	22.76	3.62
Zeeland	129,329	8,394	363	43.25	2.80
Utrecht	117,405	7,063	390	55.21	3.32
Friesland	202,530	17,419	606	34.79	2.99
Overijssel	160,937	6,714	229	34.11	1.42
Groningen	156,045	6,377	252	39.52	1.61
Drenthe	53,368	2,247	41	18.25	0.77
Total North	2,262,712	187,659	5,593	29.80	2.47
S. Brabant	495,455	105,781	988	9.34	1.99
Limburg	321,246	38,593	258	6.69	0.80
Liège	331,101	56,151	302	5.38	0.91
E. Flanders	687,267	59,839	708	11.83	1.03
W. Flanders	563,826	78,600	710	9.03	1.26
Hainault	546,190	106,085	616	5.80	1.13
Namur	189,393	25,269	192	7.60	1.01
Antwerp[b]	323,678	23,901	674	28.20	2.08
Luxembourg	292,610	2,450	49	20.00	0.17
Total South[c]	3,750,766	505,063	4,860	9.62	1.30
Total	6,013,478	692,722	10,453	15.09	1.74

[a]Only the total figure for the two provinces was available. Separate data calculated by employing weight of 1828.
[b]Figure refers to 1823 since 1822 is obviously in error.
[c]Including all of Limburg and Luxembourg.
SOURCES: Poor Relief—J. J. F. Noordziek, ed., *Verslag der Handelingen van de Tweede Kamer der Staten Generaal* [Report on the actions of the second chamber of the Estates General], 1822–23 (The Hague: Martinus Nijhoff, 1873), pp. 861 ff. Population—Quetelet, *Recherches Statistiques*, annex table 2.

Table 5.11 thus reflects two basic facts: the Netherlands was wealthier than Belgium and could afford to spend more on their poor; yet the absolute number of people in need was far larger in Belgium with its large pockets of rural and urban "pseudo labor-surplus." It is the spending per welfare client that determines the impact of a welfare system on the wage level, as well as total spending on welfare payments.

How important the Dutch welfare system was in determining the wage level in the Netherlands is, however, not an easy question. The "going wage" was determined by a large vector of parameters, and though theory can predict the direction of the influence of some of these parameters, it is much more difficult to assess the *relative* importance of each of these parameters, including the welfare payments. Nonetheless, the correlation between wages and outdoor relief is strong enough to suggest that welfare was an important factor. The rank correlation (Spearman) coefficient between wages and welfare payments per capita is $R = 0.571$ which for 19 observations yields a t statistic of 2.87, which is significant at the 1 percent level. The rank correlation coefficient between wages and welfare payments per client is $R = 0.463$ (t = 2.15), which is significant at the 5 percent level.

In addition to institutional factors such as taxation and poor relief, one is naturally inclined to look at the agricultural sector as a possible source of the wage differential between the Netherlands and Belgium. If the

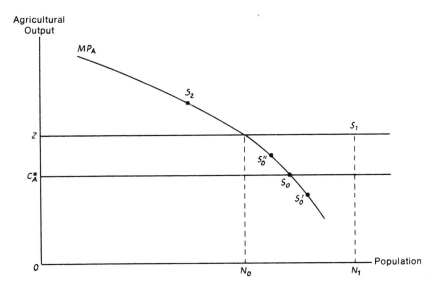

Figure 5.2   Z-good Production, Population Growth, and Wages

productivity of labor in Dutch agriculture was found to be substantially higher than in Belgium, this would explain the wage differential in an indirect way, through the presence or absence of a Z-good sector. Consider figure 5.2, an adaptation of figure 1.2. If population exceeds N_0, the Z-good sector should be expected to become important because the marginal product of labor in agriculture has fallen below that in Z-good production.

In practice, curves like MP_A are not observed. What is known is that the distance N_0N_1, that is, the amount of population "employed" in the Z-good sector, was large in Belgium and negligible in the Dutch maritime provinces, which also happened to be blessed with high quality alluvial clay soil. But the mere fact that Z-goods were insignificant in the Netherlands cannot help us to distinguish between points like S_2 and S_0. At S_2, the economy has no Z-good sector because it does not need one—agricultural marginal productivity is sufficiently high. Yet an economy without a Z-good sector could also exist because of its inability to resort to this hedge against population pressure. The causes for such inability to develop a protoindustry could be many: the absence of soil suitable for the cultivation of raw flax, insufficient water resources, lack of appropriate skills and traditions among peasants, opposition from nobility and/or clergy, and so on. Such an economy would find itself eventually in a Malthusian trap, say at point S_0.[68]

What is therefore needed at this stage is some information corroborating the hypothesis that the absence of a Z-good sector in the Netherlands was a matter of choice and not of necessity, and that the Dutch economy was at a point like S_2 rather than S_0. A first point to be established is that there is no evidence that Z-goods could not be produced in the Netherlands for "objective" causes. For one thing, Z-goods *were* produced in those areas in which the soil was less fertile and agriculture less productive.[69] Second, flax was grown in the alluvial provinces, but the bulk of the crop was exported in raw form rather than used as a basis for a protoindustry.[70] Water certainly cannot be regarded as a scarce resource in the Netherlands.

It seems therefore a plausible hypothesis that agriculture in the Netherlands was more productive (per unit of labor) than in Belgium. In the absence of quantitative research on Dutch nineteenth-century agriculture, it is very difficult to test this hypothesis properly. The link between the type of agriculture prevalent and the absence or presence of protoindustry

68. Because of continuous overshooting the economy may not be actually at S_0 for long periods. Rather, points like S'_0 and S''_0 will be observed with recurrent famines, epidemics, etc.

69. See above, pp. 6–7.

70. Goldberg, "Journaal der Reize," *TSS* 18: 244; *TSS* 19: 15. D'Alphonse, *Aperçu*, p. 176. Exports of raw flax between 1803–09 averaged 4.3 million francs, while imports were nil (d'Alphonse, *Aperçu*, pp. 394–95).

was apparent to intelligent contemporaries. Van Hogendorp, asked by a Flemish gentleman what the Dutch peasants did if they neither spun nor wove, answered that they produced butter and cheese and that this provided them with sufficient work.[71]

The historical background of Dutch agriculture was summarized in chapter 1. It is important to realize that Dutch agriculture remained prosperous throughout the hard years of French domination, due to high prices for agricultural goods. This enabled agriculture to cushion the heavy blows absorbed by the maritime and traffic industry sectors. Consequently thousands of urban dwellers fled to the countryside.[72] The agricultural boom was not transitory, however, and Dutch agriculture continued to grow during the first half of the nineteenth century. The value of land was reported by one author to have doubled in this period, together with a notable increase in livestock and a continuous adoption of technical innovations. Land reclamation through drainage of lakes and poldering culminated in the drainage of the Zuidplas near Gouda (province of South Holland) between 1828 and 1839 and the Haarlemmermeer, near Haarlem, between 1848 and 1852. Significantly, the difficulty was in finding colonizers to settle on the reclaimed land.[73] In the mid-nineteenth century, foreign visitors were still amazed at the wealth of Dutch farmers.[74]

The sources of Dutch agricultural prosperity should be sought in the high capital-labor ratio and the high land-labor ratio, with land measured in fertility units. In practice the two causes are indistinguishable; much agricultural capital was invested in land improvement and reclamation, although no doubt some part of the fertility of the alluvial soils was because of natural causes as well. To complicate things even more, important complementarities existed between capital and land (such as the fertilizing effects of livestock). There is, unfortunately, no evidence on the quality of land in Belgium and the Netherlands. The only proxies for the determinants of labor productivity in agriculture are acreage under cultivation per rural habitant (uncorrected for quality differences) and livestock and horses, which formed an important part of the agricultural capital stock.[75]

---

71. Van Hogendorp, *Bijdragen*, 5: 167.

72. Brugmans, *Paardenkracht*, pp. 51–53. Z. W. Sneller, "Anderhalve Eeuw in Vogelvlucht, 1795–1880" [A century and a half from a bird's eye, 1795–1880] in *Geschiedenis van den Nederlandschen Landbouw*, pp. 38–43.

73. Sneller, "Anderhalve Eeuw," pp. 57–61.

74. See, for example, M. DuCamp, *En Hollande* (Paris: Poulet-Malassis et de Broise, 1859), p. 159, and X. Marmier, *Lettres sur la Hollande* (Paris: Garnier Frères, 1842), p. 49.

75. It is immaterial whether reference is made to the marginal or the average productivity of labor, since in any constant returns to scale production function both the marginal and the average productivity of labor will vary positively with the inputs of land and capital.

The comparison between northern and southern agriculture is presented in table 5.12. The quality of the data leaves much to be desired: the data for livestock are uncorrected for quality differences that probably were important. The observation for the relatively poor and backward province of Drenthe seems questionable. The land under cultivation is not only uncorrected for differential quality but also for differential use of the land which may not be determined entirely by the physical properties of the soil but in part also by the labor-land ratio.

As can be verified from table 5.12, the capital-labor ratio in Dutch agriculture was 82 percent higher than in Belgium, while the cultivated land (in physical units) per rural worker was 44 percent higher. The

Table 5.12   Land, Labor, and Capital in Agriculture in the Low Countries
in the Early 1820s

Province	Area Cultivated (in thousands of hectares)	Rural Population (1824)	Capital per Agricultural Worker (florins)	Cultivated Area per Agricultural Worker (hectares)
N. Brabant	277.1	267,101	36.49	1.037
Gelderland	289.8	212,680	47.76	1.362
S. Holland	244.2	215,222	57.15	1.135
N. Holland	203.0	134,153	58.07	1.512
Zeeland	148.0	89,405	57.09	1.656
Utrecht	110.2	63,179	72.82	1.745
Friesland	235.7	150,901	63.55	1.570
Overijssel	175.9	117,661	52.52	1.495
Groningen	173.1	125,894	60.74	1.376
Drenthe	74.2	44,310	72.40	1.681
Total North	1,931.4	1,420,506	53.70	1.368
S. Brabant	316.9	355,464	27.02	0.893
Limburg	310.5	257,070	34.84	1.208
Liège	237.6	253,297	27.52	0.934
E. Flanders	265.0	527,998	19.12	0.502
W. Flanders	296.9	415,699	23.66	0.714
Hainault	356.3	429,210	32.20	0.830
Namur	278.4	159,078	40.57	1.751
Antwerp	197.3	213,717	29.38	0.922
Luxembourg	463.4	248,721	49.60	1.862
Total South	2,722.2	2,860,254	29.49	0.952
Total	4,653.6	4,280,760	37.52	1.087

SOURCES: Capital—Physical quantities from A. J. L. van den Bogaerde de ter Brugge, *Essai sur l'Importance du Commerce, de la Navigation et de l'Industrie dans les Provinces Formant le Royaume des Pays-Bas* (The Hague-Brussels: P. H. Noordendorp et Périchon, 1844–45), 3: 60–61. Prices from ibid., pp. 28, 48–49. Land—Quetelet, *Recherches Statistiques*, annex table 1. Rural Population—Smits, *Statistique Nationale*, annex table 1.

Spearman coefficients show again a positive association between the determinants of agricultural productivity and the industrial wage. Between agricultural capital per worker and industrial wages $R = 0.700$ ($t = 4.12$, $n = 19$), while between the land in cultivation per rural worker and the industrial wage $R = 0.463$ ($t = 2.15$, $n = 19$). Omitting the province of Luxembourg (which was largely pastures which were counted as cultivated areas and hence introduce a bias in the results) yields $R = 0.571$ ($t = 2.78$, $n = 18$). Correcting for land quality would probably have reinforced these results since high wage provinces tended to be associated with high quality soils.

To return to figure 5.2, it can be seen now that all evidence points to the fact that the Dutch economy around 1800 was still at a point like S_2. Hence high wages prevailed, determining indirectly the speed and character of industrialization and accumulation. The question arises why rural population did not grow as a result of high standards of consumption that must have accompanied the high productivity of labor in agriculture. As was argued in chapter 1, the most likely explanation for this phenomenon was the high proportion of urban population in the Netherlands that absorbed large numbers of migrants during the late seventeenth and eighteenth centuries.[76] However, the question of demographic change in the eighteenth century should be regarded partially as unsolved at this stage.

To summarize: it has been demonstrated that wages in the Netherlands were considerably higher than in Belgium during the entire first half of the nineteenth century. The reasons for the high wage level in the Netherlands are deeply entrenched in the special path followed by the Dutch economy in becoming the central maritime and commercial power of Europe in the seventeenth century, and its subsequent stagnation. The inheritance of the golden age to the Dutch economy of 1800 consisted of an income distribution in which wages were substantially higher than elsewhere on the Continent. The mechanisms through which the historical background transmitted itself into high wages were of an institutional as well as an economic character. Extensive poor relief and high taxes figure prominently in the former category, while high agricultural labor productivity, unconstrained by Malthusian mechanisms are the most important in the latter category. Other causes, less easily quantifiable, can be put forward. One possible hypothesis might argue that high wages were established during the golden age and had since outlived it, kept high by the inertia embodied in certain types of institutions such as guilds and tradition. A second type of hypothesis could focus on the volatile character

76. See above, chapter 1.

of the shipping and traffic industries in the maritime provinces. The wage rates paid in these sectors might conceivably have included a "risk premium." None of these hypotheses is particularly sweeping or easily testable, but they cannot be ruled out as possible contributing factors. Finally, it is possible to appeal to the argument concerning Dutch entrepreneurs, which will be elaborated upon in the next chapter. If Dutch entrepreneurs did not maximize profits, it is likely that the wages they paid were higher than in an economy in which entrepreneurs were more aggressive.[77]

77. See below, pp. 220–21.

6 UNEVEN DEVELOPMENT IN THE LOW COUNTRIES: SOME ALTERNATIVE HYPOTHESES

Warm yourself at the fire of the learned, but beware of their glowing coals lest you get scorched.

Jewish Proverb

The dramatic economic gap that emerged between 1800 and 1850 should have stirred the curiosity of contemporaries and historians from both the Netherlands and Belgium. Marc Bloch recommended that the comparative method can and should penetrate monographic studies as "a technical instrument, generally used, easily manageable and capable of giving positive results."[1] Yet, surprisingly enough, the question is rarely put in comparative terms, even in the works of modern historians. One recent study by two Belgian historians, which was presumably meant to cover both countries, totally ignores the comparative aspects of this classic case of differential growth and fails even to ask the question of questions: Why did Belgium industrialize while the Netherlands did not?[2] A somewhat more explicit attempt to compare the two countries has recently been made by J.A. van Houtte.[3] He endeavors to contrast the differential development of the two countries, though his work is of a general nature and his explanations are not supported by much quantitative evidence.

On the other hand, Dutch historians have rarely examined the experience of their country in the framework of a comparative case study. In-

1. Marc Bloch, "Toward a Comparative History of European Societies," in *Enterprise and Secular Change*, ed. F. C. Lane and J. C. Riemersma. (Homewood, Ill.: Richard D. Irwin, 1953), p. 495.
2. Dhondt and Bruwier, *The Industrial Revolution*.
3. J. A. van Houtte, "Economic Development of Belgium and the Netherlands from the Beginning of the Modern Era," *JEEH* 1, no. 1 (Spring 1972): 100–20. Id., *Economische en Sociale Geschiedenis van de Lage Landen* [Economic and social history of the Low Countries] (Zeist-Antwerp: W. de Haan, 1964).

stead they usually asked simply why their country's economy in the
nineteenth century behaved as it did, without specifying precisely by
which standards they were judging the performance or assessing its
causes.[4]

The various theories put forward by Dutch and Belgian historians to
explain the economic development of their countries in the first half of
the nineteenth century can be arranged by four major themes. The first
emphasizes the different "circumstances" in the two countries, that is,
both the fact that Belgium was endowed with richer mineral resources
and the widely different historical courses followed by the two countries
at least up to 1814. In the same spirit is the line of reasoning which focuses
on demand-related issues. Various arguments along this line, not all
mutually consistent, are presented for the two countries. In general, no
attempt is made to ask why Belgium enjoyed such a high level of demand
compared to the Netherlands. Nor are the theoretical pitfalls of the demand
argument sufficiently explored. A third line of reasoning, important
especially in the Netherlands, focuses on the entrepreneur as the pivotal
actor on the industrial stage. In a more general setting, this approach places
heavy emphasis on socio-psychological factors in the explanation of
Dutch relative backwardness in the period prior to 1870. Finally, some
historians have emphasized the role of economic policy and governmental
attitudes by the various rulers of the two countries in determining the
pace of industrialization in particular and economic development in
general.

NATURAL RESOURCES

Turning first to the explanation that centers around the respective
resource endowments, it is of course striking that Belgium was richly
endowed with iron and coal in two different provinces, Liège and Hainault.
The Netherlands had virtually no iron ore except for some negligible
mines in the Veluwe area in the province of Gelderland.[5] Nor did the
Dutch have much coal, but for a small area in the province of Limburg,
the exploitation of which began much later. Consequently, the textile
industry in Twente faced an obstacle in high fuel costs since the coal for
its steam engines had to be imported.[6]

The argument that the endowment of Belgium with coal and iron pro-

4. For a summary see van Stuijvenberg, "Economische Groei," pp. 196–202. Id.,
"De Industriële Revolutie in Nederland" [The industrial revolution in the Netherlands],
mimeographed, n.d.

5. Westermann, *Geschiedenis van de IJzer en Staalgieterij*, pp. 1–32.

6. Boot, *Twentsche Katoennijverheid*, p. 173. Smissaert, *Geschiedenis der Ontwikkeling*,
pp. 45, 123.

vided it with a significant headstart compared with the Netherlands can be attacked at various levels.[7] The first is that the importance of iron and coal in the industrial development before 1850 does not seem overwhelming. The textile industries formed the basis of the "first" industrial revolution. The importance of coal and iron was steadily increasing over time, but in the initial stages of the industrial revolution its overall significance was modest. The availability of cheap coal might have produced an incentive to the introduction of steam engines in various industries but it can hardly be regarded as decisive. Transportation costs of coal from the mines in the Walloon provinces to Flanders were substantial too, though lower perhaps than to the Netherlands. However, the Dutch maritime provinces resorted to the option of importing coal and iron from England by sea, so it is possible that they bought their raw materials at the same or even lower prices than the Flemish provinces. In addition, the completion of a large number of canals in both countries greatly reduced transportation costs even before the introduction of the railroads, and reduced accordingly the explanatory power of transportation costs. Moreover, the share of fuel costs in total costs was far from overwhelming. In the Verviers woolen industry, for example, it was merely 2 percent, while in the Ghent cotton industry, it was only about 4.7 percent.[8]

Furthermore, the difference in the respective natural endowments of the two countries should not be overstated. The Netherlands, though poor in coal, was rich in peat which for some uses constituted a good substitute for coal. So cheap was peat in the Netherlands that it was used as a fuel for the steam engines in the textile industry in Twente in spite of its lower efficiency.[9] The Dutch engineering firm of G. M. Roentgen in Rotterdam built all its steam engines so they could operate on both coal and peat.[10] Peat also served as an input in many other industries.[11] In

---

7. For statements in this spirit, see Roland-Holst, *Kapitaal en Arbeid*, 1: 47. J. G. van Dillen, "Omstandigheden en Psychische Factoren in de Economische Geschiedenis van Nederland" [Circumstances and psychological factors in the economic history of the Netherlands], in *Mensen en Achtergronden* (Groningen: J. B. Wolters, 1964), p. 71. Brugmans, *Paardenkracht*, p. 213. Van Houtte, "Economic Development," p. 114. A. M. Lambert, *The Making of Dutch Landscape, An Historical Geography of the Netherlands* (London-New York: Seminar Press, 1971), p. 275. E. A. Wrigley, "The Supply of Raw Materials in the Industrial Revolution," *EHR* 15, no. 7 (August 1962): 14–16.

8. Figures cited in Great Britain, *Parliamentary Papers*, vol. 42, 1839, pp. 161, 163.

9. N. W. Posthumus, ed., "Bijdragen tot de Geschiedenis der Nederlandsche Grootindustrie" [Contributions to the history of Dutch industry], *EHJ* 11 (1925): 185. J. Boessenkool, "De Eerste Stoommachine in de Twentsche Textielindustry" [The first steam engine in the textile industry in Twente], *THB* 4 (1962): 67–72.

10. De Boer, *Leven en Bedrijf van G. M. Roentgen*, p. 131.

11. P. van Schaik, "De Economische Betekenis van de Turfwinning in Nederland" [The economic significance of peat digging in the Netherlands], *EHJ* 32 (1968–69): 201–20. Among the principal peat using industries were brewing, brickmaking, salt-refining, madder, chicory refining, linen bleaching, and cotton printing.

addition, the importance of wind as an energy source in a flat country cannot be discounted. The paper, oil, and sawmills in North Holland, for example, relied heavily on this cheap source of power.[12] The water supplies in the Dutch peat marshes were highly suitable for bleaching purposes.[13] Moreover, one should also not exaggerate the richness of Belgium's mineral resources. Though the Charleroi area was exceptionally well located with coal and iron deposits in close vicinity, the condition of the Liège area was less ideal. Iron ore was relatively rare and of mediocre quality, and a large part of the coal mined in this area was not cokable.[14] The coal-rich Borinage area around the city of Mons sold most of it in raw form to Flanders and Brussels, and was too remote from iron ore to induce the creation of much local iron industry.[15]

In addition to the above-mentioned qualifications, one could point to Switzerland as a counterexample to the claim that the availability of raw materials played a major role within economies that had the prior advantage of a labor supply furnished by a protoindustrial sector. The argument is succinctly stated in a recent work:

The rapid economic development of Switzerland in the early nineteenth century shows that for an economy of sufficiently small size it was not in fact necessary to have good raw material resources. And thereby it is a useful warning against accepting the simple explanation that the reason why Belgium became an industrial economy in the same period was that there were coal and iron ore resources there.[16]

Finally, the appropriateness of an economic model that focuses on the propinquity of resources as a crucial factor in development may be questioned.[17] Since there were no import tariffs on raw materials and fuel in the Netherlands after 1830, the only possible cause that the "unavailability" of some resources could have made a difference was through higher

12. A. M. van der Woude, "Het Noorderkwartier," *A.A.G. Bijdragen* 16 (1972), vol. 2: 476, 488, 496.

13. Van Houtte, "Economic Development," p. 111.

14. Lévy-Leboyer, *Les Banques Européenes*, p. 366. A significant symptom of the same phenomenon is the fact that the Maastricht nail manufacturer, Petrus Regout, preferred English to Belgian iron, being both cheaper and of higher quality, while coal was bought from Belgium. This resulted in a doubling of transportation costs as compared to locating the firm in Rotterdam for example, so that one may conclude that the costs of transporting raw materials and fuel, though by no means insignificant, can hardly have been an overriding factor. Cf. Maenen, *Petrus Regout*, pp. 163–67, and above, pp. 121–24.

15. Van der Wee, "De Industriële Revolutie," p. 186.

16. A. S. Milward and S. B. Saul, *The Economic Development of Continental Europe, 1780–1870* (London: Allen and Unwin, 1973), p. 454. In view of the Japanese example, it does not seem necessary to confine the argument to small countries.

17. The following is based on C. P. Kindleberger, *Economic Growth in France and Britain, 1851–1950* (New York: Simon and Schuster, 1964), pp. 15–17.

transport costs. Yet it is quite clear that the transport cost per unit of resource was not independent of the process of technological change and capital formation. If transport costs in coal and iron really formed the crucial bottleneck in the Dutch economy, surely investment in railroads, canals, highways, and ocean shipping would have been highly profitable and would be expected to be forthcoming. In other words, capital formation and resources were substitutes for each other, and even if it could be shown that the high costs of raw materials and coal were the principal constraining elements responsible for Dutch sluggishness, it would still be true that insufficient capital formation and its determinants were the underlying fundamental villains of the piece. Moreover, cheap fuel does not necessarily imply low fuel costs, since considerable substitution was possible both within an industry and between industries. As Kindleberger notes in a similar context: "British writers have complained that their industry failed to practice fuel economy in contrast to the Continent and the United States, where the industry, faced with relatively expensive coal, 'made fuel out of brain.'"[18]

A more convincing approach to the question of resources focuses not on the comparative endowments of the two countries in terms of fuel and raw materials, but rather on the question of the "technological inter-relatedness" of certain resources and the technological infrastructure of the economy. From this point of view, the availability of cheap but anti-quated sources of power such as peat and windpower in the Netherlands was not an undivided blessing, since they conceivably tied Dutch industry in a technical framework that was becoming rapidly obsolete.

The same issue concerning the complementarity of the investments to be made by a modern sector was raised by Frankel.[19] He argues that a relatively complex economy (such as the Netherlands) would find it comparatively more difficult to introduce technologically revolutionary production methods, since any change of such nature would require a long chain of costly changes in interrelated aspects. In Frankel's view the shifting of an industry from an obsolete technique or source of energy to a new one might therefore be more difficult than the emergence of new techniques ex nihilo. Applying this model to the Netherlands, it can be seen why the Dutch adhered to their ancient windmills and peat hearths, even though in the long run this led to a dead end.

As an explanation of the entire phenomenon of Dutch late industriali-zation, however, the "interrelatedness effect" is not very satisfactory. Under assumptions of economic rationality (which may of course be

18. Ibid., p. 17.
19. Marvin Frankel, "Obsolescence and Technological Change in a Maturing Economy," *AER* 45, no. 3 (June 1955): 298–319.

unrealistic, see below), entrepreneurs will regard previous investments as "bygones," that is, old equipment will be scrapped only when its net quasi rent is zero or negative. In other words, the decision of whether to introduce a new technique is separate from the decision to scrap an old one.[20] The issue of "interrelatedness" logically becomes important only when there are certain elements in the infrastructure of the firm (or the economy as a whole) that will not tolerate the coexistence of the old and the new technique. This implies that large indivisibilities might have existed with regard to the introduction of new techniques, and hence it may have been difficult to renovate an economy like the Netherlands, especially if capital markets were very imperfect. At the present stage, it is difficult to evaluate the role of technical interrelatedness in the retardation of the Netherlands, but it certainly seems a promising area for future research.[21]

DEMAND

The issues relating to the demand side of industrialization constitute a far more powerful explanation. The original statement on this point is made by Lewiński, who argues that the incorporation of Belgium into a large (and expanding) empire of some 50 million inhabitants, protected against foreign (i.e., English) competition, provided it with an enormous demand.[22] Later on, Lewiński argues, the importance of the foreign market declined and local demand began to play a more crucial role. The latter point is disputed by Demoulin, who accepts, however, the basic premise of the importance of demand.[23]

There can be little doubt that the incorporation of Belgium into France in 1795, while the Netherlands remained separated from this market until 1812, did put the Dutch at a disadvantage.[24] But there are two lines of reasoning that can be put forward against attributing too much weight to this argument. The first is that it can hardly be extended to 1850. From 1814 on, the Netherlands and Belgium had access to the same markets, first as joint members of the United Kingdom of the Netherlands, and then from 1830 on as competitors in the world markets. Moreover,

20. For a critique of the Frankel hypothesis, see Donald F. Gordon, "Obsolescence and Technological Change: Comment," *AER* 46, no. 4 (September 1956): 646–52. Marvin Frankel, "Reply," *AER* 46, no. 4 (September 1956): 652–56. Salter, *Productivity and Technical Change*, p. 56.

21. For discussions of the question of technological interrelatedness, see Kindleberger, *Economic Growth*, pp. 139–47, and Landes, *The Unbound Prometheus*, pp. 334–36.

22. Lewiński, *L'Évolution Industrielle*, p. 68.

23. Demoulin, *Guillaume Ier*, p. 228.

24. Van Dillen, "Omstandigheden," p. 71. See also above, pp. 86–88.

the exclusion of Belgium from the Dutch colonial market after 1832 placed the Flemish cotton industry in a difficult spot while at the same time creating for the first time the opportunity for a Dutch modern industry. But the Java market failed to do for Haarlem what it did for Ghent, and even Twente by no means constituted a "modern" industry before 1850. Yet the demand was there. On the other hand, the Flemish cotton industry, though no doubt profoundly shaken, survived the loss of the Java market as it had survived the loss of the French market two decades earlier. From a different angle the same point can be viewed by asking: why were both Flanders and the Walloon provinces among the few regions in the entire French Empire which were able to exploit the "enormous opportunities" provided by the large market after 1800?

Moreover, there is again a theoretical difficulty in focusing upon demand as an explanation of long-run phenomena. Lewiński cites Adam Smith's celebrated passage concerning the division of labor being limited by the extent of the market. Later he presents Adam Smith's idea as "technological progress depends on the extent of the market available to its products."[25] The latter opinion is accepted by Demoulin.[26] Yet while Adam Smith's statement is still regarded as essentially true,[27] few economists would subscribe to the latter statement. Indeed it is hard to conceive why this would be true. Technological progress means that the same output can be produced with less input. It does not necessarily imply any economies of scale, and even if such existed in reality, it would have been mostly on the level of the firm, not the economy or even the sector. Mechanical cotton spinning for example may have required an optimal firm size of a hundred workers instead of a single spinning jenny at a peasant's house. But the difference between fifty million and two million consumers would imply that there would be place for, say, a hundred cotton mills instead of four. Is there any reason to believe that a hundred identical mechanized firms would be more efficient than four, that is, were there any economies of scale on the level of the economy? The only possible cause for such a phenomenon would be the increased profitability of overhead investments with a large fixed cost component, such as railways, an industry-oriented education system, and perhaps certain institutions such as investment banks. In these respects Belgium was in the forefront of Europe—but only *after* losing the French market.

To repeat, the statements made by Lewiński and Demoulin clearly confuse technological progress with gains in productivity due to the

25. Lewiński, *L'Évolution Industrielle*, pp. 48 and 55.
26. Demoulin, *Guillaume Ier*, p. 228.
27. George Stigler, "The Division of Labor is Limited by the Extent of the Market," *Journal of Political Economy* 59 (June 1951): 185–93.

realization of scale economies. This, however, does not dispose altogether of the importance of demand. The more important element, from the point of view of development, is not so much a large demand for industrial goods as such, but a large demand for certain types of industrial goods that were particularly amenable to technological change. The elasticities of demand (a microeconomic concept) can play an important role in the impact of a given shift in a supply curve due to technological change in a given commodity on the total output of the economy. More precisely, a technological change that reduces the production costs of a good will increase total output approximately by the product of the initial share of the good in total output, the proportional fall in its price, and its income elasticity. If technological change was, as was thus far assumed, exogenous to the economy, it would enhance relatively more growth if those goods in which technological change occurred happened to coincide with the goods for which demand was comparatively elastic. In this framework, demand factors may have been important. Cotton is quoted as the classical example: since the first major technical breakthroughs occurred in cotton, and since demand for it was highly elastic, it was the pivotal industry in the industrial revolution.[28]

It is worthwhile to keep in mind, however, that technological change was by no means confined to cotton, not even to textiles. Paper, glass, metallurgical industries, chemical industries, machine tools, and other branches of industries underwent cost reducing transformations, too. The reason why their role in the initial stages of the industrial revolution was more modest was precisely because the demand for most of them was less elastic (both with respect to income and with respect to price). Thus the coincidence of high demand elasticity with technological change is more apparent than real. The goods that had high demand elasticities grew fast precisely because of that reason. Moreover, it is likely that high demand elasticity goods will be subject to more technological progress, because of the higher potential returns to an invention.[29] This is not the same as saying that demand was a "factor" in industrialization. In any economy there will always be goods with high income and price elasticities. Demand is more likely to be a guide to which sectors of the economy grew earlier and faster than other sectors, than an explanation of why the economy industrialized at all.

Suppose the mechanizing industry faces a less than perfectly elastic demand curve. Technological change will therefore worsen the (net price)

28. Phyllis Deane, *The First Industrial Revolution* (Cambridge: At the University Press, 1969), pp. 89, 91.
29. Note that this concept of induced innovation differs from the traditional Hicks-Habakkuk concept.

terms of trade faced by that industry. This sets a limit to the modern sector's potential expansion.[30] But matters are not that simple in an economy in which the modern sector draws its labor force from a traditional sector dominated by a Z-good sector. As was shown in chapter 4, the rate of accumulation of capital and the rate of profit are independent of the terms of trade as long as the wage rate is determined by the protoindustrial sector, labor is homogeneous and mobile, and wages are perfectly flexible downwards. The third assumption is probably the most unrealistic. As the terms of trade between industrial and agricultural goods fall enough, the rate of accumulation will start to decline as wages hit the hard floor of subsistence. But accumulation will not necessarily come to a standstill if the technological changes affect more than one good. In that case demand conditions help to determine the *order* and *speed* in which the various goods undergo the modernization process.

The intuitive argument is as follows. Suppose one or more of the three necessary conditions for the independence of the rate of profit and the terms of trade is violated. This implies that as more and more of the first good to be modernized (good 1) is produced, the profit rate on 1 falls. At some point, therefore, it becomes profitable to modernize the next good (good 2). When this exactly occurs depends on the price of good 2 prior to modernization, the elasticity of the demand for 1 (but not for 2), and the relative efficiences of the "manual" and "modern" techniques in the two goods. As the output of goods 1 and 2 increases, their prices and hence their rates of profit decline, and modernization is extended to a third good, and so on. The exact pattern followed by the process is determined jointly by the productivity parameters, the demand function of each good, and the initial prices. But the incentive to undertake the initial introduction of a new technique to the production of a certain commodity *at all* is independent of the extent of the market and indeed of demand conditions altogether—all that is required is a significant difference in productivity between the two techniques. The prices at the "onset of modernization" (which are, of course, demand determined) then help to determine the *order* in which the goods are modernized, while the demand elasticities (or the extents of the markets if one wishes) determine the exact *time pattern* of the process.[31]

Is it therefore true that the unification with France, the subsequent crisis, the opening and closing of the Dutch East Indies to Flemish cotton, and similar events affecting demand were really of secondary importance?

---

30. Only if the country is a perfect price taker, so that the demand elasticity it faces is infinite, can output expand unconstrained.

31. A mathematical exposition of this argument is given in Mokyr, "Industrial Growth," pp. 381–83. See also Bensusan-Butt, *On Economic Growth*, pp. 18–27.

A more subtle line of defense for the importance of demand would be to argue that *violent changes* in the demand curves facing individual industries would be damaging to economic development and industrialization. For example, the loss of the Java market for the Ghent cotton industry was costly to Belgian industry because of the limited ability of the industrial sector to adjust rapidly to new demand patterns. The transition from cotton to other industries (heavy industry, mining, glass, food, and others) was neither costless nor instantaneous—hence the impact of changes in demand. In other words, the Ghent cotton industry overexpanded in the period 1820–30 compared to the demand of 1832 and ended up with excess capacity which would not have occurred if the revolution of 1830 and its economic consequences had been fully foreseen. It is significant to note that this is true only for spinning, whereas weaving did mechanize exactly in the period following 1832.[32] This would lend support to the hypothesis that the decision whether to implement an innovation is not as dependent on demand conditions as is sometimes believed. Moreover, a less tangible effect of abrupt and unexpected shifts in demand curves was that instability increased the incentive to invest in risk-free assets, which were becoming more attractive compared to the profitable but volatile capital goods.[33]

Finally, it is sometimes argued that the importance of the concept of demand pertains to *aggregate* demand, not to demand functions for individual commodities. Such a line of reasoning has been put forward recently by Professor P. W. Klein. Klein argues:

> The capacity of the [Dutch economy] to grow was dependent on many divergent and interdependent conditions. Even if one concentrates only on capital as the overriding factor in the growth process, it is necessary to examine closely not only the supply of capital but also the demand for it. The retardation of commerce and industry seems to have been caused primarily by an insufficient *demand* for capital rather than a lack of *supply* of capital.[34]

Klein adds that the demand for investments is (tautologically) equal to the difference between the desired and the actual stock of capital. While the actual stock of capital in the eighteenth and early nineteenth centuries was quite high, the desired stock was growing very slowly. The latter,

32. See above, p. 34.
33. A sufficient condition for this to be true is that capital goods (or for that matter labor) were less than perfectly malleable and could not be shifted costlessly and effortlessly from industry to industry.
34. P. W. Klein, *Kapitaal en Stagnatie tijdens het Hollandse Vroegkapitalisme* [Capital and stagnation during early Dutch capitalism] (Rotterdam: Universitaire Pers, 1967), p. 7, emphasis added.

which seems the pivotal element in Klein's argument, is explained by the lack of aggregate demand, resulting from an unequal income distribution, the loss of export markets in the eighteenth and nineteenth centuries, and the relative absence of autonomous investments.[35] In short, a Keynesian short-run income determination model with induced investment is put forward to explain the stagnation of an economy during two centuries.

Klein's argument is based on speculative and sometimes rather questionable evidence. His claim that the distribution of income was becoming more skewed since the mid-seventeenth century is unsupported, and flies in the face of the evidence presented in chapter 5 concerning the wage level in the Netherlands and the high stage of development of outdoor and indoor poor relief. Klein's argument that population growth in the Netherlands was insufficient is even less convincing. For one thing, population growth is neither a necessary nor a sufficient condition for the expansion of demand. More important, while Dutch population was probably stagnant in the eighteenth century, it grew from about 2 million to 3 million in the critical period 1800–50, which is a faster rate than in Belgium, Switzerland, and France, though slower than in England. But the main reason why Klein's story gets in trouble is that it is theoretically unsound. It consists of the application of a short-run model to long-run problems.

If one is to argue seriously that a situation of less than full employment, which is what Klein's deficient aggregate demand model implies, was responsible for the sluggishness of the Dutch economy, it is necessary to show how such a disequilibrium situation could persist for a century and a half or more without being gradually corrected by automatic forces. It is by all means legitimate to argue that Say's Law was invalid, but any such statement ought to be accompanied by an explanation. It is unclear if price and wage rigidities and money illusion, the most frequently raised explanations of the persistence of *involuntary* unemployment in the short and medium runs, could cause comparable phenomena in the very long run. Perhaps one could argue that the source of the insufficient aggregate demand was a persistent deficit on the Dutch current account. Under certain assumptions it is possible that countries which suffered from chronic deficits on their current accounts would be subject to heavier deflationary pressures than countries with consistently balanced accounts. This is simply so because exports are a part of aggregate demand. In the long run, any country that suffered from a deficit on its current account would be subject to equilibrating forces (the price-specie-flow mechanism),

35. Ibid., pp. 8–10.

unless it had an independent source of income in gold or foreign currency. Such a source was found in the eighteenth century in the interest payments yielded by Dutch foreign investments.[36] It is not clear whether these earnings were a cause of deflationary pressures, but they could have been. If the Dutch *rentiers* spent a considerable part of their income in foreign exchange on imports, aggregate demand would be smaller than in a situation in which they spent it on domestic products. However, this leaves the persistence of the slack in Dutch aggregate demand to be explained, as earnings from foreign assets dwindled in the first half of the nineteenth century. At any rate, none of these possibilities is even hinted at by Klein. To say the least, the attempt to analyze the long-run behavior of the Dutch economy by means of short-run models seems unconvincing at the present stage.

This is not to say that short-run aggregate demand effects were altogether unimportant. The political events of the turbulent period 1795–1815, and for the Belgian case the period following the 1830 Revolution as well, surely caused heavy fluctuations in the level of aggregate employment and demand. Any model with less than instantaneous frictionless adjustment of prices, wages, and output would support such a conclusion. But this is not what Klein argues, and it constitutes by no means a satisfactory explanation of the long-run divergence of the paths of the Dutch and the Belgian economies.

Finally, it should be made clear that the criticism raised against Klein's interpretation does not imply that the demand for capital was wholly negligible in the accumulation process. But the determinants of investment in the long run are not the expectations of the manufacturers with regard to demand as such, but rather the expectations of the manufacturers with regard to the profitability of the investment. If the expected rate of return on a florin invested in real capital was high enough compared to the closest alternative and covered a risk premium, investment in real capital would occur. The demand for capital (or for investment, to be more exact) thus clearly depends on the rate of profit, and thus on the wage rate. The high wage rate in the Netherlands (and analogously, the low wage in Belgium)

36. Toward the end of the eighteenth century the United Provinces was earning considerable amounts of interest on its foreign investments, which possibly enabled the Republic to run a deficit in goods and services. The average rate of return on loans was in the neighborhood of 3 percent. Cf. L. P. van de Spiegel, "Schets tot een Vertoog over de Intrinsique en Relative Magt van de Republiek" (1782) [Sketch of the intrinsic and relative power of the Republic], ed. Joh. de Vries, *EHJ* 27 (1958): 94. Total assets were estimated at 1.5 billion florins (see above, p. 5), yielding an interest income of 45 million florins annually. The French agent Lubbert noted in 1799 that interest income before 1795 was 50–60 million florins. (Cf. Colenbrander, *Gedenkstukken*, 3 : 47.) The deflationary effect of such interest income depended, however, on the extent to which the interest was used to finance import surpluses rather than reinvested abroad.

thus enters the accumulation process on both sides of the equation. On the one hand it determined how much investment funds were available to the modern sector in the absence of intersectoral flows of funds. On the other hand it also determined the relative profitability of investment in new capital goods embodying the new technology vis-à-vis the alternative assets such as foreign and domestic government bonds, cash balances, and real estate. This is precisely the situation illustrated in figure 4.9, above.

ENTREPRENEURSHIP

The most frequently raised argument by Dutch historians as well as contemporaries is formulated in socio-psychological terms. The attention is drawn to the "human side": the mentality of the Dutch entrepreneur, his risk averseness, technical ineptitude, leisure preference, and general perfunctory and complacent attitudes. Sometimes the Dutch entrepreneurs are outright accused of slothfulness, myopia, and insipidness. The argument is not confined to the industrial entrepreneur; it is applied equally to the financier, the engineer, and the workers. It was the *Zeitgeist*, an atmosphere of listlessness and acquiescence, that was supposed to have pervaded Dutch society. The *opus classicus* in this respect is by the Dutch historian, W. J. Wieringa, who writes:

> ... the deep cause of the listlessness was the fact that very little had changed in the Netherlands since the eighteenth century.... there are signs of a social petrification which prevented adaption to the dynamism of the time [nineteenth century] and did not enhance the mechanization of industry. A railroad network could not be attained by this generation. It seems unlikely to me that technical difficulties were the principal factor in this respect, and even if they were, it proves the technological backwardness of the Netherlands.... In this little stimulating climate, the entrepreneurs were expected to introduce the innovations in their businesses. Is it surprising that these attempts were unsuccessful, especially if one considers the unfavorable position of the Netherlands compared to its neighbors?
> ... Was it only the longing for routine and the so-called early capitalist spirit which impeded the attempts to rise above the circumstances? Both were of course important, but in addition to them a third factor mounted roadblocks for the few who were willing to mechanize. As it turns out, ignorance and lack of theoretical education were often the main causes of the failures of Dutch industry and its modernization.... This is proven by the fact that many foreign experts, mostly English, helped to build modern industry in the Netherlands in the

nineteenth century. . . . But even if the entrepreneurs had not lacked the essential technical and managerial knowledge, they would have been impeded by the poor quality of their workers . . . dexterity, skills, and diligence had been reduced already in the eighteenth century to a very low level . . . the vocational training was the worst in Europe. . . . The fact that modern industry had its incipience in the first half of the nineteenth century proves that the so-called objective factors did not constitute absolute impediments, but for the majority of entrepreneurs the circumstances were probably too high a hindrance to be leapt over.[37]

In spite of the persistent vagueness of the arguments and the many unsubstantiated generalizations, the view that simple human failure was a central factor in Dutch economic history in the early nineteenth century has been widely accepted by Dutch historians.[38] It is, in retrospect, somewhat astonishing that the entrepreneurial explanation of Dutch backwardness has enjoyed such an easy triumph. The difficulties in testing such a hypothesis are far from mastered, as can be verified from the famous Landes-Gerschenkron debate concerning French industrialization. A recent work on the iron and steel industry in Victorian England has developed several ingenious ways of testing entrepreneurial failure, and its methods could well be applied to the Low Countries.[39] In the absence of such a study, it is largely on grounds of intuition and circumstantial evidence that the entrepreneurial hypothesis has been accepted. In some cases literary caricatures of complacent, self-satisfied, lazy, fat Dutch bourgeois prototypes are cited as "evidence."[40] The possible tests for a theory that pivots around the entrepreneur as the central figure in Dutch industrial backwardness are seldom mentioned, let alone carried out. To what extent, for example, was Dutch entrepreneurial behavior a result of economic conditions rather than a cause of them? This question was posed by van Dillen, but never satisfactorily answered by his opponents.

37. W. J. Wieringa, *Economische Heroriëntering in Nederland in de Negentiende Eeuw* [Economic reorientation in the Netherlands in the nineteenth century] (Groningen: J. B. Wolters, 1955), pp. 8–11.

38. Brugmans, *Arbeidende Klasse*, pp. 66–71. H. F. J. M. van den Eerenbeemt, *Bedrijfskapitaal en Ondernemerschap in Nederland, 1800–1850* [Working capital and entrepreneurship in the Netherlands] (Leyden: H. E. Stenfert Kroese, 1965). P. J. Bouman, "Van Vroeg tot Modern Kapitalisme" [From early to late capitalism] in *De Lage Landen bij de Zee*, ed. J. and A. Romein, 3d ed. (Zeist: de Haan, 1955), 3:82–84. P. W. Klein, *Traditionele Ondernemers en Economische Groei in Nederland, 1850–1914* [Traditional entrepreneurs and economic growth in the Netherlands] (Haarlem: de Erven F. Bohn, 1966), pp. 3–4.

39. Donald N. McCloskey, *Economic Maturity and Entrepreneurial Decline: British Iron and Steel, 1870–1913* (Cambridge: Harvard University Press, 1973).

40. The somewhat trite example is Oom Stastok, a decadent bourgeois in *Camera Obscura*, a novel by Hildebrand (pseud. of Nicolaas Beets). Cf. Brugmans, *Arbeidende Klasse*, p. 70.

Moreover, if entrepreneurship and technical skills were an internationally mobile factor (as Wieringa stresses) why did these factors constitute bottlenecks at all? As was shown in chapter 3, English as well as Belgian entrepreneurs were active in various sectors of the Dutch economy. Presumably, if all other conditions for the emergence of a modern industrial sector had existed but the entrepreneur failed to grasp the opportunities and bring the separate elements together, foreigners could successfully have fulfilled this task. Yet the role played by English entrepreneurs and technicians in the Netherlands is dwarfed in comparison with the role played by them in other continental countries.[41] If Dutch entrepreneurs were worse than, say, Belgian, German, or Swiss entrepreneurs, and if this was the fundamental reason for the failure of the Dutch to develop a modern industrial sector, one would expect exactly the reverse to have occurred.

There are a number of other logical flaws in the entrepreneurial argument. It has been argued that Dutch engineers were unable to build capital equipment. Since England lifted its official embargo on the export of machines as late as 1843, the Dutch ran into difficulties trying to purchase machinery while unable to build their own.[42] Yet Belgium was producing steam engines in large quantities and of high quality, and it is hard to think of reasons why the Dutch could not have bought more Belgian machines than they did if they were unable to make them themselves. It is probably true that Belgian machines were more expensive than English ones, but this cannot explain Dutch backwardness relative to Belgium. The technical ignorance of Dutch entrepreneurs is a somewhat more plausible argument, and it is possible that the Dutch education system was not conducive to the adoption and absorption of mechanized techniques. But how crucial was this bottleneck? Wieringa's statement that lack of theoretical knowledge was an important element totally ignores the separateness of science and industry in the first half of the nineteenth century. The technical knowledge and dexterity required to *operate* modern equipment were anything but staggering, though this is comparatively less true for the *construction* of new equipment.[43]

More appealing is the argument which concentrates around the low quality of labor due to the deficiency of elementary and intermediate

41. Henderson, *Britain and Industrial Europe*, pp. 198–200.

42. Van Stuijvenberg, "Economische Groei," p. 198. Brugmans, *Paardenkracht*, p. 213.

43. J. D. Bernal, *Science and Industry in the Nineteenth Century* (Bloomington: Indiana University Press, 1969), p. 20. With respect to the inventive processes, the divorce between science and industry may have been overstressed, but since both countries contributed little new to technology, this line cannot rescue Wieringa's argument. Cf. A. E. Musson and Eric Robinson, *Science and Technology in the Industrial Revolution* (Manchester: Manchester University Press, 1969).

education, which was judged to be one of the worst-suited to industry in Europe.[44] One may, however, legitimately wonder why there was such backwardness in the school system, and whether the causality runs entirely in one direction. In any case, in the early stages of industrialization on-the-job training seems to have been the main source of skills. The importance of vocational and technical schools was rising over time, but probably did not attain major significance until the last three decades of the nineteenth century. In this context it is important to note that similar arguments are raised viewing education in England in the last third of the nineteenth century as a cause for the so-called "climacteric" of England.[45] As science and engineering (applied science) became increasingly important in the industrial sector, the absence of adequate schools possibly became a bottleneck. But in the first half of the nineteenth century, England, with its highly deficient educational system, was the leading industrial nation in the world. This fact somewhat reduces the credibility of the "human capital" argument, although it does not entirely dispose of it.

On the other hand, the arguments that the Dutch laborer was undernourished, underclothed, unhealthy physically and mentally, and utterly lacking in energy and motivation, seem untenable as a reasonable explanation of Dutch relative backwardness.[46] Needless to say, the life of a Dutch laborer in Dutch industry was not pleasant by modern standards. But this was no less true in Belgium, England, North and Northeast France, Switzerland, and the Rhineland. Nowhere did factory workers fare well, and no unambiguous rise in the standards of living of workers has been observed in any industrializing country or region before 1850. The evidence put forward in chapter 5, moreover, indicates that workers in the Netherlands, if anything, were better off than in Belgium and probably most other areas in Europe as well. Nominal wages were higher and the welfare system better developed. No doubt living standards were still low enough to raise the wrath of many well meaning contemporaries, but relatively speaking there is no evidence that the Dutch labor force was worse off (and therefore less productive) than anywhere else.

If entrepreneurial behavior played a role at all in the economic development of the Low Countries, it seems to have taken place mainly through savings and investment behavior. As was shown in chapter 4, the rate of accumulation is determined jointly by the rate of profit and the rein-

44. Wieringa, *Economische Heroriëntering*, p. 10. A well-documented contemporary account is given by von Baumhauer, *Voorlezingen*, pp. 41–87. See also Brugmans, *Arbeidende Klasse*, p. 176 and sources quoted there.
45. Landes, *The Unbound Prometheus*, pp. 339–48.
46. Especially emphasized by Brugmans, *Arbeidende Klasse*, pp. 141, 169–72.

vestment coefficient. Entrepreneurial attitudes, or the "business ethos" ruling at any given time, help to determine the reinvestment coefficient. For example, if the Dutch industrialist was more risk-averse than his Belgian colleague, it is reasonable to expect that his reinvestment coefficient would be lower, so that *ceteris paribus* the rate of capital accumulation would be lower.[47] The reason is that a higher risk averseness implies that a larger part of industrial profits is diverted to safer, largely unproductive uses, so that less capital is plowed back into the firm itself in the form of productive capital goods.[48] Or consider for example the argument that the Dutch entrepreneur had an extraordinary high leisure preference.[49] Since in the early, owner-operated, industrial firms there was a high degree of complementarity between the input of capital and the input of managerial labor, it is likely that the leisure preference on the part of the owner constrained his desire to invest in the firm, resulting again in a lower reinvestment coefficient. To the extent, then, that entrepreneurial "failure" resulted in a lower value of the reinvestment coefficient than elsewhere,[50] it was an important factor in the sluggishness of Dutch industrialization. Analogously, a high reinvestment coefficient in Belgium would help to account for its success. Since no information on the reinvestment coefficients is available, it is difficult to distinguish between the two hypotheses relating the differences in accumulation to differences in profits or to differences in reinvestment behaviors respectively.

However, the blame put by Wieringa on the Dutch financiers and *rentiers*, for not having invested in the Dutch economy, seems misplaced, and Klein is justified in objecting to this line of reasoning.[51] More fundamental than Klein's objection that supply-oriented factors were secondary since the demand for loanable funds was small is that the market in which the Dutch industrialist and the Dutch financier could conclude financial

47. There is some evidence in this direction. On risk averseness in the Netherlands, see A. J. Backer, *Wevers Onder Gaslicht* [Weavers by gaslight] (Amsterdam: G. van Reemst, 1952), p. 22. Van den Eerenbeemt, *Bedrijfskapitaal*, p. 5. Brugmans, *Paardenkracht*, p. 85. For Belgium see Dhondt, "L'Industrie Cotonnière," pp. 256, 274. Coppejans-Desmedt, "De Betekenis van Gent," pp. 21–23. In this context it is important to note that it can be proven rigorously that risk averse behavior may follow from institutional characteristics—especially imperfect capital markets—and not necessarily from a psychological aversion to risk. This opens a fascinating new field for the interpretation of the history of capital accumulation and savings. Cf. Robert T. Masson, "The Creation of Risk Aversion by Imperfect Capital Markets," *AER* 62 (March 1972): 77–86.

48. For an application of the impact of risk aversion and capital market imperfections on the rate of formation of real capital to the Victorian and Edwardian economy, see William P. Kennedy, "The Economics of Maturity: Aspects of British Economic Development, 1870–1914" (Ph.D. diss., Northwestern University, 1975), chapter 3.

49. Brugmans, *Arbeidende Klasse*, p. 67.

50. For a definition and discussion of this parameter, see above, pp. 160–64.

51. Wieringa, *Economische Heroriëntering*, p. 18. Klein, *Kapitaal en Stagnatie*, p. 7.

transactions did not exist. Therefore the entire connection between the "capital" owned by the Amsterdam banking houses and the "capital" accumulated (or not) in industry breaks down. There is virtual unanimity that capital markets were inaccessible to Dutch manufacturers in the period under discussion here.[52] Nor did they play a major role anywhere else in Europe. "Industrial capital has been its own chief progenitor," wrote Ashton.[53] Hence it can be concluded that the behavior of the much maligned "coupon clipper," the narrow-minded and provincial *rentier*, cannot be held responsible for the sluggishness of Dutch industrialization. The fact that the Dutch financiers could not or would not finance an industrial revolution in the Netherlands explains why the Dutch did not do *better* than other countries—not why they did so much *worse*.

A final note on entrepreneurship and its possible role in European industrialization in general and Dutch in particular. The most common failures diagnosed in entrepreneurs in a dynamic framework are failures to recognize potentially profitable innovations, or failures to adopt these innovations after they have been recognized. But it should be emphasized that static inefficiencies had clear-cut dynamic ramifications. In particular, consider the case in which the entrepreneurs do not maximize profits.[54] It immediately follows that for any given reinvestment coefficient, the amount plowed back in the firm will be smaller and accumulation will be slower. It can thus be seen that "entrepreneurial failure" did not operate only through a low reinvestment coefficient.

In passing it should be noted that nonmaximizing behavior on the part of the entrepreneurs could have resulted in higher wages. One consequence of this behavior is the divorce of the demand curve for labor from the value of the marginal product (marginal revenue product) of labor. If the nonmaximizing behavior was a result of purely random errors, the aggregate demand curve for labor in the long run would still be likely not to diverge too much from its optimal location. But if entrepreneurs displayed systematic static deviations from maximizing behavior, it should be possible to formalize the conditions under which wages could be expected to be higher or lower than their "neoclassical" values. In principle, the errors of entrepreneurs can be dichotomized into two

52. W. H. Berghuis, *Ontstaan en Ontwikkeling van de Nederlandse Beleggingsfondsen tot 1914* [Emergence and development of Dutch investment funds] (Assen: van Gorcum, 1967), p. 87. Wieringa, *Economische Heroriëntering*, pp. 17–18. Klein, *Kapitaal en Stagnatie*, p. 10. Van den Eerenbeemt, *Bedrijfskapitaal*, p. 22.

53. T. S. Ashton, *The Industrial Revolution, 1760–1830* (New York: Oxford University Press, 1964), p. 68. Cf. also above, p. 134, n. 4.

54. Two logically different cases may be distinguished, though for most practical purposes they coincide. One is the case in which the utility function maximized by entrepreneurs contained other arguments than profits which were not independent of profits. The other case is the one in which the "rules of thumb" followed by the entrepreneurs were highly defective and provided solutions to the decision variables which were remote from the optimal solutions.

classes: those that result in the entrepreneurs producing the wrong quantities of output, and those that result in the employment of labor and capital in the wrong proportions. The first would lead to a divergence of the Rate of Commodity Substitution from the Rate of Product Transformation; the second would result in the nonuniformity of the Rates of Technical Substitution of labor and capital.

If the Dutch industrial entrepreneur was listless, had a high leisure preference, had little or no drive for expansion, and was satisfied with his market share (possibly maximizing average profits as has been argued for the French entrepreneur),[55] the quantities produced would be smaller than optimal. Hence, assuming there is no factor-proportion error, the demand curve for labor is *lower* than the marginal revenue product of labor. On the other hand, if the typical entrepreneur was risk-averse, conservative, technically incompetent, and took an attitude of philanthropic paternalism toward his workers, it seems likely that he would be operating on a labor-capital ratio that was higher than optimal. This implies that the demand curve for labor would tend to be *above* the marginal revenue product of labor. It is thus impossible to decide on an a priori basis whether the net effect of "entrepreneurial failure" on the wage level was positive or negative, in other words, whether it tended to reinforce or to offset the forces causing high wages.

To summarize, if entrepreneurship is to be accepted as a member in the family of explanations of Dutch industrial backwardness, more evidence will have to be produced and some questions will have to be answered. In particular, it has to be shown why the chronically inefficient Dutch entrepreneur was not supplanted by more aggressive competitors, either native or foreign. As Kindleberger puts it:

> . . . the greatest weakness in attaching first importance to the nature of entrepreneurship in shaping France's and Britain's economic development is that the model is incomplete. What needs to be explained is not why business behaved as it did but, taking this for granted, why other firms did not come along and challenge existing enterprise.[56]

THE ROLE OF ECONOMIC POLICY

While economic historians in the Netherlands have emphasized the importance of entrepreneurship in the development of their country in the nineteenth century, little stress is put on the policies of the govern-

---

55. Landes, *The Unbound Prometheus*, p. 131.
56. Kindleberger, *Economic Growth*, p. 134.

ment as a factor affecting industrialization. On the other hand, the various governments that ruled Belgium in the same period were and are credited with a large share in Belgium's industrialization.[57] It is quite difficult to classify the various economic policies by their net effect on industrialization. It is even harder to evaluate the overall impact of such policies. While the Netherlands was a relatively free trade oriented country, Belgium was more or less continuously surrounded by high tariffs protecting its industry. Yet was this unequivocally a point in Belgium's favor? One writer views the adoption of complete free trade by both countries almost simultaneously (1861 in Belgium and 1862 in the Netherlands) as "creating a new economic climate [which] allowed the two countries to take full advantage of the formidable growth of world economy and trade."[58] Other governmental policies are easier classified as beneficial, for example the sweeping administrative reforms introduced in both countries after 1795 which contained many steps that were unambiguously conducive to industrialization. But not only is it difficult to assess the relative importance of the effect of, say, the abolition of guilds, it is even harder to establish that the difference in policies between the governments in the Netherlands and Belgium was sufficient to explain the growing gap between the two countries. To get an overview of the economic policies followed in the two countries, we have to examine four periods: pre-1795, 1795–1814, 1814–30, and 1830–50. Needless to say, the following by no means pretends to constitute a comprehensive survey of economic policies in the Low Countries, and merely attempts to examine policy as a possible factor in the uneven development of industry.

The Austrian government, which ruled between 1713 and 1795 most of what is Belgium today, followed in general policies that were in line with the moderate mercantilism characteristic of Austrian enlightened despotism. The Austrian government made considerable efforts to encourage industry in the classical mercantilist tradition. The popular governor,

57. Briavoinne, *De l'Industrie*, 1: 77–174. Van Houtte, "Economic Development," p. 114. Id., *Economische en Sociale Geschiedenis*, pp. 313–16. Demoulin, *Guillaume Ier*, pt. 1. Terlinden, "La Politique Économique," passim.

58. Van Houtte, "Economic Development," p. 106. See also Brugmans, *Paardenkracht*, p. 213. Under which conditions high tariffs were beneficial to an expanding modern sector is a complex issue and cannot possibly be done justice here. For an insightful treatment of this subject for the American case, cf. Paul A. David, "Learning By Doing and Tariff Protection: A Reconsideration of the Ante Bellum United States Cotton Textile Industry," *JEH* 30, no. 3 (September 1970): 521–601. It is interesting to note that while David's assessment of the impact of the American tariff is far from favorable, he concedes that in cases of highly imperfect capital markets "the imposition of a tariff might be defended on the ground that it shifted income toward firms in the protected industry and thereby permitted more *internally financed* investment to be undertaken. . . . Tariffs [were] one means of subsidizing the internally financed expansion of firms in the industry" (ibid., p. 534, emphasis in original).

Charles Alexander de Lorraine (who ruled between 1744 and 1780), and his ministers, the count of Botta-Adorno and especially the count of Cobenzl (whom Briavoinne calls "an Austrian Colbert"), used local monopolies, exemptions from export duties and other taxes, prohibitions on the emigration of skilled artisans, and, at times, prohibitions on the export of raw materials, to encourage industry.[59] In addition, the Austrian government invested in social overhead capital. More than 2,500 km. of roads were built, the canal between Ghent and Bruges improved and rebuilt, and a new canal between Ostend and Ghent constructed. The Austrian government even made a feeble attempt to have the Scheldt reopened for maritime shipping, but this was stifled by the Dutch navy (1784).

The government of the United Provinces of the Netherlands, at the same time, shrank from any activity that might have impeded free trade. The commercial interests of Amsterdam ruled supreme. Yet, increasingly voices were raised in favor of local industrial interests.[60] Dutch economic policy in the second half of the eighteenth century—as far as it existed— was neither hostile nor agnostic to industry, although many mercantilist measures taken abroad were ignored here to preserve the real or imaginary interests of the commercial and financial oligarchy.[61] Although the decentralized character of the political structure of the United Provinces and the precarious state of public finances made infrastructural invest- ments far from easy,[62] it has been argued that in the eighteenth century the Netherlands were well-supplied with overhead capital.[63] It can be concluded that there is no evidence that the Austrian government provided the Belgians with a headstart in industrialization by creating some "preconditions" for industrialization which were wholly lacking in the Netherlands. It is, however, plausible that the Austrian policies somewhat compensated the Belgian provinces for the grievous setbacks suffered during the wars of the sixteenth and seventeenth centuries.

The French era (1795–1814) was inaugurated by a complete revolution of the entire institutional setup of Belgian and Dutch society. The incorporation of the Belgian provinces in the French republic swept the *ancien régime* away by a mighty tidal wave. Two institutions, the removal of which were *sine qua non* for the development of modern industry, disappeared as if by magic. The first were the guilds which during the *ancien régime* had "never failed to do all they could to shackle the pros-

59. Briavoinne, *De l'Industrie*, 1 : 87.
60. Bierens de Haan, *Van Oeconomische Tak*, pp. 38–55.
61. Joh. de Vries, *Economische Achteruitgang*, pp. 118–24.
62. Ibid., pp. 177–79.
63. Klein, *Kapitaal en Stagnatie*, p. 9.

perity of manufactures," as Pirenne puts it.[64] The second was the incredibly complex and inefficient judicial system in which civil law was organized. Many cases were handled by special professional tribunals requiring up to twelve judges for a single case. Since the laws often differed from province to province, the confusion during the Austrian period was almost insuperable. In addition to the abolition of the guilds and the simplification and unification of the legal system, the French revolutionaries introduced many other reforms to increase the efficiency of the institutional framework in Belgium. The standard metric system of measures and weights was introduced, which must have meant a considerable improvement: under the old regime, for example, five lengths of the ell between 69 and 76 cm. were used in the different provinces. The declaration of the freedom of professions was no doubt indispensable for the creation of a mobile labor force. The abolition of feudal rights was another step forward, though its immediate implications for industrialization are less obvious. The opening of the Scheldt for international shipping after an effective blockade of 210 years has justly been regarded as a major event for the Belgian economy.

A special corollary of the annexation of the Belgian provinces to France, from the point of view of industrialization, was the confiscation of large amounts of real estate property from the church and their sale at auctions, often for fractions of their value. It is not clear whether the fortunes earned by speculators were a source of industrial capital, as Lebrun suggests.[65] If they were, they could perhaps be regarded as the initial discontinuity that set the system into motion, the "appropriate incident which was quickly submerged in past history."[66] The more important aspect of the *"biens nationaux"* as they were called was that they reduced the price of buildings and land, which constituted an important component of the fixed investment in modern industry. Indeed, some factories were located in abandoned convents bought or rented at extremely low prices.[67] It is irrelevant that only a small proportion (18.4 percent) of the confiscated goods was bought by the "economically active group" (i.e., bankers, industrialists, and merchants) between 1796–1814.[68] After all, modern industry constituted only a small proportion of the Belgian economy at

64. Pirenne, *Histoire de Belgique*, 3: 149.
65. Lebrun, "La Rivoluzione Industriale," pp. 574, 589.
66. See above, pp. 146–47.
67. Demoulin, *Guillaume Ier*, p. 238.
68. J. Lambert, "De Verkoop van Nationale Goederen in de Provincie Oost Vlaanderen tijdens het Hollands Bewind" [The sale of national goods in the province of East Flanders during the Dutch rule], *HMGOG* 20 (1966): 29. The importance of "national goods" was not confined to Flanders. Nicholas Delloye, the second largest ironmonger in Liège, had made a fortune in speculation in ecclesiastical property.

this stage. More important is the fact that the sale of church lands and buildings must have reduced the price on all real estate, irrespective of whether it had once belonged to the church or not, relative to what it would have been otherwise. The overall importance of the stimulus given to industry by the "national goods" should therefore be measured by the effect of the confiscation and auctioning of ecclesiastical property on the price of real estate, and by the proportion of land and buildings in total fixed capital investment. It is therefore with some justification that the Dutch historian, Verberne, singles out the sale of the "national goods" as one of the crucial differences between the Netherlands and Belgium that explains the divergence of the paths of the two economies.[69] Before more research is done in this area, it is too early to draw definitive conclusions, but it seems plausible that the confiscation of church lands facilitated industrialization in Belgium in the first decade of the nineteenth century.

The French government did, however, more for Belgian industry than overthrowing the institutions of the *ancien régime* and the redistribution of land. An active policy to stimulate industry was followed by both the republican and the imperial governments. The minister of the interior during the consulate, Francois de Neufchâteau (1798–99), set a precedent by organizing an industrial exhibition, which was followed by several others during the empire. Napoleon visited Ghent in July 1803 to open a local exhibition, and displayed considerable interest in the textile industry in that town.[70] Especially Lieven Bauwens enjoyed amicable relations with the imperial government, which turned out to be very lucrative for him.

On the other hand, the record of the French in the area of public works is far less impressive. The total length of the roads built in the French period was 230 km., as compared to 2,600 km. built by the Austrians in eighty years.[71] None of the many canals initiated by the Napoleonic government was completed before 1814, and the only canal that actually passed the planning stage was the one connecting Mons to the Scheldt at Condé—completed in 1818.

The reforms brought about in the Netherlands in the same period were somewhat less radical, but the circumstances were of course different. No confiscation of church or nobility-owned lands occurred in this pre-

69. L. G. J. Verberne, *Noord Brabant in de Negentiende Eeuw, tot omstreeks 1870, de Sociaal-Economische Structuur* [North Brabant in the nineteenth century until about 1870, the social-economic structure] (Nijmegen: de Koepel, 1947), pp. 16–17.

70. Leleux, *Liévin Bauwens*, pp. 152–54.

71. Lebrun, "La Rivoluzione Industriale," p. 574. Demoulin, *Guillaume Ier*, p. 106 mentions only 165 km. of roads, probably because he excludes sanded roads.

dominantly protestant country in which the landed nobility had been reduced to secondary importance centuries ago. On the other hand, it should be kept in mind that the "patriots" who established the Batavic Republic in 1795 introduced many reforms which were inspired by the French Revolution. The 1798 constitution abolished the guilds (though their tenacity was greater than expected, so that the decision had to be renewed by William I in 1818). The same constitution also abolished the feudal rights, which were not of much consequence at any rate by this time. Another significant improvement brought about by the Dutch Revolution of 1795 was the demonopolization of the *beurtveren*, the passenger and cargo barge services between the major cities.[72] This made a more efficient usage of the Dutch internal waterways possible. The government of the Batavic Republic also made some, rather feeble, attempts to encourage industry. Goldberg, whose work was cited in chapter 3, was appointed agent for the national economy. Among his achievements were the Goldberg survey and his data-collecting journey, both in 1800–01. Goldberg was directly influenced by Neufchâteau, and his endeavors in the field of data collection and statistics were inspired by the French example.[73] Goldberg's surveys were not entirely successful, and for political reasons he was fired in 1801. But his activities demonstrate that in the Netherlands, too, a new wind was blowing.[74]

In 1806 the Batavic Republic was swept from the map by a stroke of Bonaparte's pen, and in its place came the kingdom of Holland, ruled by Napoleon's brother, Louis. Four years later the whole area was formally annexed to the empire. As was shown in chapter 3, this episode was altogether too short-lived and too war-ridden to improve the deeply troubled Dutch economy. Still, the implementation of the revolutionary institutions was completed in those years. The metric system was adopted, the legal system entirely reorganized and unified after the French example, the fiscal system revised and taxation redistributed among the provinces (1806). A postal system was organized, and the monetary structure improved. A first industrial exhibition was organized in 1808, followed by a second a year later. Finally, the interest on the Dutch national debt was reduced by two-thirds by Napoleon in 1810, thus making government bonds a far less attractive asset.

It is therefore anything but self-evident that the incorporation of

---

72. Cf. Lambert, *The Making of Dutch Landscape*, pp. 192–93, 253.

73. W. M. Zappey, *De Economische en Politieke Werkzaamheid van Johannes Goldberg*, p. 48.

74. Brugmans observes that thanks to French influence the Netherlands was able to create a modern bureaucracy which made a more active economic policy possible. Cf. Brugmans, *Paardenkracht*, pp. 16–17.

Belgium in the French Empire bestowed upon the Belgians enough advantages to give them a definitive edge over the Dutch. Both countries underwent sweeping reforms, and it is certainly not true that the *ancien régime* was relatively more preserved in the Netherlands than in Belgium, or that the attitudes taken toward industry were markedly more positive in Belgium. Of course, the two countries faced very dissimilar political circumstances and had different economic and social structures in 1795, as emphasized in chapter 1. Hence their development between 1795 and 1814 was different. But economic policy played a modest role in this divergence.

The restoration of the house of Orange in the newly formed United Kingdom of the Netherlands put both countries under the rule of William I. William was "a positivist, not a theorist," as one contemporary dubbed him.[75] But there can be little doubt that William I followed a very explicit and determinate economic policy. Nor is there any doubt that this policy was heavily biased in favor of industry, and was therefore opposed by such ardent free traders as van Hogendorp. Some of the support, both financial and moral, given by William I to industry was described in chapter 2 and needs no recapitulation.[76] In addition to the founding of the Société Générale and the establishment of the industrial fund, industry was helped in many ways. William I did not hesitate to forfeit the real or imaginary interests of Dutch commerce and *haute finance* in favor of Belgian industry. A central issue was the tariff question. While the industrial interests in Belgium exerted great pressure to introduce a protective tariff on industrial imports, the old free trade ideology of the carrying trade was not yet quite dead, although the North-South confrontation on the issue was not as clear-cut as is sometimes thought. In any case, after a lengthy struggle the tariff of 1822 was adopted, which constituted a modest victory for the protectionist elements. Various amendments raised the tariff even more between 1822 and 1830. In addition to the tariff on imports into the Low Countries themselves, it is important to keep in mind the protection given to Belgian industry in the Dutch East Indies, as described in detail in chapter 2. Another noteworthy step taken by the Dutch government was the passing of a law that con-

75. Brugmans, "Koning Willem I," p. 38. Brugmans attributes to William I a "neo" mercantilist policy, which seems a somewhat questionable definition. Direct state intervention was relatively rare under William I and resorted to only in extreme instances. Most policies were directed toward the indirect encouragement of private enterprise. The foundation of the *Société Générale* and the establishment of the industrial fund *"Merlin Million"* should be viewed as an attempt to correct for the obvious case of market failure which plagued the capital markets in the Low Countries. In this sense it seems more justified to view William I as a precursor of Saint-Simonian policies than as a belated mercantilist.

76. See above, pp. 59, 64–65.

strained the purchases of the government to locally manufactured goods.

Finally, it is important to note the large infrastructural investments carried out by the Dutch government between 1814 and 1830 in both parts of the kingdom. The Dutch built 800 km. of paved roads in the Belgian provinces alone, five times the annual length built by the French.[77] Among the many canals completed by William I's government before 1830 were the Amsterdam-Den Helder canal, the Keulse Vaart which improved several existing canals between Amsterdam and the Rhine, and the Zuid Willemsvaart between Maastricht and Bois le Duc. In the South, the Ghent-Terneuzen canal gave the center of the cotton industry an improved outlet to the North Sea, while the canal between Peruwelz and Antoing improved communications in the coal mine areas. Furthermore, two major projects were started in the Dutch period and not completed until after the revolution: the canal Charleroi-Brussels which supplied the rapidly growing administrative center of the Belgian provinces with coal, and the canalization of the Sambre which connected Charleroi to the eastern Walloon provinces.[78] Some of these ambitious and expensive projects were financed by the state, others conceded to private contractors who were, however, able to obtain generous government loans.

It can therefore be seen that the policy of William I had a definite though perhaps unquantifiable positive effect on the industrial development of the Low Countries. It does not, however, have much power to explain the *differential* development in the two parts of the United Kingdom of the Netherlands. It is true that a large part of the assistance given to industry, sometimes from the king's private resources, benefited the South relatively more than the North. But why would this happen? It could hardly be argued that William I had a personal preference for his Belgian subjects who were not only Catholic but also obstreperous and suspicious of their new rulers. Nor could the eventuality of a revolt have failed to occur to him. The reason, then, why the king bet (literally) most of his money on Belgian industry was because it was more profitable than Dutch industry. The fundamental causality lies in this direction, not the reverse. The success of Belgian industrialization has to be explained in terms of the inherent conditions that facilitated it and in that way drew government support. Though the policies of William I enhanced *ex post* the gap between the Netherlands and Belgium with respect to industrialization, they were not the original cause for it.

It is only for the period after 1830 that the two respective governments follow policies that were markedly different in approach and that might

77. Demoulin, *Guillaume Ier*, p. 106.
78. *Exposé de la Situation*, pp. 248–54.

have acted as a partly exogenous factor in increasing the gap in industrialization. The Belgian government from the very beginning followed
an aggressive policy in support of industry. The foundation of the Banque
de Belgique in 1835 and the highly protective tariff of 1834 were mani-
festations of this policy. Even more important was the vigorous pursuit
of a government-sponsored program to provide Belgium with a railroad
network. Between 1834 and 1850, 861.4 km. of track were laid, of which
the bulk (72.5 percent) was owned by the government. A total of 167.3
million francs had been invested by the Belgian government alone, most
of it in track laying.[79] Road construction and canal digging were also taken
up energetically. Between 1830 and 1850, the total length of paved and
ballasted roads grew from 1,494 km. to 7,894 km., a more than fivefold
increase. In addition to the completion of various projects started by the
Dutch, the Belgian independent government constructed the *Canal de la
Campine*, connecting the Meuse to the Scheldt, and the Liège-Maastricht
canal, which had been a long standing demand of the *Liègeois*.[80]

In contrast to this vigorous and energetic approach, the Dutch policy
after 1830 was hesitant and bungling. A large amount of energy and money
was spent in a quixotic attempt to regain control of the Belgian provinces.
True, there was a conscious effort on the part of Dutch authorities to
establish a modern industrial sector in the Netherlands after the secession
of the Belgian provinces.[81] As far as the maritime provinces are concerned,
the attempts to introduce a mechanized cotton industry were a miserable
failure and not in the least because of the lukewarm attitude of the government to its own project. As far as Twente is concerned, the net effects of
the policies of the Dutch government and the Dutch Commercial Company (N.H.M.) were more complex. As was argued above, there is good
reason to believe that the advice of Ainsworth to establish the Dutch
textile industry within the existing Z-good sector was fallacious, and in
effect, impeded the rapid formation of modern industry.[82] By driving up
the wages in the Z-good sector through increased productivity in the
protoindustry (due to the introduction of the flying shuttle), and a possible
bidding away of workers previously employed in agriculture, the result
of Ainsworth's activities was a much slower accumulation of capital once
the inevitable shift to power looms and mules occurred. The objectives of
the N.H.M. and the government were, as was seen, largely philanthropic
and not economic, and this may help to explain their persistence on an
erroneous course.

79. *Exposé de la Situation*, pp. 231–32.
80. Demoulin, *Guillaume Ier*, pp. 382–85.
81. See above, pp. 94–96.
82. See above, pp. 106–14.

In other ways, too, the Dutch government slackened activity on behalf of economic development in general and industrialization in particular after 1830. The construction of railroads was conceded to private entrepreneurs without proper government supervision and financial aid. The inevitable result was that in 1850 the Netherlands had only 176.4 km. of railroad track, one-fifth of the length in Belgium.[83] One might add that the 1822 tariff was gradually liberalized after 1830, so that industry lost its protection while at the same time a sliding scale import tariff on grain was introduced (1835), just as the anti-corn law movement in England was starting to pick up steam.

To summarize: a case is sometimes made that one of the Belgian advantages was that the various governments that ruled the provinces were more oriented toward an economic policy conducive to industrialization. There seems little evidence for the hypothesis that the Belgian provinces enjoyed significant advantages of which the Dutch provinces were deprived. The only exceptions were the windfalls enjoyed by Belgian industry by the sale of the "national goods" and the fact that the Belgian government after the revolution proved more effective than the defeated and frustrated Dutch. Otherwise both countries were subject to political forces that, though often quite different in character, did not furnish the Belgians with a clear-cut edge over the Dutch.

83. J. H. Jonckers-Nieboer, *Geschiedenis der Nederlandsche Spoorwegen* [A history of Dutch railways] (Haarlem: H. D. Tjeenk Willink, 1907), appendix G.

7 THE CONSEQUENCES OF INDUSTRIALIZATION

O, the fierce wretchedness that glory brings us
Who would not wish to be from wealth exempt
since riches point to misery and contempt?
Who would be so mocked with glory?

Timon of Athens

We have examined in some detail the differential development of Belgium and the Netherlands and attempted to evaluate possible causes underlying the phenomenon of uneven growth in this area in the first half of the nineteenth century. The present chapter forms in some sense a digression from the central theme of this study in examining some of the consequences of industrialization and the absence of it. It will therefore focus on the events in Belgium, while the comparison between the two countries will be resumed in the last section.

SOME THEORETICAL OBSERVATIONS

The growing up model presented in chapter 4 and employed in the analysis presented in chapters 5 and 6 is really a disequilibrium model. The disequilibrium properties of the model stem from the coexistence of techniques to produce industrial goods simultaneously: the modern, mechanized technique, and the traditional protoindustrial (Z-good) technique. The process of growing up is in fact a transition between the two techniques, and it consists of a continuous plowing back of profits made in the modern sector. With these profits new equipment is purchased, enabling the capitalists in the modern sector to hire more Z-good workers from the traditional sector, and so on. Provided the growth of population does not replenish the traditional sector's labor force too fast, the modern sector will gradually come to dominate the economy. Eventually capital formation will come to a stop or converge to some exogenously given rate ("steady state"): the growing up process is completed.

However, as was observed already by John Stuart Mill, it is possible that in an open economy growth will make the growing country worse off.[1] Suppose, argues Mill, that due to technological progress a country can now offer its export product at a lower price. In that case the economy may be worse off if the elasticity of world demand facing the country is smaller than unity, since the reduction in costs implies that the total amount of imports which can be purchased in exchange for the increased volume of exports has declined. In other words, the net barter terms of trade have declined relatively more than output has increased. The exact conditions for "damnification" (as Edgeworth has termed it) are somewhat more complex, but have largely been upheld by modern theory.[2]

It may, however, be doubted whether the necessary conditions for growth to be immiserizing held in the Belgian case. Belgium, after all, was a small country and even though it was the most advanced industrial economy on the Continent by 1850, it still controlled a small part of the world market. England was not only much larger, but also further advanced on the path of industrialization. An indication of this fact was the small share of Belgian textile trade compared with England. Average Belgian imports of raw cotton between 1840 and 1849 were an annual 8.13 million kg. or 17.95 million lbs.[3] The corresponding figure for England was 549.8 million lbs.[4] The average value (current prices) of Belgian exports of linen manufactures between 1846 and 1850 was 14.8 million francs annually or 590,000 pounds sterling.[5] English exports averaged about 3.9 million pounds sterling in the same period.[6] On the other hand, the world market was to some extent segregated. While Belgium, during most of the period under discussion, dominated the French market for linen goods, its exports to the United States and South America were very small. The share of Belgium in the world market, with proper allowance for segregation and other market imperfections, and the world demand curve determined jointly whether the demand curve facing

    1. Cf. J. S. Mill, *Principles of Political Economy*, bk. 3, chap. 18. (London: Longmans, Green and Co., 1894), pp. 358–60.
    2. F. Y. Edgeworth, "The Theory of International Values," *EJ* 4 (March 1894): 39–43. Harry G. Johnson, "Equilibrium Growth in an International Economy," reprinted in *International Trade and Economic Growth* (Cambridge: Harvard University Press, 1967), pp. 120–49. Murray C. Kemp, "Technological Change, the Terms of Trade, and Welfare," *EJ* 65 (September 1955): 457–74. Id., *The Pure Theory of International Trade* (Englewood Cliffs, N. J.: Prentice Hall, 1967), pp. 81–88. J. Bhagwati, "Immiserizing Growth: A Geometrical Note," *ReStud* 25 (June 1958): 201–05.
    3. *Statistique de la Belgique, Tableau Général du Commerce*, passim.
    4. B. R. Mitchell and Phyllis Deane, *Abstract of British Historical Statistics* (Cambridge: At the University Press, 1962), p. 180.
    5. *Exposé de la Situation*, pp. 124–25.
    6. Mitchell and Deane, *Abstract*, p. 303.

Belgium was sufficiently elastic to exclude the possibility of "immiserizing growth."[7]

All in all, it seems reasonable to suppose that the impact of the expansion of Belgium's industrial sector on the terms of trade it faced, though not negligible, was insufficient to transform industrialization into impoverishment. On the other hand, Belgium's smallness rendered it much more vulnerable to external changes in the world economy.

Consider a simple model in which two exporting countries B and E compete on a world market in which the overall demand curve has an elasticity less than unity. Suppose for simplicity that both countries export their entire output of industrial goods and import their entire consumption of agricultural goods. If country B grows while country E does not, it may still gain from its growth if the sum of the elasticity of world demand (in absolute value) and the elasticity of supply of country E multiplied by the share of country E in total production exceeds the share of country E.[8] Clearly, thus, the smaller the share of B in world production, the more likely it is able to increase its industrial output without "damnification," provided its competitors do not grow. But it is equally true that the smaller country B, the larger will be the impact on it of shifts in the supply curve of country E.[9] The blessings of "smallness" are thus mixed. The net effect of capital accumulation and technological change in B depends on what happens in country E no less (and probably more) than on what it does itself.

The possible paths for country B can be taxonomized as follows:

1. The demand curve facing the world is elastic. Since the demand curve facing country B is always more elastic than that of the world, growth cannot be immiserizing.[10]

2. World demand is inelastic, but the demand curve facing country B is elastic. If B alone grows, immiserization is excluded, at least in the short run. If both countries grow, but B grows faster than E, the net outcome is

7. The condition for immiserizing growth to occur is that the sum of the elasticities of international demand is larger than unity yet smaller than one plus the product of the terms of trade and the marginal propensity to import of the growing country. Cf. Johnson, "Equilibrium Growth," pp. 142–43.

8. The proof of this proposition is presented in Mokyr, "Industrial Growth," pp. 417–18.

9. The algebraic proof of this proposition is straightforward. The intuitive reasoning is that the larger the share of country E in total output, the larger will be the price-depressing effect of an increase in the supply of E. The exact decline in the revenue of country B depends on the magnitude of the price fall and the elasticity of B's supply.

10. Note that the condition here is somewhat simpler than that stated in footnote 7 above. The reason for this is that it has been assumed for simplicity that B exports all its industrial production and imports all its agricultural consumption. The same result would also hold if the cross elasticity of the demand of country B for agricultural goods with respect to the price of industrial goods were zero or negligible. Cf. Kemp, "Technological Change," p. 467.

indeterminate. If both countries grow *pari passu* or if E grows faster than B, B's growth will not save it from gradual impoverishment. Note that in the long run even nonimmiserizing growth is likely to be transformed into "damnification." If the economy is initially small enough to face an elastic demand even though world demand is inelastic, and it is growing faster than the rest of the world, by necessity the demand curve faced by this economy will eventually become inelastic as its share in world production exceeds some critical proportion.[11]

3. World demand is inelastic, and so is the demand for country B's industrial products. Damnification is inevitable.

The fall in the terms of trade might thus dash the hopes of more consumption of agricultural goods following the modernization of industry. It can have, however, much graver consequences for an economy in the midst of the growing up process as previously defined. As was shown in chapter 4, the rate of accumulation of capital is independent of the terms of trade, while as long as the wage rate is dominated by the Z-good sector wages are proportional to the terms of trade.[12] Therefore *any* decline in the terms of trade, whether sufficient to offset the gains from growth or not, whether caused by a shift in the supply curve of the economy itself or by a shift of the supply curve of a competing country, changes the income distribution to the disadvantage of those who still remain in the Z-good sector. For some, then, growth is always immiserizing.

The two possible ways in which the process of growing up resolves itself are illustrated in figure 7.1.

Panel I describes the path toward the blissful stationary state. At any moment total output of textiles by the economy as a whole is given. This output is equal to the number of Z-good workers times their productivity plus the number of workers in the consumption industry of the modern sector times their productivity. At output Q_1 the price of manufactured goods in terms of agricultural goods given to the economy is P_1, so that the wage rate is equal to bP_1, where b is the (constant) productivity of labor in the Z-good sector. The reinvestment of profits makes additional investment possible, so that the next period output is larger, while prices are lower at P_2. If prices continue to fall, taking wages with them, sooner or later the standard of living of workers

---

11. This critical proportion is equal to the sum of the rest of the world's supply and demand elasticities for industrial and agricultural goods respectively, divided by one plus the rest of the world's elasticity of supply of agricultural goods.

12. The reason for this is that the earnings in the Z-good sector are the relevant opportunity cost of labor. These earnings equal the (constant) productivity of labor in producing Z times the price of Z in terms of food, i.e., the terms of trade. See above, pp. 151–52.

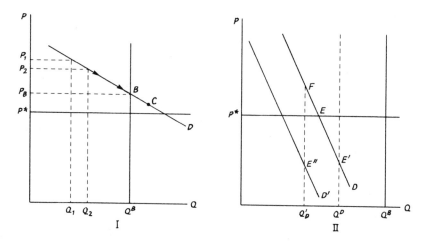

Figure 7.1   The Blissful and the Dismal Stationary State

will reach subsistence levels, below which the workers in the modern sector will refuse to work. The corresponding level of prices is depicted by P^*. The criterion for successful growing up is whether the modern sector can absorb the available reservoir of pseudo surplus-labor in the Z-good sector *before* the increased supply pushes the price down to a level that reduces wages to subsistence. Whether growing up will result in a blissful or a dismal stationary state depends on the initial size of the Z-good sector (and its growth, if the assumption of constant population is relaxed), the elasticity of the demand curve facing the economy, the initial price of Z-goods, the level of subsistence, and the stability of the demand curve faced by the economy depending on what happens in the rest of the world. Panel I in figure 7.1 depicts the successful case. At quantity Q^B the Z-good sector is exhausted. After point B (the "turning point") wages start to rise, so that profits start to decline. At some further point, say C, growth comes to a halt since profits have fallen to zero. It is indeterminate whether wages at C are higher or lower than at B, but it is not possible that they have fallen beneath subsistence. A position like C might therefore be called the blissful stationary state.

Consider now panel II. As the price of output falls to its minimum at point E, wages in the modern sector will become sticky downward. Profits will start to decline and the process of accumulation will gradually grind to a halt. In the meantime, however, accumulation will go on so that output reaches a level of Q^D. The point E' may truly be called a dismal stationary state: of the three classes composing the industrial sector, the capitalists earn no profits and are struggling for survival, the workers in the modern sector earn the bare subsistence wage, and those workers who still remain in the traditional Z-good sector have dropped under subsistence.

However, it is crucially important to keep in mind that movements *of* the demand curve faced by the economy would have an effect similar to movements *along* the curve. Consider again panel II. Suppose the economy was at point F, still in the middle of the process of growing up. Now assume a sudden shift of the demand curve faced by the economy from D to D' takes place. The industrial sector is plunged all of a sudden in a dismal stationary state at point E''. Moreover, if the shift occurs at a later stage, it might conceivably threaten even the workers in the modern sector with sub-subsistence wages and/or the capitalists with negative profits. It will thus be realized that the slope of the demand curve and its stability jointly determine whether growing up will result in a blissful or a dismal stationary state.

What are the causes for possible shifts in the demand curve facing a country like Belgium? Historically speaking, four different causes may be isolated.

1. Changes in the tastes of the rest of the world. This could be particularly important in the case of a differentiated textile product, for instance, a substitution of cotton cloth for linen would change the income distribution in the disadvantage of workers, since linen was largely a Z-good product (in Belgium until 1840 there was no modernization in the linen industry), while cotton had by then largely been mechanized. A decline in the price of substitutes due to supply effects (such as technological progress in cotton manufacturing) would have similar effects.

2. Technological progress and capital accumulation in competing industrial countries. Even if the world demand curve was stable, this would shift the demand faced by the economy, as was argued above.

3. An exogenous decline in the supply of agricultural goods of the rest of the world caused by crop failures, political turmoil, or population growth abroad. It should be kept in mind that the curves D in figure 7.1 are reciprocal demand curves: the value of the textiles demanded from the economy is equal to the amount of agricultural goods supplied to it. The same is true if some of the agricultural goods imported are raw materials used by industry, such as wool or cotton. A rise in the price of raw materials will have similar effects to a rise in the price of foodstuffs.

4. The imposition of tariffs on industrial goods or export duties on food or raw materials by the economy's trading partners.

To summarize: the path leading to a modern industrial sector is by no means strewn with roses. Two types of dangers menace the successful completion of the growing up process. The first is the traditional idea of immiserizing growth that, properly modified for a small economy, can be shown to contain the possibility of impoverishment. The second, which may occur whether growth is "damnifying" or not, is that the distribution of income may be altered to the disfavor of workers, and thus reduce the Z-good sector's income to below subsistence, resulting in its eventual destruction.

INDUSTRIALIZATION AND IMPOVERISHMENT IN BELGIUM

Natalis de Briavoinne was no doubt the most insightful contemporary observing the consequences of industrialization in Belgium. His major work, *De l'Industrie en Belgique*, is ambitious and highly competent, combining meticulous research with often surprising insights. One of his chapters bears the title, "The Industrial Revolution"—forty years before Toynbee and virtually simultaneous with Blanqui, who is generally credited with the first use of the term.

It seems Briavoinne was skeptical about the results of the industrial revolution in Belgium.[13] His dilemma was quite obvious. He noted that the material effects of the industrial revolution clearly should have been beneficial.

Man has created more resources to defend himself against the inclemencies of the seasons, to cloth and feed himself better, and to improve housing ... the mortality rate has declined together with privations and fatigue. ...Workers receive higher wages, women and children have been able to find more lucrative occupations.[14]

Yet even in the late 1830s, when the worst was still to come, some doubts were arising in the mind of this brilliant contemporary. He continues:

Why, then, is it that these generally beneficial improvements have allowed shocking inequality and deep misery to persist? Why is it that, in spite of a certain progress made, the fate of the majority is still to suffer? The reason is that the newly acquired wealth is as unevenly distributed as in the past. The expectations have been disappointed, the efforts have been in vain.[15]

Was it then the greedy capitalists who had made vast fortunes at the expense of their ruthlessly exploited workers?

The captains of industry are often blamed for the situation. But the industrial revolution has made their condition more brilliant than

13. Briavoinne, *De l'Industrie*, 1: 203–10; 2: 551–62. See also Heinrich Waentig, "Briavoinne" (in German), *JNS* 58, no. 3 (1919): 309–13.
14. Briavoinne, *De l'Industrie*, 1: 204.
15. Ibid., p. 206.

solid. Gradually their existence is becoming precarious and painful due to tough competition and rapidly changing techniques on the one hand, and by workers who constantly are demanding higher wages on the other. . . . For every ten industrialists who have accumulated large fortunes, there are a hundred who have lost theirs.

As to the condition of the workers, Briavoinne states:

Has the condition of the workers improved? The wages have, overall, increased somewhat, but they hardly exceed the minimum of subsistence. The workers have benefitted from the industrial revolution in the sense that they are clothed better now, but they are neither better fed nor better housed than before. The concentration of population has driven up rents and food prices.[16]

According to Briavoinne, the rise in agricultural goods had not benefited the farmers either, since the value of land and rents had risen considerably. Probably the influence of Ricardo inspired these conclusions. Yet it is striking that neither entrepreneurs nor workers appear to have derived substantial benefits from industrialization—most of the gains seem to have been transferred to consumers (to a large extent foreign), in terms of lower prices, and landowners.

Two years after the publication of his major book, Briavoinne headed an inquiry commission, which in 1841 published the *Enquête Linière*. The conclusions of the commission were anything but optimistic—a terminal disease was in fact diagnosed in the Flemish linen industry, the principal Z-good sector remaining in Belgium. However, as a description of the catastrophe that hit the linen industry in the 1840s, it is not the best source for the simple reason that it was compiled before the disaster reached its peak. The causes of the crisis can be viewed as having two components: a transitory component due to the extraordinarily bad harvest failures in 1845–46, and a permanent component due to the secular decline of the Flemish Z-good industry which is the more intriguing part for the present purpose. Before turning to an analysis of the events, it may be worthwhile to describe the extent of the plight of Flanders in the 1840s.

One indication of the catastrophic events is population change. The hypothesis is that the industrial sector as a whole experienced a decline in its terms of trade, causing the Z-good sector (but not the modern sector) to drop under subsistence. If so, one should be able to observe, first, a relatively stronger effect of the crisis on the countryside than on the urban population since most protoindustry had remained rural.

16. Ibid., pp. 208–09.

Secondly, the crisis should be particularly severe in those provinces in which the Z-good had remained important, namely the two Flemish provinces and to a lesser extent Limburg and Hainault. Table 7.1 shows the dimensions of the catastrophe that hit Flanders in the 1840s. During the entire period 1815–45, birth rates had been falling slowly and death rates were constant, though the movement of the birth and death rates in the towns went in the opposite direction and partially offset the general trend dominated by the countryside. In the mid-1840s, however, a sharp rise in death rates occurred simultaneous with a decline in birth rates. The result was a net decline in population during 1846–48.

Table 7.2 shows that the rise in death rates and decline in birth rates were general phenomena in Belgium in the 1840s. While the decline in birth rates was more or less uniform for the entire country, the rise in death rates was by far more marked in the two Flemish provinces. As the rate of population growth in Flanders was already considerably lower than average in 1841–45, population in these two provinces actually diminished in subsequent years. Consequently, the share of Flanders in total Belgian population declined from 35 percent in 1840 to 32 percent in 1850. In passing, it should be noted that the province of West Flanders was hit more severely than East Flanders, in spite of the fact that the Z-good sector in the latter was somewhat larger. The reason is that the modern industry was much more important in East Flanders and, as the model presented above suggests, modern industry partially absorbed the impact of the crisis. In West Flanders, the cushioning effect of modern industry was largely absent.

Table 7.3 demonstrates the fact that, in the provinces in which there was still an important Z-good industry, death rates in the countryside were higher or as high as in the cities, a phenomenon rarely observed hitherto. Indeed, death rates in the Flemish countryside were higher than anywhere else, including the towns in all other provinces. A breakdown of the Flemish countryside into counties that were predominantly linen producing and counties in which protoindustry was less important underlines the difference. The death rate in the "linen counties" in East Flanders in 1847 was 3.64 percent as compared to 2.92 percent in the "nonlinen counties." In West Flanders the figures were, respectively, 4.65 percent and 3.23 percent.[17] The distinction between the two is somewhat less marked before 1846, but the overall difference between the Flemish provinces and the others indicates that the extreme poverty of the Flemish countryside did not start in 1845. Moreover, the distinction between linen and nonlinen counties is somewhat blurred. St. Nikolaas,

17. Jacquemyns, "Histoire de la Crise," pp. 360–61.

Table 7.1   Birth and Death Rates in Flanders, 1815–48
(in percentages)

East Flanders	Cities			Countryside			Total		
	B	D	G	B	D	G	B	D	G
1815–24	3.4	2.9	0.5	3.3	2.4	0.9	3.3	2.5	0.8
1836	3.3	2.4	0.9	3.1	2.3	0.8	3.2	2.4	0.8
1845	3.3	2.8	0.5	3.0	2.5	0.5	3.1	2.5	0.6
1846	3.1	3.1	0	2.5	2.8	−0.3	2.6	2.9	−0.3
1847	3.0	3.2	−0.2	2.3	3.3	−1.0	2.5	3.3	−0.8
1848	2.9	2.9	0	2.3	2.9	−0.6	2.5	2.9	−0.4
West Flanders									
1815–24	3.7	3.0	0.7	3.3	2.4	0.9	3.6	2.6	1.0
1836	3.5	2.8	0.7	3.4	2.6	0.8	3.4	2.7	0.7
1845	n.a.	n.a.	n.a.	n.a.	n.a.	n.a.	3.2	2.7	0.5
1846	3.0	3.3	−0.3	2.6	3.2	−0.6	2.7	3.2	−0.5
1847	2.8	3.8	−1.0	2.5	4.0	−1.5	2.6	4.0	−1.4
1848	3.0	3.2	−0.2	2.5	3.3	−0.8	2.6	3.4	−0.8

NOTE: B = birth rates, D = death rates, G = growth rates.
SOURCES: All years except 1836—E. Ducpétiaux, *Mémoire sur le Paupérisme dans les Flanders* (Brussels: M. Hayez, 1850), pp. 28–29. 1836—Heuschling, *Essai sur la Statistique*, 1st ed., pp. 37–53.

Table 7.2   Birth and Death Rates in Belgium, 1841–50

Province	1841–45			1846–50		
	B	D	G	B	D	G
Antwerp	3.23	2.23	1.00	2.87	2.38	0.49
Brabant	3.47	2.43	1.04	3.05	2.50	0.55
W. Flanders	3.13	2.62	0.51	2.79	3.18	−0.39
E. Flanders	3.04	2.41	0.63	2.67	2.83	−0.16
Hainault	3.21	2.16	1.05	2.82	2.23	0.59
Liège	3.37	2.34	1.03	3.02	2.49	0.53
Limburg	3.03	2.27	0.76	2.68	2.29	0.39
Luxembourg	3.23	2.03	1.20	2.95	1.99	0.96
Namur	3.15	1.83	1.32	2.88	1.82	1.06
Total	3.21	2.32	0.89	2.86	2.53	0.33

NOTE: B = birth rates, D = death rates, G = growth rates.
SOURCE: *Exposé de la Situation*, pp. 4, 5, 21, 27.

Table 7.3   Birth and Death Rates in Belgium, 1848

Province	Cities			Countryside			Total		
	B	D	G	B	D	G	B	D	G
Antwerp	2.9	2.4	0.5	2.7	2.2	0.5	2.7	2.3	0.4
Brabant	3.3	2.8	0.5	2.9	2.2	0.7	3.0	2.4	0.6
W. Flanders	2.9	3.2	−0.3	2.5	3.4	−0.9	2.6	3.3	−0.7
E. Flanders	2.9	2.9	0	2.4	2.8	−0.4	2.5	2.9	−0.4
Hainault	2.7	2.6	0.1	2.9	2.1	0.8	2.8	2.2	0.6
Liège	3.0	2.5	0.5	3.0	2.1	0.9	3.0	2.2	0.8
Limburg	2.6	2.3	0.3	2.6	2.4	0.2	2.6	2.4	0.2
Luxembourg	3.0	2.3	0.7	2.9	2.2	0.7	2.9	2.2	0.7
Namur	2.9	2.2	0.7	2.9	1.7	1.2	2.9	1.8	1.1
Total	2.9	2.7	0.2	2.7	2.4	0.3	2.8	2.5	0.3

NOTE: B = birth rates, D = death rates, G = growth rates.
SOURCE: Ducpétiaux, *Mémoire sur le Paupérisme*, pp. 31–32.

Lokeren, and other nonlinen counties did have, in fact, considerable protoindustry, including both linen and cotton.[18]

A second indicator of the misery of the population is the number of paupers (*indigents*) registered at the offices of the charity bureau. Unfortunately, the registration of paupers was not very consistent, and the rules differed substantially from community to community. Moreover, the number of paupers varied directly with the size of the funds to be distributed.[19] Urban areas tended in general to have better organized and better funded poor relief. However, it is Jacquemyns's conclusion that these problems encumber comparisons between communities, but that comparisons between larger units (counties, provinces) can still be meaningful. Tables 7.4 and 7.5 present cross sections and time series of the paupers as a percentage of population, and illustrate the rapid impoverishment of the Flemish countryside.

Table 7.4 indicates that the number of paupers in both Flemish provinces doubled between the mid-1830s and the late 1840s. It is evident that the famine of 1845–46 greatly aggravated the poverty in these areas. Yet, the immiserization, especially in the countryside, clearly antedates the "hungry forties." That the impact of the famine was particularly severe in those provinces in which protoindustry was important and the modern sector was growing insufficiently fast, can be ascertained from table 7.5. While the national average grew only by 2.2 percent from 1839

18. *Enquête Linière*, 2: 415.
19. Jacquemyns, "Histoire de la Crise," p. 299.

Table 7.4   Paupers in Flanders as a Percentage of Population, 1818–48

	East Flanders			West Flanders		
	Urban	Rural	Total	Urban	Rural	Total
1818	14.5	9.5	10.7	n.a.	n.a.	n.a.
1836	18.5	10.6	12.7	n.a.	n.a.	n.a.
1837	17.9	10.7	12.5	n.a.	n.a.	17.9
1838	16.7	10.9	12.3	n.a.	n.a.	n.a.
1839	17.8	11.2	12.8	n.a.	n.a.	19.9
1840	17.8	11.8	13.2	n.a.	n.a.	19.4
1841	18.0	12.2	13.8	n.a.	n.a.	n.a.
1842	17.0	13.1	14.2	n.a.	n.a.	n.a.
1843	17.2	14.1	14.9	29.7	19.7	22.5
1844	17.8	14.5	15.2	n.a.	n.a.	23.8
1845	20.4	21.6	21.2	n.a.	n.a.	32.3
1846	23.6	28.2	27.2	35.8	35.0	35.2
1847	24.6	29.5	28.2	36.7	36.8	36.7
1848	24.9	26.8	26.2	32.0	34.9	34.1

SOURCES: Paupers—Ducpétiaux, *Mémoire sur le Paupérisme*, pp. 19, 23. Population—*Exposé de la Situation*, pp. 4–5.

Table 7.5   Paupers in Belgium as a Percentage of Population, 1828–46

Province	1828	1839	1846
Antwerp	6.8	10.3	5.7
Brabant	22.6	15.2	21.0
W. Flanders[a]	15.0	19.9	26.5
E. Flanders[a]	11.5	12.5	19.6
Hainault	22.3	20.0	16.3
Liège	16.2	10.7	12.1
Limburg	12.9	14.6	15.8
Luxembourg	0.7	3.1	1.7
Namur	13.0	11.4	11.3
Total	14.4	14.6	16.8

[a]The figures are not fully consistent with those of table 7.4, since the latter is based on census data, while the present data come from provincial council figures.
SOURCES: Paupers—Ducpétiaux, *Mémoire sur le Paupérisme*, pp. 15–17. Population—for 1828 and 1846, ibid.; for 1839, *Statistique de la Belgique, Population, Relevé Décennal 1831–1840* (Brussels: Ministère de l'Intérieur, 1842), p. 244.

Table 7.6 Budgets of Flemish Rural Families, around 1840
(weekly, in francs)

	Family 1 (eight persons)		Family 2 (five persons)	
Income:				
Husband's earnings	6.60		6.60	
Wife's earnings	2.70		3.30	
Children's earnings	3.60		1.80	
Total		12.90		11.70
Expenditures:				
Bread	3.25		2.05	
Potatoes	1.45		1.44	
Buttermilk, flour	1.75		0.60	
Other food and beverages	2.50		2.40	
Washing needs	0.35		0.43	
Heat and lighting	1.80		0.92	
Clothing	0.50		2.07	
Rent	1.60		1.73	
Total		13.20		12.14
Deficit		0.30		0.44

SOURCE: *Enquête Linière*, 2: 385, 403.

to 1846, the proportion of paupers in Flanders increased by about 7 percent. The only other province in which a comparable increase in the number of paupers occurred was Brabant. However, there the situation was very different: most of the paupers consisted of the urban poor in Brussels, where the number of paupers had been traditionally high.

On a less aggregate level, the picture is even bleaker. The *Enquête Linière* provides some detailed consumption budgets of Flemish rural families, engaged in Z-good production. These budgets provide the grim details of sub-subsistence living. As noted, these figures pertain to the the period 1840–41, before the harvest failure of 1845–46. The budgets presented in table 7.6 describe two families of, respectively, eight and five persons. In spite of the fact that expenditures were limited to the barest necessities, the peasants failed to make ends meet.

The verbal reports of the *Enquête Linière* contain many passages about the intense poverty and the dire misery in the Flemish villages. Many of the persons interviewed claimed never to eat meat or pork, never to drink beer, and to subsist almost exclusively on potatoes, ryebread, and buttermilk.[20] Similar conclusions were reached by the *Enquête sur la*

20. *Enquête Linière*, 2:386–87. See also above, p. 16.

Condition des Classes Ouvrières [Inquiry into the condition of the working classes] conducted in 1844. The Flemish weavers and spinners subsisted on unbalanced diets containing little or no protein. Most of their dietary variation was provided by home grown vegetables.[21]

The most serious and reliable research on the physical and social dimensions of the economic crisis in Belgium in the 1840s was undertaken by Édouard Ducpétiaux, a leading contemporary political economist whose work was quoted earlier in this chapter. Ducpétiaux's investigations of the consumption patterns of the working class on the household level are an indispensable source of information for any social research on this period. The usefulness of his figures for the present purpose is somewhat limited, however, because most of his budgets were compiled in the early 1850s when recovery was setting in. Yet it is important to emphasize that even then the consumption of food in Flanders was considerably lower than the national average.[22]

Ducpétiaux's figures show that between 60 and 80 percent of total expenses of Flemish households in the lower classes were devoted to food, while most of the rest went to fuel, rent, and a little clothing. Among the "luxury" expenditures the most prominent was tobacco. Altogether the "luxury" expenditures comprise on the average no more than 2 percent of consumption.[23] It is also interesting to note that the majority of households suffered from deficits, i.e., their incomes were smaller than the value of the consumption baskets they reported. Since wages were lower and prices higher during the peak of the crisis (1845–48) than in 1852–53, the deficits in the late 1840s were probably even higher. How, then, were these budgets balanced? The answer was partially through outdoor relief and, when that was insufficient, simply through starvation. The author of the classic work on the hungry forties in Belgium states it quite bluntly:

> In spite of the strict minimum which the weavers imposed on their expenditures, six out of ten households [sampled by Ducpétiaux] closed their books in the red.... The assistance provided by the *bureaux de bienfaisance* [outdoor relief agencies] was insufficient to

21. "Rapport de la Commission Médicale de la Flandre Occidentale," in *Enquête sur la Condition des Classes Ouvrières*, 3: 304. Also, Mareska and Heyman, "Enquête sur le Travail et la Condition Physique et Morale des Ouvriers dans les Manufactures de Coton à Gand," in Ministère de l'Intérieur, *Enquête sur la Condition des Classes Ouvrières* (Brussels: Th. Lesigne, 1846), 3: 386–87. In comparison the situation in other provinces seems to have been less critical, a fact which is also reflected in the population data. See also "Mémoire de la Commission Médicale de la Province de Liège," in *Enquête sur la Condition des Classes Ouvrières*, 3: 492–96, 573–76.

22. E. Ducpétiaux, "Budgets Économiques des Classes Ouvrières en Belgique," *BCCS* 6 (1855): 402–04.

23. The proportion of luxury expenditures seems remarkably constant in these budgets. This might indicate that income was so low that the "bare necessities" were not yet subject to Engel's Law. Cf. Ducpétiaux, "Budgets Économiques," pp. 290–91, 318–19.

balance the budgets. Ducpétiaux does not tell us what happened to those budgets when the workers were unable to get any more credit, or when the prices of food went up while wages remained stationary or fell. Our study enables us to explain how the budgets were balanced: the weaver himself had to balance it. The only way he could do this was at the expense of his health and that of his family. Hence the physical conditions of the Flemish weaver-peasant.

Our sad conclusion is that those workers ate not whenever they were hungry but whenever they could afford to. This type of life implied starvation and premature death. Such were the consequences of the persistence of the linen industry by artificial means. In spite of all the protection, aid, and credit given to it, the linen industry was unable to provide a living for its workers. . . . Ultimately they were forced to abandon the ancient manufacture, which was so highly regarded, yet did not allow them to earn a wage sufficient to satisfy their most elementary needs.[24]

Starvation was not the only way to make ends meet. The number of persons jailed in West Flanders for minor offenses grew from an average of 3,006 in 1839–41 to 6,503 in 1846–48. The corresponding figures for East Flanders were 3,853 for 1839–41 and 13,866 (1846–48).[25] For Belgium as a whole the rise was less dramatic and almost wholly dominated by Flanders. In 1839–41 the average number of people jailed annually was 24,101, rising to 40,270.[26] The overall rise in criminality is thus largely explained by what happened in Flanders. It is equally suggestive that out of the 5,228 inmates of the central prison system in 1849, 3,135 were textile workers, most of them spinners and weavers.[27] Many of the most desperate had themselves imprisoned deliberately to avoid starvation, becoming known as "window smashers." One of them was quoted, "If I had ten francs, I would hire a lawyer to have my whole family jailed for half a year, so that they could leave prison fat and well-fed."[28]

On the other hand, unlike the case of Ireland with which Flanders has otherwise much in common, emigration did not attain major proportions. The causes for the absence of emigration are unclear at the present stage of research. Jacquemyns claims that, "The population of Flanders was too routine-minded to adapt to an entirely novel mode of life. Frightened by the unknown, they lacked the adventurous spirit and remained attached

24. Jacquemyns, "Histoire de la Crise," p. 227.
25. E. Ducpétiaux, *Mémoire sur le Paupérisme dans les Flanders* (Brussels: M. Hayez, 1850), p. 42.
26. E. Ducpétiaux, "Des Subsistances, des Salaires et de l'Accroissement de la Population," *BCCS* 6 (1855): 568.
27. Computed from *Exposé de la Situation*, p. 473.
28. Jacquemyns, "Histoire de la Crise," pp. 329–30.

Table 7.7   Estimated Net Internal Migration in Belgium, 1841–50
(net immigration [+] or emigration [−])

Province

Antwerp	+ 11,228
Brabant	+ 43,559
W. Flanders	− 33,347
E. Flanders	− 31,567
Hainault	− 298
Liège	+ 13,223
Limburg	+ 4,187
Luxembourg	− 5,885
Namur	− 1,103
Total	0

SOURCE: Computed from *Exposé de la Situation*, pp. 4–5, 21, 29. The procedure is based on the assumption that net emigration from the country was negligible (no exact data were available for 1841–45), which made it possible to correct for obvious underreporting of birth figures.

to their soil."[29] This argument is somewhat simplistic, perhaps, but it is consistent with the fact that the majority of people who left Flanders between 1845 and 1850 migrated to a different province, while of those who actually left Belgium, the majority ended up in northern France.[30] Between 1845 and 1850, an average number of 5,850 persons left Belgium annually, but immigration into the country (possibly repatriating Belgians) offset most of that, so that net emigration averaged only 1,663 annually.[31] Data on internal migration are not readily available, but as table 7.7 indicates, it too was not large enough to mitigate the effects of the crisis. On the other hand, it is significant that of the almost 16,000 persons who left the countryside in East Flanders, 72 percent came from the linen counties (which accounted for 62 percent of total rural population). In West Flanders, where the difference between linen and nonlinen counties was more clear-cut, the linen counties accounted for 99 percent of emigration from the countryside.[32]

The third alternative open to the linen workers was to increase the input of labor per man, i.e., to prolong the working day. Here, however, physiological limits proved an unsuperable barrier, although in some instances heroically long working days were observed.[33]

29. Ibid., p. 382. See also Arrivabene, *Sur la Condition des Laboureurs*, p. 25.
30. Jacquemyns, "Histoire de la Crise," pp. 384–85.
31. *Exposé de la Situation*, p. 44.
32. All figures from Jacquemyns, "Histoire de la Crise," pp. 385–86.
33. A cotton weaver in a village not far from Brussels was reported to have worked from 5 A.M. to 10 P.M. daily. A linen weaver in Thielt (W. Flanders) worked from 5:30 A.M. to 9:00 P.M. daily. Cf. *Enquête Linière*, 2: 386, 653.

The actual fall beneath subsistence levels took other forms besides starvation. One of these was the startling decline in hygienic standards. A medical report from the late 1840s described it as follows:

In these devastating conditions squalor is pushed to the point where it borders on the unimaginable and of which no example exists in mankind's history. The disgusting filthyness is not only apparent from the clothing and the rags of these miserable creatures, but also from anything else that surrounds them, including the little-refreshing substances with which they feed themselves. The straw which serves as their bed, in which the grandfather, the father, the mother, and the little children spend the night in a disorderly fashion, resembles more a pile of dung than a resting place for the night. Around this hovel, on the bare ground lie the excretions of pigs, chickens, rabbits, ducks, and dogs, soaked with rainwater, filling the air with a noxious stench. . . . The place is surrounded with an infected puddle where everyone living in these hideous quarters dumps his garbage.[34]

Malnutrition and unhygienic conditions did not fail to produce severe repercussions on the physical health of the population. A new syndrome, consisting of anemia, extreme emaciation, transparency of the skin, and exhaustion was aptly named *maladie des Flanders* or *fièvre famine* ("Flemish disease or hunger fever").[35] In 1846 typhus struck many communities all over Europe. In Belgium the disease struck chiefly in the districts in which the linen industry was still important, mainly Flanders. A few years later the Flemish provinces were hit again by a contagious disease, this time cholera.

The connection between starvation and disease did not operate exclusively through the mechanism of reduced resistance due to unbalanced and insufficient nutrition. Dr. Mersseman, the above-quoted physician, argues quite convincingly that the more men were pauperized and the more desperate their condition became, the more they were tempted to neglect the most indispensable needs to prevent disease. The sapping of the physical energies extinguished the will to live.[36] Mersseman has little doubt about the underlying causes of the disaster. He quotes an ancient Flemish proverb: "Snijdt Vlaemsche spinsters duimen af en Vlaenderen

34. M. de Mersseman, "Rapport," *Bulletin de l'Académie Royale de Médecine* 8 (1848–49): 109.

35. Jacquemyns, "Histoire de la Crise," p. 341.

36. Mersseman, "Rapport," p. 108. In the discussion following Mersseman's presentation, Dr. Mareska, a long-time investigator of the condition of the Flemish working class, fully concurred with his shocking findings and diagnosis.

sterft van gebrek" [Cut off the thumbs of Flemish spinsters and Flanders starves]. It is to this question that we turn next.

THE CAUSES OF THE DESTRUCTION OF THE FLEMISH LINEN INDUSTRY

While the permanent component in the explanation of the destruction of the Z-good industry in Flanders is no doubt the more interesting part, it is important not to underestimate the enormous catalytic effect of the harvest failure of 1845–46 on the decline of the protoindustry. The two main food crops in Flanders, potatoes and cereals, suffered from extraordinarily bad crops in consecutive years.

The year 1845 was disastrous for potato crops all over Europe, and Belgium was not spared the disease. For the kingdom as a whole, the harvest of potatoes was 87.3 percent below normal. For Flanders, the losses were even more staggering: 92.4 percent in West Flanders, 90.7 percent in East Flanders.[37] Fortunately, however, the Flemish depended much less on the potato than, for instance, the Irish, and this was true even for the lower classes. In an ordinary year, total output of potatoes in Flanders was about 447,000 tons, while the production of rye was about 136,000 tons.[38] Since the nutritional value of a weight unit of potatoes was about 6.6 times smaller than rye,[39] the importance of rye as a popular food can be seen to be roughly twice that of potatoes. In addition, other cereals were grown in Flanders, mainly wheat. The production of wheat in an ordinary year was almost as large as that of rye, although wheatbread was generally a more expensive product and consumed by richer classes.

The next year the potato crop recovered some, though not all, ground lost, but unfortunately the winter of 1846 was very humid and warm, and the cereal crops were greatly damaged. The rye harvest in West Flanders was 53 percent below its normal level, 58 percent in East Flanders. For the country as a whole, the loss amounted to 61 percent.[40] Other cereals suffered, too, though to a lesser extent. Wheat crops were about 18 percent below their mean for the country as a whole, though the decline in Flanders was somewhat smaller (13 percent).

The exact deficits in nutrition are, of course, not easy to estimate, since it is not clear what the absolutely necessary levels of consumption were. Xavier Heuschling and Adolphe Quetelet, the leading Belgian

37. Jacquemyns, "Histoire de la Crise," pp. 254–55.
38. *Statistique de la Belgique, Recensement Général 1846*, "Agriculture," pp. 19, 26.
39. The ratio of nutritional values for volume units is given as 1 : 5.7, while the specific weight of rye is about 14 percent higher.
40. *Statistique de la Belgique, Recensement Général 1846*, "Agriculture," pp. 19, 26, 53.

statisticians of the time, estimated in their report to the Minister of
Interior in 1848 that the deficit for Belgium as a whole in 1846 was
5,505,000 hectolitres of cereals or their equivalent in potatoes, constituting
33 percent of normal consumption. The deficit for the two Flemish
provinces was 2,253,000 hectolitres or 42 percent of normal consumption.[41]
Yet it is not easy to draw unambiguous conclusions from these "deficits."
The problem was that the substitutability between the various starch
foods was quite high, so that the actual losses of consumers' surpluses
were lower than the staggering losses in output would suggest. In 1845,
presumably, people ate more ryebread and in 1846 they ate more potatoes
and wheatbread. While the price of potatoes rose from 3.38 francs per
hectolitre in 1844 to 8.51 per hectolitre in 1846, a rise of 151 percent *at
most* (since the true comparison should take average prices of 1844–45
and 1845–46), output of potatoes had declined by 87 percent in 1845.

The elasticity of demand can be approximated by the formula $-\dfrac{\triangle Q}{\triangle P}\dfrac{P'}{Q'}$,

where $Q' = Q + \dfrac{\triangle Q}{2}$ and $P' = P + \dfrac{\triangle P}{2}$. The elasticity of demand for

potatoes can thus be seen to be about 2.3, and although this figure is very
crude, it suffices to draw the conclusion that the demand for potatoes was
rather elastic.[42] The price of rye doubled between 1845 and 1847, while
output fell by 60 percent, implying a price elasticity of 1.3. The actual
(own) elasticity of demand was probably higher, since the rise in the
price of rye reflected also the decreases in the supply of potatoes and wheat.

To summarize, three caveats have to be kept in mind when it comes to
evaluating the role of the famine of the mid-1840s in the general catastrophe that hit the Flemish countryside in the second third of the nineteenth century. The first, as argued above, was the possibility to substitute
starch foods for each other if the various harvest failures did not coincide.
As can be verified from table 7.8, the year 1846 was by far the worst
year, since it was the only year in which an "overall harvest failure"
occurred. Even so, potatoes had largely recovered from their abysmal lows
in 1845 (other crops in 1845 were normal), while the wheat and barley
crops in 1846 were only slightly below normal. The impact of the harvest
failures on prices is demonstrated in table 7.9. As can be easily verified,
the rise in the price of wheat and rye antedates the actual harvest failure
of these crops. On the other hand, the price of potatoes remains high even
after output returns more or less to its normal levels. The conclusion is

41. X. Heuschling and A. Quetelet, "Rapport au Ministre de l'Intérieur sur la Question
des Subsistances," *BCCS* 4 (1855): 175–76, annex 4. See also table 7.11 below.
42. Fitting a constant elasticity curve through the observations yields a virtually identical
estimate.

Table 7.8   Actual and Normal Output of Agricultural Goods, 1846
(in thousands of hectolitres)

	Belgium			Flanders		
Crop	Actual	Normal	Actual as a % of Normal	Actual	Normal	Actual as a % of Normal
Wheat	3,510.1	4,189.4	83.8	1,239.5	1,421.6	87.2
Rye	2,010.7	5,069.3	39.7	773.6	1,742.0	44.4
Potatoes	15,151.3	22,514.9	67.3	4,095.4	7,544.7	54.3
Spelt	1,228.4	1,396.8	87.9	26.9	32.0	84.1
Barley	1,143.5	1,256.7	91.0	488.8	550.4	88.8
Oats	4,628.2	6,060.3	76.4	585.2	1,067.4	54.8
Buckwheat	529.5	562.7	94.1	247.7	247.5	100.1

SOURCE: *Statistique de la Belgique, Recensement Général 1846*, "Agriculture," pp. 19, 26, 53.
See also Heuschling and Quetelet, "Rapport," passim.

Table 7.9   Belgian and Flemish Agricultural Prices, 1845–50
(1841–44 = 100)

	1845	1846	1847	1848	1849	1850
Wheat:						
Belgium	103.5	126.6	160.7	89.6	87.9	83.3
E. Flanders	103.3	122.8	159.8	93.0	93.8	88.8
W. Flanders	102.6	126.7	163.9	86.4	90.6	85.3
Rye:						
Belgium	111.6	156.0	176.8	86.8	78.6	83.4
E. Flanders	116.4	158.3	181.0	87.4	82.8	89.8
W. Flanders	110.0	147.8	181.9	86.6	81.0	85.5
Potatoes:						
Belgium	142.4	209.6	158.9	124.9	120.4	107.4
E. Flanders	139.4	181.4	157.5	121.5	118.6	96.6
W. Flanders	128.9	201.4	162.6	135.6	117.6	95.8
Oats:						
Belgium	100.8	123.8	134.2	94.7	82.9	91.0
E. Flanders	99.3	116.3	123.7	97.0	89.4	96.0
W. Flanders	93.3	120.0	125.0	93.2	85.1	89.2
Barley:						
Belgium	100.5	129.5	135.3	93.5	86.0	86.4
E. Flanders	106.7	114.2	131.1	91.0	85.4	85.6
W. Flanders	89.6	113.7	131.9	91.7	87.0	88.9

NOTE: Since the data pertain to calendar years, there is probably a lag of about half a year between the harvest failure and the price, e.g., the price for 1845 reflects to some extent the harvest of 1844 and so on.
SOURCE: Computed from *Exposé de la Situation*, pp. 87–89.

Table 7.10   Harvest Successes in Four Selected Belgian Provinces, 1841–50
(frequency of occurrence of each type, in number of years)

		West Flanders	East Flanders	Antwerp	Liège
Wheat:	VG	–	1	–	–
	G	6	7	8	6
	S	–	–	1	–
	M	3	2	1	4
	B	–	–	–	–
Rye:	VG	1	1	1	1
	G	5	6	5	4
	S	–	–	2	2
	M	1	2	1	2
	B	2	1	1	1
Potatoes:	VG	–	2	–	1
	G	4	2	6	5
	S	–	–	1	–
	M	3	4	2	2
	B	2	2	2	2
Spelt and	VG	–	1	–	–
buckwheat:	G	5	6	6	7
	S	2	–	2	–
	M	2	3	2	3
	B	–	–	–	–

NOTE: VG = very good; G = good; S = satisfactory; M = mediocre; B = bad. The reason for the failure of the number of years to add up to exactly ten in some cases is unknown.
SOURCE: *Exposé de la Situation*, pp. 77–78.

thus that the cross elasticities between the main crops in Belgium were comparatively high since the commodities were good substitutes for each other. In other words, the cereals could absorb part of the scarcity created by the failure of the potato crop, and vice versa.

Secondly, since the Flemish crisis extended over the entire decade, one wonders whether the harvests had been generally below average during the entire decade, so that the reserves in 1845–47 were already low, causing the harvest failures of 1845–46 to be particularly severe. As it turns out, however, this was not the case. The Belgian national statistics classified the harvests into five classes: very good, good, satisfactory, mediocre, and bad. The results for the two Flemish provinces, with Liège and Antwerp as controls, are reproduced in table 7.10. As can be seen, for all cereals at least half of the crops in the decade were classified as good or very good, and even for potatoes, the years 1842, 1843, and 1844 were generally good.[43]

43. *Exposé de la Situation*, p. 77.

Table 7.11   "Deficits" and Imports, 1846
(in thousands of kgs.)

Good	Deficit	Imports
Wheat	52,990	86,097
Rye	217,189	52,246
Buckwheat	2,090	329
Oats	63,010	—
Potatoes	463,932	4
Rice	—	6,833
Flour	—	4,233
Peas, beans	3,137	3,294

SOURCE: Heuschling and Quetelet, "Rapport," pp. 188, 189.

Finally, the harvest failures were to a considerable extent cushioned by increased import of food. The average import of cereals for the period 1841–44 was 87,700 tons. This amount grew to 166,000 tons in 1845, 216,000 tons in 1846 and 175,000, falling back to its normal level in the last years of the decade when the shortages were alleviated.[44] Heuschling and Quetelet argue that imports were "by no means sufficient to make up for the lost crops," since total imports covered only about one half of the total deficit. The argument is somewhat dubious, since the definition of the "deficit" by itself as the difference between actual output and normal output is rather odd. It does not allow, for example, for sharp reductions in nonfood uses of cereals (industrial uses, fodder), nor for the substitution of inferior cereals such as oats and buckwheat for the scarce foodstuffs. Table 7.11 compares the "deficits" with imports for the period September 1846–August 1847. It is clear that imports did not suffice to cover the entire difference between actual and normal output, nor was there any particular reason why they should. Still, there can be little doubt that imports went a long way toward removing the sharpest edges of the famine.

The ailments of the Flemish rural linen industry had deeper roots. As was argued above, the two principal possible causes that might have caused the terms of trade faced by the Belgian linen industry to decline were shifts *down* a (relatively inelastic) demand curve, and shifts *of* the demand curve faced by the Belgian industrial sector. It is not always easy, in practice, to distinguish between these different factors, though analytically they are clearly distinct.

To start with, the first half of the nineteenth century witnessed a secular decline in the price of textiles relative to the price of agricultural

44. *Statistique de la Belgique, Tableau Général du Commerce*, passim.

goods. There can be little doubt that the chief cause for this phenomenon was the enormous increase in the supply of cotton products in England and, to a lesser extent, on the Continent (mainly in Switzerland, Flanders, and Alsace). Of secondary importance was the secular decline in the cost of raw materials for the cotton industry. As cotton and linen were to a degree good substitutes, the revolution in cotton depressed the demand for linen. It was not only the fact that cotton was becoming gradually cheaper over time that made the linen industry in the long run "a moribund industry." Part of the substitution between cotton and linen was due to changing tastes, or to the improving *quality* of cotton goods (which could be viewed either as an effective shift in the supply curve of cotton or as a change in tastes on the part of the consumers). However, it seems plausible that in addition to the price and quality effects, there were also genuine changes in tastes in favor of cotton at the expense of linen.[45]

Unfortunately, there are no continuous time series available for Belgian cotton and linen prices. Since both were, however, internationally traded

Table 7.12   Textile Prices in Terms of Agricultural Goods, 1814–50
(1850 = 100)

Year	Cotton Yarn	Cotton Cloth	Year	Cotton Yarn	Cotton Cloth	Linen Yarn
1814	210.1	n.a.	1833	110.9	142.7	n.a.
1815	222.7	n.a.	1834	115.1	147.8	151.4
1816	221.8	n.a.	1835	116.8	161.5	142.5
1817	173.9	n.a.	1836	108.4	146.2	109.5
1818	179.8	n.a.	1837	105.0	126.2	89.9
1819	175.6	n.a.	1838	98.3	115.7	76.2
1820	173.1	256.9	1839	91.6	106.3	71.1
1821	169.7	280.5	1840	85.7	97.8	66.7
1822	176.5	276.0	1841	90.8	99.9	59.2
1823	154.6	237.0	1842	93.3	95.0	57.8
1824	153.8	237.6	1843	91.6	96.6	69.1
1825	137.8	202.8	1844	84.9	93.6	68.9
1826	132.8	197.1	1845	86.6	91.0	76.9
1827	124.4	187.5	1846	83.2	87.1	77.2
1828	117.6	186.3	1847	80.0	91.2	83.0
1829	106.7	165.1	1848	82.4	87.1	79.7
1830	103.4	156.8	1849	88.2	87.1	84.3
1831	100.0	154.2	1850	100.0	100.0	100.0
1832	100.8	138.4				

SOURCES: Textiles—*Report on Wholesale and Retail Prices in the U. K. in 1902, with Comparative Statistical Tables for a Series of Years*, ordered by the House of Commons, August 6, 1903 (London: His Majesty's Stationery Office, 1903), pp. 46, 48, 66. Agricultural Prices—*Rousseaux Agricultural Price Index*, reproduced in Mitchell and Deane, *Abstract*, pp. 471–72.

45. *Enquête Linière*, 2: 351.

goods, the English data should be correlated with the Belgian prices. The price terms of trade are presented in table 7.12. As will be quite apparent, a secular downward trend dominates the figures. This trend accelerated in the 1840s.

The price of Flemish linen cloth declined with the trend. On the major markets of Ghent, Oudenaarden, and Kortrijk, the price of a metre of linen cloth fell respectively by 20, 22, and 25 percent between 1825 and 1840.[46] As the commission conducting the linen survey (chaired by the intelligent and knowledgeable Briavoinne) observed, the fall in Flemish linen prices did not result in an increased volume of sales. In other words, what happened was a shift *of* the demand curve rather than *along* it.[47] In spite of the decline in linen prices, an English observer noted in 1840 that the linen cloth sold on the Flemish markets was by no means cheap.[48] As an immediate consequence of the fall in linen prices the wages of the workers in the linen industry fell. Spinners employed by putting-out entrepreneurs suffered a 25 percent decline in their wages between 1825 and 1840, while the implicit wages of the large majority of self-employed spinners who bought the hackled flax and sold the spun yarn at the market fell by 30 to 35 percent in the same period.[49] A similar decline hit the wages of linen weavers.[50] Clearly, then, what happened was precisely the phenomenon described in the beginning of this chapter: the falling terms of trade increasingly depressed the income of the workers in the protoindustrial sector, finally pushing thousands to levels beneath subsistence.

The wages of the workers in the modern sector, at the same time, remained by and large unchanged, as was shown in chapter 5. In general, it would be expected that the wages of the workers in the modern sector were highly correlated with the (implicit) wages earned in the Z-good sector. The most important exception to this rule was the case in which Z-good earnings in terms of food hit the floor of subsistence. In that case additional declines in the terms of trade were absorbed by the capitalists. No such cushions, however, existed in the Z-good sector, which thus dropped inexorably under subsistence.[51] Was this what actually happened? No exact figures are available at this stage, but it is worthwhile to note the opinion of two conscientious social researchers of the Ghent cotton industry, writing in 1843:

46. Ibid., p. 346–47.
47. Ibid., p. 348.
48. Emerson-Tennent, *Belgium*, 1: 130n.
49. *Enquête Linière*, 2: 396.
50. Ibid., p. 400.
51. See above, p. 236.

Since the revival of our cotton industry, that is to say since the introduction of machines [in the first decade of the nineteenth century], the wage level has been subject to great variations. A spinner who previously earned 30 francs a week, receives nowadays no more than 14–15 francs per week. This considerable diminution did not take place all of a sudden. . . . from 1830 the wages have not fallen much anymore, *since they had reached their lowest possible level.*[52]

In addition to the fall in demand, the Flemish linen industry lost even more ground because of the relatively low quality of its output, compared with the increasingly improving quality of English linen cloth. Briavoinne notes that it was impossible to produce linen cloth of a regular quality with hand-spun yarn, and that the absence of an adequate system of numbering the different types of yarn by their thickness greatly encumbered the entire industry. Here, too, England was far ahead of Belgium.[53] The Belgian fabrics were generally more durable and easier laundered than English goods, but less regular, less uniform in size and composure, and less brilliant in appearance. The latter qualities, the compilers of the *Enquête Linière* noted not without sadness, are the ones that consumers look for.[54] Weaving, too, left much to be desired. The isolation of the weavers led to anarchy in quality, with each using special techniques taught by his parents. Indeed, according to one account, it was impossible to find two identical pieces of linen cloth in all of Flanders.[55] At the same time, the Flemish product was not varied enough, did not offer sufficient choice, and was not flexible enough to adapt to the changing needs and tastes of the consumers.[56]

The only way in which the Flemish protoindustrial workers could have found a hedge against lower prices was through increased productivity. But the rigid framework of the traditional rural society proved little conducive to technological change. The flying shuttle, which greatly increased the weaver's productivity as well as the quality of his product, spread very slowly. The Jacquard loom, which was suitable especially to high quality linen cloth, was quite rare in Belgium before 1850. Other innovations, such as a new and more versatile temple built by a blacksmith from Kortrijk, were also adopted at a slow pace.[57] At the same time, the modern sector, which adopted new techniques both in spinning and in

52. Mareska and Heyman, "Enquête sur le Travail," pp. 375–76. Emphasis added.
53. Briavoinne, *De l'Industrie*, 2: 353.
54. *Enquête Linière*, 2: 472.
55. F. J. Gyselinck, "Coup d'oeil sur la Situation Actuelle Linière" (1847). Quoted by Varlez, *Les Salaires*, 2: 48.
56. Ducpétiaux, *Mémoire sur le Paupérisme*, p. 129.
57. Jacquemyns, "Histoire de la Crise," pp. 92–96.

weaving, was growing too slowly to be able to absorb many workers from the traditional sector.

The shift of the demand curve faced by the Belgian linen industry was mainly caused by what happened in the French market. France had replaced Spain and the Spanish colonies as the major market for Belgian linen goods during the French period, and had retained its dominant share in Belgian linen sales after 1815. Despite the tariff of 1825, France still absorbed between 75 and 90 percent of total Belgian linen exports in the 1830s.[58] The situation in the French market was somewhat complicated since it was the scene of a trilateral competition between English, Belgian, and French manufacturers. As English production of both yarn and cloth took an enormous flight in the 1830s, the French manufacturers demanded and obtained important tariff reforms that barred imports indiscriminately. Desperate Belgian political efforts managed to improve the situation somewhat, but by 1850 exports of all linen products had declined substantially, both to France and to other countries. The decline of the

Table 7.13   International Commerce in Linen Yarn, 1832–50
(all figures in thousands of kilograms)

	Total Belgian Exports	Of which to France	Total British Exports	Of which to France	Total French Imports
1832	n.a.	686[a]	50	35	849
1833	n.a.	820[a]	424	393	1,409
1834	n.a.	708[a]	694	648	1,716
1835	n.a.	647[a]	1,183	1,080	2,113
1836	n.a.	632	2,072	1,817	2,737
1837	n.a.	538	3,793	3,176	3,911
1838	n.a.	403	6,760	5,203	5,798
1839	n.a.	495	7,391	5,553	6,811
1840	n.a.	583	8,033	5,951	6,838
1841	n.a.	638	11,425	9,437	9,905
1842	n.a.	547	13,359	10,058	11,261
1843	1,426	1,078	10,572	6,262	7,583
1844	2,014	1,724	11,765	6,137	8,051
1845	2,492	2,264	10,550	4,146	6,926
1846	2,162	1,749	8,826	2,631	4,321
1847	1,376	1,148	5,748	735	1,933
1848	658	230	5,310	117	389
1849	1,503	654	7,820	246	782
1850	1,450	751	8,254	313	976

[a] For these years the French data differ considerably from the Belgian. The former are used because of the unreliability of early Belgian exports figures (cf. above, pp. 46–47).
SOURCE: Jacquemyns, "Histoire de la Crise," pp. 418, 426, 427.

58. *Enquête Linière*, 2: 419.

Table 7.14   International Commerce in Linen Cloth, 1832–50

	Total Belgian Exports (in thousands of kgs.^{b})	Of which to France^b	Total British Exports (in thousands of yards)	Of which to France	Total French Imports (in thousands of kgs.)
1832	a	2,941	49,531	314	3,237
1833	a	3,672	63,233	182	4,055
1834	a	3,490	67,834	264	4,034
1835	4,572	3,510	77,977	1,248	4,099
1836	4,612	4,289	82,089	1,998	5,148
1837	3,977	3,675	58,426	3,368	4,748
1838	4,872	3,481	77,196	7,633	5,201
1839	3,160	2,937	85,257	6,255	4,247
1840	3,396	2,523	89,373	6,792	3,805
1841	3,520	2,792	90,322	8,824	4,718
1842	2,777	2,349	69,233	8,587	4,420
1843	2,639	2,118	84,173	4,380	2,291
1844	2,860	2,354	91,284	4,977	2,890
1845	2,789	2,479	88,402	2,366	2,857
1846	2,609	2,078	84,799	1,951	2,371
1847	2,092	1,483	89,329	1,326	1,640
1848	1,448	721	89,002	861	795
1849	2,132	1,010	111,259	1,518	1,125
1850	1,975	1,364	122,343	1,587	1,486

^{a} Figures too unreliable.
^{b} Includes hemp.
SOURCE: Jacquemyns, "Histoire de la Crise," pp. 163, 420, 422, 426–27.

Belgian linen exports concomitant with the rise of English competition is illustrated in tables 7.13 and 7.14.

The somewhat erratic movements of French imports in the two decades covered resulted largely from the repeated changes in the French tariff structure. In 1842, the French doubled their tariff on all linen products, but excluded Belgium from the increase, thus providing a temporary boost to the Belgian linen industry.[59] The downward trend continued, however, inexorably. The United States and the West Indies, which were the most important markets for the English linen products, remained—except for Cuba—largely inaccessible for Belgium.[60] The reasons for this were not only the higher price and the lower quality of the Belgian linen products, but also the absence of a commercial superstructure which could coordinate the sales, acquire and dissipate information, and absorb risks. With some envy, the compilers of the *Enquête Linière* mention the

59. For a survey of these policies, see Jacquemyns, "Histoire de la Crise," pp. 147–56.
60. *Enquête Linière*, 2: 468–71.

N.H.M., which (as they thought) performed these functions in the Netherlands.[61]

The elements mentioned above explain adequately the secular decline of the Flemish linen industry. On the other hand, the argument raised by many contemporaries and echoed in the *Enquête Linière* concerning the scarcity of raw materials seems unacceptable. The argument was that production of raw flax in Belgium was insufficient for local needs since large parts of the crop were bought by England, thus driving up the price of raw flax paid by local spinners. A rise in the price of raw flax, other things being equal, would ipso facto reduce the earnings of the self-employed workers in the Z-good sector.[62] The *Enquête* was compiled in a period when flax prices had reached a peak due to a series of unsatisfactory harvests. In the 1840s, however, the price of raw flax fell continuously. Moreover, output of raw flax dropped remarkably in the short period between 1840 and 1846. The area allocated to flax cultivation fell by 26.5 percent and output by 16.8 percent. This decline was partially offset by a decline of 32 percent in the export of raw and hackled flax between 1835–40 and 1844–46.[63] It seems that the supply of raw flax, whether Belgian or foreign, was quite elastic and raw materials were unlikely to constitute a bottleneck of serious proportions. Nor does it seem reasonable to attach much weight to Ducpétiaux's argument that England purchased much of its raw flax from Russia (where the price of flax was less than 60 percent of the Belgian price) and hence was in a favorable position vis-à-vis Flanders.[64] For one thing, Belgium was a net exporter of raw flax throughout the 1830s and 1840s, and its main customer was England.[65] The Russian flax was cheaper, but of a lower quality and not suited to the finer fabrics that were Flanders's specialty. In addition, of course, Belgium had the option to import Russian flax if it wished. To some extent, in fact, it did: imports of raw flax tripled between 1835–40 and 1847–49, reaching approximately 10 percent of domestic production by the end of the 1840s.[66]

INDUSTRIALIZATION IN THE LOW COUNTRIES IN PERSPECTIVE

It would be presumptuous to attempt in this study an evaluation of the welfare effects of industrialization. Yet one more question must be faced, though a satisfactory answer cannot be provided fully here. As was shown

61. Ibid., p. 477.

62. Ibid., pp. 150–51.

63. Jacquemyns, "Histoire de la Crise," pp. 40, 412, 414.

64. Ducpétiaux, *Mémoire sur le Paupérisme*, pp. 127, 128. Ducpétiaux's opinion is taken over uncritically by Jacquemyns, "Histoire de la Crise," pp. 142–43.

65. Between 1831 and 1840, 69 percent of total Belgian exports of raw flax went to England. Cf. *Enquête Linière*, 2: 118, 125.

66. Jacquemyns, "Histoire de la Crise," p. 414.

at length in chapters 2 and 3, the two countries followed very different trajectories in the first half of the nineteenth century. Yet it is apparent that the impact of industrialization on the overall economic well-being of the population was far from unambiguous. Wages did not rise significantly before the mid-century, and there seems little evidence that there was an improvement in overall standards of living. Moreover, the remaining protoindustrial workers were plunged into a terrible economic disaster in the 1840s. Might one, therefore, not conclude that the fact that the Dutch did not industrialize was perhaps not all that unfortunate from their point of view? Was it Belgium's destiny to suffer the disamenities and pains of industrialization while the Dutch were rich enough to be able to dispense with modern industry?

There is some merit to this view, but at the same time it is important to realize that the very different starting points of the two countries make semi-normative comparisons of historical paths somewhat dubious. It seems plausible that what happened in Belgium was the best that could be done under the initial circumstances the country faced. On the other hand, the Dutch, due to the structure of their traditional economy, had the option to choose a different alternative. The central factor (which seems to have been the critical difference between the two countries) was the existence of a protoindustrial sector in Belgium. Consider what would have happened to Belgium if it had not industrialized. The terms of trade would have turned against its industry in any event. England dominated the world supply, and its industry was growing independently of events in Belgium. If, then, there had been no industrialization in Belgium, the catastrophe in Flanders would have occurred all the same, but its dimensions would have been much larger. As it transpired, at least a part of the Flemish proletariat had moved to the modern sector and was thus saved from the starvation which plagued the rural proletariat in the Z-good sector. The large imports of food in the critical famine years, 1845–47, were clearly not independent from the fact that Belgium had a large modern industry, the "surplus" of which could be used to finance these food purchases.

Moreover, it should be kept in mind that the other centers of modern industry in Belgium did not suffer Flanders's fate since they had more or less finished the successful transition to a modern industry, and most of the Z-good workers had been absorbed. Such was the case in the woolen industry in the Vesdre area, as well as in most of the iron industry in the Walloon provinces. Of course, the transition was not yet complete even there, but a large enough portion had been absorbed to prevent the possibility of a dismal stationary state. It seems therefore that capital accumulation and technical progress, rather than being the source of the evil, were its only possible remedy. As it happened, in Flanders the growth of the modern sector for different reasons was too slow to prevent disaster for hundreds of thousands—but even there the existence of a highly productive, mechanized industry probably cushioned the worst consequences of the famine and might have saved Flanders from a disaster on the order of the Irish catastrophe.

In the Netherlands, the situation was very different because of the comparative unimportance of the protoindustry. One could argue that the Dutch did not industrialize because they did not need to. The pending disasters menacing the protoindustries in Europe did not threaten the Dutch economy. The high wage level in the Netherlands could be regarded at the same time as the reason why the Dutch did not industrialize and as the reason why they did not have to. The high wage level was an invisible hand leading the Dutch away from an industrialization not in their interest.

It is, of course, not possible to test this argument rigorously. But from the viewpoint of economic analysis, some reasonable doubt can be cast on it. Two cases have to be distinguished. The first is the one in which the productivity of labor in the modern sector (say, c) is smaller than the wage level determined in the traditional sector, w, i.e., $w > c$. In that case, indeed, industrialization will not take place because in a sense it is unnecessary. However, if $w < c$ and if w is a reflection of the productivity of labor in the traditional sector, the economy stands to gain from the adoption of mechanized techniques in its industry.[67] It is true that Dutch agriculture was highly efficient and that due to high land-labor and capital-labor ratios, the marginal product of labor in agriculture was quite high. But as was argued in chapter 5, high agricultural productivity was not the only cause for high Dutch wages. Insofar as wages were kept "artificially" high by taxes, poor relief, and other institutional factors, they did not accurately reflect the opportunity cost of labor, and therefore even in a case in which $w > c$, it may have been possible that there were gains to be had from adopting the new industrial technology.

Moreover, Dutch population grew very rapidly in the first half of the nineteenth century, and the standards of living (and GNP per capita) were probably not rising and possibly falling. It is thus not likely that the Dutch failure to industrialize was really a healthy response to objective economic conditions. In any case, it is quite obvious that intelligent contemporaries did not view it as such, though they failed more often than not to diagnose the economic ailments of their country.[68]

67. It has been assumed throughout this study that machines are eternal and do not depreciate. This assumption can be relaxed easily by a proper redefinition of c as the "net" productivity of labor.

68. See, for example, van der Boon-Mesch, "Over het Nederlandsche Fabrijkswezen," pp. 536–49. G. Wttewaal, "Over de steeds Toenemende Armoede in het Koninkrijk der Nederlanden" [On the ever-increasing poverty in the kingdom of the Netherlands], *TBN* 1, pt. 4 (1833): 523–51.

It could be countered that since wages in Belgium did not rise significantly in the first half of the nineteenth century, it is not clear what the majority of the Dutch population could have gained by industrialization, especially when the massive negative externalities associated with large-scale industrialization are taken into account. But the fact that wages failed to rise in the initial stages of industrialization is not really an indication of the "desirability" of industrialization. The nature of the process was such that the initial inertia of wages made accelerated accumulation possible. Eventually wages and consumption started to go up, provided the gains of industrialization were not lost to foreign consumers in the form of greatly deteriorated terms of trade.

The latter possibility was anything but imaginary, as the present chapter indicates. But again, the question of the initial structure of the traditional economy is of crucial importance. For a traditional sector that was predominantly protoindustrial, the options were limited since without modernization, they were liable to undergo an even worse disaster (unless the decline in the terms of trade was actually caused directly by the economy's own modernization). But for a largely agricultural traditional sector, the choice was more difficult. If many workers shifted out of their traditional occupations only to discover eventually that, due to changing terms of trade, their previous activities were now more remunerative than their new positions, a large effort would have been wasted. From this point of view, perhaps, it may have been fortunate for the Dutch to have missed the train of the first industrial revolution. Still, at the present stage of knowledge, there does not appear to be much evidence for this point. After all, the obvious candidate for modernization of industry in the Netherlands would have been, at least initially, the cotton industry and not linen. Cotton was far less subject to possible "damnification" than linen. It remained for many more decades one of the leading industries in the industrialized nations in Europe, the effect of falling terms of trade largely offset by a continuously advancing technology.

Although the quantitative evidence is insufficient, it seems likely that during the first half of the nineteenth century the Netherlands and Belgium exchanged positions. While the former was definitely the richer country in terms of GNP per capita in around 1795, it seems very likely that the latter overtook it before the midcentury—in spite of the Flemish crisis of the 1840s, in spite of the fact that Dutch agriculture enjoyed improving terms of trade, and in spite of the ever-increasing exploitation of the Dutch colonies in the East Indies, which kept the somewhat sclerotic maritime economy alive. The glory and the wealth accumulated by intrepid seafaring and skillful trading could not and did not last in a new world that belonged increasingly to the factory and the railway.

BIBLIOGRAPHY

Theoretical and General Historical Works

Ashton, T. S. *The Industrial Revolution, 1760–1830.* New York: Oxford University Press, 1964.
Bensusan-Butt, D. M. *On Economic Growth, An Essay in Pure Theory.* Oxford: Oxford University Press, 1963.
Bhaduri, Amit. "On the Significance of Recent Controversies on Capital Theory." *EJ* 79 (1969): 532–39.
Bhagwati, Jagdish. "Immiserizing Growth: A Geometrical Note." *ReStud* 25 (1958): 201–05.
Bernal, J. D. *Science and Industry in the Nineteenth Century.* Bloomington: Indiana University Press, 1969.
Blaug, Mark. "The Myth of the Old Poor Law and the Making of the New." *JEH* 23 (1963): 151–84.
Braun, Rudolph. "The Impact of Cottage Industry on an Agricultural Population." In *The Rise of Capitalism,* edited by David S. Landes, pp. 53–64. New York: Macmillan, 1966.
Bruno, Michael. "Fundamental Duality Relations in the Pure Theory of Capital and Growth." *ReStud* 36 (1969): 39–53.
Cameron, Rondo. *Banking in the Early Stages of Industrialization.* New York: Oxford University Press, 1967.
Corden, W. M. "A Two Sector Growth Model with Fixed Coefficients." *ReStud* 33 (1966): 253–63.
Crouzet, François. "Capital Formation in Great Britain During the Industrial Revolution." In *Capital Formation in the Industrial Revolution,* edited by François Crouzet, pp. 162–222. London: Methuen, 1972.
———. "Wars, Blockade, and Economic Change in Europe, 1792–1815." *JEH* 24 (1966): 567–88.
David, Paul A. "Learning By Doing and Tariff Protection: A Reconsideration of the Ante Bellum United States Cotton Textile Industry." *JEH* 30 (1970): 521–601.
Deane, Phyllis. *The First Industrial Revolution.* Cambridge: At the University Press, 1969.
Deane, Phyllis and Cole, W. A. *British Economic Growth, 1688–1959.* 2d ed. Cambridge: At the University Press, 1967.
Edgeworth, Francis Y. "The Theory of International Values." *EJ* 4 (1894): 35–50.
Exhibition of the Works of Industry of All Nations. *Reports by the Juries.* London:

Spicer Bros., 1852.

Exposition Universelle de 1855. *Rapports du Jury Mixte Internationale.* Paris: Imprimerie Impériale, 1856.

Fei, John C. H. and Ranis, Gustav. *Development of the Labor Surplus Economy.* Homewood, Ill.: Richard D. Irwin, 1964.

——. "Economic Development in Historical Perspective." *AER* 59 (1969): 386–400.

Ferguson, C. E. *The Neoclassical Theory of Production and Distribution.* Cambridge: At the University Press, 1969.

Frankel, Marvin. "Obsolescence and Technological Change in a Maturing Economy." *AER* 45 (1955): 298–319.

Great Britain. *Parliamentary Papers.* Vol. 6 (*Report on Manufactures, Commerce, and Shipping*), 1833.

Great Britain. *Parliamentary Papers.* Vol. 33 (*Accounts and Papers Relating to Trade, etc.*), 1833.

Great Britain. *Parliamentary Papers.* Vol. 47 (*Tables of the Revenue, Population, Commerce, etc., of the United Kingdom and its Dependencies*), 1837–38.

Great Britain. *Parliamentary Papers.* Vol. 42 (*Report from the Assistant Hand-Loom Weavers Commissioners*), 1839.

Great Britain. *Parliamentary Papers.* Vol. 7 (*Report from the Select Committee into the Operation of the Existing Laws Affecting the Exportation of Machinery*), 1841.

Habakkuk, H. J. *American and British Technology in the Nineteenth Century.* Cambridge: At the University Press, 1962.

Hartwell, Ronald M. "The Causes of the Industrial Revolution, An Essay in Methodology." In *The Industrial Revolution and Economic Growth*, pp. 131–57. London: Methuen, 1971.

Heckscher, Eli. *The Continental System, An Economic Interpretation.* 1922. Reprint. Gloucester, Mass: Peter Smith, 1964.

Henderson, W. O. *Britain and Industrial Europe, 1750–1850.* 2d ed. Leicester: Leicester University Press, 1965.

Hicks, John Richard. *Capital and Growth.* New York: Oxford University Press, 1969.

——. *A Theory of Economic History.* Oxford: Oxford University Press, 1965.

Hymer, Stephen and Resnick, Stephen. "A Model of an Agrarian Economy with Nonagricultural Activities." *AER* 59 (1969): 493–506.

Johnson, Harry G. "Equilibrium Growth in an International Economy." In *International Trade and Economic Growth*, pp. 120–49. Cambridge, Mass.: Harvard University Press, 1967.

Jones, Eric L. "Agricultural Origins of Industry." *P and P* 40 (1968): 58–71. Reprinted in *Agriculture and the Industrial Revolution*, pp. 128–42. Oxford: Blackwell's, 1974.

Kaldor, Nicholas. "Alternative Theories of Distribution." *ReStud* 23 (1956): 83–100.

Kellenbenz, H. "Industries Rurales en Occident de la Fin du Moyen Age au XVIIIᵉ Siècle." *Annales* 18 (1963): 833–83.

Kemp, Murray C. *The Pure Theory of International Trade.* Englewood Cliffs, N. J.: Prentice Hall, 1964.

————. "Technological Change, the Terms of Trade, and Welfare." *EJ* 65 (1955): 457–74.

Kennedy, William P. "The Economics of Maturity: Aspects of British Economic Development, 1870–1914." Ph.D. dissertation, Northwestern University, 1975.

Kindleberger, Charles P. *Economic Growth in France and Britain, 1851–1950*. New York: Simon and Schuster, Clarion Books, 1964.

Kisch, Herbert. "The Textile Industries in Silesia and the Rhineland: A Comparative Study in Industrialization." *JEH* 19 (1959): 541–63.

Kuznets, Simon. *Economic Growth of Nations, Total Output and Productive Structure*. Cambridge: Harvard University Press, 1971.

Landes, David S. *The Unbound Prometheus*. Cambridge: At the University Press, 1969.

Lévy-Leboyer, Maurice. *Les Banques Européenes et l'Industrialization Internationale dans la Première Moitié du XIXe Siècle*. Paris: Presses Universitaires de France, 1964.

Lewis, W. Arthur. "Economic Development with Unlimited Supplies of Labor." In *The Economics of Underdevelopment*, edited by A. N. Agarwala and S. P. Singh, pp. 400–49. New York: Oxford University Press, 1963.

————. "Unlimited Labor: Further Notes." *MS* 26 (1958): 1–32.

Marshall, Alfred. *Principles of Political Economy*. 9th ed. Edited by C.W. Guillebaud. 2 vols. New York: Macmillan, 1961.

Marx, Karl. *Capital*. New York: International Publishers, 1967.

Masson, Robert Tempest. "The Creation of Risk Aversion by Imperfect Capital Markets." *AER* 62 (March 1972): 77–86.

McCloskey, Donald N. *Economic Maturity and Entrepreneurial Decline: British Iron and Steel, 1870–1913*. Cambridge, Mass.: Harvard University Press, 1973.

————. "New Perspectives on the Old Poor Law." *EEH* 10 (1973): 419–36.

Mill, John Stuart. *Principles of Political Economy*. London: Longmans, Green and Co., 1894.

Milward, Alan S. and Saul, S. B. *The Economic Development of Continental Europe, 1780–1870*. London: Allen and Unwin, 1973.

Mitchell, B. R. and Deane, Phyllis. *Abstract of British Historical Statistics*. Cambridge: At the University Press, 1962.

Mokyr, Joel. "Growing Up and the Industrial Revolution in Europe." *EEH* 14 (1977): forthcoming.

Montalivet, J. P. B. de. *Exposé de la Situation de l'Empire*. Paris: Imprimerie Impériale, 1813.

Musson, A. E., ed. *Science, Technology and Economic Growth in the Eighteenth Century*. London: Methuen, 1972.

Musson, A. E. and Robinson, Eric. *Science and Technology in the Industrial Revolution*. Manchester: Manchester University Press, 1969.

Nef, John U. "The Industrial Revolution Reconsidered." In *War and Human Progress*, pp. 273–301. New York: Norton, 1968.

Pollard, Sidney. "Industrialization and the European Economy." *EHR*, n.s. 26 (1973): 636–48.

Report on Wholesale and Retail Prices in the United Kingdom in 1902, with Comparative Statistical Tables for a Series of Years. London: His Majesty's Stationery Office, 1903.

Reynolds, Lloyd G. "Economic Development with Surplus Labour: Some Complications." *OEP* 21 (1969): 89–103.

Ricardo, David. *Principles of Political Economy.* Edited by R. M. Hartwell. Harmondsworth: Pelican Books, 1971.

Rimmer, W. G. *Marshalls of Leeds, Flax Spinners 1788–1886.* Cambridge: At the University Press, 1960.

Robinson, Joan. *The Accumulation of Capital.* 3d ed. London: Macmillan, 1969.

———. *Essays in the Theory of Economic Growth.* London: Macmillan, 1962.

Salter, W. E. G. *Productivity and Technical Change.* 2d ed. Cambridge: At the University Press, 1969.

———. "Productivity Growth and Accumulation as Historical Processes." In *Problems in Economic Development,* edited by E. A. G. Robinson, pp. 266–94. London: Macmillan, 1965.

Smith, Adam. *The Wealth of Nations.* Edited by Andrew Skinner. Harmondsworth: Penguin Books, 1970.

Solow, Robert M. *Capital Theory and the Rate of Return.* Amsterdam: North Holland Publishing Company, 1963.

———. *Growth Theory, an Exposition.* Oxford: Oxford University Press, 1970.

Thirsk, Joan. "Industries in the Countryside." In *Essays in the Economic and Social History of Tudor and Stuart England in Honor of R. H. Tawney,* edited by F. J. Fisher, pp. 70–88. Cambridge: At the University Press, 1961.

Tobin, James. "Liquidity Preference as a Behavior Towards Risk." *ReStud* 25 (1958): 65–86.

Wilson, Charles. *England's Apprenticeship, 1603–1763.* London: Longmans, 1965.

Wrigley, E. A. "The Supply of Raw Materials in the Industrial Revolution." *EHR,* n.s. 15 (1962): 1–16.

WORKS PERTAINING TO THE LOW COUNTRIES

Adelman, Gerhard. "Die Zollgrenze im Ostniederländisch-westfälischen Textilgebiet, 1815–1850." *THB* 10 (1968): 42–53.

Alphonse, F. J. B. d'. *Aperçu sur la Hollande* (1811). Published by the Dutch Central Bureau of Statistics. The Hague: Belinfante Bros., 1900.

Ansiaux, M. *L'Industrie Armurière Liègeoise.* Les Industries à Domicile en Belgique, vol. 1. Brussels: J. Lebègue, 1899.

Arrivabene, Giovanni. *Situation Economique de la Belgique.* Brussels: De Deltombe, 1843.

———. *Sur la Condition des Laboureurs et des Ouvriers Belges.* Brussels: Méline, Cans et Cie., 1845.

"Avanti" [pseud.]. *Een Terugblik—Proeve eener Geschiedenis der Gentsche Arbeidersbeweging gedurende de XIXᵉ Eeuw.* Ghent: Samenwerkende Volkdrukkerij, 1908.

Baasch, E. *Holländische Wirtschaftsgeschichte.* Jena: Gustav Fischer, 1927.

[Backer, A. J.] *Wevers onder Gaslicht.* Amsterdam: G. van Reemst, 1952.

Barlet, Edouard. *Histoire du Commerce et de l'Industrie.* Liège: J. G. Lardinois, 1858.

Baudet, Henri. "De Dadels van Hassan en de Start der Nederlandse Industrialiteit." In *Bedrijf en Samenleving*, Festschrift presented to I. J. Brugmans, pp. 1–15. Alphen on the Rhine and Brussels: N. Samson, 1967.

Baumhauer, E. H. von. *Voorlezingen over de Nederlandsche Nijverheid en de Middelen om Haar te Ontwikkelen.* Haarlem: A. C. Kruseman, 1856.

Beaucourt, Alfred. *La Filature Méchanique de Lin en Belgique.* Paris: Librairie Nouvelle de Droit et de Jurisprudence, 1914.

Bel, J. G. van. *De Linnenhandel van Amsterdam in de 18e Eeuw.* Amsterdam: Swets and Zeitlinger, 1940.

Berghuis, W. H. *Onstaan en Ontwikkeling van de Nederlandse Beleggingsfondsen tot 1914.* Assen: van Gorcum, 1967.

Bertrand, L. *L'Ouvrier Belge Depuis un Siècle.* Brussels: L'Eglantine, 1924.

Bierens de Haan, J. *Van Oeconomische Tak tot Nederlandsche Maatschappij voor Nijverheid en Handel.* Haarlem: H. D. Tjeenk-Willink, 1952.

Blonk, Arie. *Fabrieken en Menschen, een Sociografie van Enschede.* Enschede: M. J. van der Loeff, 1929.

Boer, M. G. de. "Guillaume Ier et les Débuts de l'Industrie Métallurgique en Belgique." *RBPH* 3 (1924): 527–52.

———. *Honderd Jaar Machine Industrie op Oosterburg, Amsterdam.* Amsterdam: Bussy, 1927.

———. *Leven en Bedrijf van G. M. Roentgen.* Groningen: P. Noordhoff, 1923.

Boessenkool, J. "De Eerste Stoommachine in de Twentsche Textiel Industrie." *THB* 4 (1962): 67–72.

Bogaerde de ter Brugge, A. J. L. van den. *Essai sur l' Importance du Commerce, de la Navigation et de l'Industrie dans les Provinces Formant le Royaume des Pays Bas, depuis les Temps les plus Reculés Jusque'en 1830.* The Hague and Brussels: P. H. Noordendorp et Périchon, 1844–45.

Bonenfant, Paul. "Le Problème du Paupérisme en Belgique à la Fin de l'Ancien Régime." *ARCLM* 35 (1934): 1–579.

Boon-Mesch, A. H. van der. "Over het Nederlandsche Fabrijkswezen en de Middelen om hetzelve te Bevorderen en in Bloei te Doen Toenemen." *TBN* 7 (1843): 524–86.

Boot, J. A. P. G. "Fabrikeurs en Textielzaken omstreeks 1750." *THB* 5 (1963): 18–51.

———. "Gebrek aan Handwevers in Twente na 1850." *THB* 10 (1968): 16–36.

———. *De Twentsche Katoennijverheid, 1830–1873.* Amsterdam: H. J. Paris, 1935.

Boot, J. A. P. G. and Blonk, Arie. *Van Smiet- tot Snelspoel, de Opkomst van de Twents-Gelderse Textielindustrie in het begin van de 19^e Eeuw.* Hengelo: Stichting Textielgeschiedenis, 1957.

Bosch Kemper, J. de. *Geschiedkundig Onderzoek naar de Armoede in ons Vaderland.* Haarlem: de Erven Loosjes, 1860.

Bouman, P. J. "Van Vroeg tot Modern Kapitalisme." In *De Lage Landen bij de Zee*, edited by Jan and Annie Romein, vol. 3:77–103. 3d ed. Zeist: de Haan, 1961.

Boxer, Charles. *The Dutch Seaborne Empire, 1600–1800.* Harmondsworth: Pelican

Books, 1973.

Briavoinne, Natalis de. *De l'Industrie en Belgique, Causes de Décadence et de Prosperité, sa Situation Actuelle.* 2 vols. Brussels: Société Typographique Belge, 1839.

——. "Mémoire sur l'Etat de la Population des Fabriques, des Manufactures et du Commerce dans les Provinces des Pays Bas, depuis Albert et Isabella jusqu'à la Fin du Siècle Dernier." *ARMC* 14 (1840): 5–213.

——. "Sur les Inventions et Perfectionnements dans l'Industrie." *ARMC* 13 (1838): 5–187.

Brink, W. L. D. van den. *Bijdrage tot de Kennis van den Economischen Toestand van Nederland in de Jaren 1813–1816.* Amsterdam: H. J. Paris, 1916.

Brugmans, I. J. *De Arbeidende Klasse in Nederland in de 19ᵉ Eeuw.* 8th ed. Utrecht and Antwerp: Het Spectrum, 1971.

——. "The Economic History of the Netherlands in the 19th and 20th Century." *AHN* 2 (1967): 260–98.

——. "Koning Willem I als Neomercantilist" (pp. 38–50), "De Opkomst der Amsterdamse Machine Industrie" (pp. 51–60), "Honderd Jaren Nederlandse Nijverheid" (pp. 118–39). In *Welvaart en Historie*. The Hague: Martinus Nijhoff, 1950.

——. *Paardenkracht en Mensenmacht, Sociaal-Economische Geschiedenis van Nederland, 1795–1940.* The Hague: Martinus Nijhoff, 1961.

——, ed. "Rapport aan z.e. den Minister van Binnenlandsche Zaken Nopens den Tegenwoordige Staat van den Handel, de Scheepvaart, het Fabriekswezen, de Visscherij, de Mineralogische Voortbrengselen en de Houtteelt in Zuid Holland, 21 Februari 1817." *EHJ* 27 (1955–57): 101–51.

——, ed. "Rapporten over den Economischen Toestand van Nederland in 1816." *EHJ* 31 (1965–66): 150–92.

——, ed. *Statistieken van de Nederlandse Nijverheid uit de Eerste Helft der 19ᵉ Eeuw.* In *R.G.P.*, vols. 98, 99. The Hague: Martinus Nijhoff, 1956.

Buddingh, D. *Algemeene Statistiek voor Handel en Nijverheid.* Haarlem: A. C. Kruseman, 1846.

Burgers, R. A. *Honderd Jaar G. en H. Salomonson, Kooplieden, Entrepreneurs, Fabrikanten, en Directeuren van de Koninklijke Stoomweverij te Nijverdal.* Leyden: Stenfert Kroese, 1954.

Caulier-Mathy, Nicole. *La Modernisation des Charbonnages Liègeois pendant la Première Moitié du 19ᵉ Siècle.* Paris: Société d'édition les Belles Lettres, 1971.

——. *Statistique de la Province de Liège sous le Régime Hollandais.* Louvain and Paris: Nauwelaerts, 1962.

Chambon, R. *L'Histoire de la Verrerie en Belgique du IIᵉ Siècle à nos Jours.* Brussels: Editions de la Librairie Encyclopédique, S.P.R.L., 1955.

Chlepner, B. S. *La Banque en Belgique.* Brussels: M. Lamertin, 1926.

——. "Les Débuts du Crédit Industriel Moderne." *RS* 9 (1929): 293–316.

Cloet, J. J. de. *Handboek voor Staatsmannen of Statistiek Tafereel der Nederlandsche Nijverheid.* Edited and translated by Paul van Griethuizen. Utrecht: S. Alter, 1826.

Colenbrander, H. T., ed. *Gedenkstukken der Algemeene Geschiedenis van Nederland van 1795 tot 1840. R.G.P.* The Hague: Martinus Nijhoff, 1905–22, scattered over various volumes.

Commission d'Enquête de l'Industrie Linière. *Enquête sur l'Industrie Linière, Rapports de la Commission.* Brussels: Ministère de l'Intérieur, 1841.

Coppejans-Desmedt, Hilda. *Bedrijfs-Archieven op het Stadsarchief van Gent.* Louvain: Nauwelaerts, 1971.

————. "De Betekenis van Gent voor de Expansie van de Katoennijverheid in de Nederlanden." *THB* 11 (1969): 17–27.

————. "Bijdrage tot een Kritische Studie over de Nijverheidsstatistieken uit de Jaren 1795–1846." *BCRH* 126 (1960): 1–60.

————. "Economische Opbloei in de Zuidelijke Nederlanden." In *Algemene Geschiedenis der Nederlanden,* edited by J. A. van Houtte et al., vol. 8: 261–86. Utrecht: de Haan, 1955.

————. "De Gentse Textielnijverheid van 1795 tot 1835. Het Proces van de Mechanizering in Zijn Economische Gevolgen." Ph.D. dissertation, University of Ghent, n.d. [about 1955].

————. "De Gentse Vlasindustrie vanaf het Einde van de XVIIIe Eeuw tot de Oprichting van de Grote Mechanische Bedrijven (1838)." *HMGOG,* n.s. 22 (1968): 179–202.

————. "Incidenten rond de Constructie van de Eerste Mechanische Weefgetouwen te Gent." *HMGOG,* n.s. 13 (1959): 163–77.

————. "Pogingen tot Opbeuring van de Gentse Wolnijverheid bij de Aanvang van de XIXe Eeuw." *HMGOG,* n.s. 21 (1967): 163–89.

————, ed. "De Statistieken van Emmanuel Carolus van der Meersch over de Katoenindustrie in Oost Vlaanderen." *BCRH* 128 (1962): 121–81.

Craeybeckx, Jan. "De Arbeiders voor de Industriële Omwenteling." In *Geschiedenis van de Socialistische Arbeidersbeweging in België,* edited by Jan Dhondt, pp. 9–32. Antwerp: "Ontwikkeling," 1960.

————. "Les Débuts de la Revolution Industrielle en Belgique et les Statistiques de la Fin de l'Empire." In *Mélanges offerts à G. Jacquemyns,* pp. 115–44. Brussels: Université Libre de Bruxelles, Édition de l'Institut de Sociologie, 1968.

Darquenne, Robert. "Histoire Économique du Département de Jemmapes." *MPSH* 79 (1965): 1–380.

Dechesne, Laurent. *Histoire Économique et Sociale de la Belgique.* Liège: Libraire Joseph Wykmans, 1932.

Demoulin, Robert. *Guillaume Ier et la Transformation Économique des Provinces Belges.* Liège: Bibliothèque de la Faculté de Philosophie et Lettres de l'Université de Liège, 1938.

Dhondt, Jan. "L'Industrie Cotonnière Gantoise à l'Époque Française." *RHMC* 2 (1955): 233–79.

————. "Notes sur les Ouvriers Industriels Gantois à l'Époque Française." *RN* 36 (1954): 309–24.

————. "De Opkomst van de Burgerij als Politieke Macht en de Groei van de Arbeidersstand." In *Geschiedenis van de Socialistische Arbeidersbeweging in België,* pp. 35–60. Antwerp: "Ontwikkeling," 1960.

Dhondt, Jan and Bruwier, Marinette. *The Industrial Revolution in Belgium and Holland, 1700–1914.* The Fontana Economic History of Europe, edited by Carlo Cipolla, vol. 4, sec. 1. London: Collins/Fontana Books, 1973.

Dillen, J. G. van. "Omstandigheden en Psychische Factoren in de Economische Geschiedenis van Nederland." In *Mensen en Achtergronden,* pp. 57–79. Groningen: J. B. Wolters, 1964.

———. *Van Rijkdom en Regenten, Handboek tot de Economische en Sociale Geschiedenis van Nederland tijdens de Republiek.* The Hague: Martinus Nijhoff, 1970.

Documents Statistiques Récueillis et Publiés Par le Ministre de l'Intérieur du Royaume de Belgique. Brussels: de Mat, 1836.

Doorman, G. *Het Nederlandsch Octrooiwezen en de Techniek der 19ᵉ Eeuw.* The Hague: Martinus Nijhoff, 1947.

Drieling, F. H. C. "Verslag over den Toestand der Arbeidende Klasse Vooral ten Plattenlande, in de Provincie Utrecht, en over de Middelen tot Verbetering van hunne Zedelijke en Stoffelijke Welvaart." *TSS* 8 (1853): 405–52.

Dubois, Ernest. *L'Industrie du Tissage du Lin dans les Flanders.* Les Industries à Domicile en Belgique, vol. 2. Brussels: J. Lebègue, 1900.

Du Camp, M. *En Hollande.* Paris: Poulet-Malassis et de Broise, 1859.

Ducpétiaux, Edouard. "Budgets Économiques des Classes Ouvrières en Belgique." *BCCS* 6 (1855): 261–438.

———. *De la Condition Physique et Morale des Jeunes Ouvriers et des Moyens de l'Améliorer.* Brussels: Méline, Cans et Cie., 1843.

———. *Mémoire sur le Paupérisme dans les Flanders.* Brussels: M. Hayez, 1850.

———. *Le Paupérisme en Belgique.* Brussels: Librairie Polytechnique d'Aug. Decq, 1844.

———. "Des Subsistances, des Salaires et de l'Accroissement de la Population." *BCCS* 6 (1855): 441–595.

Eerenbeemt, H. F. J. M. van den. *Bedrijfskapitaal en Ondernemerschap in Nederland, 1800–1850.* Leyden: H. E. Stenfert Kroese, 1965.

———. "Het Huwelijk tussen Filantropie en Economie: Een Patriotse en Bataafse Illusie." *EHJ* 35 (1972): 28–64.

Emerson-Tennent, J. *Belgium.* 2 vols. London: Richard Bentley, 1841.

Everwijn, J. C. A. *Beschrijving van Handel en Nijverheid in Nederland.* The Hague: N. V. Boekhandel, 1912.

Faber, J. A.; Roessingh, H. K.; Slicher van Bath, B. H.; van der Woude, A. M.; and van Xanten, H. J. "Population Changes and Economic Development in the Netherlands: A Historical Survey." *A.A.G. Bijdragen* 12 (1965): 47–113.

Faipoult, M. *Mémoire Statistique du Dept. de l'Escaut* (1804). Edited by Paul Deprez. Ghent: Oostvlaams Verbond van de Kringen voor Geschiedenis, 1960.

Fell, R. *A Tour Through the Batavian Republic During the Latter Part of 1800.* London: R. Phillips, 1801.

Franquoy, J. "Mémoire sur l'Historique des Progrès de la Fabrication du Fer dans le Pays de Liège." *MSLEL,* n.s. 1 (1860): 313–448.

Fris, Victor. *Histoire de Gand.* Brussels: G. van Gest et Cie., 1913.

Fussell, G. E. "Low Countries' Influence on English Farming." *English Historical Review* 74 (1959): 611–22.

Gadisseur, Jean. "L'Indice de la Production Industrielle en Belgique de 1830 à 1913." Mimeographed. Liège: 1971.

Génart, C. *L'Industrie Cloutière en Pays Wallon.* Les Industries à Domicile en Belgique, vol. 3. Brussels: J. Lebègue, 1900.

Gobert, T. "Conditions de l'Industrie du Tissage à la Fin de l'Ancien Régime— Les Cockerills à leur Début." *BIAL* 40 (1910): 155–86.

Gogel, I. J. A. *Memoriën en Correspondentiën Betrekkelijk den Staat van s'Rijks Geldmiddelen in den Jaren 1820.* Amsterdam: Johannes Müller, 1844.

Goldberg, Johannes. "Journaal der Reize van den Agent van Nationale Economie der Bataafsche Republiek, 1800." *TSS* 18 (1859): 194–217, 241–54, 313–37, 377–93 and *TSS* 19 (1860): 1–18, 57–74, 121–41, 185–99, 249–63.

―――. "Memorie over de Nederlandsche Fabrieken van Manufactuurwaaren, 1816." Edited by N. W. Posthumus. In *Bijdragen tot de Economische Geschiedenis van Nederland,* pp. 84–198. The Hague: Martinus Nijhoff, 1916.

Gorter, R. A. and de Vries, C. W. "Gegevens Omtrent den Kinderarbeid in Nederland Volgens de Enquêtes van 1841 en 1860." *EHJ* 8 (1922): 1–253.

Griethuizen, Paul van. "Iets over de Nederlandse Vlasteelt." In *Mengelingen.* Amsterdam: 1826–27.

Griffiths, Richard T. "Iets meer over de Haarlemse Katoenfabrieken." *THB* 15 (1974): 38–58.

Hansotte, George. *La Clouterie Liègeoise au XVIIIe Siècle.* Brussels: Éditions de la Librairie Encyclopedique, 1972.

Harkx, W. A. J. M. *De Helmondse Textielnijverheid in de Loop der Eeuwen. De Grondslag voor de Huidige Textielindustry, 1794–1870.* Tilburg: Stichting Zuidelijk Historisch Contact, 1967.

Heuschling, Xavier. *Essai sur la Statistique Générale de la Belgique.* Brussels: Établissement Géographique Faubourg de Flandre, 1st ed., 1838; 2d ed., 1841.

Heuschling, Xavier and Quetelet, Adolphe. "Rapport au Ministre de l'Intérieur, sur la Question des Subsistances." *BCCS* 4 (1851): 175–90.

Hogendorp, Karel Gijsbrecht van. *Bijdragen tot de Huishouding van Staat in het Koninkrijk der Nederlanden.* 8 vols. Amsterdam: K. H. Schadd, 1825.

Hommen, B. H. "Bijdrage tot een Geschiedenis van de Textielnijverheid te Oldenzaal." *THB* 5 (1963): 52–94.

Houtte, F. X. van. *L'Évolution de l'Industrie Textile en Belgique et dans le Monde, de 1800 à 1939.* Louvain: Nauwelaerts, 1949.

Houtte, Jan A. van. "Economic Development of Belgium and the Netherlands from the Beginning of the Modern Era." *JEEH* 1 (1972): 100–20.

―――. *Economische en Sociale Geschiedenis van de Lage Landen.* Zeist and Antwerp: de Haan, Standaard Boekhandel, 1964.

―――. "Het Economische Leven in België, 1830–1880." In *Algemene Geschiedenis der Nederlanden,* edited by J. A. van Houtte et al., vol. 10, pp. 202–37. Utrecht: de Haan, 1955.

Jacquemin, P. *Notice Historique sur les Établissements de la Société Cockerill.* Liège: L. de Thier, 1880.

Jacquemyns, G. "Histoire de la Crise Économique des Flanders, 1845–1850." *ARM* 26 (1929): 11–472.

Jonckers-Nieboer, J. H. *Geschiedenis der Nederlandsche Spoorwegen*. Haarlem: H. D. Tjeenk-Willink, 1907.

Jong, G. F. A. de. "Enige Sociale Aspecten van de Arbeid in de Textielindustrie Gedurende de 19ᵉ Eeuw." In *De Opkomst van Tilburg als Industriestad*, edited by H. F. J. M. van den Eerenbeemt and H. J. A. M. Schurink, pp. 167–99. Nijmegen: Centrale Drukkerij, 1957.

Jonge, Jan Arie de. "Industrial Growth in the Netherlands, 1850–1914." *AHN* 5 (1971): 159–212.

———. *De Industrializatie in Nederland tussen 1850 en 1914*. Amsterdam: Scheltema en Holkema, 1968.

Keuchenius, W. M. *Inkomsten en Uitgaven der Bataafsche Republiek, Voorgesteld in eene Nationale Balans*. Amsterdam: W. Holtrop, 1803.

Keune, A. W. M. "De Industriële Ontwikkeling Gedurende de 19ᵉ Eeuw." In *De Opkomst van Tilburg als een Industriestad*, edited by H. F. J. M. van den Eerenbeemt and H. J. A. M. Schurink, pp. 11–60. Nijmegen: Centrale Drukkerij, 1957.

Klein, Peter Wolfgang. *Kapitaal en Stagnatie Tijdens het Hollandse Vroegkapitalisme*. Rotterdam: Universitaire Pers, 1967.

———. *Traditionele Ondernemers en Economische Groei in Nederland, 1850–1914*. Haarlem: De Erven F. Bohn, 1966.

Koenen, H. J. *Voorlezingen over de Geschiedenis der Nijverheid in Nederland*. Haarlem: A. C. Kruseman, 1856.

Kohlbrugge, J. "Over de Invloed der Steden op hare Bewoners en op de Bewoners van het Land." *De Economist* (1907): 372–93.

Kruithof, J. "De Grootte van het Belgische Proletariaat Tijdens de Eerste Helft van de 19ᵉ Eeuw." In *Geschiedenis van de Socialistische Arbeidersbeweging in België*, edited by Jan Dhondt, pp. 53–68. Antwerp: "Ontwikkeling," 1960.

Lambert, Audrey M. *The Making of Dutch Landscape, An Historical Geography of the Netherlands*. London and New York: Seminar Press, 1971.

Lambert, Jan. "De Verkoop van Nationale Goederen in de Provincie Oost Vlaanderen Tijdens het Hollands Bewind, 1820–21." *HMGOG*, n.s. 20 (1966): 19–41.

Laureyssens, J. "Le Crédit Industriel et la Société Générale des Pays Bas Pendant le Régime Hollandais." *RBHC* 3 (1972): 119–40.

Lebrun, Pierre. "Croissance et Industrialisation, l'Expérience de l'Industrie Drapière Verviétoise, 1750–1850." In *First International Conference of Economic History, Stockholm, 1960, Contributions and Communications*, pp. 531–68. Paris and The Hague: Mouton et Cie., 1960.

———. *L'Industrie de la Laine à Verviers*. Liège: Bibliothèque de la Faculté de Philosophie et Lettres de l'Université de Liège, 1948.

———. "La Rivoluzione Industriale in Belgio." *Studi Storici* 2 (1961): 548–658.

Leleux, F. *Liévin Bauwens, Industriel Gantois*. Paris: S.E.V.P.E.N., 1969.

Lewiński, Jan St. *L'Évolution Industrielle de la Belgique*. Brussels and Leipzig: Misch and Thron, 1911.

Lindemans, Paul. *Geschiedenis van de Landbouw in België*. Antwerp: De Sikkel, 1952.

Luzac, Elias. *Hollands Rijkdom*. 4 vols. Leyden: Luzac and van Damme, 1783.

Maenen, A. J. F. *Petrus Regout, 1801–1878. Een Bijdrage tot de Sociaal-Economische Geschiedenis van Maastricht*. Nijmegen: Centrale Drukkerij, 1959.

Mahaim, E. "Les Débuts de l'Établissement John Cockerill à Seraing." *VSWG* 3 (1905): 627–48.

Mansvelt, W. M. F. *Geschiedenis van de Nederlandsche Handelsmaatschappij*. Haarlem: Joh. Enschedé en Zonen, 1924.

Mareska, D. J. B. and Heyman, J. "Enquête sur le Travail et la Condition Physique et Morale des Ouvriers dans les Manufactures de Coton à Gand." In Ministère de l'Intérieur, *Enquête sur la Condition des Classes Ouvrières*, vol. 3, pp. 307–484. Brussels: Th. Lesigne, 1846.

Marmier, X. *Lettres sur la Hollande*. Paris: Garnier Frères, 1849.

Meersch, Emmanuel Carolus van der. [Report on Industry in Twente.] Manuscript. Dutch National Archives, The Hague. Kabinet des Konings, 17 February 1834, no. 62.

Meersch, P. C. van der. "De l'État de la Mendicité et de la Bienfaisance dans la Province de la Flandre Orientale." *BCCS* 5 (1853): 25 268.

Memorie over de Fabrieken en Trafieken in het Voormalig Koninkrijk Holland. Anonymous Manuscript. Dutch National Archives, The Hague. Binnenlandse Zaken 1796–1813, file no. 783.

Mendels, Franklin F. "Agriculture and Peasant Industry in Eighteenth Century Flanders." Paper read at the Conference on Economic Issues in European Agrarian History, Yale University, 1972. Mimeograph. In *European Peasants and Their Markets*, edited by William N. Parker and Eric L. Jones. Princeton: Princeton University Press, forthcoming.

———. "Industrialization and Population Pressure in Eighteenth-century Flanders." Ph.D. dissertation, University of Wisconsin, 1969.

———. "Protoindustrialization: The First Phase of the Industrialization Process." *JEH* 32 (1972): 241–61.

Mersseman, M. de. "Rapport." *Bulletin de l'Académie Royale de Médecine* 8 (1848–49): 87–127.

Metelerkamp, Robert. *De Toestand van Nederland in Vergelijking gebragt met die van Enige Andere Landen van Europa*. Rotterdam: Cornel and van Balen, 1804.

Michotte, Fritz. "L'Évolution des Prix de Détail en Belgique de 1830 à 1913." *BISEL* 8 (1937): 345–57.

Mokyr, Joel. "Capital, Labor and the Delay of the Industrial Revolution in the Netherlands." *EHJ* 38 (1975): 280–99.

———. "Industrial Growth and Stagnation in the Low Countries." Ph.D. dissertation, Yale University, 1974.

———. "The Industrial Revolution in the Low Countries in the First Half of the Nineteenth Century: A Comparative Case Study." *JEH* 34 (1974): 365–91.

Muller, Hendrik. *De Nederlandsche Katoen nijverheid en het Stelsel van Bescherming in Nederlandsch Indië*. Rotterdam: H. A. Kramers, 1857.

Neirynck, M. *De Loonen in België sedert 1846*. Leuven: Em. Warny, 1944.

Nève, J. E. *Gand sous la Domination Française, 1792–1814*. Ghent: A. Buyens, 1927.

Nierop, Leonie van. "Een Enquête in 1800." *De Gids* 77 (1913): 293–323.

———. "De Zijdenijverheid van Amsterdam, Historisch Geschetst." *TVG* 46

(1931): 113–43.

Nisard. "Souvenirs de Voyages, Le Pays de Liège." *Revue de Paris* 24 (1835): 129–48.

Noordziek, J. J. F., ed. *Verslag der Handelingen van de Tweede Kamer der Staten Generaal*, 1822 and subsequent years. The Hague: Martinus Nijhoff, 1873 and subsequent years.

Olyslager, Paul M. *De Localiseering der Belgische Nijverheid*. Antwerp: Standaard Boekhandel, 1947.

Peeters, M. "L'Évolution des Salaires en Belgique de 1831 à 1913." *BISEL* 10 (1939): 389–420.

Pen, Jan and Bouman, P. J. "Een Eeuw van Toenemende Welvaart." In *Drift en Koers*, edited by P. J. Bouman et al., pp. 85–104. Assen: Van Gorcum and Co., 1962.

Perrot, Édouard. *De l'Industrie et du Commerce en Belgique*. Brussels: H. Remy, 1835.

———. *Revue de l'Exposition des Produits de l'Industrie Nationale en 1841*. Brussels: At the Author's, 1841.

Pirenne, Henri. *Histoire De Belgique*. 4 vols. Brussels: La Renaissance du Livre, 1948.

Poel, J. M. G. van der. "De Landbouw in de Bataafse Tijd: Illusie en Werkelijkheid." *EHJ* 35 (1972): 65–80.

Posthumus, N. W., ed. "Bijdragen tot de Geschiedenis der Nederlandsche Groot-industrie." *EHJ* 11 (1925): 169–244.

———. *Documenten Betreffende de Buitenlandsche Handelspolitiek van Nederland in de Negentiende Eeuw*. The Hague: Martinus Nijhoff, 1921.

———, ed. "De Geheime Lijnwaadcontracten der N. H. M., 1835–1854." *EHJ* 2 (1916): 3–207.

———. *De Geschiedenis van de Leidsche Lakenindustrie*. 3 vols. The Hague: Martinus Nijhoff, 1939.

———. "De Industrieele Concurrentie tussen Noord- en Zuid- Nederlandsche Nijverheidscentra in de XVIIe en XVIIIe Eeuw." In *Mélanges d'Histoire Offerts à H. Pirenne*, pp. 369–78. Brussels: Vromant et Cie., 1926.

Postmus, J. *Een Onderzoek naar Omvang en Aard van de Bevolkingsconcentratie in Nederland Sedert 1830*. Amsterdam: Swets and Zeitlinger, 1928.

Quetelet, Adolphe. *Recherches Statistiques sur le Royaume des Pays Bas*. Brussels: M. Hayez, 1829.

Rammelaere, C. de. "Bijdrage tot de Landbouwgeschiedenis in Zuid-Oost Vlaanderen." *HMGOG*, n.s. 16 (1962): 21–40.

Rapport der Hoofdcommissie ter Beoordeling der Voorwerpen van Nationale Nijverheid, Tentoongesteld te Haarlem in de Maanden Juli en Augustus 1825. The Hague: 1825.

Rapports du Jury et Documents de l'Exposition de l'Industrie Belge en 1841. Brussels: A. Seghers, 1842.

Reesse, J. J. *De Suikerhandel van Amsterdam, 1813–1894*. 2 vols. The Hague: Martinus Nijhoff, 1911.

Rénier, J. S. "Histoire de l'Industrie Drapière aux Pays de Liège." *MSLEL*, n.s.

6 (1881): 149–296.

Ridder, J. *Een Conjunctuuranalyse van Nederland, 1848–1860.* Amsterdam: H. J. Paris, 1936.

Roentgen, Gerhard Moritz. "Berigt van den Toestand van de IJzerwerken in de Waalsche Provinciën (1823)." Edited by M. G. de Boer. *EHJ* 9 (1921): 103–49.

Roland-Holst van der Schalk, Henriette. *Kapitaal en Arbeid in Nederland.* 4th ed. 2 vols. Rotterdam: W. L. en J. Brusse, 1932.

Ruwet, J. *L'Agriculture et les Classes Rurales au Pays de Herve sous l'Ancien Régime.* Liège: Bibliothèque de la Faculté de Philosophie et Lettres de l'Université de Liège, 1943.

Schaik, P. van. "De Economische Betekenis van de Turfwinning in Nederland." *EHJ* 32 (1968–69): 141–205. *EHJ* 33 (1970): 186–235.

Schöller, P. "La Transformation Économique de la Belgique de 1832 à 1844." *BISEL* 14 (1948): 526–97.

Schweitzer, W. F. "Spinnewiel Verbeteringen en Organizatie van Spinwerk in Nederland, Omstreeks 1800." *THB* 3 (1961): 55–61.

Sérionne, Jacques Accarias de. *La Richesse de la Hollande.* London: Aux dépens de la Compagnie, 1778.

Sickenga, F. N. *Bijdrage tot de Geschiedenis der Belastingen in Nederland.* Leyden: P. Engels, 1864.

————. *Geschiedenis der Nederlandsche Belastingen, Tijdvak der Omwenteling, Algemeen Stelsel van het jaar 1805.* Amsterdam: N. van Kampen, 1865.

————. *Geschiedenis der Nederlandsche Belastingen Sedert het Jaar 1810.* Utrecht: J. L. Beijers, 1883.

Slicher van Bath, Bernard H. "Historische Ontwikkeling van de Textielnijverheid in Twente." *THB* 2 (1960): 21–39.

————. *Een Samenleving onder Spanning, Geschiedenis van het Platteland in Overijssel.* Assen: van Gorcum, 1957.

Sluijk, B. C. "Charles de Maere en de Vernieuwing van de Handweverij in Twente." In *Overijssel, Jaarboek voor Cultuur en Historie 1957,* pp. 5–23.

Smissaert, H. *Geschiedenis der Ontwikkeling van de Twentsche Katoennijverheid.* The Hague: Mouton and Co., 1906.

Smit, C. *De Handelspolitieke Betrekkingen tussen Nederland en Frankrijk, 1814–1914.* The Hague: Martinus Nijhoff, 1923.

Smit, W. J. *De Katoendrukkerij in Nederland tot 1813.* Rotterdam: Ontwikkeling, 1928.

Smits, Édouard. *Statistique Nationale, Développement des 31 Tableaux.* Brussels: H. Tarlier, 1827.

Sneller, Zeger Willem. "Landbouwtoestanden in Nederland in het Laatst der 18ᵉ Eeuw" (pp. 7–36), "Anderhalve Eeuw in Vogelvlucht, Part 1: 1795–1880" (pp. 38–65). In *Geschiedenis van den Nederlandschen Landbouw, 1795–1940,* edited by Zeger Willem Sneller. Groningen: J. B. Wolters, 1943.

————. "La Naissance de l'Industrie Rurale dans les Pays Bas aux XVIIᵉ et XVIIIᵉ Siècles." *Annales* 1 (1929): 193–202.

————. *De Ontwikkeling der Nederlandsche Exportindustrie.* Haarlem: H. D. Tjeenk-Willink, 1925.

————. "De Opkomst der Nederlandse Katoenindustrie" (pp. 80–133), "De Toestand der Nijverheid te Amsterdam en Rotterdam Volgens de Enquête van 1816" (pp. 161–202). In *Bijdragen tot de Economische Geschiedenis*. Utrecht and Antwerp: Het Spectrum, 1968.

————. "De Twentsche Weefnijverheid Omstreeks het Jaar 1800." *TVG* 41 (1926): 395–419.

Spiegel, L. P. van de. *Over de Armoede en Bedelaary met Betrekkinge tot de Provintie van Zeeland*. Goes: J. Huisman, 1780.

————. "Schets tot een Vertoog over de Intrinsique en Relative Magt van de Republiek (1782)." Edited by Johan de Vries. *EHJ* 27 (1958): 81–100.

Staatkundig en Staathuishoudkundig Jaarboekje, 1849 and subsequent years. Amsterdam: Johannes Müller, 1850 and subsequent years.

Staat van de Nederlandsche Fabrieken Volgens de Verslagen der Gemeenten. Uitgegeven door de Nederlandsche Maatschappij ter Bevordering van Nijverheid. Haarlem: De Erven Loosjes, 1859.

Stainier, Édouard. *Histoire Commerciale de la Métallurgie dans le District de Charleroi, 1829–1867*. Charleroi: Auguste Piette, 1873.

Statistiek van den Handel en de Scheepvaart van het Koninkrijk der Nederland, 1846 and subsequent years. The Hague: Giunta d'Albani for the Department of Finances, 1847 and subsequent years.

Statistique de la Belgique, Mines, Usines Minéralurgiques, Machines à Vapeur. Vol. 1 (1839–44), vol. 2 (1845–49). Brussels: Ministère des Travaux Publics, 1846, 1852.

Statistique de la Belgique, Population, Relevé Décennal, 1831–1840. Brussels: Ministère de l'Intérieur, 1842.

Statistique de la Belgique, Recensement Général 1846, Industrie, Agriculture, Population. Brussels: Ministère de l'Intérieur, 1851.

Statistique de la Belgique, Tableau Général du Commerce avec les Pays Étrangèrs, 1837 and subsequent issues. Brussels: Ministère de l'Intérieur, 1838 and subsequent years.

Statistique Générale de la Belgique, Exposé de la Situation du Royaume (1841–1850). Brussels: Ministère de l'Intérieur, 1852.

Stork, C. T. *De Twentsche Katoennijverheid, hare Vestiging en Uitbreiding*. Enschede: M. J. van der Loeff, 1888.

Stuijvenberg, J. H. van. "Economische Groei in Nederland in de 19ᵉ Eeuw, een Terreinverkenning." In *Bedrijf en Samenleving*, Festschrift presented to I. J. Brugmans, pp. 195–205. Alphen on the Rhine and Brussels: N. Samson, 1967.

————. "De Industriële Revolutie in Nederland." Unpublished manuscript, n.d.

Swaine, A. "Die Heimarbeit in der Gewehrindustrie von Lüttich und dessen Umgebung." *JNS* 67 (1896): 196–221.

Tahon, V. "L'Industrie Cloutière au Pays de Charleroy." *DRSAC* 36 (1914–21): 7–71.

Terlinden, Charles. "La Politique Économique de Guillaume Iᵉʳ, Roi des Pays Bas en Belgique, 1814–30." *RH* 139 (1922): 1–39.

Thomassin, L. F. *Mémoire Statistique du Département de l'Ourthe (1812)*. Liège: Grandmont-Donders, 1879.

Unger, S. "De Economische Ontwikkeling van België tijdens de Vereeniging met Noord Nederland." *TVG* 33 (1918): 143–46.

Vandenbroeke, C. "Brusselse Merkuriale van Granen, Aardappelen, Hooi, Stro, Boter, Vlees, Koolzaad, Boskool en Steenkool, 1800–1912." In *Documenten voor de Geschiedenis van Prijzen en Lonen in Vlaanderen en Brabant*, edited by C. Verlinden and E. Scholliers. Vol. 3: 289–349. Bruges: De Tempel, 1972.

Vandenbroeke, C. and Vanderpijpen, W. "Gentse Merkuriale van Granen, Brood, Aardappelen, Hooi, Stro, Boter, Vlees, Jenever, Olie en Oliehoudende Zaden, 1800–1914." In *Documenten voor de Geschiedenis van Prijzen en Lonen in Vlaanderen en Brabant*, edited by C. Verlinden and E. Scholliers. Vol. 3: 95–188. Bruges: De Tempel, 1972.

Varlez, Leon. *Les Salaires dans l'Industrie Gantoise.* 2 vols. Brussels: J. Lebègue, 1901–04.

Verberne, L. G. J. *Noord Brabant in de 19ᶜ Eeuw tot Omstreeks 1870, de Sociaal-Economische Structuur.* Nijmegen: De Koepel, 1947.

———. "Over de Noordbrabantse Nijverheid in de Eerste Jaren na 1830." In *Land van Mijn Hart*, Festschrift presented to Professor J. A. J. Goossens, pp. 115–22. Tilburg: Henri Bergmans, 1952.

Verhaegen, A. "Note Sur le Travail et les Salaires en Belgique au XVIIIᶜ Siècle." *BISEL* 19 (1953): 71–85.

Verhaegen, B. *Contribution à l'Histoire Économique des Flanders.* 2 vols. Louvain and Paris: Nauwelaerts, 1961.

Verhagen, F. B. A. M. "De Linnen en Katoenindustrie in de Bataafse en Franse Tijd." In *Land van Mijn Hart*, Festschrift presented to Professor J. A. J. Goossens, pp. 123–30. Tilburg: Henri Bergmans, 1952.

Viry, C. *Mémoire Statistique du Département de la Lys.* Paris: Imprimerie Impériale, 1803–04.

Vleeshouwer, Robert de. "Le Consulat et l'Empire: Periode de 'Take-off' pour l'Économie Belge?" *RHMC* 17 (1970): 610–19.

Voortman, J. *Les Débuts de l'Industrie Cotonnière et les Crises Économiques de l'Industrie Cotonnière Gantoise sous le Régime Français et le Régime Hollandais d'après les Archives de la Maison A. Voortman.* Ghent: L. van Melle, 1940.

Vos, A. de. "Bloei en Verval der Plaatselijke Handweefnijverheid te Evergem, 1794–1880." *HMGOG*, n.s. 13 (1959): 113–61.

Vries, A. de. *Geschiedenis van de Handelspolitieke Betrekkingen tusschen Nederland en Engeland.* The Hague: Martinus Nijhoff, 1931.

Vries, B. W. de. *De Nederlandse Papiernijverheid in de 19ᶜ Eeuw.* The Hague: Martinus Nijhoff, 1957.

Vries, Jan de. *The Dutch Rural Economy in the Golden Age, 1500–1700.* New Haven and London: Yale University Press, 1974.

Vries, Johan de. *De Economische Achteruitgang der Republiek.* Amsterdam: J. van Campen, 1959.

———. "De Economische Achteruitgang der Republiek." In *Algemene Geschiedenis der Nederlanden*, edited by J. A. van Houtte et al., vol. 8: 222–60. Utrecht: de Haan, 1955.

Vuylsteke, J. *Korte Statistieke Beschrijving van België.* Ghent: I. S. van Doosselaere,

1865–69.

Waentig, Heinrich. "Briavoinne." *JNS* 58 (1919): 289–319.

———. "Die Grundfrage der Belgischen Volkswirtschaft." *JNS* 54 (1917): 129–57, 513–43, 641–77.

Warzée, A. "Exposé Historique de l'Industrie du Fer dans la Province de Liège." *MSLEL*, n.s. 1 (1860): 449–538.

———. "Exposé Historique et Statistique de l'Industrie Métallurgique dans le Hainaut." *MPSH*, 2d ser. 8 (1860–62): 5–146.

Wee, Herman van der. "De Industriële Revolutie in België." In *Historische Aspecten van de Economische Groei*, pp. 168–205. Antwerp and Utrecht: De Nederlandsche Boekhandel, 1972.

Weerdt, Denise de. "Loon- en Levensvoorwaarden van de Fabrieksarbeiders, 1789–1850." In *Geschiedenis van de Socialistische Arbeiders-Beweging in België*, edited by Jan Dhondt, pp. 71–82. Antwerp: "Ontwikkeling," 1960.

Werveke, Hans van. "De Curve van het Gentse Bevolkingscijfer in de 17ᵉ en de 18ᵉ Eeuw." *KVAV* 10 (1948): 5–60.

Westermann, J. C. *Blik in het Verleden: Geschiedenis van de Nederlandsche Blik-industrie in hare Opkomst*. Amsterdam: Vereenigde Blikfabrieken, 1939.

———. *Geschiedenis van de IJzer en Staalgieterij in Nederland*. Utrecht: Demka, 1948.

Wibail, Ami. "L'Évolution Économique de la Sidérurgie Belge de 1830 à 1913." *BISEL* 6 (1933): 31–61.

Wielen, H. G. W. van der. "Sociale Toestanden ter Plattelande." In *Geschiedenis van den Nederlandschen Landbouw*, edited by Zeger Willem Sneller, pp. 426–65. Groningen: J. B. Wolters, 1943.

Wieringa, Wiert Jan. *Economische Heroriëntering in Nederland in de 19ᵉ Eeuw*. Groningen: J. B. Wolters, 1955.

Willemsen, G. "Contribution à l'Histoire de l'Industrie Linière en Flandre au XVIIIᵉ Siècle." *HMGOG* 7 (1906): 223–340.

Wilson, Charles. "The Decline of the Netherlands" (pp. 22–47), "Taxation and the Decline of Empires: An Unfashionable Theme" (pp. 117–27). In *Economic History and the Historians*. London: Weidenfeld and Nicolson, 1969.

Witlox, H. J. M. *Schets van de Ontwikkeling van Welvaart en Bedrijvigheid in het Verenigd Koninkrijk der Nederlanden*. Nijmegen: Centrale Drukkerij, 1956.

Woude, A. M. van der. "Het Noorderkwartier." *A. A. G. Bijdragen* 16 (1972), 3 vols.

Woude, A. M. van der, and Mentink, G. J. "La Population de Rotterdam au XVIIᵉ et XVIIIᵉ Siècles." *Population* 21 (1966): 1165–90.

Wright, H. R. C. *Free Trade and Protection in the Netherlands, 1816–1830*. Cambridge: At the University Press, 1955.

Wttewaal, G. "Over de Steeds Toenemende Armoede in het Koninkrijk der Nederlanden." *TBN* 1 (1833): 523–51.

Zappey, W. M. *De Economische en Politieke Werkzaamheid van Johannes Goldberg*. Alphen on the Rhine: Samson, 1967.

INDEX